FROMM

EasyGuide

TO

LAS VEGAS

by
Rick Garman

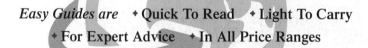

Easy Guides are ✦ Quick To Read ✦ Light To Carry
✦ For Expert Advice ✦ In All Price Ranges

FrommerMedia LLC

Published by
FROMMER MEDIA LLC

ISBN 978-1-62887-086-2 (paper), 978-1-62887-087-9 (e-book)

Editorial Director: Pauline Frommer
Development Editor: Melissa Klurman
Production Editor: Lynn Northrup
Cartographer: Liz Puhl
Indexer: Maro Riofrancos

For information on our other products or services, see www.frommers.com.

Frommer Media LLC also publishes its books in a variety of electronic formats. Some content that appears in print may not be available in electronic formats.

Manufactured in the United States of America

5 4 3 2 1

AN IMPORTANT NOTE

The world is a dynamic place. Hotels change ownership, restaurants hike their prices, museums alter their opening hours, and busses and trains change their routings. And all of this can occur in the several months after our authors have visited, inspected, and written about, these hotels, restaurants, museums and transportation services. Though we have made valiant efforts to keep all our information fresh and up-to-date, some few changes can inevitably occur in the periods before a revised edition of this guidebook is published. So please bear with us if a tiny number of the details in this book have changed. Please also note that we have no responsibility or liabil-ity for any inaccuracy or errors or omissions, or for inconvenience, loss, damage, or expenses suf-fered by anyone as a result of assertions in this guide.

CONTENTS

ABOUT THE AUTHOR

Rick Garman began visiting Las Vegas as soon as he was old enough to not be barred from doing so by pesky things like laws. He started writing about the city in 1997 when he and his best friend Mary Herczog were invited to write *Frommer's Las Vegas*. He went on to create Vegas4Visitors.com, one of the most respected Las Vegas travel resources on the Web, and has appeared in various outlets as a self-proclaimed Vegas expert, although most of that expertise has been gained sitting at a slot machine with a glazed look in his eye while mumbling incoherently to himself. Rick was honored to return to the Frommer's fold in 2010 after Mary passed away after a long struggle with breast cancer. He dedicates this book to her memory.

ABOUT THE FROMMER TRAVEL GUIDES

For most of the past 50 years, Frommer's has been the leading series of travel guides in North America, accounting for as many as 24% of all guidebooks sold. I think I know why.

Though we hope our books are entertaining, we nevertheless deal with travel in a serious fashion. Our guidebooks have never looked on such journeys as a mere recreation, but as a far more important human function, a time of learning and introspection, an essential part of a civilized life. We stress the culture, lifestyle, history, and beliefs of the destinations we cover, and urge our readers to seek out people and new ideas as the chief rewards of travel.

We have never shied from controversy. We have, from the beginning, encouraged our authors to be intensely judgmental, critical—both pro and con—in their comments, and wholly independent. Our only clients are our readers, and we have triggered the ire of countless prominent sorts, from a tourist newspaper we called "practically worthless" (it unsuccessfully sued us) to the many rip-offs we've condemned.

And because we believe that travel should be available to everyone regardless of their incomes, we have always been cost-conscious at every level of expenditure. Though we have broadened our recommendations beyond the budget category, we insist that every lodging we include be sensibly priced. We use every form of media to assist our readers, and are particularly proud of our feisty daily website, the award-winning Frommers.com.

I have high hopes for the future of Frommer's. May these guidebooks, in all the years ahead, continue to reflect the joy of travel and the freedom that travel represents. May they always pursue a cost-conscious path, so that people of all incomes can enjoy the rewards of travel. And may they create, for both the traveler and the persons among whom we travel, a community of friends, where all human beings live in harmony and peace.

Arthur Frommer

THE BEST OF LAS VEGAS

The flamboyant showman Liberace once said, "Too much of a good thing is wonderful!" He may very well have been talking about Las Vegas, a city in which he was a frequent headliner, and one that has built its reputation on the concept of excess. There's too much too look at, too much to do, too much to eat, too much to drink, and certainly too many ways to lose your money. Indulgence is the level at which most people start their visit, and why not? You can run out of room on your memory card trying to snap pictures of all the postcard-worthy sights from dancing fountains to blasting volcanoes; the hotels are so big that getting from your room to the front door requires rest periods; the dining scene has turned this town into a culinary destination; and the nightclubs have elevated Sin City to the biggest, most successful party spot in the world. And all of that is before you get to the shows, the shopping, and the sheer madness of glittering casinos. Look at the faces of those waiting for their flights out of town: tired, maybe a little hung over still, but then there's that little smile when they think about one of those "what happens in Vegas . . ." moments they just had. When it comes to Las Vegas, Liberace may have had a point.

THE best AUTHENTIC LAS VEGAS EXPERIENCES

o **Strolling on the Strip After Dark:** You haven't really seen Las Vegas until you've seen it at night. This neon wonderland is the world's greatest sound-and-light show. Begin at Luxor and work your way past the incredible hotels and their attractions. You'll probably be exhausted, both physically and mentally, by the time you get to the halfway mark around Caesars Palace, but forge ahead and you could go all the way to the Stratosphere Tower for a bird's-eye view of the city from more than 1,000 feet up. Make plenty of stops en route to see the Mirage Volcano erupt, take a photo of the full moon over the Eiffel Tower, and marvel at the choreographed water-fountain ballet at Bellagio.

o **Casino-Hopping on the Strip:** The interior of each lavish hotel-casino is more outrageous and giggle-inducing than the last. Just when you think they can't possibly top themselves, they do. From Venice to Paris, from New York City to the Manhattan-style chic of CityCenter, it is all, completely and uniquely, Las Vegas. See "The Best Las Vegas Casinos" later in this chapter.

o **Sleeping In:** Come on! You're on vacation! Yes, there are lots of things to see and do in Las Vegas, but with tens of thousands of the most luxurious hotel rooms in the world, don't you just want to stay in one of those big fluffy beds and maybe order room service? We know we do. See "The Best Las Vegas Hotels" below.

o **Visiting an Only-in-Vegas Museum:** A stuffy and "tasteful" museum would never do the trick here in Vegas, so visit these few that are worthy of their Sin City locales: Go nuclear at the **National Atomic Testing Museum** (p. 144) get "made" at the **Mob Museum** (p. 140), or get lit up at the **Neon Museum** (p. 141).

o **Spending a Day (and Night) in Downtown:** Glitter Gulch is undergoing a renaissance with fun, modern hotels and casinos like **The Downtown Grand** (p. 60); terrific new and affordable dining options such as **Eat** (p. 113) and **La Comida** (p. 110); fun and funky bars like **Insert Coin(s)** (p. 197) and **Atomic Liquors** (p. 194); and must-see attractions like the **Fremont Street Experience** (p. 140). Oh, and there's a giant, fire-breathing praying mantis at the **Downtown Container Park** (p. 172). If that doesn't make you want to go, nothing will!

o **Shopping Until You're Dropping:** Take what Napoleon called "the greatest drawing room in Europe," replicate it, add shops, and you've got **The Grand Canal Shoppes** at the Venetian (p. 170)—it's St. Mark's Square, complete with canals and working gondolas. See chapter 7 for the low-down on the shopping scene.

o **Dressing Up for a Show:** You don't have to get gussied up to see one of the mind-boggling Cirque du Soleil productions or one of your favorite headliners, but there's something about putting on your best suit or fanciest dress for an evening at the "thea-tuh" that can't be beat. See chapter 8 for reviews of the major shows and check out "The Best Las Vegas Shows" later in this chapter.

o **Breaking Some Records:** You can find thrills almost anywhere in town, but a few of the adrenaline-pumping attractions here are worthy of spots in *The Guinness Book of World Records*. **High Roller** (p. 135) is the world's tallest observation wheel; **The Stratosphere Tower & Thrill Rides** (p. 137) are the highest in the United States; and **SlotZilla** (p. 141) is the world's tallest "slot machine," which is the launching platform for zip and zoom lines down Fremont Street.

o **Getting Away from It All:** Las Vegas can be overwhelming, so be sure to put some time on your itinerary to find your Zen at such scenic spots as the **Valley of Fire State Park** or **Red Rock Canyon.** See chapter 9 for more ideas for day trips from Vegas.

THE best LAS VEGAS RESTAURANTS

o **Best Strip Restaurants:** The intricate construction and mind-blowing flavors of the epicurean delights at **Rose.Rabbit.Lie** (p. 96) are enhanced by the unique experience of dining there. Meanwhile, the impossibly fresh Mediterranean seafood specialties at **Bartolotta** (p. 106) will make people who don't like fish change their minds.

o **Best Downtown Restaurants:** The Latin specialties at **The Commissary** (p. 112) and the authentic, homemade-style Mexican dishes at **La Comida** (p. 110) prove that the dining scene in Downtown has arrived.

Las Vegas & Environs

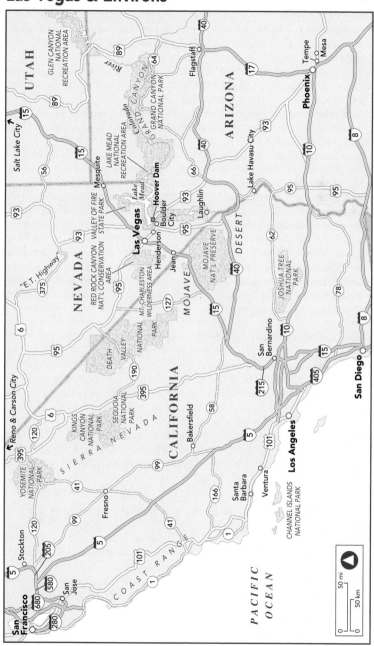

○ **Best Off-Strip Restaurant: Raku Grill** (p. 123) is a 10- to 20-minute drive from the Strip, but the flavorful Japanese grill specialties here make it totally worth the trip.

○ **Best Comfort Food:** The heaping portions of classic American comfort food at **Citizens Kitchen** (p. 86) will satisfy even the most ravenous of eaters, while the funky twists on the genre served at **Culinary Dropout** (p. 116) will charm the most jaded.

○ **Best Theme Restaurant:** Generally speaking, we think theme restaurants are over-priced tourist traps, but **Gilley's** (p. 100) has such great down-home cooking that we're willing to overlook the mechanical bull.

○ **Best Steakhouse:** Based on the NYC restaurant that has been in business for more than 150 years, **Old Homestead Steakhouse** (p. 95) serves hugely flavorful cuts of meat that are just plain old huge. They did invent the doggy bag, after all.

○ **Best Inexpensive Meal: Capriotti's** (p. 118) serves monster, well-stuffed subma-rine sandwiches with fresh ingredients both traditional (ham and cheese) and offbeat (the Bobby is like Thanksgiving on a bun). Even better, most are under $10.

○ **Best Splurge:** Food should not cost as much as it does at **Joël Robuchon at the Mansion** (p. 84) and the slightly less expensive sibling **L'Atelier de Joël Robu-chon** (p. 84), but a few bites of the exquisite cuisine will make you understand why it does.

○ **Best Buffets:** It's expensive, but the **Buffet at Wynn Las Vegas** (p. 128) serves high-quality food worthy of tablecloths and candlelight. Bargain hunters, however, won't need to sacrifice quality at the **Main Street Garden Court Buffet** (p. 128).

○ **Best Hamburgers: KGB: Kerry's Gourmet Burgers** (p. 105) gives you a choice of creating your own burger or ordering one of theirs. Either way, you come out a winner.

○ **Best Desserts:** How can you go wrong with a place called **Sugar Factory** (p. 104)? By not ordering enough of their deliriously sweet treats.

○ **Best Views:** You can see the entire city, and big chunks of southern Nevada, from the revolving **Top of the World** (p. 108), situated more than 800 feet up the Strato-sphere Tower, while at **Alizé** (p. 115), at the top of the Palms, you get a virtually unobstructed view of the Strip and delightfully crafted French cuisine that may make you forget the vista entirely.

○ **Best Breakfasts:** The twisted farm food at **Hash House a Go Go** (p. 101) features things like pancakes the size of pizzas and waffles with bacon baked right in, while **Eat** (p. 113) offers dizzyingly fresh and flavorful choices that have won legions of fans.

THE best LAS VEGAS HOTELS

○ **Best Classic Vegas Hotel:** Most of historic Las Vegas has been imploded (often spectacularly), but at **Caesars Palace** (p. 48) you can still get a taste of it as themed Roman decadence meets classic Sin City opulence.

○ **Best Modern Vegas Hotel: The Cosmopolitan of Las Vegas** (p. 49) offers a blue-print for what the next generation of Las Vegas hotels will be like: as over-the-top visually as any theme hotel, but with a sexy, contemporary edge.

○ **Best for a Romantic Getaway:** No, it's not the real Eiffel Tower, but the one at **Paris Las Vegas** (p. 54) is almost as charming as the rest of this ooo-la-la themed resort, providing you ample opportunity to re-create a romantic French retreat.

o **Best for Families:** Las Vegas is not a family destination, but if you can't leave the little ones with Grandma, your only choice for a major Vegas hotel is **Circus Circus** (p. 58), where there are almost as many things for the wee ones to do as there are for adults.

o **Best for Business Travelers: LVH: Las Vegas Hotel's** (p. 66) location next to the Convention Center makes this a no-brainer from a geographical perspective, but the large rooms, classic casino, and raft of restaurants give it a decidedly Vegas spin.

o **Best Rooms on the Strip:** The condo-like units at **The Cosmopolitan of Las Vegas** (p. 49) are not only sizeable, but they have cool design touches (art! real books!) and terraces offering amazing views of the Strip.

o **Best Rooms Downtown: The Downtown Grand** (p. 60) took the bones of the old Lady Luck hotel and turned it into a modern yet comfortable resort that ups the ante considerably for this neighborhood.

o **Best Rooms Off the Strip: Red Rock Resort** (p. 74) lives up to the resort part of its name as a true desert retreat, complete with gorgeous, modern rooms that you'll never want to leave.

o **Best Bathrooms:** This one is a toss-up for us, with the bigger-than-many-apartment-size retreats at **The Venetian** (p. 50) and the sumptuous luxury fixtures at **Wynn Las Vegas** (p. 57) both winning our hearts.

o **Best Bang for Your Buck:** Almost everything you can find at a Strip hotel (nice rooms, full casino, multiple restaurants, sharks!) can be gotten at the **Golden Nugget** (p. 60) in Downtown Las Vegas for a fraction of the cost.

o **Best Non-Casino Hotel:** They can't get your money gambling, so they get it through high room rates, but to stay at the **Mandarin Oriental** (p. 41) is to immerse yourself in luxury.

o **Best Splurge:** Rooms at **Wynn/Encore Las Vegas** (p. 57) will almost always be among the most expensive in town, but you'll totally feel like you are getting your money's worth, especially with the gorgeous spas, pools, casinos, and other amenities at your disposal.

THE best FREE THINGS TO DO IN LAS VEGAS

o **Watching the Waters Dance:** The intricately choreographed water ballet that is the **Fountains at Bellagio** (p. 138) would be worth repeated viewings even if they charged to see it. The fact that they don't makes it an almost perfect Vegas experience.

o **Enjoying the Changing of the Seasons:** There are five seasons in the elaborately designed botanical gardens of the **Bellagio Conservatory** (p. 138): Winter (holiday), Chinese New Year, Spring, Summer, and Fall. No matter which is on display during your visit, make sure your digital camera has a full battery charge. You'll want lots of pictures.

o **Seeing a Volcano Erupt:** When the free **Mirage Volcano** (p. 138) first "erupted" in 1989, shooting flames and faux lava into the sky, it literally stopped traffic on the Strip. That it doesn't today only means that it has more competition for your attention, not that it is any less fun.

o **Watching the Sky Light Up:** Many people considered it almost sacrilegious to convert the famed Glitter Gulch in Downtown Vegas into a pedestrian mall with a free light-and-sound show broadcast on a massive LED canopy overhead. Now the **Fremont Street Experience** (p. 140) is considered a must-visit.

o **Playing a Penny Slot:** Yes, in order to win the big bucks—sometimes millions of them—on a modern penny slot you have to bet much more than just one penny. But if you're okay with smaller rewards and losses, you could stretch a dollar into 100 spins.

o **Beating the High Score:** It's free to just look at the restored classic machines at the **Pinball Hall of Fame** (p. 145), and if you want to do more than just look, it'll only cost you a couple of quarters. What other museum lets you play with its works of art?

o **Making Your Own Postcard:** Just down the road from the southern-most edge of the Strip is one of the most photographed and imitated signs in the world. Get a picture of you at the **Welcome to Fabulous Las Vegas Sign** (p. 139), and you'll have a postcard-worthy souvenir.

THE best WAYS TO SEE LAS VEGAS LIKE A LOCAL

o **Gambling on a Budget:** Finding a local at a Strip casino is rare. Why? Because Vegas residents know the limits are lower and the payback is often higher at neighborhood casinos like **Red Rock Resort** (p. 74) and **Green Valley Ranch Resort** (p. 72).

o **Eating off the Strip:** Those same locals who don't gamble on the Strip usually don't eat on the Strip either, unless they are trying to impress visitors. Instead they dine at the less expensive but still fantastic local eateries such as **Lola's: A Louisiana Kitchen** (p. 110) or **Todd's Unique Dining** (p. 120).

o **Becoming an Arts Lover:** Leave the tacky Las Vegas snow globes for the souvenir-hunting tourists and get yourself some unique Vegas keepsakes at one of the arts collectives instead. **Emergency Arts** (p. 139) and **The Arts Factory** (p. 138) are leading the charge for the burgeoning arts scene in the city.

o **Hunting for Treasure:** It may be surprising to find out that in a city like Las Vegas, where history is often disposed of with carefully timed implosions, antique shopping is a favored pastime of locals and visitors alike. Check out the fun finds at **Retro Vegas** (p. 173).

o **Catching a Broadway Show:** The 2012 opening of the stunning (both visually and aurally) **Smith Center for the Performing Arts** (p. 141) has been a boon to the cultural life of Las Vegas, giving a proper home to everything from the philharmonics and dance troupes to their popular Broadway Series featuring titles like *Book of Mormon* and *Wicked*.

o **Walking the Streets:** No, not that way. Instead, check out the fun **First Friday Las Vegas** street fair (p. 143), which brings the local (and tourist) community together with live entertainment, art vendors, and lots of state fair–type food. Did we mention deep-fried cookie dough? We thought that would get your attention.

THE best LAS VEGAS CASINOS

o **Best Classic Casinos:** On the Strip there is no place that honors its history quite like **Caesars Palace** (p. 48), where you can still enjoy the classic Roman splendor that has been wowing gamblers since 1966. And though they no longer have the World Series of Poker, serious players still head directly to **Binion's** (p. 34) for its swingers vibe and lively table game action.

o **Best Modern Casinos:** When we first saw the contemporary, cutting-edge decor at **Aria Las Vegas** (p. 37), we thought that nothing could top it in terms of modern casino luxury. But then along came the bold, artistic statement of **The Cosmopolitan of Las Vegas** (p. 49), and we realized we just might have a competition on our hands.

o **Best Glitter Gulch Casinos:** Downtown Las Vegas casinos often have lower limits and friendlier dealers, two things that can make losing money less egregious. The best of the breed in the area are the **Golden Nugget** (p. 60), all warm hues and laid-back fun, and **The Downtown Grand** (p. 60), which manages to be both modern and charmingly retro at the same time.

o **Best Local Casinos:** Most neighborhood casinos are low-limit, no-frills joints, but the casinos at **Red Rock Resort** (p. 74), **Green Valley Ranch** (p. 72), and **M Resort** (p. 72) are as stylish as many on the Strip. That they can be that visually appealing and still maintain most of the thrifty attitude that the locals' casinos are known for is almost a miracle.

o **Best Budget Casinos:** You won't find any ostentatious opulence at **The Orleans** (p. 69), but you will find thousands of low-limit slot and video poker machines and dozens of gaming tables that won't cost you an arm and a leg to join. Meanwhile **The Four Queens** (p. 62) in Downtown Las Vegas offers similarly low-priced gambling options in comfortable and friendly surroundings.

o **Best Splurge Casino:** Yes, you can find high-limit slots and table games pretty much anywhere, but why not surround yourself with the opulent decor and high-class furnishings of **Wynn/Encore** (p. 57)?

o **Best Blast from the Past Casinos:** Both the **D Las Vegas** (p. 61) and the **Eastside Cannery** (p. 70) have a selection of "classic" machines that still take and dispense actual coins!

THE best LAS VEGAS SHOWS

o **Best Overall Show:** A perfect intersection of music and artistry can be found at *Michael Jackson ONE* (p. 181), featuring the music and choreography of the King of Pop and the stunning visual theater of Cirque du Soleil.

o **Best Big Shows:** The wow-factor winner is a toss-up between **Cirque du Soleil's** *KÀ* (p. 178) and *Mystère* (p. 182). The latter is more traditional—if you can call a human circus that mixes dazzling acrobatics with dramatic visuals "traditional"—in that it has only a loose semblance of narrative, whereas *KÀ* actually has a plot. Both are dazzling and, given the extremely high production values, seem worth the extremely high ticket prices.

o **Best Small Shows:** Only the spaces in which *Absinthe* (p. 177) and *Vegas Nocturne* (p. 191) are performed can be called small; the over-the-top acrobatics, stunts, dance, comedy, and mind-blowing originality of each certainly can't be.

o **Best Classic Shows:** You know: big, huge stage sets, pointless production numbers, showgirls, nipples on parade, Bob Mackie headdresses. Ah, *Jubilee!* (p. 187), this world would be dreary without you. But if you want more than just a musty blast from the past, check out *Vegas! The Show* (p. 193), which celebrates multiple eras of classic Sin City entertainment in one spectacular package.

o **Best Magic Shows:** This town isn't good enough for **Penn & Teller** (p. 189) and their master class in the art and artifice of illusion taught by guys who will both amuse and amaze. Meanwhile, mixing traditional illusions (big sets and big shocks) with a rock-'n'-roll aesthetic, **Criss Angel:** *Believe* (p. 184) will make you rethink everything you thought about magic shows.

o **Best Music Shows:** Former Strip headliner **Clint Holmes** (p. 186) is doing a master class of jazz stylings at the Smith Center for the Performing Arts once a month, and **Human Nature** (p. 185) will shock you with how good four white Australian dudes can do classic Motown songs.

o **Best Daytime Shows:** It's almost as much of a comedy show as it is a magic show, but the set done by **Mac King** (p. 188) will leave you astounded with some great close-up tricks and laughing your head off at the same time. A similar mix of laughs and gasps can be found at the comedy juggling show done by **Jeff Civillico** (p. 186).

THE best OUTDOOR EXPERIENCES IN LAS VEGAS

o **Best Pools:** There are acres of water park fun at **Mandalay Bay** (p. 40), including a wave pool, lazy river, beach, regular swimming pools, and even its own open-air casino. Meanwhile, the lush landscaping, fountains, and water slides at **The Mirage** (p. 54) will make you feel like you're in a tropical paradise. For more picks for our favorite pools, see p. 53.

o **Best Golf:** The greens fees are outrageously high, but the course at **Wynn Las Vegas** (p. 166) is one of the most lush in town. "Real" golfers head to **TPC Las Vegas** (p. 166) for its challenging holes, gorgeous scenery, and occasional Justin Timberlake sightings.

o **Best Drives:** The 13-mile **Red Rock Scenic Drive** (p. 222) provides a way to enjoy the colorful rocks and canyons without leaving the air-conditioned comfort of your car. On the other hand, you could get a good breeze going at about 140 mph in one of the race or exotic cars you can drive yourself at the **Las Vegas Motor Speedway** (p. 147).

o **Best Retreat:** If you need a respite from the hustle and bustle of Las Vegas, head north to **Mount Charleston** (p. 223) for a relaxed mountain retreat or to work up a sweat while hiking or snowboarding.

o **Best Man-Made Wonder:** One of the greatest engineering feats in history is the 726-foot-tall **Hoover Dam** (p. 213). You can take tours of the mighty facility and learn how it made Las Vegas (and much of the American Southwest) possible.

o **Best Spas:** Okay, technically it's not an outdoor experience, but you won't care once you experience the **Spa at Encore** (p. 167), a 70,000-square-foot oasis for the mind, body, and spirit, with a gorgeous Moroccan-infused design and full menu of pampering delights. Meanwhile, we only wish our own gym were as handsomely equipped as the one at the **Canyon Ranch SpaClub** (p. 166) in the Venetian, which also has a number of other high-priced treatments on which you can blow your blackjack winnings. For more great spa options, see p. 166.

SUGGESTED LAS VEGAS ITINERARIES

The Strip alone has hundreds of restaurants, dozens of shows, and more attractions, sights, and sounds than can easily be catalogued, much less visited. So yes, when you come to Las Vegas, you certainly won't be lacking in things to do. But the sheer enormity of the city and its laundry list of items to add to your daily to-do list could leave even the most intrepid traveler feeling a little overwhelmed.

The itineraries in this chapter are designed to help narrow the big list down a little while maximizing your time. This way you can spend less energy planning and more having fun. Each itinerary has a theme, but you can always mix and match to create your perfect Las Vegas getaway.

Instead of a step-by-step tour, the itineraries are broken down by morning, afternoon, and nighttime activities with multiple suggestions for each, again allowing you to customize your vacation in a way that makes sense for you.

ICONIC LAS VEGAS

There are many things with which Las Vegas has become synonymous: gambling and all things excess are probably at the top of the list, but there's also the dancing waters, the dolphins, the buffets, the Cirque du Soleil shows, the steakhouses, the offbeat museums, the wild nightlife, and much more. This itinerary will guide you to the must-see and must-do, all of which are fun for first-timers or repeat offenders. Have your cameras ready!

Mornings

Start your day with a photo opportunity at the **Welcome to Fabulous Las Vegas Sign,** perhaps the city's most iconic symbol of all. Then keep your "say cheese" smile in place as you take a walking or driving tour past the only-in-Vegas, postcard-worthy exteriors of hotels like the pyramid-shaped **Luxor,** the castle-themed **Excalibur,** the Gotham re-creation of **New York–New York,** the modern wonder of **CityCenter,** the Italian villa charm of **Bellagio,** the Gallic splendor of **Paris Las Vegas,** and the Roman decadence of **Caesars Palace.** There are more photo ops, of course, but you only have so much room on your digital camera's memory card and there is much more to see.

Suggested Las Vegas Itineraries

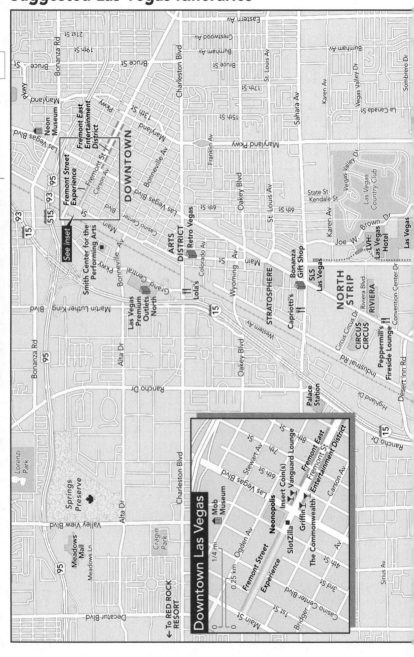

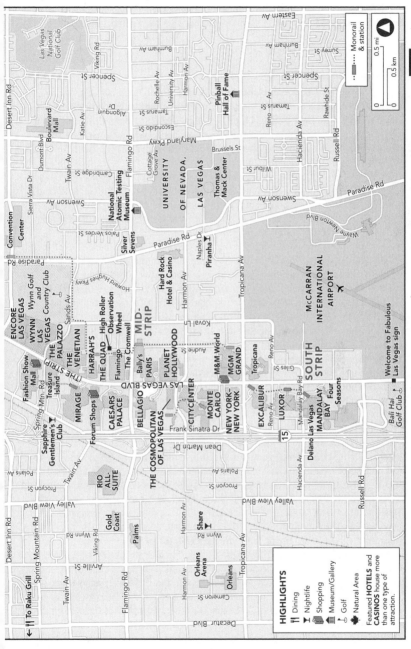

HIGHLIGHTS

- Dining
- Nightlife
- Shopping
- Museum/Gallery
- Golf
- Natural Area

Featured **HOTELS** and **CASINOS** house more than one type of attraction.

Monorail & station

0   0.5 mi

0   0.5 km

If you started early enough and still have time before lunch, check out one (or preferably both) of the city's more colorful attractions with the glorious botanical gardens at the **Bellagio Conservatory** or the majestic animals at the **Mirage Secret Garden & Dolphin Habitat.** Both are fun to look at, but more importantly, offer a bit of a peaceful respite from the madness that is Las Vegas. Trust us, you'll need a break every now and then!

Afternoons

You can go one of two ways for lunch, either with a classic Vegas buffet or a view of the throngs of humanity that crowd the Strip. For the former, check out the **Spice Market Buffet** at Planet Hollywood or **Le Village Buffet** at Paris Las Vegas. Both offer a seemingly endless array of well-prepared food; while they may not be the cheapest buffets in town, neither are they the most expensive, so you can have your proverbial—or literal—cake and eat it, too.

The other way to go would be to have a nosh at a Strip-side cafe so you can do some people-watching while you eat. The best of the bunch are **Mon Ami Gabi,** offering Americanized twists on classic French bistro cuisine, and the **Sugar Factory,** which serves up a long menu of hearty dishes from burgers to steaks with stops at crêpes and waffles in between. Both are at Paris Las Vegas.

After you have refueled, head to one (or more, if time allows) of the city's offbeat, unique museums. Tops on our list are the **National Museum of Organized Crime and Law Enforcement,** aka the Mob Museum, which takes a look at the Mafia and its influence on the country and Vegas in particular; the **National Atomic Testing Museum,** which explores the history of the nuclear age with a special focus on the nearby Nevada Testing Site; and the **Neon Museum,** which puts the city's history on display in the form of rescued signs from long-gone casinos and other businesses.

Close out your afternoon with some shopping, window or otherwise. Las Vegas is one of the top shopping destinations in the world. Even if you can't afford to buy anything, stroll through the highly themed malls like **The Forum Shops** or **Grand Canal Shoppes,** which are designed to look like a street in ancient Rome and a Venice canal (complete with gondoliers!), respectively.

Nights

If you didn't eat the buffet at lunch you may want to consider one for dinner, but our preference would be to send you to a steakhouse. Virtually every hotel in town has at least one, and they are practically a requirement for nonvegetarian Vegas visitors. The best of the bunch are **Old Homestead Steakhouse** at Caesars Palace, a Vegas version of the famed New York City restaurant that has been in business since 1868; **Strip House** at Planet Hollywood, which has fantastically flavorful cuts of meat and a peek-a-boo bordello theme; and the simply named **The Steakhouse** at Circus Circus, which has an old-school charm, terrific food, and affordable prices.

We hope you didn't eat too much, because your night is just getting started. Next, it's on to one of the shows by Cirque du Soleil, the French-Canadian circus troupe that reinvented and now rules the Las Vegas entertainment scene. There are many to choose from, but our favorites include the dreamy wonder of *Mystère* at Treasure Island, the martial arts spectacle of *KÀ* at MGM Grand, the water ballet of *O* at Bellagio, or the King of Pop spectacle that is *Michael Jackson ONE* at Mandalay Bay.

From there it's on to the truly iconic Las Vegas experiences, which are all best viewed at night. The dancing waters of the **Fountains of Bellagio** are worth visiting no matter how many times you have seen them; the **Mirage Volcano** is still a lava-spewing delight; and the **Fremont Street Experience** in Downtown Las Vegas will immerse you in the neon-lit glory that is Glitter Gulch.

End your day dancing the night away at one of the city's hot nightclubs like the Cirque du Soleil–inspired **Light** at Mandalay Bay or the world's largest nightclub **Hakkasan** at MGM Grand. Or put some money down in the casino. It certainly doesn't get more iconic Vegas than that.

OVER-THE-TOP LAS VEGAS

Las Vegas was built on the idea that "average" and "normal" were adjectives that should never be used to describe the city. They don't just build hotels here; they build the biggest hotels in the world. And then they throw a roller coaster, a volcano, a $500-per-person golf course, or a $400-per-meal restaurant into the mix. Vegas is all about extravagance, so this itinerary will help you find the biggest of the big, the wildest of the wild, and the most outrageous, over-the-top experiences the city has to offer.

Mornings

You're going to have a busy day of excess, so it's important to start out with an ample breakfast to keep your energy level high. Room service is always an option—there's nothing quite as extravagant as having servers bring you food without ever getting out of bed—but if you feel like getting out and about, try the sumptuous **brunch buffets at Wynn Las Vegas** or **Caesars Palace.** Both offer an almost mind-boggling number of food choices (Caesars Bacchanal Buffet claims over 500 individual dishes at any time), all of which are a cut above your standard buffet. Handmade omelets and crêpes, freshly baked breads, and heaping mounds of bacon, sausage, and even steak will go well with your unlimited mimosas. At more than $45 per person (for the weekend champagne brunch), the price will remind you that this is no pedestrian all-you-can-eat experience.

The a.m. hours are the best time to schedule your outdoor activities. Not only are crowds often lighter, as a lot of people sleep in (it is a vacation, after all), but temperatures are also more moderate. This is especially true in the summer, when an afternoon stroll down the Strip can emulate a trek across the desert. So use this time to catch some rays poolside or, if you are recreationally minded, work up a moderate sweat with a round of golf. If you are a guest of **Wynn Las Vegas** or **Encore,** you can play the links at the **Wynn Las Vegas Golf Club** for a princely sum of $300 per person.

End your morning with a visit to a spa for some pampering and luxuriating. The **Qua Baths & Spa at Caesars Palace** offers virtually every massage, aromatherapy, skin-care treatment, and relaxation technique known to man—some of which will cost you more per 30-minute session than your hotel room. Soak in the Jacuzzi or sit in the unique ice room before heading out for the rest of the day.

Afternoons

You may still be full from breakfast, but that doesn't mean you can't have a little dessert to tide you over. Stop by **Serendipity 3** at Caesars Palace and order the Golden Opulence Sundae, made with rare ice cream and chocolate that's topped with edible 23-carat gold leaf. It's only $1,000, so get two!

Then it's off to the shopping malls, where the true excess can really begin. **The Forum Shops at Caesars Palace,** the **Grand Canal Shoppes at The Venetian, Crystals at CityCenter,** and the **Miracle Mile at Planet Hollywood** are all filled with

VEGAS BY air

Most people are satisfied with the views of Las Vegas from terra firma. Walking or driving up the Strip, especially at night, is a requirement for the first-time Vegas visitor. But, for some, there is no better way to see Sin City in all its neon glamour than from the air. If you are one of these intrepid souls, then look for a helicopter tour of Las Vegas.

There are more than a dozen competing companies offering tours of the city and surrounding areas, and most offer the same type of services at very similar prices. We're including a few of the more well-known companies below, but comparison shopping and checking out safety records are highly encouraged.

Maverick Helicopters (© 888/261-4414; www.maverickhelicopter.com) is one of the most well-known tour

operators in Las Vegas. Its large fleet of ECO-Star helicopters has one of the best safety records in the business, and a variety of packages are available, including twilight and night flights over the Strip. If you want to venture farther, Hoover Dam and Grand Canyon packages are available. Rates start at around $119 per person and go up from there, depending on the length and distance of the tour you choose. Most include transportation to and from your hotel.

VegasTours.com (© 866/218-6877; www.vegastours.com) features a similar list of air adventures, including a nighttime flight over Vegas and several to the Grand Canyon, while **Papillon Tours** (© 888/635-7272; www.papillon.com) not only offers helicopter tours, but airplane and ground excursions as well.

high-end retailers designed to drain your checking account and max out your credit cards. If those are a little out of your price range, consider going the completely opposite direction at the **Bonanza Gift and Souvenir Shop.** Billed as the largest souvenir shop in the world, this is the place where you can find pretty much anything—from tacky to, well, more tacky—emblazoned with the words "Las Vegas" on it. The kitsch factor here is off the charts.

Finally, experience some of the quintessential, only-in-Vegas attractions, such as riding a gondola through a shopping mall at **The Venetian,** or watching the water ballet at the **Fountains of Bellagio.**

Nights

Start your evening with a meal at **Joël Robuchon,** the multi-Michelin-star-winning darling of the foodie world—and with good reason. It'll only cost you a mere $300 a person (and that's before wine) to find out why. Or if your extravagance knows no bounds, try the FleurBurger at **Fleur by Hubert Keller.** Made from Wagyu beef, topped with foie gras truffle, and accompanied by a bottle of 1995 Chateau Petrus, it costs a measly $5,000.

Next, you'll want to see a show, and you should focus on those that can only be seen here. If **Celine Dion** or **Elton John** is in town, you should seize the opportunity to catch one of their concerts at Caesars Palace, because these shows are exclusive to Vegas. Or check out any of Cirque du Soleil's Vegas-only productions, the best of which are *O* at Bellagio and *KÀ* at MGM Grand. Each is set in its own multimillion-dollar theater, with stage sets—a giant pool and an enormous revolving platform, respectively—unlike anything you've seen before.

Nighttime is the best time for getting the true Strip experience, so how about renting a limousine (maybe one of those superstretch Hummers, if you are feeling really crazy) and instructing the driver to just cruise Las Vegas Boulevard. Hanging out of the sunroof with a cocktail in your hand is discouraged, but people do it anyway.

An after-dark stop at the **High Roller** is in order to give you a bird's-eye view of Las Vegas from the top of the world's tallest observation wheel, and then it's off to the party spots.

Most of the Vegas club scene starts late (11pm or midnight), so have your driver take you to one of the hip hot spots, such as **XS** at Encore, **Light** at Mandalay Bay, or **Marquee** at the Cosmopolitan of Las Vegas. These are see-and-be-seen places, so dress to impress and be on the lookout for a celebrity or three hanging out in the VIP areas. You can easily drop a grand if you want to sit at a table with bottle service.

If it's more of the classic Las Vegas vibe you're looking for, try **Peppermill's,** with its retro-'70s/'80s interior. So cheesy, it's hip again.

Your final destination should be in the spot that makes Vegas tick, the casino. Yes, there are casinos all over the country now, but there's nothing quite like tossing the dice at a craps table at **Caesars Palace** or spinning the reels in the high-limit lounge at **Wynn Las Vegas.**

GUYS' GETAWAY

Not every trip to Vegas with the guys needs to get as crazy as the movie *The Hangover,* but if you're looking for a real man's-man experience, no other city does it quite like this one. Whether it's a bachelor blowout weekend or just an excuse to blow off steam without your significant other's disapproving glances, this itinerary is designed to explain why they call this place "Sin City."

Mornings

You were probably out late the night before and there may have been alcohol involved, so start your morning with a hearty guy's breakfast at **Hash House a Go Go.** Its huge portions of twisted farm food are chest-poundingly substantial, and there is even a specialty called O'Hare of the Dog—a Budweiser served in a paper bag with a side of bacon.

To get your body in shape for the day ahead, spend the morning taking advantage of the various sports and recreation options available around town. Nearly every hotel has a fitness center and some, such as Bally's, offer full tennis courts. If you're a fan of the fairway, head over to **Bali Hai golf course,** located conveniently on the Strip, for 18 holes and some wheeling around in their GPS-enabled golf carts. Or, if you need something more extreme, visit the **Adventure Spa,** at Red Rock Resort, where you can arrange everything from rock climbing to horseback riding to river rafting.

If you're serious about your gambling, then late mornings are a great time to hit the casinos as well. The crowds are thinner, so you'll usually be able to find a table or a slot easily, and the blackjack limits are often lower, so you can save money for your big day ahead.

Afternoons

Continue your guys-gone-wild day with a stop at **Gilley's** for some great down-home grub and even a ride on the mechanical bull if you feel like proving your machismo.

Daytime is playtime in Las Vegas, where the big trend is to have nightclub-worthy experiences during the afternoon at some of the hotel pools. **DAYLIGHT Beach Club** at Mandalay Bay, **Tao Beach** at the Venetian, and **Encore Beach Club** at Encore Las Vegas are all open to the general public (for a cover charge) and include everything from live DJs to fully stocked bars and certainly a bevy of bikini-wearing partiers. If that's not enough to appeal to the guy in you, **Sapphire Gentleman's Club** now has its own daytime pool party complete with strippers.

Next, head back to the casino for a little sports-book action. You can place a wager on just about any type of sporting event in existence (cricket, anyone?), and, depending on the season and the day of the week, you might be able to catch a game in action. The **sports books** at the Mirage and Caesars Palace are always good options for their huge screens and high energy, but you may want to consider the M Resort, the Venetian, or the Palazzo, which offer in-running betting. Popular in the U.K., this means that you can not only wager on the outcome of the game, but place bets during the action as well.

If you want to get a little more immersed in the sporting action, try **SCORE!** at Luxor, an interactive attraction where you become a basketball, hockey, football, or racing star.

And if you need to get your adrenaline flowing, consider one of the serious thrill rides in town, such as the extreme adventures atop the 1,000-foot **Stratosphere Tower** at the Stratosphere Hotel. You can play a little game and make whichever of your friends who screams the loudest while on **Insanity: The Ride** or **SkyJump** buy the first round of drinks later that night. Or take a run at **SlotZilla,** a zip-line attraction in Downtown Las Vegas that features both seated and superhero flying position rides.

Nights

We know. We already sent you to some sports books, but you should go back to the only one that is a real restaurant. The 45,000-square-foot **Lagasse's Stadium** at the Venetian is a sports bar on steroids, with 100 flatscreen TVs and a menu crammed with highlights from Emeril's American and Creole cuisine.

Now for some nighttime entertainment. Topless revues are becoming an endangered species around Vegas—which you can probably blame on the Internet—but there are still a couple left that will allow you to get your (not so cheap) thrills. *Jubilee!* at Bally's is the last traditional showgirl production in town, and while it's a bit cheesy, it's still classic and classy Vegas. Meanwhile, *Crazy Girls* at the Riviera has absolutely no class, but maybe that's what you and the guys are after.

The party gets started late in Vegas, and you might want to start at a bar or two, such as **The Commonwealth** or **Insert Coin(s)** on Fremont Street in Downtown Las Vegas. Then it's time to hit the dance floor. **Marquee** at the Cosmopolitan is an obvious place to start, but **Beacher's Madhouse** at MGM Grand may be a better bet for a wild party night; they have weird carny acts and flying midgets, so be prepared for anything.

What's that? You haven't had enough gambling? Well, head over to Planet Hollywood's **Passion Pit,** complete with lingerie-clad dealers at the blackjack tables and go-go girls.

And if you want more girly action, Vegas has **strip clubs** aplenty. The best of the best are detailed in chapter 8.

GIRLS' GETAWAY

With the plethora of strip clubs and showgirls in this town, you'd think that Vegas is a man's world. Not so! There are plenty of activities and attractions for the ladies—from wild, bachelorette-style craziness to relaxing, leave-your-cares-at-home-style getaways. Here are just a few suggestions.

Mornings

If you dream of going to Paris, skip the hotel of the same name and go more or less across the street to Caesars Palace and **Payard Patisserie & Bistro** for breakfast. The chef is from the City of Lights, and you'll know it when you taste his croissants. The food is not cheap, but it is high quality, generously portioned, and just plain delightful. (It's also worth an evening stop for the amazing desserts.)

Vegas is retail heaven, and you could spend your whole day going to branches of pretty much every designer name you can think of in the major hotel malls (**Crystals** at CityCenter, **The Forum Shops** at Caesars Palace, **The Grand Canal Shoppes** at Venetian/Palazzo, **Miracle Mile** at Planet Hollywood, and shops at Bellagio and Wynn Las Vegas). Bargain shoppers will want to check out the **Las Vegas Premium Outlets North** near Downtown. Truth be told, there are not a lot of bargains there; but it's an outlet, so something will turn up.

Afternoons

You can have a fabulous girly lunch at the pink-and-orange **Serendipity 3,** a branch of the beloved New York establishment. The hot dogs are authentic, but, more to the point, they serve frozen hot chocolate!

Okay, it's time for some serious pampering. You could just stretch out by the pool (didn't you just buy a new bikini this morning?), but it's hot outside. So make your way to the spas at **Encore, Bellagio,** or **The Venetian** (which is a branch of the Canyon Ranch) for a full menu of massages, facials, weird treatments imported from countries you've never heard of, and lots more—all designed to make you feel as relaxed and limp as an al dente noodle.

Nights

If your girls' getaway weekend is of the rowdy bachelorette variety, have dinner at **Tacos & Tequila,** at Luxor. Not only is the food fun and frivolous, but the margaritas are also among the best in town. If it's a more convivial atmosphere you're after, get a big table at **Citizens Kitchen** at Mandalay Bay and share their big portions of classic American comfort food.

Hey, speaking of getting rowdy, if you're tired of all those signs with scantily clad women all over Vegas, equal time can be attained at such shows as the male-stripper review *Thunder From Down Under,* at Excalibur. Or, if that's not risqué enough, try the delightfully profane circus of *Absinthe* at Caesars Palace or the wild antics at *Vegas Nocturne* at the Cosmopolitan of Las Vegas. Just don't allow the host to pull you up on stage for an audience participation bit. You'll thank us later.

Fizz bar at Caesars Palace is a calm, sophisticated spot to have a tipple to gear up for the rest of your evening. Check out their outlandish champagne cocktails and the art on the wall from Elton John's private collection (his husband co-created the joint). A somewhat more gearing-up-for-the-clubs atmosphere is across the way at **Hyde Bellagio,** which in addition to having fun cocktails (is that a Belini cart? Why, yes, it is!) has the best view of the Bellagio Fountains from its lakeside patio.

Finally, strap on that pair of Christian Louboutins you bought earlier today (lucky you), because it's time to go dancing. If you're single and looking to mingle (or whatever, we don't judge), the scenes at **Light** at Mandalay Bay, **XS** at Encore Las Vegas, and **Rose.Rabbit.Lie** at the Cosmopolitan of Las Vegas are such that people will stand in line for hours (and pay outrageous cover charges) just to get inside. We have to admit they are awfully fun.

Wanna just go dance and not be bothered by the meat-market scene? Consider going to gay clubs, such as **Piranha** or **Share,** both just off the Strip. They welcome women, but remember that you aren't going to be the priority here.

UNLIKELY LAS VEGAS

It's really hard to overlook the Strip—after all, a number of people have spent billions and billions of dollars to ensure that you don't—but there are still some surprisingly unusual and captivating sights to see in and around Las Vegas. This itinerary is designed to help you discover them. You will need a car to do this tour.

Mornings

Those pricey buffets at the casinos may offer you truckloads of food, but even the ones at the out-of-the-way hotels are the very definition of "discovered." Instead, go down home for the delightful Southern cooking at **M&M Soul Food Café.** Chicken and waffles, biscuits and gravy, or anything with grits is a great way to start the day as far as we're concerned.

Walk off that breakfast by exploring the nearby **18b Arts District,** home to a number of art galleries and studios, bravely taking a stance against prefab, soulless Vegas. You might take special note of **Retro Vegas,** a fun and funky store celebrating Sin City and mid-century modern furnishings (they work remarkably well together). If it's the first Friday of the month, you could come back and stroll here in the evening, as that's when the galleries come into the streets for a food, art, and entertainment festival.

Springs Preserve is a remarkable destination, focused on nature and ecological concerns. The interpretive center examines the history of the region as related to water consumption, which sounds "dry" but really isn't. Need proof? Try the so-real-you-are-there flash-flood exhibit or the 3-D movie theater that puts you atop the Hoover Dam being built. Outside are trails through the wetlands, animal habitats, and other exhibition halls dealing with the environment and recycling. The place is informative, entertaining, and absolutely vital in this day and age, and you can't believe that something of this quality and social significance is anywhere near Vegas.

Afternoons

Although Las Vegas is obviously our favorite city, New Orleans comes in a close second and a lot of that has to do with the food. You can find amazingly authentic offerings at **Lola's: A Louisiana Kitchen,** including 'po boys served on bread that is flown in from the Big Easy.

From there, we recommend a duo of only-in–Las Vegas museums. Begin with the **National Atomic Testing Museum.** It's about more than just the 5 minutes when the bomb was awesome (apparently people really thought that—they have photos that you won't believe, like the one of Miss Atomic Bomb), instead tracing the history of the atomic age and focusing specifically on the aboveground nuclear testing that occurred just outside of Las Vegas. It's a fascinating and sobering experience.

Then you're off to the **Pinball Hall of Fame,** where you can not only appreciate, but actually play, classic machines and arcade games from the 1960s to the present day.

If you want to skip the latter, consider taking in the afternoon show by **Mac King** or **Jeff Civillico** at Harrah's Las Vegas and the Quad, respectively. Both are considered among the best shows in Vegas and are good values for the money. King is an illusionist and comedian of great personal charm who still practices magic that doesn't require computer technology, while Civillico is a comic-juggler with a family-friendly and very funny patter. You can often get discounted (or even two-for-one) tickets for both shows in local magazines or online.

Nights

Now we'll send you far west to a place only foodies tend to know: **Raku Grill,** a Japanese *robata* (charcoal grill) restaurant that is a hangout for many of the chefs in town when they're off the clock. Alternately, you could try **Rose.Rabbit.Lie,** the distinctive and definitely unique dining and entertainment venue at the Cosmopolitan of Las Vegas. Not only is the food fantastic, but the experience of eating there is unforgettable.

After dinner, why not do something completely "unlikely," like perform on the Las Vegas Strip? There are several hotel lounges that offer karaoke, but the sing-along fun at **Gilley's** at Treasure Island is probably the best. Or, instead of a show in one of the casinos, see what's playing at **The Smith Center for the Performing Arts** in Downtown Las Vegas. You might be able to catch a Broadway touring show, a big-name concert, or a jazz set in one of the many theaters at the complex.

End your night exploring the booming bar scene of Downtown's **Fremont East Entertainment District** with the funky taverns like **Griffin, The Commonwealth, Insert Coin(s), Vanguard Lounge,** and more, all within steps of each other. Each has its own vibe and is mostly populated by locals, so try each on for style and see what fits.

EATING LAS VEGAS

Las Vegas is a mecca for food lovers, offering you almost endless opportunities to gorge yourself on virtually every type of cuisine, from cheap eats to gourmet meals. This itinerary presumes you are very hungry and want to at least sample as much of it as you can, throwing waistlines, cholesterol counts, and common sense to the wind. You will need a car to do this tour, although you may want to consider walking as much of it as you can to give the illusion that you're getting a little exercise in between binges.

Mornings

There are plenty of ways to overdo it from a food perspective first thing in the morning. You could go big with the insane portions of the deliriously over-the-top selections at **Hash House a Go Go,** or get an entire day's worth of calories at an inexpensive buffet like the **Main Street Garden Court** in Downtown Las Vegas—but let's be reasonable, shall we? After all, you don't want to get too full before the day has really even started.

So instead, go for something a little lighter but still packed with flavors, like the delightful crêpes at the **Sugar Factory** or the sumptuous quiche at **Bouchon.** Both come in very satisfying portions, yet they'll keep you from getting too loaded down.

If you decided to sleep in a bit (and really, who could blame you?), then you could go for brunch at **Mon Ami Gabi,** which offers its own crêpes and quiches.

Otherwise the rest of your morning could be spent exploring various sweet shops so you can stock up on quick hits of sugar to get you through the rest of the day. **M&M World** allows you to mix and match your own selection of candy, while local favorite **Ethel M Chocolates** serves a finer brand of confections. Or you could simply stay at the aforementioned **Sugar Factory,** which in addition to having a full-service restaurant, boasts a massive candy store with contemporary and blast-from-the-past treats plus a line of signature, celebrity-endorsed lollipops.

Afternoons

For lunch, we're going to suggest something a little more serious and substantial. The inspired pub grub at **Todd English P.U.B.** is a terrific choice, especially if you go for the "carvery" portion of the menu, which allows you to mix and match meats, breads, cheeses, and toppings to create your own sandwich.

Speaking of sandwiches, we'd be totally remiss if we didn't mention **Capriotti's** as a perfect place to have lunch. Their divine submarine sandwiches (we're partial to the Bobby, which is like Thanksgiving on a bun) will make you consider getting the epic 20-inch size and calling it a day, but try to restrain yourself with one of the smaller versions.

Burgers are another way to go and there are lots of options in Vegas, including the fantastic offerings at **Bobbys' Burger Palace, Gordon Ramsay BurGR,** or **Holstein's Shakes and Buns.** But if we had to pick just one burger favorite, it would have to be the barbecue bacon variety at **KGB: Kerry Simon Burgers,** which will pretty much destroy your taste for anything ordered through a clown's mouth ever again.

As you are digesting, take a stroll over to Bellagio to visit the **Jean-Philippe Patisserie** and sample the finest chocolate available in Las Vegas, or go to Monte Carlo and check out **The Cupcakery** for their mouth-watering temptations. Regarding the latter, if you can only choose one, go for the Oh My Gosh, Ganache, which has chocolate ganache baked *into* the cake!

If you're lucky enough to be visiting on the first Friday of the month, be sure to go to the **First Friday** street festival in the Arts District, where you'll find a parking lot's worth of food trucks and vendors serving everything from pizza to sushi to barbecue and more. Don't miss the state fair–style selections, including the genius deep-fried chocolate-chip cookie dough. Missing this will haunt you—trust us.

Nights

Finally, we're going to go whole hog, or cow as the case may be, by sending you to dinner at one of the city's steakhouses. **The Steakhouse** at Circus Circus is a local favorite, offering full meals at the same prices that others charge for an a la carte selection. **Strip House** at Planet Hollywood puts a modern spin on things with a charming peek-a-boo bordello theme and fantastic cuts of meat. But for our money you can't beat **Old Homestead Steakhouse** at Caesars Palace, a sister of the legendary New York City restaurant. The portions here are huge, which is appropriate since this is the restaurant that claims to have invented the doggie bag.

If a steak seems like too much of a commitment to you, you could try one of the growing number of restaurants that serves small bites instead of full meals. Chief among them would be **L'Atelier** at MGM Grand by master chef Joël Robuchon, where you can get various-size tasting menus or order small plates on your own, each of which will be better than the last. **Rose.Rabbit.Lie** at the Cosmopolitan of Las Vegas has fantastic gourmet small plates and a fun environment in which to eat them. Another great choice in this category would be **Raku Grill,** where you can get fantastic skewers of meat, vegetables, seafood, and more cooked over a Japanese charcoal grill. Just be warned that even though the portions are small, you'll wind up ordering a lot of them, and it could end up costing you more than just a standard meal.

Help for Troubled Travelers

The **Travelers Aid Society** is a social-service organization geared to helping travelers in difficult situations. Its services include reuniting families separated while traveling, feeding people stranded without cash, and even providing emotional counseling. If you're in

trouble, seek them out. In Las Vegas, services are provided by **Help of Southern Nevada,** 1640 E. Flamingo Rd., Ste. 100, near Maryland Parkway (© **702/369-4357;** www.helpsonv.org). Hours are Monday through Thursday 7am to 5pm.

But wait, we're not done. This is a 24-hour town, and lots of restaurants are open all night to satisfy those 2am cravings. **Citizens Kitchen** at Mandalay Bay serves tasty and creative takes on classic American comfort food.

Of course, you also get some symmetrical closure on your day by going back to the **Sugar Factory,** which is also open 24 hours a day.

CITY LAYOUT

Located in the southernmost precincts of a wide, pancake-flat valley, Las Vegas is the biggest city in the state of Nevada. Treeless mountains form a scenic backdrop to hotels awash in neon glitter. Although bursting with residents and visitors, the city is quite compact, geographically speaking.

There are two main areas of Las Vegas: the **Strip** and **Downtown.** The former is probably the most famous 4-mile stretch of road in the nation. Officially called Las Vegas Boulevard South, it contains most of the top hotels in town and offers almost all the major showroom entertainment. First-time visitors will, and probably should, spend the bulk of their time on the Strip.

Downtown, meanwhile, is where Vegas started its Glitter Gulch fame, complete with neon ambassadors Vegas Vic and Sassy Sally watching over the action.

For many people, that's all there is to Las Vegas. But there is actually more to the town than that: Paradise Road, just east of the Strip, and Boulder Highway on the far east side of town, are home to quite a bit of casino action; Maryland Parkway boasts mainstream shopping; and there are different restaurant options all over the city. Many of the "locals' hotels," most of which are off the regular tourist track, offer cheaper gambling limits plus budget food and entertainment options. Confining yourself to the Strip and Downtown is fine for the first-time visitor, but repeat customers (and you will be) should get out there and explore. Las Vegas Boulevard South (the Strip) is the starting point for addresses; any street that crosses it starts with 1 East and 1 West at its intersection with the Strip (and goes up from there).

All major Las Vegas hotels provide comprehensive tourist information at their reception and/or sightseeing and show desks.

Other good information sources are the **Las Vegas Convention and Visitors Authority,** 3150 Paradise Rd. (© **877/847-4858** or 702/892-7575; www.lasvegas. com), open Monday through Friday 8am to 5:30pm; the **Las Vegas Metro Chamber of Commerce,** 6671 Las Vegas Blvd. S., Ste. 300 (© **702/735-1616;** www.lvchamber. com), open Monday through Friday 8am to 5pm; and, for information on all of Nevada, including Las Vegas, the **Nevada Commission on Tourism** (© **800/638-2328;** www.travelnevada.com), open 24 hours.

NEIGHBORHOODS IN BRIEF

South Strip

For the purposes of organizing this book, we've divided the Strip into three sections. The **South Strip** can be roughly defined as the portion of the Strip south of Harmon Avenue, including the MGM Grand, Mandalay Bay, the Monte Carlo, New York–New York, Luxor, CityCenter, and many more hotels and casinos. First-timers should consider staying here or in the Mid-Strip area simply because this is where the bulk of the stuff you're going to want to see, do, and eat are located.

Mid-Strip

The **Mid-Strip** is a long stretch of the Las Vegas Boulevard South between Harmon Avenue and Spring Mountain Road, which includes such big-name casinos as Planet Hollywood, the Cosmopolitan of Las Vegas, Bellagio, Caesars, the Mirage, Treasure Island, Bally's, Paris Las Vegas, Flamingo Las Vegas, and Harrah's, and more. As mentioned above, this is a great area for newbies, and it's also the preferred location for people with mobility issues since fewer steps will get you to more places.

North Strip

The **North Strip** stretches north from Spring Mountain Road all the way to the Stratosphere and includes Wynn/Encore, Stratosphere, and Circus Circus, to name a few. Although there are certainly things to see along this chunk of the Strip, development has mostly stalled so you'll see more things closed or partially constructed in this area than you will open and completed. With the exception of Wynn/Encore, it is the lower-rent part of the Strip, with all of the good and bad that comes along with it.

Downtown

Also known as **"Glitter Gulch"** (narrower streets make the neon seem brighter), Downtown Las Vegas, which is centered on Fremont Street, between Main and 9th streets, was the first section of the city to develop hotels and casinos. With the exception of the Golden Nugget, which looks like it belongs in Monte Carlo, this area has traditionally been more casual than the Strip. But between the **Fremont Street Experience** (p. 140), the **Fremont East Entertainment District** (p. 142), and a general resurgence, Downtown offers a more affordable yet still entertaining alternative to the Strip.

The area between the Strip and Downtown is a seedy stretch dotted with tacky wedding chapels, bail-bond operations, pawnshops, and cheap motels. However, the area known as the **18b Arts District** (roughly north and south of Charleston Blvd. to the west of Las Vegas Blvd. S.) is making a name for itself as an artists' colony. Studios, galleries, antique stores, bars, small cafes, and the fun **First Friday Las Vegas** festival (p. 143) can be found in the vicinity. Eventually it may warrant its own neighborhood designation, but for now we include it in the Downtown category.

Just Off the Strip

With land directly on the Strip at a premium, it isn't surprising that a veritable cottage industry of casinos, hotels, restaurants, nightclubs, attractions, and services have taken up residence in the areas immediately surrounding the big megaresorts. Within a mile in any given direction you'll find major hotels such as the Rio, the Orleans, the Las Vegas Hotel (formerly the Las Vegas Hilton), and the Hard Rock, to name a few, as well as important visitor destinations such as the Las Vegas Convention Center. You'll also find many smaller chain/name-brand hotels and motels offering reliable service at rates that are usually cheaper than you'll pay in a big casino-hotel on the Strip.

South & East of the Strip

Once you get a little bit of distance between you and the Strip, you'll start getting into the types of neighborhoods that will look much more familiar to you—except, perhaps, with a lot more desert landscaping. Shopping centers and housing tracts dominate the landscape of the bedroom community of Henderson, while lower-priced motels and chain restaurants take up a lot of space along the Boulder Highway corridor on the far-east side of town. But sprinkled throughout are some fun, low-cost casino hotels and some out-of-the-way restaurants and attractions worth knowing about.

North & West of the Strip

The communities of Summerlin and North Las Vegas are where many of the people who work on the Strip live, shop, eat, and play. Yes, there are some major casino hotels in the area, including the stunning Red Rock Resort and a few notable restaurants, but for the most part what you'll find here are dependable chain stores and eateries that offer comfort shopping and food at better-than-Strip prices.

LAS VEGAS IN CONTEXT

3

The global recession hit Vegas hard, but like the rest of the world, Sin City is recovering slowly with improved visitation numbers, the most new development projects in years, and a little bit less red on the balance sheets at the major casino corporations. That recovery, though, is creating a Las Vegas that looks different than it used to, with more of a focus on value and a renewed sensibility that the city is open to more than just the traveler willing to blow $400 per night on a hotel room.

LAS VEGAS TODAY

No major city in America has reinvented itself as many times, especially in such a short period, as Las Vegas. Just look at the recent decades. In the '80s, it was a discount afterthought. In the '90s, it was family and theme heaven. The new millennium brought in ultra-luxury and sky-high prices on everything from rooms to shampoo in the sundry stores.

For the better part of the new millennium, the watchword was "expensive." The average room rate soared to over $200 a night, significantly higher than what visitors, once lulled by lower double-digit bargains, were used to paying. It was not unusual for the high-end hotels to charge $400 or even $500 for a standard room.

And why not? The crowds kept coming. Occupancy rates in Vegas were well over 90%, nearly 30% higher than the national average. Flush with big returns on their stock investments, equity in their home, or simply easy-flowing credit, those who could afford it flocked to the city in record numbers, generating record profit for the casinos. Vegas became hip, drawing a younger, more affluent demographic that lined up to pay for the fancy hotel rooms, the exclusive nightclubs, the celebrity-chef restaurants, and the high-limit gaming tables.

The Average Joe, on the other hand, got priced right out of town. For a lot of people—the people whose money helped build those massive hotels and casinos—the idea of a Vegas vacation became cost-prohibitive.

But then came the global economic meltdown, and Vegas was hit hard. The number of visitors coming to the city dropped dramatically, and those who came spent a lot less money in the casinos. By 2010, the average room rate plunged to the lowest level in nearly a decade and more rooms were going empty, with occupancy rates in the low 80% range—still good when compared to the national average, but scary for a city that depends on filling those rooms to keep its economy going.

Many gaming companies fell into bankruptcy, and while their casinos have remained open, their bank accounts have slammed shut. Just like many Americans who ran up too much credit-card debt, the gaming companies are operating under obligations that run into the billions, and they are having a hard time paying the bills.

As the national economy improved and we moved into the second decade of the new millennium, so did the Las Vegas economy. Visitation and occupancy rates perked up and people seemed to be willing to spend money again.

In the long run, this could wind up being good news for the Average Joe tourist. Room rates have remained lower, and most of the new stuff planned for the city—attractions, shows, restaurants, and so on—is aimed squarely at the midmarket crowd. While rates will certainly go up as the economy improves, the hotel companies are skittish about the idea of returning them to their sky-high levels because they are worried that the national mood of extravagant spending has changed.

Welcome back, Joe. Las Vegas has missed you.

Adapting to Las Vegas

Las Vegas is, for the most part, a very casual city. Although there are a few restaurants that have a restrictive dress code, most of them—and all of the showrooms, casinos, and attractions—are pretty much come as you are. Some people still choose to dress up for their night on the town, resulting in a strange dichotomy where you might see a couple in a suit and evening gown sitting next to a couple in shorts and sandals at a show or in a nice restaurant.

Generally speaking, spiffy-casual (slacks or nice jeans, button-up shirts or blouses, or a simple skirt or dress) is the best way to go in terms of what to wear, allowing you to be comfortable in just about any situation. Go too far to one extreme or the other and you're bound to feel out of place somewhere.

The only exception to this rule is the nightclubs, which often have very strict policies on what you can and cannot wear. They vary from club to club, but, as a general rule, sandals or flip-flops, shorts, and baseball caps are frowned upon. A nice pair of jeans, a clean T-shirt, and a simple pair of sneakers will get you in the door, while fancier clothes (jackets, cocktail dresses) may get you past the velvet rope a little faster.

Yes, it does get hot in Las Vegas, so you really should factor that in when you're planning your wardrobe for your trip. It's important to note that every enclosed space (casino, showroom, restaurant, nightclub, and so on) is heavily air-conditioned, so it can actually get a bit chilly once you get inside. Think light layers and you should be okay.

Las Vegas is a 24-hour town, so you can find something to eat or drink all the time; but many of the nicer restaurants open only for dinner, with 5 or 6pm to 10 or 11pm the standard operating hours. Nightclubs usually open around 10pm and go until dawn, with the bulk of the crowds not showing up until midnight at the earliest. There are a few afternoon shows, but most are in the evenings and often run two shows a night with start times that range from 7 until 10:30pm. Casinos and most regular bars are open 24 hours a day.

LOOKING BACK: LAS VEGAS HISTORY

The Early 1900s: Las Vegas Takes Shape

For many years after its creation via a land auction in 1905, Las Vegas was a mere whistle-stop town. That all changed in 1928 when Congress authorized the building of nearby Boulder Dam (later renamed Hoover Dam), bringing thousands of workers to the area. Although gambling still happened in the backrooms of saloons after it became illegal in 1909, the lifting of those prohibitions in 1931 is what set the stage for the first of the city's many booms. Fremont Street's gaming emporiums and speakeasies attracted dam workers and, upon the dam's completion, were replaced by hordes of tourists who came to see the engineering marvel (it was called "the Eighth Wonder of the World"). But it wasn't until the early years of World War II that visionary entrepreneurs began to plan for the city's glittering future.

The 1940s: The Strip Is Born

Contrary to popular lore, developer Bugsy Siegel didn't actually stake a claim in the middle of nowhere—his Flamingo opened in 1946 just a few blocks south of already-existing properties.

The true beginnings of what would eventually become the Las Vegas Strip started years earlier. According to lore, Thomas Hull was driving toward Downtown's already-booming Fremont Street area when his car broke down just outside of the city limits. As he stood there sweating in the desert heat, he envisioned, or perhaps just wished for, a cool swimming pool in the scrub brush next to the highway. Luckily, Hull was a hotel magnate and he put his money where his mirage was. El Rancho Vegas, ultra-luxurious for its time and complete with a sparkling pool facing the highway, opened in 1941 across the street from where the upcoming SLS Las Vegas (formerly the Sahara) now stands. Scores of Hollywood stars were invited to the grand opening, and El Rancho Vegas soon became the hotel of choice for visiting film stars.

Beginning a trend that continues today, each new property tried to outdo existing hotels in luxurious amenities and thematic splendor. Las Vegas was on its way to becoming America's playground.

Las Vegas promoted itself in the 1940s as a town that combined Wild West frontier friendliness with glamour and excitement. Throughout the decade, the city was Hollywood's celebrity retreat. The Hollywood connection gave the town glamour in the public's mind. So did the mob connection, which became clear when notorious underworld gangster Bugsy Siegel built the fabulous Flamingo, a tropical paradise and "a real class joint."

While the Strip was expanding with major resorts like the Frontier, Bugsy's Flamingo, and the Thunderbird, Downtown kept pace with new hotels such as the El Cortez and casinos like the Golden Nugget. By the end of the decade, Fremont Street was known as "Glitter Gulch," its profusion of neon signs proclaiming round-the-clock gaming and entertainment.

The 1950s: Building Booms & A-Bombs

Las Vegas entered the new decade as a city (no longer a frontier town), with a population of about 50,000. Hotel growth was phenomenal, with legendary names like the Sahara, the Dunes, the Sands, and the Tropicana all gaining neon-lit fame.

The Desert Inn, which opened in 1950 with headliners Edgar Bergen and Charlie McCarthy, brought country-club elegance (including an 18-hole golf course and tennis courts) to the Strip.

In 1951, the Eldorado Club Downtown became Benny Binion's Horseshoe Club, which would gain fame as the home of the annual World Series of Poker.

In 1955, the Côte d'Azur–themed Riviera became the ninth big hotel to open on the Strip. Breaking the ranch-style mode, it was, at nine stories, the Strip's first high-rise. Liberace, one of the hottest names in show business, was paid the unprecedented sum of $50,000 a week to dazzle audiences in the Riviera's posh Clover Room.

Elvis appeared at the New Frontier in 1956 but wasn't a huge success; his fans were too young to fit the Las Vegas tourist mold.

In 1958, the $10-million, 1,065-room Stardust upped the spectacular stakes by importing the famed *Lido de Paris* spectacle from the French capital. It became one of the longest-running shows ever to play Las Vegas.

Two performers whose names have been linked to Las Vegas ever since—Frank Sinatra and Wayne Newton—made their debuts there. Mae West not only performed in Las Vegas, but also cleverly bought up a half-mile of desolate Strip frontage between the Dunes and the Tropicana.

In the 1950s, the wedding industry helped make Las Vegas one of the nation's most popular venues for "goin' to the chapel." Celebrity weddings of the 1950s that sparked the trend included singer Dick Haymes and Rita Hayworth, Joan Crawford and Pepsi chairman Alfred Steele, Carol Channing and TV exec Charles Lowe, and Paul Newman and Joanne Woodward.

On a grimmer note, the '50s also heralded the atomic age in Nevada, with nuclear testing taking place just 65 miles northwest of Las Vegas. A chilling 1951 photograph shows a mushroom-shaped cloud from an atomic bomb test visible over the Fremont Street horizon. Throughout the decade, about one bomb a month was detonated in the nearby desert (an event, interestingly enough, that often attracted loads of tourists).

The 1960s: The Rat Pack & the King

The very first month of the new decade made entertainment history when the Sands hosted a 3-week "Summit Meeting" in the Copa Room that was presided over by "Chairman of the Board" Frank Sinatra, with Rat Pack cronies Dean Martin, Sammy Davis, Jr., Peter Lawford, and Joey Bishop (all of whom happened to be in town filming *Ocean's Eleven*). The series of shows helped to form the Rat Pack legend in Vegas and, in many ways vice versa, making the town hip and cool—the ultimate '60s swinging retreat.

It needed the help. After nearly a decade of almost constant building and expansion (no fewer than 10 major resorts opened in the 1950s), a crackdown on the Mafia and its money, which had fueled the city's development, brought construction to a halt. Only two major properties opened during the decade—the Road to Morocco–themed Aladdin in 1963 and the Roman Empire bacchanalia that was Caesars Palace in 1966. Perhaps trying to prove that the mob was gone for good, Las Vegas became a family destination in 1968, when Circus Circus burst onto the scene with the world's largest permanent circus and a "junior casino" featuring dozens of carnival midway games on its mezzanine level.

Elvis officially became part of the Vegas legend with the release of the film *Viva Las Vegas* in 1964, which not only furthered the city's "cool" quotient but also gave it an enduring theme song that remains a part of the city's identity more than 60 years later. But it was not until 1969 that the King's place in Sin City history would be cemented with his triumphant return to Las Vegas at the International's showroom with a series of concerts that made him one of the city's all-time legendary performers. His fans had come of age.

The 1970s: The Glamour Fades

The image of Las Vegas that emerged in the 1970s was one that it would take decades to shed itself of: a tacky tourist trap with aging casinos, cheap restaurants, and showrooms filled with performers whose careers were on their last legs. With a

THE mob IN LAS VEGAS

The role of the Mafia in the creation of Las Vegas is little more than a footnote these days, but it isn't too bold of a statement to suggest that without organized crime, the city would not have developed in the ways that it did and its past would have certainly been less colorful.

Meyer Lansky was a big name in the New York crime syndicate in the 1930s, and it was largely his decision to send Benjamin "Bugsy" Siegel west to expand their empire. Although the Strip had already begun to form with the opening of El Rancho in 1941 and the Frontier in 1942, it was Bugsy's sparkling Flamingo of 1946 that began a Mafia-influenced building boom and era of control that would last for decades. Famous marquees, such as the Desert Inn, the Riviera, and the Stardust, were all built, either in part or in whole, from funding sources that were less than reputable.

During the '60s, negative attention focused on mob influence in Las Vegas. Of the 11 major casino hotels that had opened in the previous decade, 10 were believed to have been financed with mob money. Then, like a knight in shining armor, Howard Hughes rode into town and embarked on a $300-million hotel- and property-buying spree, which included the Desert Inn itself (in 1967). Hughes was as "Bugsy" as Benjamin Siegel any day, but his pristine reputation helped bring respectability to the desert city and lessen its gangland stigma.

During the 1970s and 1980s, the government got involved, embarking on a series of criminal prosecutions across the country to try to break the back of the Mafia. Although not completely successful, it did manage to wrest major control of Las Vegas away from organized crime, aided by new legislation that allowed corporations to own casinos. By the time Steve Wynn built the Mirage in 1989, the Mafia's role was reduced to the point where the most it could control were the city's innumerable strip clubs.

These days, strict regulation and billions of dollars of corporate money keep things on the up and up, but the mob's influence can still be felt even at the highest levels of Las Vegas government. Former Mayor Oscar B. Goodman, first elected in 1999, was a lawyer for the Mafia in the 1960s and 1970s, defending such famed gangsters as Meyer Lanksy and Anthony "Tony the Ant" Spilotro. The popular and colorful Goodman cheerfully refers to his Mafia-related past often, joking about his desire to settle conflicts in the desert at night with a baseball bat like "in the good old days."

As if to bring things full circle, Goodman championed **The Mob Museum** (p. 140), a stunning facility that examines the history and influence of the Mafia in America and Las Vegas in particular. It is located in a former courthouse that was the site of the Mafia-related Kefauver hearings of the 1950s.

few exceptions, investment had slowed to a crawl and Vegas didn't seem as exciting anymore, especially when it was forced to compete with the sparkling newness of Atlantic City, where gambling was legalized in 1976.

There were some bright spots. In 1971, the 500-room Union Plaza opened at the head of Fremont Street, on the site of the old Union Pacific Station. It had what was, at the time, the world's largest casino, and its showroom specialized in Broadway productions.

The year 1973 was eventful: Over at the Tropicana, illusionists extraordinaire Siegfried & Roy began turning women into tigers and themselves into legends in the *Folies Bergere*. Meanwhile, just up the street, the original MGM Grand (now Bally's) trumped the Plaza as the largest hotel and casino in the world, with Dean Martin as the opening evening's host.

Las Vegas made its way into America's living rooms with two very different television programs. Merv Griffin began taping his daytime talkfest in 1971 at Caesars Palace, taking advantage of a ready supply of local headliner guests. Then in 1978 *Vega$* debuted, instantly emblazoning the image of star Robert Urich cruising down the Strip in his red Thunderbird convertible on the minds of TV viewers everywhere.

As the decade drew to a close, an international arrivals building opened and turned McCarran Field into McCarran International Airport, and dollar slot machines caused a sensation in the casinos.

The 1980s: The City Erupts

As the '80s began, Las Vegas was suffering an identity crisis. The departure of the mob and its money combined with a struggling economy and Reagan-era conservatism put a damper on the shining star of the desert. There was little new development and a lot of the "classic" hotels became rundown shadows of their former selves.

A devastating fire in 1980 at the original MGM Grand killed more than 80 people, and just a few months later a fire at the Las Vegas Hilton killed eight more. In some ways these tragedies helped to further the transformation of the public's view of the entire city. Las Vegas became tacky, desperate, and possibly unsafe.

Even the showrooms, once the magnificent Elvis/Sinatra klieg light that lured people from around the world, had become something of a joke. For entertainers, Vegas was where you played when your career was over, not when you were on top.

What Las Vegas really needed was a white knight, and they got one in the form of Golden Nugget owner Steve Wynn and his $630-million gamble on the Mirage. Financed mostly through the sale of junk bonds, the hotel's construction would eventually change the course of Las Vegas history.

The hotel opened in 1989, fronted by five-story waterfalls, lagoons, and lush tropical foliage—not to mention a 50-foot volcano that dramatically erupted regularly! Wynn gave world-renowned illusionists Siegfried & Roy carte blanche (and more than $30 million) to create the most spellbinding show Las Vegas had ever seen, and brought in world-class chefs to banish the idea that all you could eat in the town were all-you-can-eat spreads and $4.99 prime rib.

It was an immediate success; from a financial perspective, of course, but more importantly from a perception one. Almost overnight, Las Vegas became cool again and everyone wanted to go there.

The 1990s: King Arthur Meets King Tut

The 1990s began with a blare of trumpets heralding the rise of a turreted medieval castle, fronted by a moated drawbridge and staffed by jousting knights and fair damsels. Excalibur reflected the '90s marketing trend to promote Las Vegas as a family-vacation destination.

Was that trend successful? Well, Chevy Chase did take his family on a *Vegas Vacation* in 1997, but the city kept the Sin part of its name alive, at least in popular culture, with Robert Redford making an *Indecent Proposal* (1993); Nicholas Cage hitting rock bottom in *Leaving Las Vegas* (1995); and Elizabeth Berkley strutting her stuff in the widely derided *Showgirls* (1995).

Canadian circus/theater group Cirque du Soleil transformed the entertainment scene in Las Vegas with the 1993 debut of *Mystére* at the newly opened Treasure Island. It would be the first of no fewer than eight Cirque shows that would launch over the next 2 decades.

The era of megahotels continued on the Strip, including the *new* MGM Grand hotel, backed by a full theme park (it ended Excalibur's brief reign as the world's largest resort), Luxor Las Vegas, and Steve Wynn's Treasure Island.

In 1993, a unique pink-domed 5-acre indoor amusement park, Grand Slam Canyon (later known as Adventuredome), became part of the Circus Circus hotel. In 1995, the Fremont Street Experience was completed, revitalizing Downtown Las Vegas. Closer to the Strip, rock restaurant magnate Peter Morton opened the Hard Rock Hotel, billed as "the world's first rock-'n'-roll hotel and casino." The year 1996 saw the advent of the French Riviera–themed Monte Carlo and the Stratosphere Las Vegas Hotel & Casino, its 1,149-foot tower the highest building west of the Mississippi. The unbelievable New York–New York arrived in 1997.

But it all paled compared with 1998 to 1999. As Vegas hastily repositioned itself from "family destination" to "luxury resort," several new hotels, once again eclipsing anything that had come before, opened. Bellagio was the latest from Vegas visionary Steve Wynn, an attempt to bring grand European style to the desert, while at the far southern end of the Strip, Mandalay Bay charmed. As if this weren't enough, the Venetian's ambitiously detailed re-creation of everyone's favorite Italian city came along in May 1999, and was followed in short order by the opening of Paris Las Vegas in the fall of 1999.

The 2000s: The Lap of Luxury

The 21st century opened with a bang as the Aladdin blew itself up and gave itself a from-the-ground-up makeover (which in turn only lasted for a handful of years before Planet Hollywood took it over and changed it entirely), while Steve Wynn blew up the Desert Inn and built a new showstopper named for him. Along the way, everyone expanded, and then expanded some more, ultimately adding thousands of new rooms. The goal became "luxury," with a secondary emphasis on "adult." Little by little, wacky, eye-catching themes were phased out (as much as one can when one's hotel looks like a castle) and generic sophistication took its place. Gaming was still number one, but the newer hotels were trying to top each other in terms of other recreations— decadent nightclubs, celebrity chef–backed restaurants, fancy spas, and superstar shows.

"More is more" seemed to be the motto, and its embodiment was the massive City-Center, perhaps the most ambitious project in Las Vegas yet. Composed of a 4,000-room megaresort, two 400-room boutique hotels, condos, shopping, dining, clubs, and more, it covers more than 60 acres and, as such, is a city-within-the-city. Gone are the outrageous themes, replaced by cutting-edge modernism—all sleek lines of glass and metal designed with the future in mind, not only from an architectural standpoint but from an ecological one as well. Sure, building the massive CityCenter probably made the earth shudder a bit, but its advanced green building and sustainable operating systems helped to ensure that the planet didn't just collapse in on itself from the weight of it all.

The excess of Vegas was spotlighted in popular culture as well. *Ocean's Eleven* got a new millennium makeover in 2001 with a cast of superstars like George Clooney, Brad Pitt, and Julia Roberts. Then in 2009, *The Hangover* took it all to a new level with a raunchy morality tale of a Vegas bachelor party gone horribly awry. The 2013 *Hangover 3* brought the action back to Vegas to close out the trilogy.

Even the city's motto, which became a popular part of the American lexicon, was a winking nod to the seemingly endless ways to satisfy the id: "What happens in Vegas, stays in Vegas."

Once known solely as an outpost of all-you-can-eat buffets and $4.99 prime rib specials, Las Vegas became one of the top dining destinations in the world. Every celebrity chef worth his or her sea salt had a restaurant here, and the level of culinary quality rose almost as fast as the prices. Take a look at some of the famous names attached to Vegas restaurants: Emeril Lagasse, Wolfgang Puck, Gordon Ramsay, Bobby Flay, Todd English, Hubert Keller, Bradley Ogden, Joël de Robuchon, Thomas Keller, and Julian Serrano. It's a veritable who's who of the culinary world. Dining in Las Vegas became one of the top reasons people want to visit the city.

And proving that Las Vegas really is a 24-hour town, the nightlife scene exploded in Vegas. Megaclubs such as XS (p. 204) at Encore Las Vegas, Marquee (p. 203) at the Cosmopolitan, and Hakkasan (p. 202) at MGM Grand (billed as the largest nightclub in the world) pull in droves of the young and beautiful (or people who think they are, or who just want to be around them) who do not seem to be deterred by the eye-popping high prices ($20–$50 cover, $10–$15 drinks), long lines (expect to wait at least an hour), and lack of personal space. It's a see-and-be-seen scene, where you better dress to impress or expect to be relegated to the darker corners.

Céline Dion made it safe to be a Vegas headliner again as she kicked off a 5-year residency at Caesars Palace in 2003 (and came back in 2011). She would be followed by big-ticket names like Elton John, Bette Midler, Cher, and Garth Brooks, all of whom made Vegas their performing home for a while.

Clearly, no one can rest on their laurels in Vegas, for this is not only a town that never sleeps, but also one in which progress never stops moving, even for a heartbeat.

WHEN TO GO

Most of a Las Vegas vacation is usually spent indoors, so you can have a good time here year-round. The most pleasant seasons are spring and fall, especially if you want to experience the great outdoors.

Weekdays are slightly less crowded than weekends. Holidays are always a mob scene and come accompanied by high hotel prices. Hotel prices also skyrocket when big conventions and special events are taking place. The slowest times of year are parts of January and February, late June through August; the week before Christmas; and the week after New Year's.

If a major convention is to be held during your trip, you might want to change your date. Check the box below for convention dates.

Climate & Current Weather Conditions

First of all, Vegas isn't always hot, but when it is, it's *really* hot. One thing you'll hear again and again is that even though Las Vegas gets very hot, the dry desert heat is not unbearable. We know this is true because we spent a couple of days there in 104°F (40°C) weather and lived to say, "It wasn't all that bad, not really." The humidity averages a low 22%, and even on very hot days, there's apt to be a breeze. Having said that, once the temperature gets into triple digits, it is wise to limit the amount of time you spend outdoors and to make sure you are drinking plenty of water even while you are inside enjoying the blessed air-conditioning (which is omnipresent). Dehydration and

wild WEATHER

Las Vegas rests in the middle of a desert, so how wacky can the weather possibly get? A lot crazier than you think. Although Las Vegas's location results in broiling-hot temperatures in the summer, many people tend to forget that deserts get cold and rainy, while wind is also a potential hazard.

Winter temperatures in Las Vegas have been known to dip below 30°F (–1°C), and when you toss in 40 mph winds, that adds up to a very chilly stroll on the Strip. And snow is not an unheard-of occurrence. Most years see a flurry or two falling on Las Vegas, and since 1949, a total of 12 "storms" have resulted in accumulations of 2 inches or greater, with the largest storm dropping 9 inches on the Strip in January 1949. In

December 2003, parts of Las Vegas got 6 inches of the white stuff, and although it didn't stick around too long on the Strip, the sight of the famous "Welcome to Fabulous Las Vegas" sign in the middle of a driving blizzard was quite a spectacle. And more recently (the winter of 2008–09), Vegas received nearly 3 inches of snow on the Strip itself, with nearly 10 inches accumulating in other areas of town. Locals usually find the snow a charming addition to the city (and the stuff melts completely in a day or two, so they don't have to shovel it—lucky them).

But although snow is a novel quirk that many Vegas residents and visitors welcome, rain isn't always as well received. The soil in Las Vegas is

---

heatstroke are two of the most common ailments that affect tourists—don't be a victim of one of them. Also, except on the hottest summer days, there's relief at night, when temperatures often drop by as much as 20 degrees.

Las Vegas' Average Temperatures (°F & °C) & Rainfall

		JAN	FEB	MAR	APR	MAY	JUNE	JULY	AUG	SEPT	OCT	NOV	DEC
Average	(°F)	49	54	60	67	78	87	93	91	83	70	57	48
	(°C)	9	12	16	19	26	31	34	33	28	21	14	9
High Temp.	(°F)	58	63	70	78	89	99	104	102	94	81	67	57
	(°C)	14	17	21	26	32	37	40	39	35	27	19	14
Low Temp.	(°F)	39	44	49	56	66	75	81	79	71	59	47	39
	(°C)	4	7	9	13	19	24	27	26	22	15	8	4
Rainfall (in.)		0.6	0.8	0.4	0.2	0.1	0.1	0.4	0.3	0.3	0.3	0.4	0.5

But this is the desert, and it's not hot year-round. It can get quite cold, especially in the winter, when at night it can drop to 30°F (–1°C) and lower. Although rare, it does snow occasionally in Las Vegas. The winter of 2008 to 2009 dropped nearly 3 inches of snow on the Strip. There's nothing quite like the sight of Luxor's Sphinx covered in snow. The breeze can also become a cold, biting wind of up to 40 mph and more. And so there are entire portions of the year when you won't be using that hotel pool at all (even if you want to; most of the hotels close huge chunks of those pool areas for "the season," which can be as long as the period from Labor Day to Memorial Day). If you aren't traveling in the height of summer, bring a jacket. Also, remember sunscreen and a hat—even if it's not all that hot, you can burn very easily and very fast.

Holidays

Banks, government offices, post offices, and many stores, restaurants, and museums are closed on the following legal national holidays: January 1 (New Year's Day), the parched most of the year, making it diffi-cult for the land to absorb large amounts of water coming down in a short time. Between June and August, when most of the area's rainfall takes place due to the Southwest's monsoon season, there is a good possibility of flash flooding.

At times, the skies just open up, resulting in flooding that wreaks havoc on Sin City. On July 9, 1999, Mother Nature unleashed more than 3 inches of rain *in just a few hours* on a city that averages about 4 inches of rain a year. The deluge killed two people, swamped hundreds of cars, and destroyed millions of dollars in property. A 2013 storm caused havoc up and down the Strip with collapsed ceilings in the Mirage, a flooded casino at Caesars Palace, and a waterfall inside Gilley's at Treasure Island (go look it up on YouTube). This kind of storm (and rain in general) is rare, but even a light shower can make things treacherous on the roads, the sidewalks, and the slippery marble walkways that front almost every casino in town.

The topography of the Las Vegas region also makes it prone to high, often damaging winds. Situated at the bottom of a bowl ringed by mountains, 15 to 20 mph steady winds are not uncommon and gusts of 70 to 80 mph have been recorded. In 1994, a brief windstorm knocked down the massive sign at the Las Vegas Hilton and in 2010 a storm tore apart the Cloud 9 balloon, billed as the largest tethered helium balloon in the world.

third Monday in January (Martin Luther King, Jr., Day), the third Monday in February (Presidents' Day), the last Monday in May (Memorial Day), July 4 (Independence Day), the first Monday in September (Labor Day), the second Monday in October (Columbus Day), November 11 (Veterans Day/Armistice Day), the fourth Thursday in November (Thanksgiving Day), and December 25 (Christmas). The Tuesday after the first Monday in November is Election Day, a federal government holiday in presiden-tial-election years (held every 4 years, and next in 2016).

Any holiday, especially ones that involve a day off work for most people, will mean big crowds in Vegas. This includes "holidays" like St. Patrick's Day, Cinco de Mayo, and Spring Break.

Las Vegas Calendar of Events

You may be surprised that Las Vegas does not offer as many annual events as most other tourist cities. The reason is Las Vegas's very raison d'être: the gaming industry. This town wants its visitors spending their money in the casinos, not at Renaissance fairs and parades.

When in town, check the local paper and contact the **Las Vegas Convention and Visitors Authority** (© **877/847-4858** or 702/892-7575; www.lasvegas.com) or the **Las Vegas Chamber of Commerce** (© **702/735-1616;** www.lvchamber.com) to find out about other events scheduled during your visit.

FEBRUARY

The Super Bowl. Granted, the actual game is not held in Las Vegas, but the numbers of people it brings to the city rival those that go to wherever the big game is being held. Sports fans and sports bettors come out in droves to watch the action on the big screens around town and to lay down a wager or two on the outcome. It usually takes place on the first Sunday in February.

Valentine's Day. This is the marriage (and possibly divorce) capital of the world, where the betrothed line up to exchange their vows all across town on Cupid's day. The

MAJOR convention DATES FOR 2015

Listed below are Las Vegas's major annual conventions, with projected attendance figures for 2015; believe us, unless you're coming for one of them, you probably want to avoid the biggies. Because convention schedules frequently change, contact the **Las Vegas Convention and Visitors Authority** (📞 **702/892-0711;** www.vegasmeansbusiness.com) to double-check the latest info before you commit to your travel dates.

Event Attendance	Dates	Expected
Consumer Electronics Show	Jan 6–9	155,000
Adult Entertainment Expo	Jan 6–9	50,000
Las Vegas Market Furniture Show	Jan 18–22	50,000
International Builders Show	Jan 20–22	62,000
Shooting, Hunting & Outdoor Trade Show	Jan 20–23	61,000
National Association of Broadcasters	Apr 13–16	96,000
National Hardware Show	May 5–7	32,000
Int'l Esthetics Cosmetic and Spa Conference	Jun 20–22	25,000
Las Vegas Market Furniture Show	Aug 1–6	50,000
National Association of Convenience Stores	Oct 12–14	30,000
American Academy of Ophthalmology	Nov 14–17	25,000
Power-Gen International Conference	Dec 8–12	27,000
SEMA/Automotive Aftermarket Industry Week	Nov 3–6	130,000

city's Marriage Bureau stays open 24 hours during the weekend and some chapels perform dozens of weddings. February 14.

MARCH

NASCAR. The **Las Vegas Motor Speedway,** 7000 Las Vegas Blvd. N. (📞 **800/644-4444;** www.lvms.com), has become one of the premier facilities in the country, attracting races and racers of all stripes and colors. The biggest races of the year are the Boyd Gaming 300 and the Kobalt Tools 400, held in early March.

March Madness. Remember everything we just said about the Super Bowl? Apply it here for the NCAA college basketball championships throughout the month.

MAY

Rock in Rio USA. Announced just before this book went to press, the hugely popular concerts in Brazil, Spain, and Portugal are coming to Las Vegas starting in May 2015. The events will be a partnership between Rock in Rio, MGM Resorts, and Cirque du Soleil, and will take place every other year in a new festival ground on the North Strip (across from the former Sahara hotel, now SLS). They will feature five stages, a cityscape, carnival rides, and more. No lineup had been announced at press time, but the concerts in other cities have drawn the likes of Beyonce, Justin Timberlake, and Stevie Wonder, to name a few, and have drawn upwards of 700,000 people.

JUNE

World Series of Poker. When Harrah's Entertainment bought the legendary Binion's Horseshoe, in Downtown Vegas, out of bankruptcy, it quickly turned around and sold the hotel but kept the hosting rights to this famed event, moving its location and place on the calendar. Now held at the **Rio All-Suite Hotel and Casino,** 3700 W. Flamingo Rd. (📞 **800/752-9746**), in June and July (with the final table held in Nov for some incomprehensible reason), the event features high-stakes gamblers and showbiz personalities competing for six-figure purses. There are daily events, with entry stakes ranging from $125 to $5,000. To enter the World Championship Event, players must pony up $10,000 but could win a fortune (the 2013 top prize was $8.3 million). It costs nothing to crowd around the tables and watch the action, but if you want to avoid the throngs, you can catch a lot of it on TV. For more information, visit www.wsop.com.

Electric Daisy Carnival. One of the biggest annual Electronic Dance Music (EDM) events in the world draws upwards of 400,000 people to the city with a multi-day series of concerts from the biggest DJs and club music stars in the business. Past festivals saw EDM megastars like Tiesto, Avicii, Afrojack, Eric Prydz, Nicky Romero, Ferry Corsten, and Victor Calderone in front of the dancing mobs. If you don't know who any of those acts are, it's probably best to consider a different weekend, as rooms are scarce. Usually held the third weekend in June at the Las Vegas Motor Speedway. For more information, visit www.electricdaisycarnival.com.

OCTOBER

Life is Beautiful Festival. Started in 2013, this festival takes over a huge chunk of Downtown Las Vegas with music from bands both big (Beck, Imagine Dragons, Janelle Monae) and small; food and cooking demonstrations from celebrity chefs; art projects and displays; a speaker series; performances from Vegas shows including Cirque du Soleil; and more. The friendly neighborhood vibe, terrific organization (at least so far), and endless array of things to see, do, and eat make this a favorite for more than 65,000 people.

Halloween. Las Vegas gets even scarier than normal on and around Halloween, with "spooky" twists to many of the major attractions (Adventuredome becomes "Fright Dome," with haunted houses and more), debaucherous costume parties at the nightclubs, and a parade and festivities in Downtown Las Vegas.

DECEMBER

National Finals Rodeo. This is the Super Bowl of rodeos, attended by about 200,000 people each year and offering more than $6 million in prize money. Male and female rodeo stars compete in everything from calf roping to steer wrestling, bull riding, team roping, saddle bronco riding, bareback riding, and barrel racing. In connection with this event, hotels book country stars into their showrooms, and a cowboy shopping spree—the **NFR Cowboy Christmas Gift Show,** a trade show for Western gear—is held at the convention center. The NFR runs for 10 days, during the first 2 weeks of December, at the 17,000-seat Thomas & Mack Center of the University of Nevada, Las Vegas (UNLV). Order tickets as far in advance as possible (✆ **866/388-3267**). For more information, see www.nfrexperience.com.

New Year's Eve. Between 300,000 and 400,000 people descend on Las Vegas to ring in the New Year, making it one of the largest gatherings for the holiday outside of New York's Times Square. Fireworks are the dominant entertainment, with pyrotechnics launched from the roofs of many hotels on the Strip and under the canopy at Fremont Street in Downtown Las Vegas. The Strip is closed to vehicles for the night, and so traffic and parking are a nightmare, as is booking a room (expect to pay a hefty premium), which should be done well in advance.

WHERE TO STAY

There are about 150,000 hotel rooms in Las Vegas. If you stayed in a different room every night it would take you 411 years to get through them all. You could give one to every single resident of Dayton, Ohio, and still have enough left over for you and about 10,000 of your closest friends. The point is, finding a hotel room in Las Vegas is not hard; it's finding the right one for *you* that can be more challenging. Do you want a luxurious suite where you can lounge in bed and order room service, or basic accommodations where you'll dump your luggage and then not see the room again until you stumble back to it as the sun is coming up the next morning? Do you want classic Glitter Gulch glitz or contemporary Sin City glamour? Do you want high tech or low cost? Las Vegas has all of the above and just about everything in between.

4

HOTELS BY PRICE

EXPENSIVE

Aria Las Vegas ★★★, p. 37
Bellagio ★★★, p. 47
Caesars Palace ★★★, p. 48
The Cosmopolitan of Las Vegas ★★★, p. 49
The Cromwell ★★, p. 50
Four Seasons Hotel Las Vegas ★★★, p. 38
Green Valley Ranch Resort, Spa & Casino ★★★, p. 72
Hard Rock Hotel & Casino ★★, p. 65
JW Marriott ★★, p. 73
Mandalay Bay/Delano Las Vegas ★★★, p. 40
Mandarin Oriental ★★★, p. 41
MGM Grand Hotel & Casino ★★, p. 42
Palms Casino Resort ★★, p. 65
Red Rock Resort ★★★, p. 74
The Venetian/Palazzo Las Vegas ★★, p. 50
Wynn/Encore ★★★, p. 57

MODERATE

Bally's Las Vegas ★, p. 51
The D Las Vegas Casino Hotel ★, p. 61
The Downtown Grand ★★, p. 60
Excalibur ★, p. 43
Flamingo Las Vegas ★, p. 52
Golden Nugget ★★, p. 60
Harrah's Las Vegas ★, p. 52
Luxor Las Vegas ★, p. 44
LVH: Las Vegas Hotel & Casino ★, p. 66
M Resort ★★, p. 72
The Mirage ★★, p. 54
Monte Carlo Resort & Casino ★, p. 44
New York–New York Hotel & Casino ★★, p. 45
Paris Las Vegas Casino Resort ★★★, p. 54
Planet Hollywood Resort & Casino ★★, p. 55
Rio All-Suite Hotel & Casino ★★, p. 66

4

SOUTH STRIP

The southern third of the Strip, from roughly Russell Road to Harmon Avenue, is home to some of the biggest and most extravagant hotels in the world.

Best for: First-time visitors who want to experience all of the Vegas insanity they have read about and seen on TV.

Drawbacks: Prices are higher here than in non-Strip locations; the sheer number of people can cause major traffic jams (and we're not just talking about on the street).

Expensive

Aria Las Vegas ★★★   Sitting at the virtual center of the massive CityCenter complex, Aria Las Vegas seems to elicit the classic "love it or hate it" reaction from visitors. To be sure, it is unlike any Vegas megaresort that has come before it—all gleaming, glass skyscraper and contemporary interior design instead of the themed wackiness or faux old-school luxury of its predecessors. It feels almost out of place here, like someone picked up a big chunk of some ultracosmopolitan city (which Vegas most certainly is not, no matter how much it wants to be) and dropped it down in the middle of the Strip. It is dramatic and unexpected, modern without being cold or sterile, and for the record we are firmly in the "love it" camp.

The sinuous glass-and-steel exterior of the building gives way to a gorgeously appointed series of public spaces, each filled with the kind of attention to design detail that evokes reactions from "cool!" to "wow!" There is no such thing as a blank wall here—everything has a texture or pattern, using wood, stone, glass, fabric, metal, and other natural elements to create a richness that is lacking in other Vegas hotels. Throw in a lot of natural light and some exciting artworks (yes, that is a sculpture by Maya Lin hanging behind the check-in desk) and you have a unique and endlessly gawkable space.

More than 4,000 rooms come in all shapes and sizes, with standard rooms continuing the warm modern theme. Deep hues in the woods and fabrics would lend a cavelike

WHAT YOU'LL really PAY

The rack rate is the maximum rate that a hotel charges for a room. It's the rate you'd get if you walked in off the street and asked for a room for the night. Hardly anybody pays these prices, however, especially in Vegas, where prices fluctuate wildly with demand.

Low seasons like the insanely hot summer months and parts of December and January offer the lowest rates, where a room at a hotel like Aria Las Vegas that would go for north of $250 during a busy time can be had for as low as $129. Of course, the law of supply and demand cuts both ways—during peak periods that same room could go for over $400 a night.

The best prices can usually be found online at each individual hotel website or through its social media pages on Facebook and Twitter. All usually offer cheaper rates, special discounts, and sometimes even give low-price

guarantees. A recent check of hotels like Mandalay Bay, where they'll quote $200 a night as their base rate, showed rooms online for as low as $79 midweek.

As far as room prices go, keep in mind that our price categories are rough guidelines, at best. If you see a hotel that appeals to you, even if it seems out of your price range, give them a call anyway. They might be having a special, a slow week, or some kind of promotion, or they may just like the sound of your voice (we have no other explanation for it). You could end up with a hotel in the Expensive category offering you a room for $60 a night. It's a toll-free call or a few clicks on a website, so it's worth a try.

Note: Quoted discount rates almost never include breakfast, hotel tax, or any applicable resort fees, the latter of which can send up the price by as much as $25 per night.

---

air in other places, but the full wall of floor-to-ceiling windows fixes that nicely here. Standard amenities are plentiful and virtually everything (drapes, temperature, entertainment systems, lights) is controlled by an integrated touch-screen device that will even warn you if you've left the door unlocked. Bathrooms are generously sized, with abundant frosted glass and marble, as well as one seriously odd design element: Although the shower and tub are separate, they are in one enclosure so you have to pass through the former to get to the latter—space saving but strange.

Back downstairs you'll find a lively casino that at more than 150,000 square feet is one of the biggest in Vegas, more than a dozen restaurants here and a dozen more at the neighboring **Crystals** (p. 168) mall and hotels in CityCenter, a high-energy dance club **Haze** (p. 203), several other bars and lounges, a gorgeous spa, salon, workout facility, and lushly landscaped pool area. Entertainment comes in the form of a Cirque du Soleil production *Zarkana* (p. 183).

Downsides are the size (which is leviathan and feels it) and the parking (both self-parking and the valet pickup are a long trek from where you want to be).

3730 Las Vegas Blvd. S. © **866/359-7757** or 702/590-7757. www.arialasvegas.com. 4,004 units. $159 and up double; $359 and up suite. Resort fee $25. Extra person $35. No discount for children. Free self- and valet parking. **Amenities:** 15 restaurants; casino; concierge; executive-level rooms; health club; heated outdoor pools; room service; spa; showroom, free property-wide and in-room Wi-Fi (included in resort fee).

Four Seasons Hotel Las Vegas ★★★   For years the Four Seasons was the only thing close to a boutique luxury hotel on the Strip, cornering the market on

Las Vegas Hotels

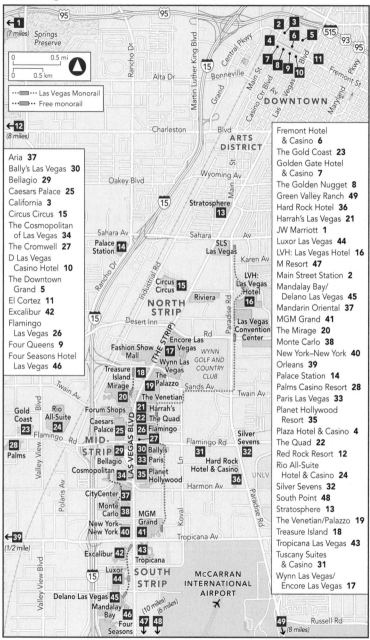

Aria **37**
Bally's Las Vegas **30**
Bellagio **29**
Caesars Palace **25**
California **3**
Circus Circus **15**
The Cosmopolitan
 of Las Vegas **34**
The Cromwell **27**
D Las Vegas
 Casino Hotel **10**
The Downtown
 Grand **5**
El Cortez **11**
Excalibur **42**
Flamingo
 Las Vegas **26**
Four Queens **9**
Four Seasons Hotel
 Las Vegas **46**

Fremont Hotel
 & Casino **6**
The Gold Coast **23**
Golden Gate Hotel
 & Casino **7**
The Golden Nugget **8**
Green Valley Ranch **49**
Hard Rock Hotel **36**
Harrah's Las Vegas **21**
JW Marriott **1**
Luxor Las Vegas **44**
LVH: Las Vegas Hotel **16**
M Resort **47**
Main Street Station **2**
Mandalay Bay/
 Delano Las Vegas **45**
Mandarin Oriental **37**
MGM Grand **41**
The Mirage **20**
Monte Carlo **38**
New York–New York **40**
Orleans **39**
Palace Station **14**
Palms Casino Resort **28**
Paris Las Vegas **33**
Planet Hollywood
 Resort **35**
Plaza Hotel & Casino **4**
The Quad **22**
Red Rock Resort **12**
Rio All-Suite
 Hotel & Casino **24**
Silver Sevens **32**
South Point **48**
Stratosphere **13**
The Venetian/Palazzo **19**
Treasure Island **18**
Tropicana Las Vegas **43**
Tuscany Suites
 & Casino **31**
Wynn Las Vegas/
 Encore Las Vegas **17**

intimate upscale experiences while all the other hotels went for the bigger is better end of the scale. Then along came Mandarin Oriental, Nobu at Caesars Palace, and the Cromwell, and suddenly the market started to get competitive. The Four Seasons responded by revamping the property, including an update of the lobby with an energetic lounge, the creation of a new outdoor socializing space, and an overhaul of the rooms, all designed to keep its rightful place atop the niche it created.

It's located on the top five floors of Mandalay Bay, though in many ways, the Four Seasons is light-years away from the vibe of the host hotel. A separate driveway and portico entrance, plus an entire registration area, set you up immediately with hushed elegance. This is one fancy hotel in town where you are not greeted, even at a distance, with the clash and clang and general hubbub that is the soundtrack of Vegas. Of course, all of that is just a short walk away if you need the clash and clang and general hubbub to make your Vegas vacation complete.

The rooms are gorgeous, taking classic design cues and updating them with a contemporary spin. Note the kicky retro lamps and French boudoir–inspired headboards, the delicate patterns in the wallpaper, and the hand-crafted metal work in the lamps and tables. It all adds up to a luxurious yet comfortable package that stands out in a sea of Vegas same-ness. Try to get a room facing north so you can soak in the views of the Strip from the floor-to-ceiling windows. In addition to all of the dining, entertainment, and recreation available at Mandalay Bay, there are two on-site restaurants, a lounge, a guests-only pool, and a spa.

Service is superb—if they say 20 minutes for room service, you can expect your food in 19½ minutes. Children are encouraged and welcomed with gifts of toys and goodies, rooms are childproofed in advance, and the list of comforts available for the asking is a yard long.

3960 Las Vegas Blvd. S. *©* **877/632-5000** or 702/632-5000. www.fourseasons.com. 424 units. $199 and up double; $399 and up suite. Resort fee $25 per night. Extra person $35. Children 17 and under stay free in parent's room. Valet parking $22; no self-parking. Pets under 25 lb. accepted. **Amenities:** 2 restaurants; concierge; executive-level rooms; fitness center; heated outdoor pool; room service; spa, high-speed Internet.

Mandalay Bay/Delano Las Vegas ★★★   Opened in 1999, this gleaming gold megaresort had started to show signs of aging (15 is like 57 in Vegas years), but the place received some much needed updating over the last couple of years. There's a new look in the casino, which is now lighter, brighter, and more energetic than it used to be, plus a host of new nightclubs, restaurants, a new high-profile show. The end result brings the hotel back in line with its vision of itself as an upscale resort with a modern spin.

The spacious rooms in the main tower may not seem as luxe when compared to dazzling options at places like Aria or the Cosmopolitan, but they are still lovely. They aren't all sleek modernity, like everyone else in town, but the furnishings are cozy (love the window seats) and the fixtures fine. The bathrooms have big tubs, glassed-in showers, double sinks, and separate water closets, plus lots of fab amenities. Rooms on higher floors have some of the best Strip views in town, but usually cost extra.

The adjacent all-suite tower, once known as THEhotel, is getting converted into a sister to the high-end Delano Hotel in South Beach Miami. Expect swank decor, fashionable amenities, and higher-than-average prices at this hotel, due to be completed by the time you read this.

Reservations at many of the nearly two dozen restaurants in Mandalay Bay are among the most sought after in town. The amazing **Citizen's Kitchen** is reviewed in chapter 5 along with **Aureole, Border Grill, Fleur by Hubert Keller, Red Square,** and the **House of Blues.** A showroom is home of the fantastic Michael Jackson–themed Cirque du Soleil production and there is a separate arena for bigger concerts and events. There's also a big, comfortable casino; several bars, clubs, and lounges, including the stunning **Light** (p. 203) nightclub done by Cirque du Soleil and the fun **Mizuya** (p. 207); the 1.5-million-gallon **Shark Reef** aquarium (p. 134); and a massive outdoor beach area including a wave pool, a lazy river ride, a sandy-bottomed pool, a cafe and bar, a dedicated casino, a day club adjunct to Light nightclub called Daylight (get it?) with its own private pool, and more. All but Daylight are great places for families, but they are extremely popular, so a quiet respite by the water is probably not on the agenda. A well-equipped workout facility, full-service spa, and a salon complete the recreation package.

3950 Las Vegas Blvd. S. (at Hacienda Ave.). ✆ **877/632-7800** or 702/632-7108. www.mandalaybay. com. 4,429 units (including Delano). $99 and up double; $149 and up suite. Resort fee $25. Extra person $30. Children 14 and under free in parent's room. Free self- and valet parking. **Amenities:** 24 restaurants; aquarium; casino; concierge; 12,000-seat events center; executive-level rooms; health club; showroom; 5 outdoor pools w/lazy river and wave pool; room service; sauna; spa; watersports equipment/rentals, in-room high-speed Internet.

Mandarin Oriental ★★★   With a host of upgrades at its most direct competition, the Four Seasons, and new places like Nobu at Caesars Palace and the Cromwell coming online, the Mandarin Oriental is no longer the only game in town when it comes to intimate and upscale. But don't let the crowded marketplace distract you. The Asian hotelier chain is better known in Europe and the Far East, but their product here in Vegas is a bold statement of true boutique luxury in a city that likes to pretend that a 3,000-room hotel can be either of those things.

This property has just under 400 hotel rooms and another 200 residential units—small by Vegas standards—allowing for a level of service and amenities that simply can't be replicated at a larger hotel. The accommodations are not huge, but are still comfortable and roomy; all with a subtle Asian decor scheme, decadently comfortable beds, plush robes and towels, and even a valet closet so the "help" doesn't need to come into the room to pick up your laundry or drop off a newspaper. Classy.

But you don't need to wait to get to your room—the playground of the rich vibe greets you as soon as you walk in the door. The top hat–wearing doorman will greet you and attendants will guide you to an elevator that whisks you to the 23rd-floor Sky Lobby. With floor-to-ceiling windows facing the Strip, it is without a doubt the most dramatic lobby in town. A tearoom, bar, and a French restaurant from world-renowned chef Pierre Gagnaire complete this floor, all with similar stunning views.

The pool and spa area are on the seventh and eighth floors with still more windows, including in the treatment rooms and whirlpool areas. Have a soak while sipping vitamin-infused water and gazing out at the city lights? Why, yes, thank you.

Although there is little else in the building (no casino, no showroom, no roller coaster), the very deep catalog of restaurants, nightclubs, bars, shopping, gambling, and entertainment options at the other properties within CityCenter are just a short walk away.

3752 Las Vegas Blvd. S. ✆ **888/881-9578** or 702/590-8888. www.mandarinoriental.com. 392 units. $199 and up double; $399 and up suite. Resort fee $25 per night. Extra person $50. Children 11 and under stay free in parent's room. Free self- and valet parking. **Amenities:** 4 restaurants; concierge; executive-level rooms; health club; heated pool; room service; spa. in-room high-speed Internet.

As room rates have plummeted due to the sagging economic fortunes of Las Vegas, hotels have found new ways to increase their bottom line, mainly through the addition of what we consider to be nefarious and often outrageous "resort fees." These extra charges are tacked on top of the nightly room rate and variously include things like Internet access, entry to the fitness center, printing of boarding passes, local and toll-free phone calls, and the like. Some hotels throw in extra goodies like bottles of water, discounted cocktails or meals, and credits for future stays. It can be a good deal if you take advantage of what the fee covers, but even if you don't, you still have to pay the fee. We indicate which hotels charge resort fees in the listings in this chapter and include their current prices, but do note that the amount and what they include changes often; be sure to ask when booking your room or take some time to read the fine print if making arrangements online.

MGM Grand Hotel & Casino ★★ How to keep the biggest hotel in Las Vegas fresh? By basically redoing the entire thing from the front door to the top floor with new restaurants, nightclubs, entertainment, and rooms to start. While most of these changes are mainly cosmetic, they have certainly bumped up the look and feel of the hotel, now more than 20 years old. Sure, it may not be as visually arresting as the Cosmopolitan or Aria, but it is definitely an improvement over what had become a fairly pedestrian experience.

Once-bland accommodations are now sexy stunners with bold accents of green or magenta making the visuals pop, floor-to-ceiling padded headboards, and mirrors making them seem bigger than they are, and lots of new technology such as 40-inch flatscreen televisions and a connectivity center, making them feel cutting edge.

Although this style makes up the bulk of the offerings, there are other layouts, including the smaller but equally modern West Wing rooms; the condominium-style units in the Signature towers out back; and the dramatic, multilevel Skylofts, which come with their own 24-hour butler.

Worth noting are the entire floor of *Stay Well* rooms, with HEPA-standard air filtration systems, a vitamin C–infused shower, healthier snacks in the minibar, electromagnetic field protection, and even alarm clocks that, instead of blaring at you, simulate dawn to gradually pull you out of your slumber. Depending on how hard you're partying in Vegas, it might just be worth the extra $30 to detoxify a little bit.

Downstairs, the casino has been updated with new machines and tables, and a massive nightclub **Hakkasan** (p. 202) has replaced the beloved Lion Habitat (don't worry, the lions are fine and living in comfort just outside Las Vegas at the **Lion Habitat Ranch**, p. 145).

MGM houses a prestigious assemblage of dining rooms, among them **Joël Robuchon**'s two sterling entries and **Emeril's New Orleans Fish House.** These, and other on-site restaurants, are reviewed in chapter 5.

The featured show is *KÀ*, a dazzling offering from Cirque du Soleil (p. 178). Plus, there are other entertainment, bar, and club offerings; a headliner showroom; and a larger events arena that hosts sporting events and bigger concerts.

And as if all that weren't enough, there is shopping, attractions, a full-service spa, a fitness center, and more than 6 acres of pools and sunbathing areas.

Pet-Friendly Hotels

Up until recently, if you wanted to bring Fido or Fluffy to Vegas with you, your options on lodging were fairly limited, with only one major hotel on the Strip allowing pets (the Four Seasons). Now, more hotels are jumping on the pet-friendly bandwagon, including all of the Caesars Entertainment properties. Their popular PetStay program allows dogs up to 50 pounds to get a taste of Sin City. There are fees associated, of course ($25–$40), and there are plenty of restrictions, but you get things like food and water dishes, recommended dog walking routes, and more. The program is good at Caesars Palace, Paris Las Vegas, Planet Hollywood, Harrah's, the Flamingo, Bally's, Rio Suites, and Imperial Palace. For more information on *PetStay,* check out www.caesars.com/petstay. You can also contact the Las Vegas Convention and Visitors Authority (✆ **877/847-4858;** www.lasvegas.com) for information on other pet-friendly accommodations in town.

3799 Las Vegas Blvd. S. (at Tropicana Ave.). ✆ **800/929-1111** or 702/891-7777. www.mgmgrand.com. 5,034 units. $99 and up double; $159 and up suite. Resort free $25. Extra person $35. Children 13 and under stay free in parent's room. Free self- and valet parking. **Amenities:** 23 restaurants; nightclub; cabaret theater; casino; concierge; events arena; executive-level rooms; large health club; Jacuzzi; 5 outdoor pools w/lazy river; room service; salon; shopping arcade; spa; wedding chapel, in-room high-speed Internet.

Moderate

Excalibur ★ One of the largest resort hotels in the world, Excalibur is a gleaming white, turreted castle complete with moat, drawbridge, battlements, and lofty towers. And it's huger than huge. To heck with quiet good taste; kitsch is cool. And it's becoming harder and harder to find in a town that once wore tacky proudly. If your soul is secretly thrilled by overblown fantasy locations—or if you just want a pretty good budget option on the Strip—the Excalibur is still here for you.

Some of the original "family-friendly" elements have been stripped out—gone is the animatronic dragon and wizard show out front, although the carnival-style midway and the SpongeBob SquarePants–themed virtual reality ride remain. It's really too bad, because without the excess, this is just another hotel—a mighty big and chaotic hotel, thanks to a sprawling casino full of families and small-time gamblers. Parents should be warned that on the way to the SpongeBob ride you may see posters for the male-stripper act *Thunder from Down Under,* also in residence at the hotel.

The standard Tower rooms are about as basic as they come, while the Contemporary rooms are a bit nicer, with oversized headboards, flatscreen TVs, better bathroom fixtures, and upgraded furnishings. Spend the extra few bucks it costs to get one of the latter; you can thank us later. Frankly, we prefer stopping in for a visit rather than actually settling here; but if budget is a major concern, we'd understand if you felt differently.

The second floor holds the Medieval Village, where several of Excalibur's restaurants and shops are peppered along winding streets and alleyways, a sort of permanent Renaissance Faire, which could be reason enough to stay away (or to come). Up here you can access the enclosed, air-conditioned, moving sidewalk that connects with the Luxor. The pool area has some nice landscaping, fancy cabanas, and the like. There are plenty of restaurants, including a branch of the popular Buca di Beppo, a buffet, and

Dick's Last Resort (p. 86). The **Tournament of Kings** and *Thunder From Down Under* are covered in chapter 8, and there's a very loud, claustrophobic casino that is most notable as being the place where the largest slot machine jackpot in history was won ($39.7 million in 2003).

3850 Las Vegas Blvd. S. (at Tropicana Ave.). 📞 **800/937-7777** or 702/597-7700. www.excalibur. com. 4,008 units. $59 and up double. Daily resort fee $20. Extra person $20. No discount for children. Free self- and valet parking. **Amenities:** 6 restaurants; buffet; food court; casino; concierge; outdoor pools; room service; showrooms; wedding chapel, in-room high-speed Internet.

Luxor Las Vegas ★   Kitsch worshipers were dealt a blow when the people behind this hotel came to the inexplicable decision to eliminate most of the Egyptian theme from the inside of it, casting aside identity in favor of generic luxury. Obviously, they can't get rid of certain elements—the main hotel is, after all, a 30-story onyx-hued pyramid, complete with a really tall 315,000-watt light beam at the top. (Luxor says that's because the Egyptians believed their souls would travel up to heaven in a beam of light. We think it's really because it gives them something to brag about: "The most powerful beam on earth!") Replicas of Cleopatra's Needle and the Sphinx still dominate the exterior, and touches of Egypt remain in the lobby and main entrance (you figure out what to do with those 3-story-high statues of Ramses). But other than that, virtually every other trace of the land of the Pharaohs is gone. And some magic is now gone from Vegas. Now guests will be attracted only by the generally good prices, not by the giddy fun the theme produced.

But they can't take away fundamentals, and so staying in the pyramid part means you get to ride the 39-degree high-speed inclinators—that's what an elevator is when it works inside a pyramid. Really, they are part conveyance, part thrill ride—check out that jolt when they come to a halt. Most of the rooms received minor cosmetic touch-ups in 2012 and 2013, but don't be expecting anything more than a standard hotel room. Pyramid rooms have marvelous views through the slanted windows, but the bathrooms are shower only, no tubs. Tower rooms have a more typical layout, which allows bathtubs.

Among the many restaurants are the margarita heaven of **Tacos & Tequila,** the upscale pub grub at **Public House,** and the archaeological dig–themed **MORE, The Buffet at Luxor,** all covered in chapter 5. **Criss Angel:** *Believe* pairs the popular exotic magician with the spectacle of Cirque du Soleil (p. 184). Comedian Carrot Top is also in residency. Enormous nightclub **LAX** (p. 203) is state of the art and attracts a fashionable crowd. Three notable attractions here are **Titanic: The Exhibition, Bodies . . . The Exhibition,** and the sports themed **SCORE!,** all of which are covered in chapter 6. There are several pools and a spa, but they are about as basic as the rooms, so if that's important to you, look elsewhere.

3900 Las Vegas Blvd. S. (btw. Reno and Hacienda aves.). 📞 **888/777-0188** or 702/262-4000. www. luxor.com. 4,400 units. $69 and up double; $150 and up whirlpool suite; $249–$800 other suites. Resort fee $22. Extra person $30. No discount for kids. Free self- and valet parking. **Amenities:** 6 restaurants; buffet; food court; nightclub; casino; concierge; executive-level rooms; health club; 5 outdoor pools; room service; showrooms; spa, in-room high-speed Internet.

Monte Carlo Resort & Casino ★   If you are the type to judge a book by its cover, you might think that Monte Carlo has a really interesting new story to tell. After all, hundreds of millions of dollars are being thrown at the front of the hotel and neighboring New York-New York to create a pedestrian plaza with restaurants, boutiques, and parklike grounds, all leading to a new 20,000-seat arena behind the hotels. The beauty of that project, expected to open in stages from 2014 through 2016, is really only skin deep, as the bulk of the hotel is the same as it has been for years.

That's not necessarily a bad thing. Monte Carlo has staked a claim as a middle-of-the-road alternative for Vegas lodging. The inside is a fairly sedate affair, with little in the way of wow-worthy moments even in the casino, which has all the gambling basics covered, but is instantly forgettable. Everything in the hotel is fairly beige, both in terms of color scheme and ambience. We love that the guest rooms are accessible without going through the casino, but we don't really love the rooms themselves, as they are smaller than what we've grown accustomed to, especially in terms of bathroom square footage. The pool area, once the very last word in local pool fun, is now put to shame by better versions (including superior lazy rivers) at Mandalay Bay and the MGM Grand. It does have a number of child-/family-/budget-friendly restaurants.

The top level operates as a mini–boutique hotel called Hotel 32. A free limo ride whisks you to a greeter, who puts you in your private elevator straight to the top and checks you into your handsome and masculine room or suite, which comes with some pretty swish details. Don't miss the club room with the free snacks. You're going to pay much more for these perks, but it might work out to be a better deal for luxury than the Four Seasons, so comparison-shop.

Among the many restaurant options, **Diablo's Cantina, Double Barrel Roadhouse,** and **The Pub** are described in chapter 5, and the show starring the wild and wacky **Blue Man Group** is reviewed in chapter 8.

3770 Las Vegas Blvd. S. (btw. Flamingo Rd. and Tropicana Ave.). ✆ **800/311-8999** or 702/730-7777. www.montecarlo.com. 3,002 units. $99 and up double; $145 and up suite. Daily resort fee $22. Extra person $30. No discount for children. Free self- and valet parking. **Amenities:** 7 restaurants; food court; casino; concierge; executive-level rooms; fitness center; Jacuzzi; outdoor pool w/wave pool and lazy river; room service; showroom; spa; watersports equipment/rentals; wedding chapel, in-room high-speed Internet.

New York–New York Hotel & Casino ★★   Isn't this exactly the kind of hotel you think about—or dream about or fear—when you think "Las Vegas?" There it is; a jumbled pile mock-up of the venerable Manhattan skyline—the Empire State Building, the Chrysler Building, the Public Library—all crammed together, along with the 150-foot Statue of Liberty and Ellis Island, all built to approximately one-third scale. And as if that weren't enough, they threw in a roller coaster running around the outside and into the hotel and casino itself.

And it's getting even more . . . well, "more." New restaurants and stores are being added to the Strip facing front, including a Shake Shack and a flagship Hershey's Chocolate World. That project may cause some construction headaches into 2015.

Inside is a different story these days. Once as highly themed as the outside, the main casino space has less of the New York detail that used to be such giddy fun. Gone are the Big Apple Bar and Central Park–themed gaming areas, replaced by a sleekly modern decor that, while pretty, is nowhere near as entertaining. The replica of Greenwich Village, down to the cobblestones, the manhole covers, the tenement-style buildings, and the graffiti, remains, and you'll still find enough of the Gotham silliness elsewhere to probably evoke a smile or three, but dizzy laughter over the sheer spectacle is a thing of the past.

Rooms are housed in different towers, each with a New York–inspired name. The place is so massive and mazelike that finding your way to your room can take a while. There are 64 different layouts for the rooms, which have moved them ever farther from

family-friendly HOTELS

We've said it before, and we'll say it again: Vegas is simply not a good place to bring your kids. Most of the major hotels have backed away from being perceived as places for families, no longer offering babysitting, much less exciting children's activities. Further, fewer hotels offer discounts for children staying in a parent's room, and many others have lowered the age for children who can stay for free.

In addition to the suggestions below, you might consider choosing a non-casino hotel, particularly a reliable chain, and a place with kitchenettes.

- **Circus Circus Hotel & Casino** (p. 58) Centrally located on the Strip, this is our first choice if you're traveling with the kids. The hotel's mezzanine level offers ongoing circus acts daily from 11am to midnight, dozens of carnival games, and an arcade. And behind the hotel is a full amusement park.

- **Excalibur** (p. 43) Though the sword-and-sorcery theme has been considerably toned down, Excalibur features an entire floor of midway games and a large video-game arcade. It also has some child-oriented eateries and shows, but there's a heavily promoted male-stripper show, too, so it's not perfect.

- **Four Seasons** (p. 38) For free goodies, service, and general child pampering, the costly Four Seasons is probably worth the dough. Your kids will be spoiled!

- **Mandalay Bay** (p. 40) Mandalay Bay certainly looks grown up, but it has a number of factors that make it family-friendly: good-size rooms, to start, which you do not have to cross a casino to access; a variety of restaurants; a big ol' shark attraction; and, best of all, the swimming area—wave pool, sandy beach, lazy river, lots of other pools—fun in the Vegas sun!

- **The Orleans** (p. 69) Considered a "local" hotel, its proximity to the Strip makes it a viable alternative, especially for families seeking to take advantage of its plus-size pool area, kid's activity area, bowling, and movie theaters.

- **Stratosphere Casino Hotel** (p. 58) For families looking for reasonably priced, if not particularly exciting, digs, this is a good choice. Plus, it's not in the middle of the Strip action, so you and your kids can avoid that. Thus far, it's not moving in the "adult entertainment" direction, and it has thrill rides at the top.

the original Deco-inspired decor to something bland, albeit comfortable, and though the bathrooms are small, they are pleasantly decorated. There can be a loooong walk from the elevators, so if you have ambulatory issues, you had best mention this while booking. Light sleepers should request a room away from the roller coaster. The health club and spa are nice but nothing to write home about, and the pool is right next to the parking structure.

In addition to a particularly good food court and several restaurants, there are some festive bars, clubs, and activities offered, including **The Bar at Times Square** (p. 199); the aforementioned **Roller Coaster** (p. 45); and the topless and adults-only

Cirque du Soleil production *Zumanity,* which we think is improving but not the best that Cirque has to offer (p. 184).

3790 Las Vegas Blvd. S. (at Tropicana Ave.). *©* **800/693-6763** or 702/740-6969. www.newyork newyork.com. 2,024 units. $79 and up double. Daily resort fee $22. Extra person $30. No discount for children. Free self- and valet parking. **Amenities:** 12 restaurants; food court; buffet; casino; executive-level rooms; fitness center; Jacuzzi; outdoor pool; room service; showroom; spa, in-room high-speed Internet.

Tropicana Las Vegas ★   For years we've been telling you about major potential changes at the Tropicana, and for years we have been made to look fools when absolutely nothing changed. But now everything has changed—and we mean that almost literally. New owners took the place out of bankruptcy and immediately dumped more than $100 million into the property, revamping rooms, the casino, restaurants, the exterior, the pool area, the convention center, and more. Just about the only thing that didn't get a makeover was the parking structure.

Gone is the faded and dusty Caribbean/tropical theme, replaced with a bright, white-and-orange South Beach/tropical theme. New carpets, marble, gaming tables, and slots liven up the casino by about a million percent with a sunny vibe (think white marble and plantation shutter–clad support columns). And that continues upstairs, where all the rooms were basically stripped to the cement and redone with sandy rattan and bamboo furnishings, crisp white linens, bright orange chaise lounges or sofas, white plantation shutters on the windows, and even a white-framed 42-inch TV. Bathrooms were similarly updated, and although they couldn't make them any bigger, they certainly are more modern and comfortable.

More changes are in store, with plans to add a three-story shopping mall at the front of the property along the Strip; expect some construction issues into 2015.

While significantly nicer than the old Trop, the new Trop is still struggling to find its footing in the marketplace. Several of the dining options, entertainment, nightlife offerings, and attractions have come and gone (and in some cases, come back again), so pardon us for being generic when we say that there are restaurants, bars, a showroom, a casino, and other amusements and leave it at that.

3801 Las Vegas Blvd. S. (at Tropicana Ave.). *©* **888/826-8767** or 702/739-2222. www.troplv.com. 1,375 units. $99 and up double. Resort fee $20. Extra person $25. No discount for kids. Free self-and valet parking. **Amenities:** 3 restaurants; food court; casino; executive-level rooms; health club; 3 outdoor pools; showroom; wedding chapel, in-room high-speed Internet.

MID-STRIP

The middle of the Strip is from Harmon Avenue to Spring Mountain/Sands Road and features many of the grand Vegas gambling destinations you have seen in the movies.

Best for: People without transportation who want to be able to walk to everything they want to see.

Drawbacks: Peak times bring out massive crowds and higher prices.

Expensive

Bellagio ★★★   Over the last few years, Bellagio has been walking a bit of a tightrope, attempting to retain the elegant features and ambience that established it as the most luxurious hotel in Las Vegas, while trying to update and modernize it to compete with the more contemporary resorts that have come along to challenge its dominance in the high-end market. That they have navigated the tightrope with ease is worthy of applause.

Most of the changes have been subtle—a new nightclub here; a new restaurant there—but the biggest update has been to the rooms in both towers, which were completely revamped between 2011 and 2013. These previously staid accommodations are now gorgeously rendered, modern masterpieces with funky retro-mod furnishings; bold purple, green, and golden design schemes; high-tech touches including a connectivity station for computers and devices of all kinds; and marble-lined bathrooms that are big enough to share and luxurious enough that you'll never want to leave.

The things that drew crowds and appreciative goggling are still there: the 8-acre lake in front with a dazzling choreographed water-ballet extravaganza (p. 138); an eye-popping Dale Chihuly blown-glass flower sculpture on the lobby ceiling (the largest of its kind in the world); an art gallery; and a downright lovely conservatory (p. 138), complete with brightly colored flowers and plants, changed every few months to go with the season (the holiday and Chinese New Year exhibits are favorites).

There are also still a host of fine restaurants, including **Picasso** and **Olives,** plus the **Bellagio Buffet,** all of which are reviewed in chapter 5; upscale bars and clubs like **Petrossian** and **Hyde Bellagio** (reviewed in chapter 8); the stunning Cirque du Soleil show *O* (p. 182); a classically designed casino with plenty of fine fabrics, wood, and marble; and Via Bellagio, a high-end shopping gallery.

On the downside, you still can't avoid a walk through the casino to get just about anywhere and there are extra charges galore, such as a pricey resort fee and another one for poolside cabanas. If you wish to splurge for the latter, you'll find them next to no fewer than six swimming pools set in a neoclassical Roman garden with flowered, trellised archways, and a fitness center and 40,000-square-foot spa, all designed to pamper you into submission.

3600 Las Vegas Blvd. S. (at the corner of Flamingo Rd.). © **888/987-6667** or 702/693-7111. www.bellagio.com. 3,933 units. Resort fee $25. $169 and up double; $450 and up suite. Extra person $35. No discount for children. Free self- and valet parking. **Amenities:** 14 restaurants; buffet; nightclubs; casino; concierge; executive-level rooms; large health club; 6 outdoor pools; room service; showrooms; spa; wedding chapel; in-room high-speed Internet.

Caesars Palace ★★★ Since 1966, Caesars has stood simultaneously as the ultimate in Vegas luxury and the nadir (or pinnacle, depending on your values) of Las Vegas cheese. It's the most Vegas-style hotel you'll find, covering all the bases, from the tacky fabulous schmaltz of the recent past (Roman colonnades, pillars, and statues) to the current trend in high-end luxury (sleekly designed, high-tech rooms). It's what Vegas ought to be.

Accommodations occupy six towers. The older Roman and Forum Tower rooms are comparatively basic, although some still have the Roman-style baths in the room (as opposed to in the bathroom). Decor is simple but plush, and they have a raft of amenities including flat-panel TVs, minibars (in some rooms), motorized drapes, and the like. The Palace Tower ups the ante with more floor space, a small sitting area, bigger bathrooms, spa tubs, and more. The newer Augustus and Octavius Towers have the biggest rooms with ultraluxe furnishings and design—all sleek lines and muted colors with big floor-to-ceiling windows offering some cool views if you get the right room. They have their own check-in and valet entrance off of Flamingo, plus some newfangled gimmickry in an online application that allows you to do things like order room service or have your car pulled up at the valet through your computer or mobile device.

The Nobu Hotel Las Vegas, a hotel-within-a-hotel concept from the Asian restaurant chain, opened in 2013, taking over the old Centurion Tower and giving it a fresh, modern makeover. The rooms here are comfortably lovely, with an Asian Zen-garden approach in both the bedroom and the bathroom, including teak and stone fixtures giving the latter a Japanese bathhouse feel. Service is extra-attentive, while snacks and room service from Chef Nobu range from traditional American to sushi for breakfast, giving the whole thing an exclusive air—a good thing considering the premium prices you'll pay to stay here.

Caesars has a well-deserved reputation for superior in-house restaurants. The meat-lover's paradise **Old Homestead Steakhouse,** the Bobby Flay brainchild **Mesa Grill,** the casual **munchbar,** and more are described in chapter 5.

Other on-site amenities include the Roman-themed shopping experience of **The Forum Shops** (p. 170); several bars and lounges; a spa and fitness center; an opulent, rambling casino; and a 4,000-seat showroom, home to **Céline Dion, Elton John, Shania Twain,** and others (see chapter 8).

Notable is the **Garden of the Gods** pool area, a tasteful, undeniably Caesaresque masterpiece. With eight pools on three levels, there is plenty of space for frolicking in the hot sun. Each has the classic granite columns and intricately carved sculptures that you'd expect from an area that names each of its pools after Roman deities or words that lend context to its unique mission (Fortuna has swim-up blackjack, Bacchus is for VIP guests only, and Apollo gets the most sun of any of them).

3570 Las Vegas Blvd. S. (just north of Flamingo Rd.). ℂ **877/427-7243** or 702/731-7110. www.caesarspalace.com. 3,960 units. $129 and up double; $299 and up suite. Resort fee $25. Extra person $30. No discount for children. Free self- and valet parking. **Amenities:** 12 restaurants; buffet; food court; nightclubs; casino; concierge; executive-level rooms; health club; 8 outdoor pools; room service; spa; 3 wedding chapels; in-room high-speed Internet.

The Cosmopolitan of Las Vegas ★★★   The trend toward bland luxury took a turn for the dramatic with the opening of this 3,000 room megaresort in 2010. The Cosmo is audacious, bold, stunningly visual, and one of the most interesting hotels in Vegas—or anywhere else, for that matter.

The interior design was envisioned as an art project—a series of curated experiences creating a dramatic whole. The big spectacles will get your attention first: the three-story chandelier with a multilevel bar inside; the video panels on the lobby columns; the 6-foot-tall sculptures of women's pumps in random places. But take time to notice the smaller details: the restored cigarette machines that dispense packs of art instead of smokes; the banquettes in the lobby of tufted velvet with a working, rotary-style phone; the wall of record album covers leading to the "hidden" pizza place. It's like staying in a contemporary art museum with slot machines.

The hotel's small footprint required a vertical design that is much more easily navigable than most Strip behemoths. Parking is under the hotel, with the casino and multiple bars on the first floor, shopping and some casual restaurants on the second, fine dining on the third, and one of the pools and a nightclub on the fourth and fifth floors, respectively.

Rooms are in two towers and all are big, with at least 600 square feet of upscale amenities including flatscreen televisions; a small kitchenette with a minibar, sink, and microwave (at the very least); huge bathrooms, some with Japanese soaking tubs; and all of the nice touches you would expect. There are even some touches you wouldn't expect, like actual books scattered about the room. You can pick them up and read them and everything! About two-thirds of the rooms also come with terraces—gorgeous outdoor patios with comfy furnishings that offer some stunning views of the city from the higher floors.

The hotel has over a dozen restaurants, including the phenomenal **Rose.Rabbit.Lie** and others that are reviewed in chapter 5; a major nightclub, **Marquee** (p. 203); a 3,000-seat showroom that frequently hosts concerts from big-name artists like Bruno Mars; the deliriously fun show *Vegas Nocture* (p. 191); three pools, a spa, and a gym; a 100,000-square-foot casino; an outdoor performance venue for concerts; and a pool overlooking the Strip that hosts "Dive In Movies" during the summer.

It is worth noting that the bold design, big crowds, and loud music at every turn can be a bit overwhelming. People who are looking for a sedate Vegas getaway should avoid this place at all costs.

By the way, that "hidden" pizza place? It's down an unmarked hallway on the third floor between the Jaleo and Blue Ribbon Sushi restaurants. Don't tell them we told you.

3708 Las Vegas Blvd. S. ✆ **877/551-7778** or 702/698-7000. www.cosmopolitanlasvegas.com. 2,995 units. $159 and up double. Resort fee $25. Extra person $30. Children under 17 stay free in parent's room. Free self- and valet parking. **Amenities:** 13 restaurants; buffet; casino; concierge; executive-level rooms; health club; heated outdoor pools; room service; spa.; in-room high-speed Internet.

The Cromwell ★★   The hotel that started life as Barbary Coast and faded into obsolescence as Bill's Gamblin' Hall has gotten a new, upper-crust lease on life as a chic boutique hotel. About the only thing they kept were the original chandeliers in the casino, restored and given a luxurious makeover that matches the rich textures and fabrics that now adorn all of the surfaces. The difference is night and day—or rather mostly night, as the original building was constructed at time when natural light was not considered a positive thing. You do get a bit of a cave-like feeling in the casino, and hallways and rooms are a bit dark, but they've done a good job with lighting and design elements like readable carpeting (there are sentences encouraging a *laissez faire* attitude toward life) and funky mirrors to create drama. The room design is French boudoir meets Meat Packing district loft, with wood floors, bold purple accents, luggage-inspired furniture, and cool touches like backgammon sets or checkerboards. Check out the bold original photography that adorns the walls, with models acting out a bacchanalian masquerade party and other vaguely scandalous themes. Rooms and bathrooms are very small compared to modern Vegas standards; and while they do a lot with the floor space, if you're a size-matters type of person or just need room to spread out, this is not the hotel for you. A restaurant from Giada De Laurentiis offers summery California cuisine, and a rooftop club offers pool fun during the day, dancing at night, and an after-hours club that keeps things going until dawn. Proving that this is a playground for those with the cash to enjoy it, the pool will offer customized fireworks that you can design and shoot off from the roof. With "only" 188 rooms (this is Vegas, after all) and a higher-than-average staff-to-guest ratio, you can expect very personal and attentive service at every turn.

3595 Las Vegas Blvd. S. ✆ **844/426-2766** or 702/777-3777. www.thecromwell.com. 188 units. $249 and up double. Resort fee $25. Extra person $35. No discount for children. Free self- and valet parking. **Amenities:** 2 restaurants; nightclubs, casino; concierge; heated outdoor pool; room service; in-room high-speed Internet.

The Venetian/Palazzo Las Vegas ★★   One of the most elaborate hotel spectacles in town, the Venetian falls squarely between an outright adult Disneyland experience and the luxury resort experience currently dominating the Vegas landscape. The hotel's exterior, which re-creates most of the top landmarks of Venice (the Campanile, a portion of St. Mark's Square, part of the Doge's Palace, a canal or two), ranks right up there with New York–New York as a must-see. As stern as we get about re-creations *not* being a substitute for the real thing, we have to admit that the attention to detail here is impressive indeed. Stone is aged for that weathered look, statues and tiles are exact copies of their Italian counterparts, security guards wear Venetian police uniforms—all that's missing is the smell from the canals, but we are happy to let that one slide.

Inside, it's more of the same, particularly in the lobby area and the entrance to the extraordinary shops, as ceilings are covered with hand-painted re-creations of Venetian art. With plenty of marble, soaring ceilings, and impressive pillars and archways, it's less kitschy than Caesars but more theme park than Bellagio.

Sister hotel Palazzo has its own lobby, casino, and other services but is more sedate than the eye-popping Venetian. As the two properties are connected, usually charge the same rates, and operate as one gigantic facility, which one you choose is really a matter of closing your eyes and pointing.

Rooms in the main and Venezia towers are virtually identical to those in the Palazzo, with a sleeping area and the sunken living room separated by a couple of steps and rich fabrics and woods adorning the surfaces. Three flatscreen TVs (two quite big, one smaller and badly positioned in the bathroom), a particularly squishy white bed with superior linens and pillows, remote-control curtain and shades, and a deep bathtub in a generously sized, gleaming bathroom add up to the kind of accommodations that are hard to leave. Stay here only if what you mostly wanted to see in the city is your fabulous hotel room.

Restaurants from many celebrity chefs can be found at the Venetian and Palazzo, including Thomas Keller, Emeril Lagasse, Mario Batali, Daniel Boulud, and Buddy Valastro, some of which are reviewed in chapter 5. The 80s-themed Broadway musical *Rock of Ages* (p. 190) and Australian singing group *Human Nature* are among the entertainment offerings. Other amusements include two casinos; the largest spa facility in town at the Canyon Ranch SpaClub; multiple pools (all of which are fine but none of which are terribly special); and **The Grand Canal Shoppes** (p. 170), a mall complete with its own canal and singing gondoliers.

3355 Las Vegas Blvd. S. ℂ **888/283-6423** or 702/414-1000. www.venetian.com. 7,093 units. $169 and up double. Resort fee $25. Extra person $35. Children 12 and under stay free in parent's room. Free self- and valet parking. **Amenities:** 37 restaurants; casino; concierge; executive-level rooms; health club; outdoor pools; 24-hr. room service; extensive shopping mall; showrooms; spa; wedding chapels; in-room high-speed Internet.

Moderate

Bally's Las Vegas ★   Originally known as the MGM Grand when it opened in 1973, this was the first real megaresort on the Vegas Strip and was, at the time, the biggest hotel in the world. Of course, it has since been overshadowed by its newer, bigger, fancier neighbors, but Bally's is still in the game with one of the best locations in town, dependable accommodations, a serviceable casino, and (most importantly) relatively affordable room rates.

If you don't have to pay too much of a premium, go for one of the new-as-of-2013 Jubilee Tower rooms, which come with retro-modern furnishings, flatscreen TVs, minibars, upgraded bathrooms, and more. The rest of the accommodations range from *Holiday Inn* to *Motel 6* but are also reportedly due for a makeover, perhaps by the time you read this. Those upgrades may also come with a revamped exterior, planned for early 2015, featuring an outdoor bazaar of shops and restaurants lining the Strip.

There are a handful of restaurants and more at neighboring Paris Las Vegas, which is connected via an indoor walkway of shops. The casino is large, well lit, and colorful, and there's also a headliner showroom and the splashy *Jubilee!* revue (p. 187). The monorail stop out back makes getting elsewhere a breeze, although it's worth noting that if you are driving, the valet seems to always be full and self-parking is next door at Paris, requiring a long walk to your room.

3645 Las Vegas Blvd. S. (at Flamingo Rd.). ℂ **800/634-3434** or 702/739-4111. 2,814 units. www. ballyslv.com. $99 and up double; $199 and up suite. Resort fee $20. Extra person $30. No discount for children. Free self- and valet parking. **Amenities:** 4 restaurants; buffet; food court; casino; concierge; health club; outdoor pool; room service; showrooms; spa; 8 night-lit tennis courts; in-room high-speed Internet.

Flamingo Las Vegas ★   As the oldest continually operating hotel on the Strip, the Flamingo has changed a great deal since Bugsy Siegel opened his 105-room oasis "in the middle of nowhere" in 1946, and yet you can still see his influence everywhere. None of the original structure still stands nearly 70 years later, but the resort has embraced its history with pink neon-lit flash and blast-from-the-past rooms that charm.

Rushing headlong into the Dean Martin/Rat Pack retro vibe, the GO rooms are kicky candy modern, with hot pink accents, frosted glass bathroom doors, candy-striped wallpaper, black-and-white photos of the Flamingo from its early days, squishy white beds with vinyl padded headboards, huge flatscreens, iPod docking stations, and more. They are ring-a-ding fun, and Dino would surely have approved.

The standard FAB rooms are not quite as fun but still very nice, with comfy furnishings, some retro touches in the artwork, and unique wood laminate floors. The latter make the rooms feel more spacious than they really are, but if you are visiting in the chillier months you may want to consider bringing your slippers.

There are also several restaurants and bars, a huge casino, and a showroom featuring **Donny and Marie** (p. 185), *Legends in Concert* (p. 187), and other entertainment. The monorail has a stop out back.

For those planning some leisure time outside the casino, the Flamingo's exceptional pool area and spa are big draws. Five gorgeous swimming pools, two whirlpools, and water slides are located in a 15-acre Caribbean landscape amid lagoons, meandering streams, fountains, waterfalls, a rose garden, and islands of live flamingos. Ponds have ducks, swans, and koi, and a grove of 2,000 palms graces an expanse of lawn. Although the water can be a little chilly, kids should be able to spend hours in the pool area.

3555 Las Vegas Blvd. S. (btw. Sands Ave. and Flamingo Rd.). ℂ **800/732-2111** or 702/733-3111. www.flamingolv.com. 3,517 units. $85 and up double; $199 and up suite. Resort fee $20. Extra person $30. No discount for children. Timeshare suites available. Free self- and valet parking. **Amenities:** 6 restaurants; buffet; food court; casino; executive-level rooms; health club; 5 outdoor pools; room service; showrooms; spa; wedding chapels; in-room high-speed Internet.

Harrah's Las Vegas ★   Here's another property that is doing its best to keep up with the pace in Vegas, to mixed success. New restaurants, new machines in the casino, and a few other upgrades haven't moved it up to luxe-level, but there is much to like here, and occasional quite good rates might make the so-so bits worth overlooking. Certainly, it wants to be the fun and convivial place we wish more of Vegas was (instead of pretty much catering to high rollers and simply tolerating the rest of us with normal budgets).

The rooms are simple, with comfy mattresses and those white bed covers that are now more or less standard in most local hotels. No flash here, but they are reliable for

SO YOUR TRIP GOES swimmingly . . .

Part of the delight of the Vegas resort complexes is the gorgeous pools—what could be better for beating the summer heat? But there are pools and there are *pools,* so you'll need to keep several things in mind when searching for the right one for you.

During the winter, it's often too cold or windy to do much lounging, and even if the weather is amenable, the hotels often close part of their pool areas during winter and early spring. The pools also are not heated for the most part, but in fairness, they largely don't need to be.

Most hotel pools are shallow, chest-high at best, only about 3 feet deep in many spots (the hotels want you gambling, not swimming). Diving is impossible—not that a single pool allows it anyway.

Although the stories about the "Death Ray" at CityCenter's Vdara hotel were overblown, where the sun reflecting off the mirrored hotel exterior reportedly caused plastic to melt, be warned that sitting by pools that offer scant shade requires diligent application of sunscreen.

At any of the pools, you can rent a cabana (which often includes a TV, special lounge chairs, and—even better—poolside service), but these should be reserved as far in advance as possible and most cost a hefty fee. If you are staying at a chain hotel, you will most likely find an average pool, but if you want to spend some time at a better one, be aware that most of

the casino-hotel pool attendants will ask to see your room key. If they are busy, you might be able to sneak in, or at least blend in with a group ahead of you.

When it comes to our favorites, we tend to throw our support to those that offer luxurious landscaping, plenty of places to lounge, multiple dipping options, and some shade for those times when the desert sun gets to be too much. This is a good description of the pools at both **The Mirage** and the **Flamingo,** which offer acres of veritable tropical paradises for you to enjoy. Ditto the renovated pool area at the **Tropicana,** serving up a sunny Miami Beach feeling among lush grounds.

If you're looking for something a little more adventurous, try the epic facility at **Mandalay Bay,** complete with a wave pool, a lazy-river ride, and good old-fashioned swimming holes along with a sandy beach. **MGM Grand** has a similar facility, although not as big and without the waves.

Partying is not confined to the nightclubs these days. Many of the hotels offer pool-club experiences (p. 208), but even when they aren't in full-on party mode, the pools at **Hard Rock** (sandy beaches, swim-up blackjack), the Palms (multilevel, high-end cabanas), **Aria Las Vegas** (acres of sexy modernity), and **The Cosmopolitan of Las Vegas** (not one but two party pools overlooking the Strip) serve up high-energy frolicking.

what is ultimately a gamblers' hotel and provide guests with most of the necessary amenities.

There's a casino, of course, and the usual array of restaurants, including a branch of the popular Ruth's Chris Steakhouse chain, the fantastic burgers at **KGB** (p. 105), a buffet, and a food court for quick bites to eat. A showroom used to be home to Sammy Davis, Jr., back in the day and is now showcasing **Mac King**'s wonderful comedy/magic act (p. 188) in the daytime and the Broadway musical *Million Dollar Quartet* (p. 189) at night. Harrah's has an Olympic-size swimming pool and sundeck area with a waterfall, trellised gardens, and a whirlpool. It's a pretty underwhelming pool by Vegas standards, but the adjacent health club and spa are nice enough.

3475 Las Vegas Blvd. S. (btw. Flamingo and Spring Mountain rds.). ℂ **800/427-7247** or 702/369-5000. www.harrahslasvegas.com. 2,526 units. $79 and up double; $199 and up suite. Resort fee $18. Extra person $30. No discount for children. Free self- and valet parking. **Amenities:** 6 restaurants; buffet; casino; concierge; executive-level rooms; health club; outdoor pool; room service; showroom; spa; in-room high-speed Internet.

The Mirage ★★ In many ways, the Mirage invented the concept of the modern Las Vegas resort. When it opened in 1989 there was nothing like it—a spectacle of excess that, though often repeated since, set a new standard for the outrageous fortune of Las Vegas.

Occupying 102 acres, The Mirage is fronted by more than a city block of cascading waterfalls and tropical foliage centering on a "volcano," which, after dark, erupts every hour, spewing fire 100 feet above the lagoons below. Throw in the 20,000-gallon aquarium behind the check-in desk, a **Dolphin Habitat** (p. 136) out back, and a 90-foot dome over an indoor rainforest in the middle, and you have the makings for a truly unforgettable resort experience.

The lodgings have that white bed/bold, solid colors/'70s-inspired look that almost everyone is sporting a variation of these days. Pillowtop mattresses and 42-inch LCD TVs do wonders for overcoming any decor concerns. Although up to date, the bathrooms remain small, but that shouldn't bother you unless you have space issues and/or have seen the bigger ones elsewhere on the Strip.

There are a host of restaurants, including ones from Tom Colicchio and *Iron Chef America* star Masaharu Morimoto, plus a satisfying buffet. The Cirque production *LOVE* is reviewed in chapter 8, as is a show starring **Terry Fator,** winner of *America's Got Talent.* The Mirage has one of our favorite casinos and some excellent nightclubs and bars.

Out back is the pool, one of the nicest in Vegas, with a quarter-mile shoreline, a tropical paradise of waterfalls and trees, water slides, and so forth. It looks inviting, but truth be told, it's sometimes on the chilly side and isn't very deep. But it's so pretty you'll hardly care. There is also Bare, a "European-style pool" offering a more adult aquatic experience.

The only significant downside here is the ridiculous slog of casino mayhem you must endure to get to your room, the pool, food, or the outside world. It gets old fast.

3400 Las Vegas Blvd. S. (btw. Flamingo and Spring Mountain rds.). ℂ **800/627-6667** or 702/791-7111. www.mirage.com. 3,044 units. $109 and up double; $275 and up suite. Resort fee $25. Extra person $35. No discount for children. Free self- and valet parking. **Amenities:** 10 restaurants; buffet; casino; concierge; executive-level rooms; health club; outdoor pools; room service; showrooms; spa, in-room high-speed Internet.

Paris Las Vegas Casino Resort ★★★ *Sacre bleu!* The City of Light comes to Sin City in this, one of the few theme-run-amok hotels left to its giddy devices. Stay here if you came to Vegas for the silly fantasy. The outside reproduces various Parisian landmarks (amusing anyone familiar with Paris, as the Hotel de Ville is crammed on top of the Louvre), complete with a half-scale perfect replica of the Eiffel Tower. The interior puts you in the middle of a dollhouse version of the city. You can stroll down a mini Rue de la Paix, ride an elevator to the top of the Eiffel Tower, stop at an overpriced bakery for a baguette, and have your photo taken near several very nice fountains.

Quel dommage, this attention to detail does not extend to the rooms, which are nice enough but uninteresting, with furniture that only hints at mock French Regency. Bathrooms are small but pretty, with deep tubs. If you don't mind the upgraded price, go for the newer Red rooms on the upper floors, done in a modern French-bordello theme complete with suede sofas that look like puckered lips. Try to get a Strip-facing room so that you can see Bellagio's fountains across the street; note also that north-facing rooms give you nice Peeping Tom views right into neighboring Bally's. The monorail has a stop out back, which adds to the convenience factor. Overall, not a bad place to stay, but a great place to visit—*quel hoot!*

Dining options include an upscale steakhouse from fiery Brit **Gordon Ramsay,** the highly lauded **Le Village Buffet,** the **Sugar Factory,** and bistro **Mon Ami Gabi,** all of which are covered in chapter 5. For entertainment (as if it wasn't entertaining enough already) there are lounges and a nightclub **Chateau** (p. 201), the **Eiffel Tower** attraction (p. 135), and the Broadway hit *Jersey Boys* in the Parisian opera house–themed showroom (p. 186).

3655 Las Vegas Blvd. S. ⓒ **888/266-5687** or 702/946-7000. www.parislv.com. 2,916 units. $119 and up double; $350 and up suite. Resort fee $20. Extra person $30. No discount for children. Free self- and valet parking. **Amenities:** 10 restaurants; buffet; casino; concierge; executive-level rooms; health club; outdoor pool; room service; showrooms; spa; 2 wedding chapels.; in-room high-speed Internet.

Planet Hollywood Resort & Casino ★★   Fronted by a jumble of LED screens and bright signs, you may think you're in for the same kind of sensory over-load that the pop-culture restaurants of the same name provide. But once you get inside you may be pleasantly surprised by classy, modern design that manages to evoke Hollywood glamour without resorting to overuse of glitter.

From a size and amenities perspective, the rooms are pretty average until you get to the memorabilia displays. Each has a movie or entertainment theme, such as *Pulp Fiction,* which might have John Travolta's suit in a glass case and a glass coffee table filled with more original memorabilia from the film. Although more than one room may share the same movie theme, no two rooms will have the same objects. The vibe of the room can vary radically depending on if the theme is Judy Garland in some charming musical or Wesley Snipes in *Blade,* so ask when booking. As gimmicks go, it's a catchy one, and a good use for all that junk the company's accumulated over the years.

There are also a couple of thousand additional rooms in the connected but separately managed Elara, a Hilton Grand Vacations timeshare/hotel. They offer the typical sleek design and decor of modern Vegas hotels but throw in a Hollywood twist through art and amenities. Studios through four-bedroom suites each have kitchens (from wee to wow), projector televisions that use the blackout shades for truly gigantic screen view-ing, and whirlpool tubs. You have to book rooms here separately through Hilton, but they are definitely nicer than those in the main tower, albeit with a little less personality.

The parking lot is all the way on the other side of the Miracle Mile shopping area, thus requiring guests to drag their suitcases all the way through the mall and a good chunk of the hotel before getting to registration. Valet parking is often full so you may not have a choice.

Several of the hotel's restaurants are covered in chapter 5, including **Gordon Ramsay BurGR** and the popular **Spice Market Buffet,** among others, and the aforementioned shopping mall known as **Miracle Mile** is in chapter 7. And don't forget about the 4,000-seat **Axis Theater** where Britney Spears is headlining through at least 2015.

3667 Las Vegas Blvd. S. ✆ **877/333-9474** or 702/785-5555. www.planethollywoodresort.com. 3,768 units. $99 and up double. Resort fee $20. Extra person $30. No discount for children. Free self- and valet parking. **Amenities:** 24 restaurants; buffet; bars/lounges; casino; concierge; executive-level rooms; health club; 2 Jacuzzis; performing-arts center; 2 outdoor pools; room service; showroom; spa; wedding chapel; in-room high-speed Internet.

The Quad ★ The rebirth of the worn Imperial Palace into this, the trying-to-be-hip-and-modern the Quad, has primarily involved redoing the casino, the facade, and some of the other public spaces. To be sure, the new look, while a bit bland, is a huge improvement over the old one, with modern lines, rich earth tones, contemporary furnishings and decor, and lots of natural light from big windows facing the Strip.

A much-needed makeover of the rooms was just getting underway as this book went to press, so we can't tell you much about them other than to say that anything would be an improvement over the old, very worn accommodations that used to be here. Of course, the bad news is that as the hotel gets nicer, the prices get higher, and now your options for basic, rock-bottom cheap rooms on the Strip are mostly gone.

The casino is much more complete than it used to be; there's a big pool, and they have lots of entertainment options, including a fun show from comic-juggler **Jeff Civilico** (p. 186) and an automotive museum reviewed in chapter 6. Dining options include the fantastic **Hash House a Go Go** (p. 101) and a restaurant from celebrity chef Guy Fieri, among others.

3535 Las Vegas Blvd. S. ✆ **800/351-7400** or 702/731-3311. www.imperialpalace.com. 2,550 units. $79 and up double; $159 and up suite. Resort fee $20. Extra person $30. No discount for children. Free self- and valet parking. **Amenities:** 8 restaurants; casino; concierge; health club; heated outdoor pool; room service; spa; showrooms; salon; auto museum; wedding chapel. *In room:* A/C, TV, high-speed Internet (for a fee).

Treasure Island ★★ Originally the most modern family-friendly hotel on the strip, Treasure Island (commonly referred to as "TI" by most folks) was a blown-up version of Disneyland's *Pirates of the Caribbean.* But that's all behind them now, with most of the pirate wackiness replaced by bland contemporary decor that, while nice, is nowhere near as interesting. Even the pirate stunt show out front was finally sent to its watery grave in 2013 to make way for a new shopping mall due to open in early 2015.

The good-size rooms are pleasant but not postcard-worthy, although additions of niceties like in-room refrigerators make them more comfy than they were. Good bathrooms feature large soaking tubs—a bather's delight.

The hotel offers several restaurants, including the party bar Señor Frog's, a steakhouse, a buffet, and western favorite **Gilley's** (p. 100), which also offers country dancing and a mechanical bull, naturally. Treasure Island is home to Cirque du Soleil's *Mystère* (p. 182), one of the best shows in town.

Neither the spa nor pool is all that memorable, so if those things are important to you, stay elsewhere, like at the neighboring Mirage, which is connected to the TI by a free tram.

3300 Las Vegas Blvd. S. (at Spring Mountain Rd.). ✆ **800/944-7444** or 702/894-7111. www.treasure island.com. 2,885 units. $89 and up double; $140 and up suite. Resort fee $25. Extra person $30. Free for children 14 and under in parent's room. Free self- and valet parking. **Amenities:** 9 restaurants; buffet; casino; concierge; executive-level rooms; health club; outdoor pool; room service; showroom; spa; wedding chapels; in-room high-speed Internet.

NORTH STRIP

The northern end of the Strip, from Spring Mountain/Sands Road to Charleston Avenue, is not quite as densely populated with major casinos, but still has enough Vegas flair to make it worth your while.

Best for: Visitors who want to be on the Strip but want a slightly more manageable experience from a crowd and congestion perspective.

Drawbacks: It's a longer walk to most of what you'll want to see; some of the hotels here are past their prime.

Expensive

Wynn/Encore ★★★ In many ways Steve Wynn created modern-day Las Vegas, with hotels like the Mirage and Bellagio setting the standard and creating the blueprint for all of the magnificent resorts that would follow—including these, the sisters Wynn and Encore. They used to be operated and marketed separately and while they still have their own lobbies, casinos, pools, and so on, the property is now considered to be one united whole.

Natural light and garden motifs infuse the public spaces throughout, with eye-catching, brightly hued floor mosaics; liberal use of reds, yellows, greens, and other summery colors; artistic fresh-flower arrangements throughout; and atriums that feature frequently changed botanical displays.

The rooms in the Wynn tower are gorgeous: large with much-appreciated floor-to-ceiling views (west side shows off the mountain and waterfalls, east side the golf course; both are choice); deeply comfortable beds, with high-thread-count sheets and feather beds atop good-quality mattresses; flatscreen TVs; and excellent up-to-the-minute bathrooms, complete with quite long and deep tubs, and high-end bath products. Take note of the silky-satiny robes (the best we've ever had in a hotel) and plush velour slippers. It's all done in creamy tones that make it modern without being garish.

While they follow a similar aesthetic, the rooms at Encore are grander than those at Wynn both in terms of size and amenities. Most are "suites" with a sleeping area separated from a living room space by a partial wall (and a giant flatscreen TV). Furnishings are modern but with an elegant panache, and high-tech, thus allowing you to operate everything from the lights to the TVs to the drapes to the air-conditioning from a single remote that remembers your preferences. Bathrooms are massive and packed with enough marble to build your own Colosseum.

Three separate pool areas cater to different audiences and moods, with the main Wynn pool full of egalitarian grandiosity, the main Encore pool a bit more exclusive and grown-up, and the Encore Beach Club pool dedicated to the younger party set. There are two fantastic spas but if you have to choose one go with Encore's, which has a jaw-dropping Moroccan garden theme.

Dining options are superb (though generally exceptionally pricey), including **Bartolotta, Red 8,** the Chairman of the Board–themed **Sinatra,** and the **Wynn Las Vegas Buffet,** all reviewed in chapter 5. Shopping options are mostly reserved for those with high credit limits—Chanel, Cartier, Manolo Blahnik, Gaultier—but if that's not enough for you, there's also a Ferrari dealership—no, really. A showroom features the Cirque-like production *Le Rêve* (p. 187). The Wynn casino is larger and more complete than Encore's, and taken as one big whole there's a little something for everyone.

As with its big sister, prices here are not for the faint of heart. While the recession may have knocked down the overall bill during its inaugural run, room rates will almost always be more expensive here than just about anywhere else on the Strip. Ditto restaurant prices, table game limits, and the cost of a bottle of water in the sundry store.

3131 Las Vegas Blvd. S. (corner of Spring Mountain Rd.). © **888/320-9966** or 702/770-7100. www.wynnlasvegas.com. 4,750 units. $159 and up double. Resort fee $25. Extra person $50. No discount for children. Free self- and valet parking. **Amenities:** 18 restaurants; buffet; casino; concierge; executive-level rooms; health club; outdoor pools; room service; showrooms; spa; wedding chapels; in-room high-speed Internet.

Moderate

Stratosphere Las Vegas Hotel & Casino ★
At 1,149 feet, the Stratosphere Tower looms large above the Vegas skyline, but over the years the hotel has struggled to find its place in the city's pantheon of megaresorts. It started as a family-friendly destination, morphed into a low-frills budget option, and now, with some recent renovations, is trying to aim for somewhere in the middle.

The standard guest rooms are nice enough but fairly basic, with simple white linens on the bed, sturdy furnishings, and simple motel-style bathrooms. The upmarket "Select" rooms have nicer just about everything, including more stylish furnishings, more contemporary decor, and upgraded but still small bathrooms, although they will never be confused with luxury digs at places like Wynn/Encore. They'll cost you a few bucks more than the standard rooms, but are totally worth it.

Note: Contrary to popular belief, there are no hotel rooms in the observation tower itself. Sorry.

Downstairs, a big casino has lots of low-limit gambling plus plenty of dining options, including a decent but unspectacular buffet and the Italian comfort-food favorite **Fellini's** (p. 108). Upstairs are the usual shows, shopping, swimming (on the eighth-floor pool deck), a spa, and the like that you'd expect to find at a Vegas casino, but none of it is really worth going out of your way to visit.

Way upstairs—up more than 100 stories—is the observation tower with restaurants, lounges, bars, and some extreme thrill rides covered in more detail on p. 137. Guests of the hotel get free access to the tower as part of the daily resort fee.

The low prices might make this the right place for you. Just remember that its location on the far northern end of the Strip means you need a rental car or a lot of cash for cabs to get to the true thrills down the street.

2000 Las Vegas Blvd. S. (btw. St. Louis and Baltimore aves.). © **800/998-6937** or 702/380-7777. www.stratospherehotel.com. 2,444 units. $49 and up double; $109 and up suite. Resort fee $15. Extra person $15. Children 12 and under stay free in parent's room. Free self- and valet parking. **Amenities:** 6 restaurants; buffet; several fast-food outlets; arcade; casino; concierge; executive-level rooms; large pool area w/great views of the Strip; room service; showrooms; wedding chapel; in-room high-speed Internet (for a fee).

Inexpensive

Circus Circus Hotel & Casino ★
This is the last bastion of family-friendly Las Vegas—indeed, for years, the only hotel with such an open mind, which is also not to say that you should confuse this with a theme-park hotel. All the circus fun is still built around a busy casino. The midway level features dozens of carnival games, a large arcade with more than 300 games, and ongoing circus acts under the big top from 11am to midnight daily. The world's largest permanent circus, it features renowned trapeze artists, stunt cyclists, jugglers, magicians, acrobats, and high-wire daredevils.

coming ATTRACTIONS

The global recession put the kibosh on new hotel development for years, with the last megaresort, the Cosmopolitan, opening in 2010. Now that the economy is improving, grand ideas for new Vegas resorts are emerging, with several already in various states of construction.

The classic Sahara hotel closed in 2010 and should be reopened by the time you read this as the **SLS Las Vegas,** a sister to the swank boutique hotels in Los Angeles, New York, and Miami. The brainchild of an L.A. nightclub impresario, the place will be packed with party-friendly hotspots, hip restaurants, and boutiques from Fred Segal.

Heavily themed hotels faded away in the 1990s, but may make a return with the proposed **Resorts World Las Vegas.** The Asian-inspired, $7-billion project from Malaysia-based gambling giant Genting Gaming will have at least 3,500 rooms, a 175,000 square-foot casino (the biggest in Vegas), a 4,000-seat showroom, an indoor waterpark, a panda habitat, and replicas of the Great Wall of China and the Terra Cotta Warriors of Xian. It will be located on the North Strip in place of the old Stardust and should open by 2017.

Finally, the **Fontainebleau,** a $4-billion high-rise hotel north of Riviera, has been mothballed for years and has no projected opening date, but may get a new lease on life with all the new development planned in the neighborhood.

Spectators can view the action from much of the midway, or get up close and comfy on benches in the performance arena.

The thousands of rooms here occupy sufficient acreage to warrant a free Disney World–style aerial shuttle (another kid pleaser) connecting its many components. The Casino and West Tower rooms are the newest and nicest, with modern decor, flatscreen TVs, and better-than-average furnishings. Get one of these if the price bump you'll be forced to pay over the more pedestrian Skyrise Tower isn't too much. The Manor section comprises five white, three-story buildings out back, and while the rooms here are usually among the least expensive in town, that old maxim applies: You get what you pay for. All sections of this vast property have their own swimming pools, and additional casino space serves the main tower and skyrise buildings.

The fact that all of this feels kind of dated and a bit worn in spots is really more of a function of changing times than any particular slam against the hotel. Compare it to places like the Cosmopolitan or Aria and it looks like a joke, but on its own it's a perfectly acceptable option and, as mentioned, one of the few places on the Strip for families.

Most of the restaurants are unremarkable, but they do have a classic steakhouse experience in the appropriately, if unimaginatively, named **The Steakhouse** (p. 107).

In addition to the ongoing circus acts, there's the **Adventuredome** (p. 136) indoor theme park out back for more amusements.

2880 Las Vegas Blvd. S. (btw. Circus Circus and Convention Center drs.). ✆ **877/434-9175** or 702/734-0410. www.circuscircus.com. 3,774 units. $59 and up double. Resort fee $14.50. Extra person $15. Children 17 and under stay free in parent's room. Free self- and valet parking. **Amenities:** 6 restaurants; buffet; several fast-food outlets; casino; circus acts and midway-style carnival games; executive-level rooms; outdoor pools; room service; wedding chapel; in-room high-speed Internet.

DOWNTOWN

The original Las Vegas, with classic and historic hotels, is Downtown; the glare of Glitter Gulch has become the must-see tourist destination of the Fremont Street Experience.

Best for: Budget-minded tourists; those looking for a friendlier atmosphere than the snooty Strip.

Drawbacks: Harder-to-find upscale experiences; the surrounding neighborhoods can be a bit rough.

Moderate

The Downtown Grand ★★   Built out of the bones of the former Lady Luck hotel, this funky and fresh take on the Downtown ethos has already taken the neighborhood by storm with its modern twist on a classic formula. It has everything you'd expect in a Downtown property, with a low-limit casino, value-priced restaurants, and simple accommodations, but it puts a contemporary spin on it with an industrial-chic design (dig those metal and crystal chandeliers), whimsical decor (sort of mid-century modern with a thrift-store aesthetic), and a more youthful energy that is almost palpable.

The rooms are small by modern Vegas Strip standards, but are still well-appointed and boldly decorated using bright green or red as a base and building from there. Spend the extra few bucks for the so-called Premium rooms, which offer a bit more floor space and more windows to brighten things up. Bathrooms are small and some only have showers, so if soaking in a tub is important to you, be sure to ask ahead.

Don't miss the fantastic pool area on the roof of the casino labeled Picnic. It has a sparkling infinity pool, fire pits, and grassy areas that make it the nicest recreation facility in all of Downtown. In fact, as a whole, the Grand is probably your best bet in Downtown and one of the best values in the entire city.

206 N. 3rd St. (btw. Stewart and Ogden aves.). ☏ **888/384-7263.** www.downtowngrand.com. 680 units. $49 and up double. $11 resort fee. Free self- and valet parking. **Amenities:** 8 restaurants; 6 bars; pool; fitness center; casino; room service; in-room high-speed Internet.

Golden Nugget ★★   While the casino dates back to 1946 (the first building built specifically for gambling) and the hotel to 1973 (it was Steve Wynn's first major property), the place feels comfortably modern thanks to renovations that have kept it contemporary and even upscale by Glitter Gulch standards.

Standard rooms are attractive and comfortable, but do splurge a bit (maybe an extra $25 per night) for the newer Rush Tower rooms, stunning digs with rough-hewn wood accents, leather furnishings, and an enormous wall of built-ins that features everything from a minibar to a flatscreen TV. You don't have to walk through the casino to get to your room, but you do have to walk a distance to get to the fab pool, a chic and snazzy highlight, complete with a water slide that goes right through a glass tunnel in the shark tank. The Rush Tower has an adults-only (not topless, just no kids) heated infinity pool with cabanas and a bar.

A crowded but pleasingly golden-hued casino dominates the main floor along with several restaurants, bars, a couple of shops, and easy access to the Fremont Street Experience outside. And of course, you have to stop by to see the *Hand of Faith* gold nugget, which at 61 pounds, 11 ounces, is the world's largest.

129 E. Fremont St. (at Casino Center Blvd.). ☏ **800/846-5336** or 702/385-7111. www.goldennugget.com. 2,425 units. $69 and up double; $275 and up suite. Resort fee $5. Extra person $20. No discount for children. Free self- and valet parking (with validation). **Amenities:** 7 restaurants;

buffet; bars, lounges, and nightclub; casino; executive-level rooms; health club; outdoor pool; room service; showroom; spa; in-room high-speed Internet (for a fee).

The D Las Vegas Casino Hotel ★ The same company that has done such a great job revitalizing the Golden Gate (see below) took on the Luck of the Irish–themed Fitzgerald's and gave it a sleek makeover that includes its somewhat too-hip-for-its-own-good new name. What does the D stand for? Well, it's a combination of sorts, paying homage to its Downtown Las Vegas location, the Detroit area from which the owners hail, and the nickname for CEO Derek Stevens. We're willing to overlook it if only so we can dream about the D, the M Resort, and LVH all getting into some sort of alphabetical street fight.

Silly name aside, the Fitz was getting long in the tooth and needed an update. Whether you like the sleek, modern look of the place is a matter of taste, but it is impossible not to see it as an improvement over what had become a tired, worn-around-the-edges blarney stone. An outdoor bar fronts Fremont Street under a new facade of light-emitting diode screens; be sure to check out the ones next to the outdoor escalator, which appear to interact with people making the ascent. Inside, the two-level casino has contemporary trappings downstairs with vintage throwbacks upstairs (the slots dispense coins!). Restaurants including Detroit favorites **Andiamo Steakhouse** (p. 109) and **American Coney Island** (p. 111) have joined the offerings, and a rare-for-Downtown pool is fairly plain in comparison to the rest of the contemporary design of the hotel.

The rooms mainly got a cosmetic freshening, but they did throw in niceties like pillowtop mattresses, flatscreen TVs, iPod docking stations, high-speed wired and wireless Internet access, and more. These rooms can't really compete with the luxury on the Strip, but they aren't trying to, especially when you consider the significantly lower room rates.

301 Fremont St. (at 3rd St.). ℂ **800/274-5825** or 702/388-2400. www.thed.com. 638 units. $59 and up double. Resort fee $20. Extra person $20. Children 11 and under stay free in parent's room. Free self- and valet parking. **Amenities:** 4 restaurants; lounge; casino; concierge; unheated outdoor pool; room service; in-room high-speed Internet.

Inexpensive

California Hotel & Casino ★ This is a hotel with a unique personality. It markets itself mostly in Hawaii, and because 85% of its guests are from the Aloha State, it offers a bold Polynesian theme, Hawaiian entrees in several of its restaurants, and a snack shop stuffed with everything from Chicken Tou Saimin to rice bowls. You'll also notice that dealers are wearing colorful Hawaiian shirts. The rooms, however, reflect neither California nor Hawaii; they have simple furnishings, small(ish) bathrooms, and a few distinctions like flat panel TVs and minifridges.

If it sounds like we are giving this place short shrift, it's only because there isn't a lot that makes it stand out (other than that Hawaii thing). What you will find are decent, middle-of-the-road accommodations (at very reasonable prices) that you will probably spend little time in because excitement is found elsewhere.

12 Ogden Ave. (at 1st St.). ℂ **800/634-6255** or 702/385-1222. www.thecal.com. 781 units. $40 and up double. No resort fee. Extra person $10. Children 13 and under stay free in parent's room. Free self- and valet parking. **Amenities:** 5 restaurants; casino; small rooftop pool; in-room high-speed Internet (for a fee).

El Cortez Hotel & Casino ★ Opened in 1941 and once owned by Bugsy Siegel, the El, as it is affectionately known, has experienced a rebirth of sorts. The hotel was overhauled a few years ago with a revamped casino, updated rooms, and a new exterior with a pedestrian plaza. It's a vast improvement and one that was well-timed as the hotel now finds itself at the epicenter of the booming Fremont East Entertainment District, surrounded by the hip bars, restaurants, and shopping that has sprung up in the last year. The result of this revamp of the hotel and the neighborhood is a more energetic vibe inside, especially on weekend nights.

Rooms in the main hotel (some quite large) have traditional furnishings; admittedly, nothing stands out, but with such amenities as flatscreen TVs, nice new (if small) bathrooms, armoires with minifridges, and Wi-Fi, they are right behind Main Street Station for recommendable, affordable Downtown lodgings.

Most notable here are the Cabana Suites. Formerly the rattrap Ogden House across the street, the building was remodeled into a modern/retro wonder complete with mod decor, Swarovski crystal chandeliers, custom furnishings, a small gym, and a funky lobby with a fireplace and concierge service. They took 102 tiny rooms and turned them into 64 bigger rooms, all with updated appointments, modern bathrooms, and a full host of amenities.

There are a couple of dependable restaurants, including a steakhouse on-site, plus bars and lounges. Many of the employees have been here for decades, which says a lot. Local legend and former owner Jackie Gaughan lived in the penthouse atop the hotel tower until his death at age 92 in 2014. Forget the manufactured versions—this is the real thing, updated but without losing its identity, and for at least half the price.

600 Fremont St. (btw. 6th and 7th sts.). ☏ **800/634-6703** or 702/385-5200. www.elcortezhotel casino.com. 428 units. $35 and up double; $55 and up suite. Resort fee $9. Extra person $10. No discount for children. Free self- and valet parking. **Amenities:** 2 restaurants; casino; in-room high-speed Internet.

Four Queens ★ Opened in 1966 with a mere 120 rooms, the Four Queens (named for the owner's four daughters) has evolved over the decades into a major Downtown property, occupying an entire city block. While not the fanciest hotel in town, there's something charmingly "Old Vegas" about it. As the staff says, this is the place to stay if you just want to gamble—or if you want a genuine retro experience. Rooms come in a bright color palette, which is jarring given the monochromes that otherwise rule local decor. They can be rather wee, but the ones in the South Tower are a shade larger than the others, though we wouldn't hold any multiperson slumber parties in there, either. In most cases, rooms in the North Tower offer views of the Fremont Street Experience. For dining, there's a coffee shop, a brew pub, and **Hugo's Cellar** (p. 109), an old-school gourmet restaurant where ladies get a red rose before being seated.

202 Fremont St. (at Casino Center Blvd.). ☏ **800/634-6045** or 702/385-4011. www.fourqueens. com. 690 units. $49 and up double; $119 and up suite. No resort fee. Extra person $15. Children 11 and under stay free in parent's room. Free self- and valet parking. **Amenities:** 3 restaurants; 2 bars; casino; room service; in-room high-speed Internet (for a fee).

Fremont Hotel & Casino ★ When it opened in 1956, the Fremont was the first high-rise in Downtown Las Vegas. Wayne Newton got his start here, singing in the now-defunct Carousel Showroom. Step just outside the front door, and there you are in the **Fremont Street Experience** (p. 140). Rooms are larger (the bathrooms, however, are the opposite of large) and more comfortable than you might expect with simple but modern furnishings, flatscreen TVs, and the like. It's worth noting that the music and noise from the Fremont Street Experience can be intrusive, but the last show is at midnight and if you are in bed before that in Vegas, it's your own fault. The staff is shockingly friendly, partly because you actually can have personal service with hotels this size (another advantage of staying Downtown), partly because they just are.

The Fremont boasts a couple of low-cost, moderate-quality restaurants and chain outlets from Tony Roma's and Dunkin' Donuts. Guests can use the swimming pool at the sister property California Hotel, but you have to walk across the street to do so.

200 E. Fremont St. (btw. Casino Center Blvd. and 3rd St.). ☏ **800/634-6182** or 702/385-3232. www. fremontcasino.com. 447 units. $40 and up double. No resort fee. Extra person $10. No discount for children. Free valet parking; no self-parking. **Amenities:** 3 restaurants; buffet; casino; access to outdoor pool at nearby California Hotel; in-room high-speed Internet (for a fee).

The Golden Gate ★   The Hotel Nevada, as it was known when it opened in 1906, was the state's first hotel, and despite its current San Francisco–referencing moniker, it is firmly embracing its history. It's up to date in terms of modernity, but everywhere you turn there are blasts from past, including antique slot machines and some of the original furnishings, plus hotel and gambling ledgers from its earliest days. Check out the kicky flapper fringe wall covering in the high-limit lounge and the black-and-white photography of the Vegas of yore. It's all charming and especially noteworthy in a town that seems to delight in blowing up its bygone eras.

The rooms are miniscule by just about any standard, but thankfully the gorgeous, retro furnishings almost make up for a lack of floor space with dark woods, warm leather, and bold touches of red livening the space. All have a flatscreen TV, iPod radios, and Wi-Fi; one or two double beds; and a comfy chair; some also have writing desks. Bathrooms are also small, so don't expect to be sharing the mirror with anyone. There are a handful of suites that are quite large and well-appointed with leather sectional sofas, a wet bar, and more substantial bathrooms.

Downstairs there's a cozy casino and both a restaurant and deli managed by the Du-Par's coffee shop chain. Note that the deli still serves the shrimp cocktail that has been featured in more than a few Travel Channel specials, though the price is up to $2.99 these days. There are only a couple of bars for on-site entertainment, but the hotel's location on Fremont Street means that you are just steps away from most of the Glitter Gulch casinos and fun.

When the hotel first opened they charged $1 per day. Unsurprisingly, it's a bit more expensive than that now, but not by a lot. You can usually get a room here for less than $40 a night, making it a great alternative for the budget-minded.

1 Fremont St. ☏ **800/426-1906** or 702/385-1906. www.goldengatecasino.com. 122 units. $25 and up for up to 4 people. Resort fee $20. Free self- and valet parking. **Amenities:** 2 restaurants; casino; bars; in-room high-speed Internet.

Main Street Station ★★   Though not actually on Fremont Street, Main Street Station is just 2 short blocks away, barely a 3-minute walk. Considering how terrific it is, this is hardly an inconvenience. This remains one of the nicest hotels in Downtown and one of the best bargains in the city.

The overall look here, typical of Downtown, is early-20th-century San Francisco. However, unlike everywhere else, the details here are outstanding, resulting in a beautiful hotel by any measure. Outside, gas lamps flicker on wrought-iron railings and stained-glass windows. Inside, you'll find hammered-tin ceilings, ornate chandeliers, period antiques and artwork, and lazy ceiling fans. It's all very appealing and just plain pretty. Guys: If "pretty" isn't your speed, check out the main casino men's room where they have a piece of the Berlin Wall holding up the urinals.

The long and narrow rooms are comfortably sized, and although the ornate decorating downstairs does not extend up here, the rooms are plenty nice enough. The bathrooms are small but well appointed. Rooms on the north side overlook the freeway, and the railroad track is nearby. The soundproofing seems quite strong—we couldn't hear anything when inside, but a few people have complained about noise in these rooms. If you're concerned, request a room on the south side.

The stylish **Triple 7 Brew Pub** is described in detail in chapter 8. The excellent buffet, **Main Street Station Garden Court,** is described in chapter 5. And the casino, thanks to some high ceilings, is one of the most smoke-free around.

200 N. Main St. (btw. Fremont St. and I-95). ℂ **800/465-0711** or 702/387-1896. www.mainstreet casino.com. 406 units. $59 and up double. No resort fee. Extra person $10. No discount for children. Free self- and valet parking. **Amenities:** 2 restaurants; casino; access to outdoor pool at nearby California Hotel; free shuttle to Strip and sister properties; in-room high-speed Internet (for a fee).

The Plaza Hotel & Casino ★★   The Fontainebleau was supposed to be a flashy $4-billion megaresort on the Strip, with amenities and decor elements designed to be competitive with other nearby luxury hotels. That project went bankrupt during construction and was picked up for a fraction of the money that had been spent on it by billionaire investor Carl Icahn (former owner of the Stratosphere), who mothballed the half-completed hotel and started selling off all the stuff that was supposed to go into it. Furniture, carpet, drapes, artwork, light fixtures, bathroom fixtures, marble floors, and more all went to the highest bidder.

Enter the Plaza. After years of neglect left this Downtown stalwart a dingy dump, the hotel has gotten a new lease on life by taking advantage of the Fontainebleau's misfortunes. The entire property was upgraded with all the stuff that was supposed to go into a multibillion hotel on the Strip, meaning that the place feels richer and more luxurious than it ever has and, for the rock-bottom prices it charges, has any right to be.

Rooms are earth-toned delights with sleek modern lines, comfy beds and chairs, and up-to-date technology (flatscreens, Wi-Fi, and so forth) plus fun, retro touches in the black-and-white photography of Old Vegas on the walls. Bathrooms are small but fancy due to the Font's sinks and tile work. There have been some complaints of maintenance issues—apparently those low prices bring a crowd that doesn't treat the furnishings with the kind of care it needs—but the hotel seems to be very responsive in addressing concerns.

The rest of the hotel got the full makeover as well, with new restaurants including **Oscar's** (p. 109) from former Mayor Oscar Goodman and branch of the fantastic **Hash House a Go Go** (p. 101); upgrades to the pool and tennis courts; and a modern update for the casino.

The fact that they have done all this and still keep the prices as low as they are (we've seen them at $29 during the week) is nothing short of a miracle. Welcome back, Plaza! We've missed you.

1 Main St. ℂ **800/634-6575** or 702/386-2110. Fax 702/382-6428. www.plazahotelcasino.com. 1,037 units. $29 and up double. Resort fee $12. Extra person $15. No discounts for children. Free self- and valet parking. **Amenities:** 4 restaurants; food court; casino; showrooms; bars and lounges; wedding chapel; salon; fitness center; outdoor pool; tennis courts; in-room high-speed Internet.

JUST OFF THE STRIP

Within about a mile east, west, and south of the Strip are dozens of hotels, many of which offer the same kind of casino-resort experience but usually at significantly cheaper rates.

Best for: People with a car at their disposal; those who want to be near the action but not in the thick of it.

Drawbacks: Traffic to and from the Strip can be a nightmare, even if you are only driving a mile.

Expensive

Hard Rock Hotel & Casino ★★   Despite ever-increasing competition, the Hard Rock remains a bastion for the hip, the famous, and their hangers-on, drawn by the "we're cooler than you" ambience, the truckloads of rock memorabilia scattered around, and the see-and-be-seen clubs, bars, and pool parties. Our problem is that we are not famous pop stars and we do not look enough like any of the Kardashians to warrant the kind of attention that the staff seems to reserve for those types.

Original rooms are spacious and almost painfully self-aware in how cool they are trying to be, with mod furnishings and funky amenities. Balconies are a nice touch here. The newer Paradise Tower has a touch more sophistication, with a black-and-gray design scheme, contemporary furnishings, and bathrooms that are sleek enough to be in a nightclub (note they only have showers, no tubs). The HRH Tower is the pinnacle in terms of amenities—and cost. The gleaming white suites are plush and feature multiple TVs and an entertainment system that allows you to plug your MP3 player into the wall and create your own playlist or listen to one of theirs.

The casino is loud and boisterous and there are several fine restaurants, including the fantastic gastropub **Culinary Dropout** (p. 116), the Asian-inspired **Fu** (p. 116), and a **Hard Rock Café** (naturally). **The Joint** (p. 192) is a major showroom that often hosts big-name rock musicians, and there are multiple nightclubs covered in chapter 8.

If you've ever dreamed of being in a beach-party movie, or on the set of one of those MTV summer beach-house shows, complete with the impossibly low body fat percentages, heavy drinking, and questionable moral standards, the pool at the Hard Rock is for you. Enough said. A spa facility mixes Moroccan details with stripper poles. Oh, but that we were making that up. There is actually a room in the spa where you can practice your, um, technique under the disguise of exercise. Whatever makes you happy.

Plus there's a tattoo shop, so yeah, it's that kind of place (or trying to be).

4455 Paradise Rd. (at Harmon Ave.). ⓒ **800/473-7625** or 702/693-5000. www.hardrockhotel.com. 1,500 units. $109 and up double; $250 and up suite. Resort fee $25. Extra person $35. Children 12 and under stay free in parent's room. Free self- and valet parking. **Amenities:** 7 restaurants; casino; concert venues; concierge; fitness center; spa; executive-level rooms; outdoor pools w/lazy river and sandy-beach bottom; room service; in-room high-speed Internet.

Palms Casino Resort ★★   If you're looking for the Palms in a nutshell, it is this: A recent stay found us in our swank, almost self-consciously contemporary room watching the windows literally rattle because the music, 22 floors down below at the Friday afternoon pool party, was so loud. This is not a place designed to nap away a Friday afternoon—it is a place to party, even more so now that a major renovation has upped the "cool" quotient.

Many of the restaurants have been redone and most of the formerly must-visit nightclubs have closed (including Rain, Moon, and the Playboy Club), but new ones are on the way, so expect this to be back near the top of the party faithful's list of nighttime destinations soon. On the other hand, there is an excellent child-care facility, Kid's Quest, plus movie theaters, a family-ready food court, and a low-limit casino packed mostly with penny and nickel slots, so you get a little bit of the best of both worlds if you want it.

Rooms in the Ivory Tower are modern wonders, with big, brightly colored murals and fuschia and teal accents leavening out the silvers and grays. Bathrooms are mod also, with frosted glass and lots of sleek marble. Note that there are only showers here, no tubs unless you upgrade to the bigger suites. The Fantasy Tower rooms are similar in size and appointments but with more traditional furnishings and decor. Go up to the Palms Place Tower if you want condo-style units with kitchenettes. And yes, this is the place with the over-the-top, if-you-have-to-ask-you-can't-afford-them fantasy suites like the one with its own basketball court and the one used in MTV's *The Real World*.

The aforementioned pool is a hot spot day and night; there is a decent spa and fitness center; and several restaurants, including the gorgeous and romantic **Alizé** (p. 115), one of the best dining experiences in town.

4321 W. Flamingo Rd. (just west of I-15). © **866/942-7777** or 702/942-7777. www.palms.com. 1,302 units. $99 and up double. Resort fee $25. Extra person $30. No discount for children. Free self- and valet parking. **Amenities:** 7 restaurants; buffet; food court; casino; concierge; executive-level rooms; movie theaters; nightclubs and bars; showroom; outdoor pool; room service; spa; fitness center; in-room high-speed Internet.

Moderate

LVH: Las Vegas Hotel & Casino ★ For the better part of 40 years this place was known as the Las Vegas Hilton, a favorite for business travelers owing to its location next door to the Las Vegas Convention Center. The licensing deal for the Hilton name expired at the end of 2011, hence the new moniker; while uninventive, at least they don't have to change their initials. Other than the signs and the stationery, everything else is pretty much the same, which is both good and bad. The place is as dependable as always but not exactly the epitome of Vegas excitement.

The rooms, for instance, are a bit boring in comparison to the wilder, newer digs on the Strip, but they are larger than you'll find at most hotels of this age and well-tended. You may want to fork over the extra few bucks for a Superior room, which comes with views of the Strip, a minifridge, and a few other extras. Nicer still are the Grand rooms, measuring out at a spacious 600 square feet; plenty of room for a sitting area.

Downstairs is an old-fashioned glitzy casino that is small enough to navigate without a GPS device; several restaurants, including a branch of the popular Benihana Japanese grill; bars and lounges, including the Shimmer Cabaret, which often has fun local cover bands; a showroom; a small shopping arcade with no-name stores; and lots of businessmen and women here for whatever convention is going on next door. A sunny recreation deck features a big pool, tennis courts, and a Jacuzzi with a well-stocked fitness center and spa adjacent.

One bit of history: Before it was LVH and even before it was the Hilton, back when it was known as the International, Elvis Presley played 837 sold-out shows here. One of Elvis's sequined jumpsuits is enshrined in a glass case in the front, near the entrance to the lobby/casino. Feel free to say "thank you very much" when you pass it. No one will judge you.

3000 Paradise Rd. (at Riviera Blvd.). © **888/732-7117** or 702/732-5111. www.thelvh.com. 3,174 units. $49 and up double. Resort fee $20. Extra person $35. Children 17 and under stay free in parent's room. Free self- and valet parking. **Amenities:** 9 restaurants; buffet; food court; casino; executive-level rooms; health club; spa; outdoor pool; room service; showrooms; 6 night-lit tennis courts; in-room high-speed Internet.

Rio All-Suite Hotel & Casino ★★ Rio bills itself as a "carnival" atmosphere hotel, which means hectic, crowded, and noisy in most of the public spaces. This is

RELIABLE CHAIN alternatives

Most people who come to Las Vegas want to stay in one of the big megaresorts on the Strip. But sometimes budget, timing, or just your own personal taste may necessitate a more traditional approach to lodging. Just about every hotel chain has at least one outlet in the city and all offer the kind of reliable, comfortable, and often affordable accommodations that they are known for. Here are some examples, all of which are located within a mile or two of the Strip so you can have the best of both worlds.

Best Western Mardi Gras, 3500 Paradise Rd.; ℂ 800/634-6501

Best Western McCarran, 4970 Paradise Rd.; ℂ 800/275-4743

Candlewood Suites, 4034 Paradise Rd.; ℂ 877/226-3539

Clarion Hotel, 305 Convention Center Dr.; ℂ 702/952-8000

Courtyard by Marriott, 3275 Paradise Rd.; ℂ 800/661-1064

Courtyard by Marriott, 5845 Dean Martin Dr.; ℂ 800/321-2211

Embassy Suites, 3600 Paradise Rd.; ℂ 800/362-2779

Embassy Suites, 4315 Swenson St.; ℂ 800/362-2779

Fairfield Inn by Marriott, 3850 S. Paradise Rd.; ℂ 702/791-0899

Fairfield Inn Suites, 5775 Dean Martin Dr.; ℂ 702/895-9810

Hampton Inn, 4975 S. Dean Martin Dr.; ℂ 702/948-8100

Holiday Inn Express, 5760 Polaris Ave.; ℂ 888/465-4329

Hyatt Place, 4520 Paradise Rd.; ℂ 702/369-3366

La Quinta Inn and Suites, 3970 Paradise Rd.; ℂ 800/753-3757

Las Vegas Marriott, 325 Convention Center Dr.; ℂ 702/650-2000

Renaissance Las Vegas, 3400 Paradise Rd.; ℂ 702/784-5700

Residence Inn, 3225 Paradise Rd.; ℂ 800/677-8328

Residence Inn, 370 Hughes Center Dr.; ℂ 702/650-5510

Staybridge Suites, 5735 Dean Martin Dr.; ℂ 800/238-8889

Super 8, 4250 Koval Lane; ℂ 800/454-3213

Travelodge, 3735 Las Vegas Blvd. S.; ℂ 800/525-4055

fine for party seekers, but families and those seeking a quiet respite may want to look elsewhere.

The hotel touts its room size. Every one is a "suite," which does not mean two separate rooms, but rather one large room with a sectional, corner sofa, and coffee table at one end. The dressing areas are certainly larger than average and feature a number of extra amenities, such as fridges. Go for the newer Samba rooms for their updated furnishings if the extra bucks they will cost you isn't exorbitant (and if you can stomach the dizzying patterns and bold color schemes attempting a festive feeling but mostly just hurting our eyes).

There are plenty of places to eat here, including the fantastic **Carnival World Buffet** (p. 128) and a branch of one of our favorites, **Hash House a Go Go** (p. 101). Afterward you can catch a show like **Penn & Teller** or the **Chippendales** male stripper show or visit the and **VooDoo Rooftop Nightclub** (all of which are covered in chapter 8). The casino, alas, is dark and claustrophobic, but if you need sun and air, check out the zip line–style attraction that sends you both forward and backward (!!!) from the roof of one hotel tower to the other. Our reaction: Yikes!

There's a decent enough pool area that is only disappointing if you know what the ones at other hotels look like, and the hotel is affiliated with the 18-hole championship

Rio Secco golf course (p. 166), located on the south side of town (transportation included).

3700 W. Flamingo Rd. (just west of I-15). ✆ **888/752-9746** or 702/777-7777. www.riolasvegas.com. 2,582 units. $99 and up suite. Resort fee $22. Extra person $30. No discount for children. **Amenities:** 9 restaurants; 2 buffets; multiple fast-food outlets; casino; concierge; executive-level rooms; golf course; health club; spa; outdoor pools; showrooms; room service; in-room high-speed Internet.

Tuscany Suites & Casino ★   This may be the right kind of hybrid between chain hotel and fancy resort—not as lush as the latter but not anywhere near as expensive, either, with far more personal detail and indulgent touches than you can find at chains. It's another all-suite hotel, and another where "suite" really means "very big room." The rooms aren't memorable, just like the chain hotels, but they are smart enough that you won't get depressed like you might when you see some of the rooms in similarly priced places. The large complex (27 acres, complete with a winding pool) isn't so much Italian as it is vaguely evocative of the idea of Italian architecture, but it, too, is more stylish than most of the chains in town. And, unlike those other chains, this one comes with a small casino, separated from the rest of the property in such a way that this is still an appropriate place for families who want the best of all worlds (price, looks, family-friendly atmosphere, and gambling). Since each room has a separate dining area, a kitchenette, and a large TV, plus convertible couches (on request), it's got many of the comforts of home only you don't have to vacuum if you make a mess. While the kids play, there is a large soaking tub for their folks to relax in. There are three on-site restaurants (Italian, Mexican, and diner), plus a lounge.

255 E. Flamingo Rd. ✆ **877/887-2261** or 702/893-8933. www.tuscanylv.com. 700 units. $79 and up suite. Resort fee $17. Extra person $20. Children 12 and under stay free in parent's room. **Amenities:** 3 restaurants; lounge; casino; concierge; fitness center; outdoor pool; room service; in-room high-speed Internet.

Inexpensive

The Gold Coast ★   Although it's less than half a mile from the Strip, this budget-minded hotel couldn't be more different than the glittery palaces in whose shadow it sits. Geared mostly to locals, everything here is noticeably cheaper—from the room rates to the gambling limits to the cost of a beer at the casino bar. People who want to be close to the Strip but don't want to pay Strip prices should absolutely pay attention here.

Rooms are small and simple, but unexpectedly stylish with modern furnishings (think IKEA), flatscreen TVs, a writing desk, a coffeemaker, hair dryer, iron and board, and other niceties. The bathrooms won't win any awards for size or style, but they are more than adequate for all but the snootiest of visitors.

On-site facilities include a big, brightly lit casino with recently updated machines and gaming tables; a 70-lane bowling alley; a basic pool and fitness center; a barber shop and beauty salon; a showroom and lounge for regular entertainment; and several affordable restaurants, including the **Ports O' Call buffet** (p. 129) and **Ping Pang Pong** (p. 118), which was chosen by *Travel + Leisure* magazine in 2013 as one of the best Chinese restaurants in the United States. A free shuttle ferries people from the hotel to the Strip and sister property the Orleans (see below).

4000 W. Flamingo Rd. ✆ **800/331-5334** or 702/367-7111. www.goldcoastcasino.com. 711 units. $39 and up double. Resort fee $10. Extra person $15. Children under 15 stay free in parents' room. Free self- and valet parking. **Amenities:** 4 restaurants; buffet; fast-food outlets; bowling alley;

casino; executive-level rooms; fitness center; heated outdoor pool; room service; barber shop; in-room high-speed Internet.

The Orleans ★   The Orleans is a little out of the way, and there is virtually nothing around it (at least nothing interesting to tourists), but with an 18-screen movie complex, a food court, a day-care center, a 24-hour bowling alley, and a 9,000-seat arena for special events, this is a reasonable alternative to staying on the hectic Strip. Plus, there is a shuttle that runs continuously to the Gold Coast, Sam's Town, and Suncoast. The facade is aggressively fake New Orleans, more reminiscent of Disneyland than the actual Big Easy. Inside, it's much the same.

As long as prices hold true (as always, they can vary), this hotel is one of the best bargains in town, despite the location. "Standard" rooms live up (or down, as the case may be) to their name with lots of beige and fairly utilitarian furnishings. Pay the premium for the also aptly named "Premium" rooms, which have much more stylish furnishings, modern decor, built-in desks, and other niceties. Don't expect to want to spend any time in the microscopic bathrooms.

In addition to the amenities listed above, you'll find plenty of restaurants, a decent (if unspectacular) buffet, a showroom, and a big, rambling casino with relatively low limits and lots of video poker.

4500 W. Tropicana Ave. (west of the Strip and I-15). ✆ **800/675-3267** or 702/365-7111. www.orleans casino.com. 1,886 units. $59 and up double; $185 and up suite. Resort fee $10. Extra person $15. Children 15 and under stay free in parent's room. Free self- and valet parking. **Amenities:** 7 restaurants; buffet; food court; 9,000-seat arena; 70-lane bowling center; casino; children's center offering amusements and day care for kids 3–12; concierge; executive-level rooms; health club; 18-screen movie theater; outdoor pools; room service; showroom; spa; in-room high-speed Internet.

Palace Station ★   Anybody who wants a Vegas experience but doesn't want to pay typical Vegas prices should take a look at Palace Station. It's close to the north end of the Strip—just on the other side of I-15, about a mile from the Stratosphere—but it is definitely not a Strip hotel in ways both good and not so good. Rooms in the hotel tower are modern and functional with crisp white linens, flatscreen TVs, and solid (if basic) furnishings. They are not particularly large and certainly not showy—these are not the kind of rooms that you'll want to take pictures of to make your friends back home jealous—but they do offer dependably comfortable lodging at bargain rates. Rooms in the low-rise motel-style buildings are even more basic and really should only be considered by those for whom money is the primary concern when picking where they stay. There's nothing expressly wrong with them, but if you can afford to pay a few more bucks per night there are better places to stay. All have the usual conveniences for rates as low as $29 a night, and that's a lot of bang for your Vegas buck.

The rest of the hotel offers plenty of low-cost entertainment and dining options, including a big, rambling low-limit casino, a small showroom, bars and lounges, two pools, a fitness room, multiple restaurants (from a buffet to a steakhouse), and free shuttle service for guests to both the Strip and the airport. Unless you want to depend on that shuttle, you will need a car to get to most of the places you'll want to visit in Las Vegas, but with all the money you'll save, it could very well be worth it. Bonus points for the frequent gaming promotions and well-tended bingo parlor (one of the few anywhere near the Strip).

2411 W. Sahara Ave. ✆ **800/678-2846** or 702/367-2411. www.palacestation.com. 1,011 units. $29 and up for up to 4 people. $17 resort fee. Free self- and valet parking. **Amenities:** 5 restaurants; buffet; food court; airport and Strip shuttle; arcade; casino; executive-level rooms; fitness center; outdoor pools; room service; in-room high-speed Internet.

4

locals' HOTELS

Most residents of Las Vegas—the locals—never go anywhere near the Strip. They prefer to play, eat, be entertained, and occasionally stay at casino-hotels in their own neighborhoods, partly because of convenience, but mostly because it usually costs a lot less money. All of the following hotels are admittedly located away from the main tourist areas, but if you have a car at your disposal, you can save yourself some dough by being flexible with your location. Several offer free shuttles to other sister properties.

Just south of the Strip along I-15 is **Silverton,** 3333 Blue Diamond Rd. ((*C* **866/946-4373** or 702/263-7777; www.silvertoncasino.com), a delightful ski lodge–themed hotel and casino with a warm casino, surprisingly stylish rooms (considering how cheap they usually are; figure in the $40–$75 range), and several affordable restaurants. The sports-minded may want to stop here just for the massive Bass Pro Shops attached to the complex offering everything from skis to the boats with which to pull people wearing them.

About 5 miles west of the Strip along Boulder Highway are several locals' hotel options. The biggest and most well-known is **Sam's Town,** 5111 Boulder Hwy. ((*C* **866/897-8696** or 702/456-7777; www.samstownlv.com). In addition to the second biggest casino in town (behind only MGM Grand), the western-themed property has a 56-lane bowling alley, an 18-screen movie theater, more than a dozen restaurants, bars and lounges, and a big indoor atrium with a silly light and laser show. The rooms are nothing to write home about, but they are fine, especially for the bargain-basement prices they go for. Another favorite is **Boulder Station** ★, 4111 Boulder Hwy. ((*C* **800/683-7777** or 702/432-7777; www.boulderstation.com), which has more than 300 guest rooms, a 75,000-square-foot casino, movie theaters, restaurants, bars, and a concert venue. Rates usually run from $75 to $125 a night, but rooms can be had for as little as $49 per night. **Arizona Charlie's East** ★, 4575 Boulder Hwy. ((*C* **888/236-9066** or 702/951-5900; www.arizonacharlies.com) features 300 minisuites, a 37,000-square-foot casino, several restaurants, and a casino lounge. It's only a step or two above budget accommodations, but still very well maintained and usually priced like the former. Lastly, the **Eastside Cannery** ★, 5255 Boulder Hwy. ((*C* **866/999-4899** or

---

Silver Sevens ★   Although it never would have been mistaken for a Four Seasons, this place was certainly not terrible when it was known as Terrible's. It specialized in low-limit gambling, low-rent accommodations, and low-cost dining and drinking. None of that has changed with the new ownership and name, but a lot of other stuff did. The rooms in the low-rise motel-style buildings were completely redone with modern furnishings in shades of cool blue and deep brown. It's all still pretty basic, but you have flat-panel TVs, wireless Internet, comfy beds, and a (very small) bathroom, so really, what else do you need? Rooms in the newer tower were not rehabbed but are basically the same, only with a different color scheme and slightly less contemporary furnishings. Other upgrades include a new sports book with cozy chairs and lots of big screens on which to watch the action; a revised casino lounge with entertainment and free Wi-Fi sponsored by Corona; and some decor and menu changes to their buffet and inexpensive coffee shop–style restaurant. Of note is the nicely landscaped pool area at the center of property, which is much nicer than it has any right to be at the kind of

702/856-5300; www.arizonacharlies.com) has a casino, several restaurants, bars and lounges, and 300 very stylish rooms that rival the Strip for amenities and decor but are miles away in terms of price.

Just down the street, you'll find locals' favorite **Sunset Station ★**, 1301 W. Sunset Rd., Henderson (✆ **888/786-7389** or 702/547-7777; www.sunsetstation.com), with 450 fairly basic hotel rooms but a host of amenities like a bowling alley; movie theaters; an outdoor amphitheater; a really nice, low-limits casino; lots of restaurants; a very good buffet; and more. Meanwhile, nearby **Fiesta Henderson ★**, 777 W. Lake Mead Dr., Henderson (✆ **888/899-7770** or 702/558-7000; www.fiestahendersonlasvegas.com) is a Southwestern-themed joint with basic yet comfortable lodgings, plus plenty of gaming options, restaurants, bars, movie theaters, and more. Things are cheap here, with rooms going for as low as $30 a night during the week.

On the north and west sides of town are several smaller properties popular with locals. **Fiesta Rancho ★**, 2400 N. Rancho Rd. (✆ **888/899-7770** or 702/631-7000; www.fiestaranchol as vegas.com) is similar in concept and execution to its sister property

mentioned above. In addition to the 100 rooms, there is a big casino and a regulation-size ice-skating rink, complete with equipment rentals and lessons (p. 162). Prices go as low as $40 a night. Right across the street is **Texas Station**, 2101 Texas Star Lane, North Las Vegas (✆ **800/654-8888** or 702/631-1000; www.aliantecasinohotel.com), which (unsurprisingly, owing to its name) has a "Yeehaw!" theme covering its basic motel rooms, bowling alley, movie theaters, big casino, and one of the best steakhouses in town, **Austins** (p. 121). If you continue north—about as far north as you can go without running into a mountain—you'll find **Aliante Casino and Hotel ★★**, 7300 Aliante Pkwy., North Las Vegas (✆ **877/477-7627** or 702/692-7777; www.aliante casinohotel.com), a beautifully done resort with smallish rooms that are gorgeously decorated with all of the latest amenities. The facility boasts several restaurants, bars and lounges, a Strip-worthy pool, and a big casino, all wrapped up in warm design elements. It's a solid 25-minute drive from the Strip without traffic, but with prices as low as $29 a night for rooms this nice, it might just be worth it.

prices you will pay here. There is a small resort fee, but it includes access to the valuable Strip and airport shuttles.

4100 Paradise Rd. (at Flamingo Rd.). ✆ **877/773-4596** or 702/733-7000. www.silversevenscasino.com. 330 units. $39 and up double. Resort fee $3. Extra person $12. Children 17 and under stay free in parent's room. Free self- and valet parking. **Amenities:** 1 restaurant; buffet; outdoor pool; room service; in-room high-speed Internet (for a fee).

SOUTH & EAST OF THE STRIP

The main areas worth knowing about are the Boulder Highway strip on the far east side of town, the bedroom community of Henderson, and Lake Las Vegas—all of which offer a range of casino and non-casino hotels that can save you money and/or provide a unique Vegas experience.

Best for: Repeat visitors who want to try something new; value hunters.

Drawbacks: You'll have to drive to get to most of the major tourist attractions; upper-end restaurants and shows are harder to find.

Expensive

Green Valley Ranch Resort, Spa & Casino ★★★   This flat-out fabulous resort makes up for its somewhat far-flung locale with earnest efforts and slightly lower prices than comparable accommodations on the Strip. The place is gorgeous; Mediterranean inspired with detailed stonework, tile roofs, and acres of lush landscaping.

Inside, all is posh and stately—a dignified, classy lobby; a low-limit yet upscale casino; large rooms with the supremely comfortable beds and luxe marble bathrooms; and plenty of cheaper-than-average restaurants, bars, and boutiques. Even the movie theater feels nicer than your usual multiplex.

Outside is the hippest pool area this side of the Hard Rock: part lagoon, part geometric, with shallow places for reading and canoodling, and your choice of poolside lounging equipment, ranging from teak lounge chairs to thick mattresses strewn with pillows. Perhaps the best feature is the drop-dead fantastic view of the Strip in the distance. There's a small but satisfactory fitness center and a modern spa with all of the latest treatments and pampering.

A shopping area, the District, conveniently located next door, features a simulated street scene, where you'll find your usual mall and catalog favorites (Williams-Sonoma, Pottery Barn), plus still more restaurants.

2300 Paseo Verde Pkwy. (at I-215). ✆ **866/782-9487** or 702/617-7777. www.greenvalleyranchresort. com. 490 units. $129 and up double. Resort fee $25. Extra person $35. Children 17 and under stay free in parent's room. Free self- and valet parking. **Amenities:** 7 restaurants; buffet; food court; casino; concierge; executive-level rooms; spa; health club; lounge; movie theaters; outdoor pools; room service; free shuttle service to the airport and the Strip; in-room high-speed Internet.

Moderate

M Resort ★★   Red Rock Resort is one of our favorite hotels in the entire city. We bring this up here because in many ways, M Resort is a lot like Red Rock: beautifully designed, lots to do, great value (in comparison to the Strip), and roughly a bazillion miles from anything you're going to want to do in Las Vegas. Well, the **Lion Habitat Ranch** (p. 145) is nearby, but everything else is a bazillion miles away or will feel like it as you sit in traffic for the 10-mile slog north on I-15 to the southern end of the Strip. But that's really the only downside here. The hotel is stunning, with an abundant use of natural elements (wood, stone, crystal, mother-of-pearl ceilings) and huge windows that flood the entire property with light. The designers wanted to bring the outside in and they succeeded, creating one of the most airy and light spaces in town.

Rooms are large at about 550 square feet, many with great views of the city off in the distance (a bazillion miles, remember), which you can even see while soaking in the tubs—there are windows from the bathroom into the bedroom. Glossy streamlined furnishings give them a mod feeling, and everything is the highest of high tech. To power up the room you have to insert your key into a holder next to the door. Remove it and everything shuts off, maintaining your settings for when you return.

On-site you'll find a 95,000-square-foot casino with all the latest bells and whistles, several restaurants, a popular buffet, multiple bars and lounges, a spa/salon/gym facility, a very nicely landscaped pool area, and the hotel's very own wine cellar.

With prices, on average, about half of what you would pay for similar digs on the Strip, it almost makes that bazillion-mile trek worth considering.

12300 Las Vegas Blvd. S. (at St. Rose Pkwy.). ✆ **877/673-7678** or 702/797-1000. www.themresort.com. 390 units. $129 and up double. No resort fee. Extra person $30. Children 17 and under stay free in parent's room. Free self- and valet parking. **Amenities:** 6 restaurants; buffet; casino; concierge; executive-level rooms; health club; spa; salon; heated outdoor pool; room service; shuttle service to the airport and Strip; in-room high-speed Internet (for a fee).

Inexpensive

South Point ★★   Located about 6 miles south of Mandalay Bay, South Point is still on Las Vegas Boulevard but certainly not within walking distance of anything else of interest except for maybe a convenience store. Still, this hotel is a worthwhile addition to this category, offering an expensive level of accommodations at an inexpensive price.

South Point follows the same formula established by its former siblings like Orleans and Gold Coast: nice rooms at reasonable prices; plenty of low-priced food outlets (and one higher priced one, the venerable Michael's that used to be at Barbary Coast a billion years ago); tons of entertainment options, including movie theaters, a bowling alley, and more; and a massive casino with lower-than-average limits on everything from slots to craps tables. There's also a giant Equestrian Center out back, large enough for just about any rodeo, complete with air-conditioned horse stalls and a pen for thousands of head of cattle. It's a unique offering, to be sure, but we'd recommend you choose a non-event time to stay here, if possible, because no matter how many odor-absorbing wood chips you throw at them, 2,000 head of cattle emit a less-than-pleasant scent that may make an afternoon by the pool rather unenjoyable.

The overall scheme is Southern California modern, with plenty of sunny paint schemes and airy architectural details. Think Santa Barbara instead of Hollywood, and you're probably in the ballpark. Rooms are large and aesthetically pleasing, each over 500 square feet and crammed full of expensive and luxurious furnishings, 42-inch plasma TVs, and all the other pampering amenities one would expect in a room three times the price. Seriously, a weekend rate check had rooms here at less than $100 per night, while Bellagio and Wynn were well over $250. Although we wouldn't put these rooms on quite the same level as the ones at those two ultraluxe establishments, we have a hard time coming up with a $150 amount of difference.

9777 Las Vegas Blvd. S. ✆ **866/796-7111** or 702/796-7111. www.southpointcasino.com. 2,100 units. $79 and up double. Resort fee $14. Extra person $20. Children 16 and under stay free in parent's room. Free self- and valet parking. **Amenities:** 10 restaurants; buffet; several fast-food outlets; 70-lane bowling center; casino; concierge; 4,400-seat equestrian and events center; 16-screen movie theater; outdoor pool; room service; spa; in-room high-speed Internet.

NORTH & WEST OF THE STRIP

Summerlin, on the far west side of town, and North Las Vegas (north of the city, appropriately enough) are suburbs that have pockets of casino-hotel options ranging from budget to luxury, and lots of outdoor opportunities from golf to hiking and beyond.

Best for: The recreation-minded; people who want a more relaxing Vegas vacation.

Drawbacks: Long drives to the Strip and fewer entertainment options.

Expensive

JW Marriott ★★   Many hotels in Vegas throw the "resort" word around a lot, but few of them feel as true to the spirit of the word as the JW Marriott. Located seemingly a million miles from the crazy that is Sin City, the entire place feels like an oasis in the middle of a neon desert. Nestled on 54 acres of lushly landscaped grounds, the Spanish missionary–style buildings are gorgeous reminders that you don't need exposed steel, acres of glass, or dancing water fountains to create a feeling of luxury.

There are more than 500 rooms in two wings that sweep out around the grounds in low-rise buildings. All are done in muted gold and earth tones and are finely appointed with plush, classical furnishings, ceiling fans, big TVs, minibars, coffee service, Wi-Fi, and more. The lush bathrooms feature Jacuzzi tubs with separate "rainfall" showers and plenty of marble to make things feel upscale. If you can, try to get a unit on the ground floor so you can take advantage of the patios they offer—sitting outside on a warm night enjoying the scenery is a must.

Spread across the 54 acres are walking paths, babbling brooks, footbridges, secluded benches, and a beautiful pool area. These are the kinds of grounds that you simply can't find on the Strip, where they pack every square inch with a building or a parking structure or a slot machine. They have the latter here, too. The adjoining Rampart Casino is separated from the main hotel by a long hallway, but it is there if you want it, offering lots of low-limit gambling and even some classic slot machines that take and dispense coins. There are several restaurants, a buffet, bars and lounges, and the extreme pampering available at the spa.

Although certainly not cheap, prices here are no more expensive than the pricier places on the Strip—you know, the ones that call themselves resorts.

221 N. Rampart Blvd. (✆ **877/869-8777** or 702/869-7777. Fax 702/869-7339. www.jwlasvegas resort.com. 200 units. $129 and up for up to 4 people. Resort fee $15. Free self- and valet parking. **Amenities:** 8 restaurants; buffet; casino; concierge; fitness center; outdoor pool; room service; spa; in-room high-speed Internet.

Red Rock Resort ★★★   The same people who brought you the fantastic Green Valley Ranch Resort trumped themselves by opening the swank Red Rock Resort in 2006, a hotel and casino complex that pretty much outdoes every other non-Strip hotel (and most of the Strip hotels, also).

Built at a cost of nearly a billion dollars (an outrageous sum for an 800-room hotel not located on Las Vegas Blvd.), the hotel is named for its perch right on the edge of the **Red Rock Canyon National Conservation Area** (see chapter 9), a stunning natural wonderland of red-hued rock formations and desert landscape. It's a toss-up, really, which view you should choose—to the west, you get the beautiful natural vistas, and to the east, you get an unimpeded view of the Strip and Downtown Las Vegas, about 11 miles away.

Yes, it is a bit of a trek out here, but people seeking a luxury resort experience with the bonus of a casino, restaurants, and more will find it worth the drive. Start with that casino, an 80,000-square-foot monster that is one of the most appealing in town, meandering through the building wrapped in natural woods, stonework, glass sculptures, and stunning amber-hued chandeliers. Restaurants serve up a wide variety of food selections, among them some great BBQ at Lucille's, a really good and affordable buffet, and a food court that knocks it up a notch with a **Capriotti's** outlet, offering some of the best submarine sandwiches we've ever tasted. Throw in a 16-screen movie theater; a day-care center; nightclubs and bars; a "luxury" bowling alley with VIP lanes; a sumptuous spa and health club; and a 3-acre circular "backyard" area with a sandy beach, swimming and wading pools, Jacuzzis, private cabanas, and a stage where big-name entertainers perform, and you've got a terrific recipe for success. A huge new shopping complex, the Shops at Summerlin, is due to open right next door by 2015.

The rooms are impressive, modern wonders with high-end furnishings and linens, 42-inch high-def plasma TVs, iPod sound systems, giant bathrooms, and more, all wrapped up in clean, sleek lines and vibrant earth tones. The only things more gorgeous are the views.

11011 W. Charleston Rd. © **866/767-7773** or 702/797-7777. www.redrocklasvegas.com. 816 units. $160 and up (up to 4 people). Resort fee $25. Extra person $35. Children 15 and under stay free in parent's room. **Amenities:** 9 restaurants; buffet; food court; bars and lounges; casino; concierge; day-care center; health club; 16-screen movie theater; outdoor pools and beach area; room service; spa; high-speed Internet.

PRACTICAL INFORMATION
The Big Picture

With a few exceptions in the very expensive category, most hotel rooms in Las Vegas are pretty much the same. After you factor in location and price, there isn't that much difference between rooms, except for perhaps size and the quality of their surprisingly similar furnishings.

Hotel prices in Vegas are anything but fixed, so you will notice wild price ranges. The same room can routinely go for anywhere from $60 to $250, depending on demand. So use our price categories with a grain of salt, and don't rule out a hotel just because it's listed as Expensive—on any given day, you might get a great deal on a room in a pricey hotel. On the negative side, some hotels start with their most typical lowest rate, adding "and up." Don't be surprised if "up" turns out to be way up. Just look online or call and ask.

Yes, if you pay more, you'll probably (but not certainly) get a "nicer" establishment and clientele to match (perhaps not so many loud drunks in the elevators). On the other hand, if a convention is in town, the drunks will be there no matter how upscale the hotel—they'll just be wearing business suits and/or funny hats. And frankly, the big hotels, no matter how fine, have mass-produced rooms; at 3,000 rooms or more, they are the equivalent of '60s tract housing. Consequently, even in the nicest hotels, you can (and probably will) encounter plumbing noises, notice scratch marks on the walls or furniture, overhear conversations from other rooms, or be woken by the maids as they knock on the doors next to yours that don't have the DO NOT DISTURB sign up.

Getting the Best Deal

Here are some tips for landing a low rate.

- **Book online.** Most Las Vegas hotels are offering their best rates via their Internet sites, with discounts and specials that you won't get if you call.
- **Be social.** Almost every major resort in town has some presence in the social media world, including Facebook pages, Twitter feeds, and smartphone apps. Connect with them and you may find yourself getting exclusive offers that the luddites out there won't be hearing about.
- **Dial direct.** When booking a room in a chain hotel (Courtyard by Marriott, for example), call the hotel's local line, as well as the toll-free number, and see where you get the best deal. A hotel makes nothing on a room that stays empty. The clerk who runs the place is more likely to know about vacancies and will often grant deep discounts in order to fill up. *Beware:* Many Vegas hotels are now charging a fee if

you book via phone, preferring you use the Internet instead. This includes all of the hotels managed by the giant MGM Resorts and Caesars Entertainment corporations including Bellagio, MGM Grand, Caesars Palace, Paris Las Vegas, and a dozen more.

○ **Don't be afraid to bargain.** Get in the habit of asking for a lower price than the first one quoted. Always ask politely whether a less expensive room is available than the first one mentioned, or whether any special rates apply to you. If you belong to the players' club at the hotel casino, you may be able to secure a better deal on a hotel room there. Of course, you will also be expected to spend a certain amount of time, and money, gambling there.

○ **Remember the law of supply and demand.** Las Vegas hotels are most crowded and therefore most expensive on weekends. So the best deals are offered midweek, when prices can drop dramatically. If possible, go then. You can also check the convention calendar run by the **Las Vegas Convention and Visitors Authority (℃ 877/847-4858;** www.vegasmeansbusiness.com) to find out whether an big trade show is scheduled at the time of your planned visit; if so, you might want to change your date. Some of the most popular conventions are listed under "When to Go" on p. 31. Remember also that planning to take your vacation just a week before or after official peak season can mean big savings.

○ **Beware of fees.** Room rates have dropped dramatically in the last couple of years, but many Vegas hotels have found ways to add to their bottom line through the addition of the infamous "resort fee." These fees range anywhere from $3 to $25 per night, and although the specifics vary from property to property, they often cover amenities like Internet service, health club access, newspapers, printing of boarding passes, maybe a bottle of water or two, and the like. So what if you're not going to use any of that? Too bad—you still have to pay it (at most hotels—some make it optional). Many hotels include this in their totals when you book your room, but a few wait and sock it to you at checkout, so be sure to ask ahead. (We have noted those hotels with resort fees in the listings, but do note that they change often.)

○ **Beware of hidden extras.** The hotels that don't charge resort fees (which are few and far between these days) charge extra for things that are always free in other destinations, such as health-club privileges. Expect to pay anywhere from $15 to $35 to use almost any hotel spa/health club. Wi-Fi also doesn't come free; usually there is a $12-to-$20 charge per 24-hour period. (We've noted when there is a fee in the listings so that you won't be taken by surprise.)

○ **Watch for coupons and advertised discounts.** Scan ads in your local Sunday travel section, an excellent source for up-to-the-minute hotel deals.

○ **Consider a suite.** If you are traveling with your family or another couple, you can pack more people into a suite (which usually comes with a sofa bed) and thereby reduce your per-person rate. Remember that some places charge for extra guests and some don't.

Reservation Services

All of the major Las Vegas hotels require a major credit card to reserve a room, although most do not charge anything until you arrive. Cancellation policies vary, but generally speaking you can usually back out of your booking anywhere from 24 to 48 hours ahead of your check-in date without penalty. Exceptions to both of these general rules are often found on major holidays like New Year's Eve or during big event weekends like the Super Bowl.

BOOKING AGENCIES

The Las Vegas Convention and Visitors Authority runs a **room-reservations hotline** (© **877/847-4858** or 702/892-0711; www.lasvegas.com) that can be helpful. The operators can apprise you of room availability, quote rates, contact a hotel for you, and tell you when major conventions will be in town.

A couple words of warning: Make sure they don't try to book you into a hotel you've never heard of. Try to stick with the hotels listed in this book. Always get your information in writing, and then make some phone calls just to confirm that you really have the reservations that they say they've made for you.

What Am I Looking for in a Hotel?

If gambling is not your priority, what are you doing in Vegas? Just kidding. But not 100% kidding. Vegas's current identity as a luxury, and very adult, resort destination means there are several hotels that promise to offer you all sorts of alternatives to gambling—lush pool areas, fabulous spas, incredible restaurants, lavish shopping. But if you look closely, much of this is Vegas bait-and-switch; the pools are often chilly (and often partially closed during non-summer months), and it will be years before there is more foliage than concrete in these newly landscaped environments. The spas cost extra (sometimes a whole lot extra), the best restaurants can require a small bank loan, and the stores are often the kinds of places where average mortals can't even afford the oxygen. So what does that leave you with? Why, that's right—gambling.

The other problem with these self-proclaimed luxury hotels is their size. True luxury hotels do not have 3,000 rooms—they have a couple of hundred, at best, because you simply can't provide first-class service and Egyptian-cotton sheets in mass quantity. But while hotels on the upper end of the price spectrum (Wynn, Encore, Bellagio, the Venetian, and so on) have done their best to offer sterling service and to make their rooms more attractive and luxurious than those at other Vegas hotels, there's only so much that any place that big can do. Don't get us wrong—these places are absolutely several steps up in quality from other large hotels, and compared to them, even the better older hotels really look shabby. But they are still sprawling, frequently noisy complexes.

If the hubbub of a casino makes you itch, there are a few non-gaming hotels and even non-gaming towers within casino-hotels that could help reduce your stress level. Check out Mandarin Oriental at CityCenter or the Delano at Mandalay Bay. Just make certain the hotel has a pool, especially if you need some recreation. There is nothing as boring as a non-casino, non-pool Vegas hotel—particularly if you have kids.

Sadly, it's relatively easy for both you and us to make a mistake about a hotel; either of us may experience a particular room or two in a 1,000-plus-room hotel and, from there, conclude that a place is nicer than it is or more of a dump than it is. Maintenance, even in the best of hotels, can sometimes be running a bit behind, so if there is something wrong with your room, don't hesitate to ask for another. Of course, if it's one of those busy weekends, there may not be another room to be had, but at least this way you've registered a complaint, perhaps letting a busy hotel know that a certain room needs attention. And who knows? If you are gracious and persistent enough, you may be rewarded with a deal for some future stay.

If you want a true luxury-resort hotel, there are only two options: the Four Seasons and the Mandarin Oriental. In addition to that same service and level of comfort only found at a smaller hotel, both offer those extra goodies that pile on the hidden charges at other hotels—health club, poolside cabanas, and so on—as part of the total package, meaning that their slightly higher prices may be more of a bargain than you'd think. Actually, there is a third option: The Red Rock Resort is attracting well-heeled and high-profile tabloid types, who, presumably, know luxury.

Casino hotels, by the way, are not always a nice place for children. It used to be that the casino was a separate section in the hotel, and children were not allowed inside. (We have fond memories of standing just outside the casino line, watching Dad put quarters in a slot machine "for us.") But in almost all the new hotels, you have to walk through the casino to get anywhere—the lobby, the restaurants, the outside world. This makes sense from the hotel's point of view; it gives you many opportunities to stop and drop $1 or $100 into a slot. But this often long, crowded trek gets wearying for adults—and it's far worse for kids. The rule is that kids can walk through the casinos, but they can't stop, even to gawk for a second at someone hitting a jackpot nearby. The casino officials who will immediately hustle the child away are just doing their job, but, boy, it's annoying.

So, take this (and what a hotel offers that kids might like) into consideration when booking a room. Again, please note that those gorgeous hotel pools are often cold (and again, sometimes closed altogether) and not very deep. They look like places you would want to linger, but often (from a kid's point of view) they are not. Plus, the pools close early. Hotels want you inside gambling, not outside swimming.

Finally, the thing that bothers us the most about this latest Vegas phase: It used to be that we could differentiate between rooms, but that's becoming harder and harder. Nearly every major hotel has changed to more or less the same effect; gone is any thematic detailing and in its place is a series of disappointingly similar (if handsome and appealing) looks. Expect clean-lined wood furniture, plump white beds, and monochromes everywhere you go. All that may distinguish one from another would be size of the room or quality of furnishings.

Ultimately, though, if it's a busy time, you'll have to nab any room you can, especially if you get a price you like. How much time are you going to spend in the room anyway?

WHERE TO EAT

For a long time, Vegas was considered an epicurean wasteland; a place where prime rib that cost more than $4.99 was considered haute cuisine and all-you-can-eat buffets dominated the landscape. Then the pendulum swung in the complete opposite direction. It got to the point where you couldn't swing a delicately seasoned roast leg of lamb with a honey-mint jus without hitting a celebrity chef and their fancy, very expensive restaurants. Wolfgang Puck, Emeril Lagasse, Joël Robuchon, Thomas Keller, Julian Serrano, Bobby Flay, Gordon Ramsay, Alain Ducasse, Charlie Palmer . . . the list goes on and on, and so did the bills that came at the end of the meals. Now, things have sort of settled in the middle. Fine dining continues to be more than fine in Vegas, but the good news for folks with less adventurous palates or less extravagant budgets is that there is plenty to eat here for everyone. All-you-can-eat buffets still abound; cheap eats can still be found if you know where to look; and moderately priced restaurants are making a big comeback. We hope you're hungry!

5

RESTAURANTS BY CUISINE

AMERICAN
Bier Garten ★★, p. 112
Citizens Kitchen ★★★, p. 86
Culinary Dropout ★★★, p. 116
Dick's Last Resort ★★, p. 86
Double Barrel Roadhouse ★★, p. 86
Eat ★★★, p. 113
Guy Fieri's Vegas Kitchen ★, p. 101
Hash House a Go Go ★★★, p. 101
Holstein's Shakes & Buns ★★, p. 102
Lagasse's Stadium ★, p. 102
munchbar ★★★, p. 105
Public House ★, p. 88
Serendipity 3 ★, p. 103
Stewart + Ogden ★★, p. 110
Sugar Factory ★★, p. 104
Table 10 ★★, p. 97

ASIAN
Red 8 ★★, p. 108
Fu ★★, p. 116

BARBECUE
Big Ern's BBQ ★★, p. 112
Gilley's ★★, p. 100
Memphis Championship Barbecue ★★, p. 120

BISTRO
Bouchon ★★★, p. 92
Mon Ami Gabi ★★★, p. 102
Payard Patisserie & Bistro ★★★, p. 103

BUFFETS
Bellagio Buffet ★★, p. 125
The Buffet at Aria ★, p. 124
The Buffet at TI ★, p. 127
Caesars Palace Bacchanal Buffet ★★, p. 126

price CATEGORIES

Expensive	Main courses $30 and up
Moderate	Main courses $15–$30
Inexpensive	Main courses under $15

5

Restaurants by Cuisine

WHERE TO EAT

JAPANESE

Raku Grill ★★★, p. 123
Yusho ★★, p. 90

MEDITERRANEAN

Paymon's Mediterranean Café &
 Lounge ★, p. 121

MEXICAN/LATIN

Border Grill ★★, p. 85
Cabo Wabo Cantina ★, p. 98
Carlos 'n Charlie's ★, p. 99
The Commissary ★★, p. 112
Doña María Tamales ★, p. 113
Diablo's Cantina ★★, p. 86
Hussong's Cantina ★, p. 87
Javier's ★★, p. 95
La Comida ★★, p. 110
Pinches Tacos ★★, p. 114
Pink Taco ★, p. 118
Tacos & Tequila ★★, p. 90

NEW AMERICAN

Aureole ★★★, p. 82

PIZZA

Radio City Pizza ★★★, p. 114

PUB

Gordon Ramsay Pub & Grill ★, p. 100
Pub 1842 ★★, p. 87
The Pub at Monte Carlo ★, p. 88
Todd English P.U.B. ★★★, p. 90
Triple 7 Brewpub ★, p. 114

SANDWICHES

Capriotti's ★★★, p. 118
Earl of Sandwich ★★, p. 104

SEAFOOD

Emeril's New Orleans Fish House ★,
 p. 82
Estiatorio Milos ★★★, p. 94

SOUL FOOD

M&M Soul Food ★★, p. 122

SOUTHWESTERN

Mesa Grill ★★, p. 95

SPANISH

Julian Serrano ★★, p. 87

STEAK

Andiamo Steakhouse ★★, p. 109
Austins Steakhouse ★★, p. 121
Delmonico Steakhouse ★★, p. 94
Gordon Ramsay Steak ★, p. 94
Old Homestead Steakhouse ★★★,
 p. 95
Oscar's Beef Booze Broads ★★,
 p. 109
The Steakhouse ★, p. 107
Strip House ★★, p. 97

THAI

Komol ★, p. 119
Lotus of Siam ★★★, p. 119

VENEZUELAN

Viva Las Arepas ★★, p. 114

SOUTH STRIP

Expensive

Andre's ★★ FRENCH   The original and much-beloved Andre's, in Downtown
Las Vegas, closed in 2008, but never fear—the branch at Monte Carlo is still going
strong. While it may not have the ambience of its forbearer, which was located in a
rustic cottage, it certainly has the menu, still overseen by owner/chef Andre Rochat,
who brings over 40 years of experience to the table. Much of the waitstaff is also
French, and they will happily lavish attention on you and guide you through your
choices. The food presentation is exquisite and choices change seasonally; examples might be an appetizer of foie gras served with fig confiture and drizzled with
a balsamic reduction, or a main course of apple-stuffed pork tenderloin with sautéed
Brussels sprouts. You get the idea. Desserts are similarly lovely with an exotic array

of rich delights. An extensive wine list (more than 1,500 selections) is international in scope and includes many rare vintages; consult the sommelier.

In Monte Carlo, 3770 Las Vegas Blvd. S. ✆ **702/798-7151.** www.andrelv.com. Main courses $36–$68. Tues–Sun 5:30–10:30pm.

Aureole ★★★ NEW AMERICAN   This branch of a New York City fave (it's pronounced Are-ree-*all*), run by Charlie Palmer, is noted for its glass wine tower. It's four stories of what is probably the finest wine collection in Vegas, made even more sensational thanks to "Wine Angels," catsuit-clad lovelies who are hoisted on wires to reach bottles requested from the uppermost heights, all navigable via a tablet computer brought to your table. They are such an ingrained part of the dining experience in Vegas that a 2013 change to their costumes (now fiery orange and red instead of simple black) actually made headlines. Amid this Vegas-show glitz is one of the best of the fine-dining experiences around. The menu changes seasonally, but be on the lookout for interesting twist items like the double pork chop served with collard greens or Jidori chicken breast. It used to be a prix-fixe menu, but now all dishes are a la carte with variable pricing, which makes it easier to rack up quite a bill here. Everything demonstrates the hand of a true chef in the kitchen, someone paying close attention to his work and to his customers. Desserts are playful, including a honey and lavender crème brulee.

In Mandalay Bay, 3950 Las Vegas Blvd. S. ✆ **877/632-1766.** www.aureolelv.com. Main courses $29–$70. Mon–Sat 5:30–10:30pm.

Crush ★★ CONTINENTAL   Foodies will likely develop a crush on this sweet bistro run by Michael Morton, whose **La Comida** (p. 110) in Downtown Las Vegas is a huge hit as well. Here the focus is on fresh and flavorful dishes with international influences. Spend most of your time in the small plates sections so you can mix and match lovely constructions like ricotta gnocchi with braised short ribs or mini-Angus burgers topped with a sunny-side-up quail egg. But if you veer off into the flatbread pizza menu or the large plate items like a succulent lamb sirloin, you won't be disappointed. If you have dietary restrictions, ask for the special menu, which offers vegan, vegetarian, gluten-free, dairy-free, and seafood/shellfish-free options.

At MGM Grand, 3799 Las Vegas Blvd. S., ✆ **702/891-3222.** www.mgmgrand.com. Small plates $15–$18, main courses $28–$65. Sun–Thurs 5:30pm–10:30pm; Fri–Sat 5:30pm–11:30pm.

Emeril's New Orleans Fish House ★ CREOLE/SEAFOOD   Celeb chefs don't get any more "celeb" than Emeril Lagasse—if there's a cooking show, he's probably been on it—and that's probably what will lure you to this Vegas version of his justifiably famed New Orleans restaurant. The bad news is it isn't as good as the original; the good news is that if you've never eaten at the original, you will probably be satisfied with your choice. Despite the name, it's the nonfish items we were most impressed with, including a Creole-spiced rib-eye that was as good as any we have eaten at a steakhouse. The Crescent City favorites, including barbecue shrimp and shrimp étouffée with Andouille pork sausage, are zesty delights, and desserts like Emeril's trademark banana cream pie with chocolate and caramel are worth saving room for. If you can swing it, get a seat at the chef's table. It won't be Emeril at the stove, but it's still quite a show.

In MGM Grand, 3799 Las Vegas Blvd. S. ✆ **702/891-7374.** www.emerils.com. Main courses $16–$23 lunch, $18–$49 dinner (more for lobster). Daily 11:30am–3pm and 5–10pm.

South Strip Restaurants

0		0.25 mi
0		0.25 km

Javier's **1**
Joël Robuchon **7**
Julian Serrano **1**
L'Atelier de Joël
  Robuchon **7**
Monte Carlo
  Food Court **4**

RESTAURANTS
Andre's **4**
Aureole **10**
Blossom **1**
Bobby's Burger
  Palace **2**
Border Grill **10**
Burger Bar **10**
Citizens Kitchen **10**
Crush **7**
Diablo's Cantina **4**
Dick's Last Resort **8**
Double Barrel
  Roadhouse **4**
Emeril's New Orleans
  Fish House **7**
Fleur **10**
Hard Rock Café **5**
Harley Davidson
  Café **3**
House of Blues **10**
Hussong's Cantina **10**

New York–New York
  Village Eateries **6**
PUB 1842 **7**
The Pub at
  Monte Carlo **4**
Public House **9**
Red Square **10**
Rí Rá Irish Pub **10**
Sirio Ristorante **1**
Tacos & Tequila **9**
Todd English
  P.U.B. **2**
Yusho **4**

BUFFETS
The Buffet at Aria **1**
Excalibur Roundtable
  Buffet **8**
Mandalay Bay's
  Bayside Buffet **10**
More, the Buffet
  at Luxor **9**

Fleur by Hubert Keller ★★★ CONTINENTAL   A reboot of Hubert Keller's divine Fleur de Lys, Fleur focuses on a continental selection of small plates, served in more casual surroundings than its predecessor. Choose a seat on the (indoor) patio, a comfy leather club chair, or a traditional table to enjoy selections like a miniature Croque Monsieur, dripping with cheese and loaded with finely smoked ham; or a small slice of tender skirt steak served with a fingerling potato and chimichurri. The construction is divine and the ingredients are noteworthy for their freshness. The good news/bad news of small plates is you get to sample more but you also have more opportunity for some bum notes, of which we had one or two, but it's strictly by comparison to the rest of the fabulous flavors. And even though individually the small plates have small prices, you can also run up a hefty bill by ordering multiple options—and that's even if you don't get the $5,000 Wagyu beef hamburger (it comes with a bottle of 1995 Chateau Petrus). Note the option of a more traditional lunch menu with sandwiches, salads, and burgers for significantly less than $5,000.

In Mandalay Bay, 3950 Las Vegas Blvd. S. ✆ **702/632-9400.** www.hubertkeller.com. Lunch main courses $13–$24; dinner small plates $9–$27; dinner full plates $26–$95. Daily 11am–10:30pm.

Joël Robuchon ★★★ FRENCH   This is listed under the *Expensive* category only because there isn't one for Unbelievably, Heart-Stoppingly, Stratospherically Expensive. But it's here because legendary chef Joël Robuchon—the first (and youngest) chef to win three consecutive Michelin stars—who closed his restaurants in France (where he was proclaimed "chef of the century") at the height of his fame, has proven that all the hype is justified. The gorgeous dining room, done in rich purple and climbing vines of deep green, hosts not just food as fuel, food to bolt down greedily (even though you may want to), but to slowly savor. Pay attention as you chew, and notice how many layers of interest are revealed. Great care was taken in choosing and combining ingredients, to create not fuss but both surprise and a sense of rightness. Exquisite, superb— name your superlative, and it's been levied toward this remarkable restaurant.

Chef Robuchon is not personally in the kitchen that often, but he oversees the menu, which changes very frequently and features many key ingredients flown in daily from France. And the service reminds one that Michelin ratings take more than just the food into account, too. None of this comes cheap. Could it possibly be worth it? When restaurant critics claim they would spend their own money to dine here, quite very possibly, yes.

In MGM Grand, 3799 Las Vegas Blvd. S. ✆ **702/891-7925.** www.joel-robuchon.com. Reservations strongly recommended. Jacket recommended. Prix-fixe tasting menus $120–$240; 16-course tasting menu $425; a la carte main courses $85–$235. Sun–Thurs 5:30–10pm; Fri–Sat 5:30–10:30pm.

L'Atelier de Joël Robuchon ★★★ FRENCH   Whether you choose the main restaurant above or this more relaxed experience is about more than just money. Certainly, it's cheaper here (if we are using the word "cheaper" loosely), but the real difference is your involvement with the divine creations they serve. The open kitchen and counter seating put you in the heart of the action, making you a participant rather than a recipient, and interacting with the charming staff on the other side only adds to the great good pleasure. Portions are small but exquisitely conceived and constructed. The seasonal tasting menu is probably your best way to go, but consider coming just to treat yourself to a couple of dishes, such as Iberico de Bellota ham, highly coveted stuff with toasted tomato bread; their simply divine spaghetti in a cream and bacon sauce; or the signature foie gras–stuffed quail. The artistry only continues with dessert. This is the kind of meal you will remember for the rest of your life.

In MGM Grand, 3799 Las Vegas Blvd. S. ✆ **702/891-7358.** www.joel-robuchon.com. Reservations strongly recommended. Main courses $32–$90; 9-course discovery menu $159; small plates $20–$45. Daily 5–11pm.

Sirio Ristorante ★ ITALIAN   From the same family that brought us Le Cirque and Circo, Sirio serves decidedly upscale Italian fare with a heavy Tuscan influence, meaning simple concepts and ingredients often thrown together in revelatory ways. Start with a build-your-own antipasti platter, and if you don't get the smoked rosemary ham as one of your choices, you only have yourself to blame. Pastas are handmade and simply divine, while the generously proportioned entrees (mainly seafood and chophouse bases with Italian decoration) are perhaps not adventurous but certainly satisfying.

In Aria Las Vegas, 3730 Las Vegas Blvd. S. ✆ **877/230-2742.** www.arialasvegas.com. Main courses $29–$50. Daily 5–10:30pm.

Moderate

Blossom ★★ CHINESE   Chef Chi Kwun Choi is not a household name like Emeril or Wolfgang, but his resume reads like a master class in the art of Chinese cuisine. He worked at some of the most prestigious restaurants in Hong Kong and, since coming to Vegas, has cooked at notable eateries like Pearl and Fin. His cuisine incorporates classic Chinese flavors into modern interpretations of the dishes. We know you're hungry, but do not skip the appetizer section, with its deliciously doughy pot stickers or the interesting version of egg rolls with finely chopped vegetables instead of the shredded, indefinable goo you find in lesser restaurants. Then you can move on to the extensive main menu for meat (everything from Peking duck to lamb chops, but a big thumbs up for the pan-fried shredded beef tenderloin), hot pot, noodle, rice, and veggie dishes. Or you can forget all that and go directly for the two pages' worth of seafood options, unbelievably fresh considering the fact that the restaurant is in the middle of a desert. Although there are plenty of options in the moderate price range, there are plenty more with eye-popping price tags—$60 for jumbo shrimp!?— so order carefully.

In Aria Las Vegas, 3730 Las Vegas Blvd. S. ℂ **877/230-2742.** www.arialasvegas.com. Main courses $15–$60. Daily 5:30–10:30pm.

Border Grill ★★ MEXICAN   This big, cheerful space (complete with a gorgeous outside patio for warm, but not too warm, summer nights) houses a branch of the much-lauded Los Angeles restaurant, conceived and run by Mary Sue Milliken and Susan Feniger, hosts of the 1990s Food Network show *Two Hot Tamales*. This is truly authentic Mexican home cooking—the Tamales learned their craft south of the border—but with a *nuevo* twist. So don't expect precisely the same dishes you'd encounter in your favorite corner joint, but do expect fresh and fabulous food, sitting as brightly on the plates as the decor on the walls. Stay away from the occasionally bland fish and head right toward rich and cheesy dishes such as the citrus chicken quesadilla or turkey tostada. Don't miss the dense but fluffy Mexican chocolate cream pie. Note that a second location is due to open in the Forum Shops at Caesars Palace by the time you read this.

In Mandalay Bay, 3950 Las Vegas Blvd. S. ℭ **702/632-7403.** www.bordergrill.com. Main courses $10–$26 lunch, $16–$36 dinner. Mon–Thurs 11am–10pm; Fri 11am–11pm; Sat 10am–11pm; Sun 10am–10pm.

Citizens Kitchen ★★★ AMERICAN   After years of one high-priced fancy restaurant after another taking up all the room in Vegas casinos, the new trend is toward the more affordable, more casual eatery like this—a fantastic comfort-food kitchen with a wide-ranging menu and a comfy, at-home vibe. Start with the baked meatballs in a tangy red gravy or the just exactly spicy enough Buffalo wings with creamy blue cheese dressing for the table. Then be prepared to keep sharing your main courses of delectable dishes like 18-hour, slow-roasted prime rib with a roasted garlic crust, zesty meatloaf on a cushion of mashed potatoes, steaks, seafood, sandwiches, New Orleans–style muffalettas (including one that serves six), burgers, pasta, and so much more. Be sure to save room for sides like mac and cheese with ham hocks, and the desserts like their simply heavenly cheesecake, served with a healthy dollop of cherry compote. A full bar with craft-cocktail level concoctions and the friendliest, most efficient service we have experienced in Vegas anywhere make this an all-round success by every measure we can think of.

In Mandalay Bay, 3950 Las Vegas Blvd. S. ℭ **702/835-9200**. www.citizenslasvegas.com. Main courses $15–$39. Daily 24 hrs.

Diablo's Cantina ★★ MEXICAN   Located right on the Strip with some fun people-watching views, Diablo's is a dark pueblo of a space serving up traditional Mexican fare at prices that will remind you that eating in Vegas doesn't need to be a bank-draining occasion. The menu, while not as mind-bogglingly expansive as similar restaurants, certainly covers all the basics, with burritos, tacos, quesadillas, enchiladas, and fajitas, plus some sandwiches, burgers, and salads thrown in for those who need a little less spice in their life. Standouts include the thick, cheesy (in a good way) quesadillas and the tender steak fajitas, served sizzling—the way God intended them to be. Be sure to check out the rooftop patio, which offers some stunning up-close view of the Strip madness.

In Monte Carlo, 3770 Las Vegas Blvd. S. ℭ **702/730-7979.** www.diabloslasvegas.com. Main courses $14–$24. Daily 11am–10pm; bar open later.

Dick's Last Resort ★★ AMERICAN   Boy food for the boisterous. This is not the place to go for a relaxing or dainty meal. The gimmick is customer abuse—yes, you pay for the privilege of having waitstaff hurl napkins and cheerful invective at you. But they mean it with love. It sounds a bit strange, but it works, in a party-hearty way. Speaking of, the food itself is hearty indeed, with house specialties (barbecue ribs, honey-glazed chicken) arriving in buckets. Entrees are substantial, both in quantity and construction—look for chicken-fried steak, fried chicken, and meats or pastas covered in cream sauces. Those with strict orders from their doctors about cholesterol levels should probably go elsewhere, but those looking for a break from the foodie snobbery in this town will love it.

In Excalibur, 3850 Las Vegas Blvd. S. ℭ **702/597-7791.** www.dickslastresort.com. Main courses $12–$25. Sun–Thurs 11am–11pm; Fri–Sat 11am–midnight.

Double Barrel Roadhouse ★★ AMERICAN   Although it has all the trappings of a theme restaurant (hint: it's not really a southern roadhouse somehow magically transported to the Las Vegas Strip), this one transcends the kitsch factor to stand on its own boot-clad feet as a place for great grub, great drinks, and some pretty spectacular people-watching opportunities. Located at the Monte Carlo, the entire front of the restaurant opens up to Las Vegas Boulevard so you can sit, enjoy a drink from any of the four bars, and watch the humanity stroll by. While doing so, enjoy down-home food such as a fried meatloaf appetizer served with bacon ketchup (yeah, it's that kind of place), deviled eggs, shrimp and cheesy grits, slow-cooked BBQ ribs, burgers, and sandwiches, including the best grilled cheese in Vegas: multiple cheeses on Parmesan-crusted Texas toast, juicy tomato, and bacon. Fun desserts include a birthday cake— yes, an actual slice of cake with candles and everything. Great, friendly service, too.

In Monte Carlo, 3770 Las Vegas Blvd. S. ☏ **702/222-7735.** www.doublebarrellv.com. Main courses $13–$40. Mon–Thurs 11am–2am; Fri–Sun 11am–4am.

Hussong's Cantina ★ MEXICAN   It is based on the legendary Ensenada bar, in business since 1892, which claims to have been the site where the margarita was invented (a bartender reportedly concocted the mixture in 1941 for either the daughter of a Mexican ambassador or Rita Hayworth, depending on who you ask—there was alcohol involved so the history is understandably fuzzy). Hussong's boldly proclaims to have "the Best Tacos in Town." Okay. Gauntlet thrown. If you can choose only one, the steak is the clear winner here, all smoky charbroiled goodness, but my-oh-my the *carnitas* (shredded, spiced pork) were pretty darned good, too. Best in town? We'll leave it up to you to decide, or you can just go with their fantastic enchiladas and skip the whole debate. The margaritas are good, but perhaps floating a bit too much on their "we invented it!" reputation. You can get better just down the hall at Tacos & Tequila (p. 90).

At Mandalay Place, 3930 Las Vegas Blvd. S., no. 121B. ☏ **702/632-6450.** www.hussongslasvegas. com. Main courses $14–$22. Daily 11am–11pm.

Julian Serrano ★★ SPANISH   Serrano is most famous in Vegas for his Picasso restaurant at Bellagio, a place that paved the way for all of the ultra-exclusive, large-check restaurants that came after it. His eponymously named restaurant at Aria Las Vegas is much more accessible, both from a menu and price perspective. Tapas are the main draw here, allowing you to load up on small plates of often exquisite dishes, many with a Spanish flair to them. The chorizo was surprisingly mild but still playfully flavorful. Check out the "new" tapas section with funky combos such as ahi tuna with avocado or the fried potatoes, eggs, and chorizo (breakfast on a stick!). If the small selections aren't doing it for you, go big with one of the signature paellas. The Valenciana has chicken and rabbit in a not-too-spicy Spanish rice, large enough to feed at least two people. The food, service, and ambience are all superb, although it is worth noting that the bill can add up quickly if you go too crazy with tapas sampling.

In Aria Las Vegas, 3730 Las Vegas Blvd. S. ☏ **877/230-2742.** www.arialasvegas.com. Reservations recommended. Main courses lunch $12–$50; main courses dinner $24–$50; tapas $7–$39. Sun– Thurs 11:30am–11pm; Fri–Sat 11:30am–11:30pm.

Pub 1842 ★★ PUB FARE   Chef Michael Mina is not as much of a "name" as some celebrity chefs, but ultimately that's a good thing, because it means he spends more time in the kitchen cooking than he does on TV talking about it. This is his fourth Vegas restaurant and the first that is aimed at the middle market, complete with a casual vibe and wide-ranging gastropub menu. If all you want is some grub to soak up all of the beers and barrel-aged cocktails they serve, focus on the snacks, bites, and "apps" section of the menu, offering delightful takes on classic bar food like lobster corn dogs served with a creme fraiche mustard. If you are hungrier than that, check out the burgers, sandwiches, steaks, slow-cooked BBQ from their own pit, and entrees from fish and chips to Maine lobster with Andouille sausage. The organic half-chicken, roasted to perfection and generously topped with sundried tomato and jalapeño, is a standout. In case you were wondering, 1842 is the year in which Pilsner beer was invented. Honor that by getting one of their beer wheels, with 5-ounce samplings of eight of their brews.

In MGM Grand, 3799 Las Vegas Blvd. S. ✆ **702/891-3922**. www.pub1842.com. Main courses $15–$47. Mon–Thurs 11:30am–10pm; Fri 11:30am–midnight; Sat 10am–midnight; Sun 10am–10pm.

The Pub at Monte Carlo ★ PUB FARE   Before the gastropub explosion in Vegas came along, this hearty brew pub was laying the groundwork for the breed with a simple, two-story chic warehouse look, a big bar serving more than 200 beers on tap (including their own in-house labels), lots of TVs showing the latest games, an entertainment area with a stage and dance floor, and a restaurant, of course. It's mainly pub-grub food—lots of sandwiches and some really fantastic burgers (try the build-your-own section, where you can create dozens of different combinations), salads, and a few entrees. Check out "Gus' Small Bites," which are really huge appetizers (because Gus is the pub's mascot whale). It's all surprisingly flavorful and well prepared for a very moderate price. Note that frequent live entertainment and DJs can make this a fun but noisy spot at night.

In Monte Carlo, 3770 Las Vegas Blvd. S. ✆ **702/730-7420.** www.montecarlo.com. Main courses $11–$32. Sun–Thurs 11am–11pm; Fri–Sat 11am–3am.

Public House ★ AMERICAN   Not to be confused with the completely unrelated Public House at Venetian, this one is more sports pub than gastropub, with a satisfying menu of American classics and a boisterous atmosphere. The latter is due to the omnipresent TVs showing all manner of sporting events and the people who watch them, cheering along. Even if the concept of a less-than-peaceful meal bothers you, the food could make up for it with a variety of burgers, sandwiches, salads, and comfort-food entrees like meatloaf, steak, and even jambalaya. Standouts include the slow-roasted, pulled-pork sandwich, which is topped with a mound of onion straws and cole slaw and dressed in a sweet (rather than vinegary) BBQ sauce (which we prefer, frankly), and braised short rib with caramelized onions and horseradish. Prices are moderate and service is fantastic, so if you can put up with the roar of the crowd you'll have little else to complain about.

In Luxor, 3900 Las Vegas Blvd. S. ✆ **702/262-4525.** www.publichouselasvegas.com. Main courses $10–$25. Mon–Thurs 4pm–midnight; Fri–Sat 11am–1am; Sun 11am–midnight.

Red Square ★★ CONTINENTAL/RUSSIAN   This Vegas stalwart got a makeover in 2013 that updated the menu to feature less of the Americanized Russian food it used to showcase and more Russian-influenced American food—and in some cases, neither Russian or American. This sounds a bit disjointed and perhaps it is, but the food is so good that you simply won't care. If you must create your own version of glasnost, start with a caviar sampler and a flight of vodka and then move on to Chicken Kiev or Beef Stroganoff, the latter of which is a divine modern take with braised short rib and mushroom pasta. If you are feeling more patriotic, start with the Buffalo wings with creamy blue cheese and then move on to a classically prepared steak. Or go in between with Italian meatballs in a delicious marinara or lobster pasta. Regardless, the flavors are bright and the preparation superb. While it may not be exactly "cheap," it is less

YOU GOTTA HAVE A theme

It shouldn't be too surprising to learn that a town devoted to gimmicks has just about every gimmick restaurant there is. No matter your interest, there is probably a theme restaurant here for you, from sports to pop culture and back again. Fans should have a good time checking out the stuff on the walls, but for the most part the memorabilia is usually more interesting than the food. Here are some of the best of the bunch.

The House of Blues ★★, in Mandalay Bay, 3950 Las Vegas Blvd. S. (ⓒ **702/632-7600**; www.hob.com; Sun–Thurs 7am–11pm, Fri–Sat 7am–midnight), has a Mississippi Delta blues theme complete with frequent concerts and a gospel brunch. The food is down-home Southern and there is lots of it for pretty decent prices.

Southern staples are also on tap at the **Harley-Davidson Café ★**, 3725 Las Vegas Blvd. S., at Harmon Avenue (ⓒ **702/740-4555**; www.harley-davidsoncafe.com; Sun–Thurs 8:30am–11pm, Fri–Sat 9am–midnight), alongside shrines to the easy-rider lifestyle evoked by the motorcycle brand.

The Hard Rock Cafe ★, 3771 Las Vegas Blvd. S. (ⓒ **702/733-7625**; www.hardrock.com; daily 8:30am–11pm), has decent burgers and all of the requisite music memorabilia you have come to expect packed in a massive, 42,000-square-foot, three-level behemoth with a gigantic gift shop, a 1,000-seat concert venue, and more. **Note:** There is a second Hard Rock Cafe at the Hard Rock Hotel, 4475 Paradise Rd., at Harmon Avenue (ⓒ **702/733-8400**).

Parrot Heads, as fans of Jimmy Buffet refer to themselves, like to party it up at **Margaritaville ★**, at the Flamingo, 3555 Las Vegas Blvd. S. (ⓒ **702/733-3302**; www.margaritavillelasvegas.com; Sun–Thurs 11am–1am, Fri–Sat 11am–2am), the singer's tropical-themed cafe/bar/club. The menu runs a range from Mexican to something sort of Caribbean themed to basic American, and it's not all that bad, considering. Partaking in lots of fruity tropical drinks doesn't hurt, either.

If the rodeo is more your style, the Pro Bull Riding organization has its own place at the **PBR Rock Bar & Grill ★** at Planet Hollywood, 3663 Las Vegas Blvd. S. (ⓒ **702/750-1685**; www.pbrrockbar.com; daily 8am–late). It serves up down-home American food in a country-western environment complete with a mechanical bull and tire swings above the tables.

You would think the celebrity shrine and memorabilia factory that is the **Planet Hollywood** restaurant would be in the Planet Hollywood Resort. But you'd be wrong. Instead, it's at Caesars Palace in the Forum Shops, 3500 Las Vegas Blvd. S. (ⓒ **702/791-7827**; www.planethollywood.com; Sun–Thurs 11am–11pm, Fri–Sat 11am–midnight).

expensive than it used to be unless you are ordering piles of imported caviar, and then it will be time to say *dos vedanya* to your wallet.

In Mandalay Bay, 3950 Las Vegas Blvd. S. ⓒ **702/632-7407.** www.redsquarelasvegas.com. Main courses $27–$65. Sun–Thurs 4:30pm–10pm, Fri–Sat 4:30pm–midnight.

Rí Rá Irish Pub ★★ IRISH   Is it too much of a cliché to say that the one dish you should not pass up at an Irish pub is the potato-cake appetizer? Perhaps, but one bite of the pan-seared, delicately seasoned dish covered in Irish sour cream and drizzled with balsamic oil and you will not care a whit about stereotypes. But don't stop there. Traditional favorites include fish and chips, shepherd's pie, bangers and mash, and corned beef and cabbage, although you could also play it safe with a variety of burgers, sandwiches, and salads, many of which have *Erin go bragh* twists like Irish bacon or Guinness barbecue sauce. Be sure to ask for a tour of the restaurant from your server (many of whom are as authentically Irish as the food) to see the restored pub once run by the owner's aunt, the tile floors from the shipyard office of the company that built the Titanic, and the massive 500-pound statue of St. Patrick found in an Irish farmer's field. Late night the place lives up to the Irish Pub part of its name, with a rowdy spirit with live music or DJs pumping up the energy.

At Mandalay Place, 3930 Las Vegas Blvd. S. ℂ **702/632-7771.** www.rira.com. Main courses lunch $11–$21; dinner $11–$30. Mon–Thurs 8am–3am; Fri 8am–4am; Sat 9am–4am; Sun 9am–3am.

Tacos & Tequila ★★ MEXICAN   Between the loud music and general din from the adjacent Luxor attractions level, the atmosphere here does not lend itself to a quiet meal. Have a margarita and you won't care. All are made with hand-squeezed lime juice, organic agave nectar, and your choice of a mind-boggling array of tequilas and flavors. We know people who are very picky about their margaritas and have declared these the best they have ever tasted. What? Oh, the food. Right. Although there are more than a dozen varieties of tacos (Kobe beef, lobster, beer-battered tilapia, and more) the menu goes beyond their namesake to include tostadas, enchiladas, burritos, quesadillas, seafood, soups, and salads, all done with an organic freshness that sets the dishes apart from the chain restaurants you're probably used to. A weekend Mariachi Brunch adds a variety of breakfast items to the offerings, including *huevos con tocino* or *chorizo*, burritos, and *huevos rancheros*. Prices are high for a Mexican joint but relatively affordable for a Strip restaurant.

In Luxor, 3900 Las Vegas Blvd. S. ℂ **702/262-5225.** www.tacosandtequilalv.com. Main courses $11–$22. Daily 11am–11pm.

Todd English P.U.B. ★★★ PUB FARE   English's Olives restaurant (p. 96) up the street at Bellagio, is one of our favorites, so we had high hopes for his new pub concept at CityCenter. Hopes met and exceeded. A huge beer and wine list is enticing, as are the sun-dappled interiors with lots of TVs on which to catch your favorite game, but it is the menu that really seals the proverbial deal here. Want a sandwich? Make your own from the Carvery, with your choice of meat (prime beef, roasted chicken, turkey, duck, salmon, and pastrami for starters), bread, and condiments. Be sure to accompany that with the spectacular prime rib chili, slathered in cheese and moderate on the spicy scale. Burgers, salads, bangers and mash, fish and chips, pot pies, and a host of other sandwiches round out the menu. Best of all are the moderate prices. Late night brings a boisterous crowd lured by the pub's infamous 7-Second Challenge: Slam a beer in 7 seconds or less and it's free. We know we shouldn't approve of such shenanigans.

In Crystals at CityCenter, 3720 Las Vegas Blvd. S. ℂ **702/489-8080.** www.toddenglishpub.com. Reservations recommended. Main courses $13–$24. Sun–Thurs 11am–2am; Fri–Sat 9:30am–2am.

Yusho ★★ JAPANESE   Just when it felt like everything worth doing from a culinary perspective had been done in Vegas, along comes this refreshing eatery that will help redefine your taste buds' expectations. Japanese "street food" is the concept here—the kind of stuff you might find in vendor stalls or outdoor marketplaces—with items like veggie tempura (including shallots, mushrooms, and a delightful deep-fried lemon slice); pork and egg ramen noodles; steamed buns with chub sausage, red peppers, and cauliflower; pork shoulder buns with kimchi; house-made pickles; and more. It's all prepared with a delicate touch that makes the unique blend of flavors pop in

quick BITES

Food courts are a dime a dozen in Vegas, but the one in **New York–New York,** 3790 Las Vegas Blvd. S. (☎ 702/740-6969), deserves a mention for two reasons. First, it's the nicest setting for this sort of thing on the Strip, sitting in the Greenwich Village section of New York–New York, which means scaled replica tenement buildings, steam rising from the manhole covers, and more than a little (faux, naturally) greenery, a nice change from unrelentingly shrill and plastic mall decor. Second, the selections are the usual, but it's a better-than-average food court, with a deli and pizza (as befitting an ode to NYC), and excellent if expensive (for this situation) double-decker burgers, plus **Ben & Jerry's** ice cream. Hours vary by outlet.

The **Monte Carlo,** 3770 Las Vegas Blvd. S., between Flamingo Road and Tropicana Avenue (☎ 702/730-7777), has traditional offerings like **McDonald's** and **Subway,** which can be comforting if you need it. The food court is open daily from 6am to 3am.

The food court at **Flamingo Las Vegas,** 3555 Las Vegas Blvd. S.

(☎ 702/733-3111), has a couple of interesting outlets like **Pan Asian Express** and **Johnny Rockets** hamburgers, among others. Hours vary, but it's usually open from 8am until 2am.

If you head farther down the Strip, to **The Grande Canal Shoppes** at the Venetian, 3355 Las Vegas Blvd. S. (☎ 702/414-4500), you can find another decent food court, with a **Panda Express,** a good pizza place (despite the confusing name of **LA Italian Kitchen**), and more. Plus, it's right by the canals of this faux Venice, one of our favorite places in Vegas. Hours are Sunday through Thursday from 10am until 11pm and Friday and Saturday from 10am until midnight.

And of course, it should come as no surprise that the biggest mall in Vegas has the biggest food court as well. **The Fashion Show Mall,** 3200 Las Vegas Blvd. S. (☎ 702/369-8382), has more than a dozen outlets from **KFC Express, Nathan's Famous, Subway, Wendy's,** and more. Hours are Monday through Saturday from 10am until 9pm and Sunday from 11am until 7pm.

unexpectedly delightful ways. Be sure to quiz your server thoroughly—they may have more off-menu items than they are letting on (if one of them is the spicy fried chicken skin, done almost like fried-chicken potato chips, get it). Also ask for advice on drink pairings, including exclusive beers, sake, and on-tap cocktails. About the only downside here is the bland room and uncomfortable metal chairs; but have a few bites and you won't care about the ambience.

In Monte Carlo, 3770 Las Vegas Blvd. S. ☎ **702/730-6888**. www.yusholv.com. Small plates $7–$39. Sun–Wed 3pm–midnight; Thurs–Sat 3pm–2am.

Inexpensive

Bobby's Burger Palace ★★ BURGERS   The Bobby in the title is celebrity chef and Food Network staple Bobby Flay, whose upscale Mesa Grill at Caesars Palace remains a Vegas favorite. Here he goes decidedly American with a menu of burgers and shakes that are several cuts above typical fast-food fare. Pay special attention to the fun concoctions like the Philadelphia with sweet onions and hot peppers, or the Miami, done as a Cuban press with ham and pickles. Beef, turkey, and chicken options are available, as are a couple of salads if you are feeling like at least pretending to be looking for some nutritional value that a burger can't supply. Note the location is at the base

We've already alluded to the rock-bottom budget meals and graveyard specials available at casino hotel restaurants, quality not assured and Pepto-Bismol not provided. As prices and deals can change without notice, we don't want to list examples, but finding a full prime-rib dinner for around $10 is not rare (pun definitely intended).

Your best bet is to keep your eyes open as you travel through town, as hotels tend to advertise their specials on their marquees. Or you can go to www.vegas.com and click on **"Dining"** and then **"Dining Bargains,"** though the tips and prices may be somewhat out-of-date. Following are three examples of current options for late-night munchies: **Coronado Café** at the South Point offers a $3.95 steak-and-eggs meal, while $2.95 gets you a hearty breakfast at **The Sundance Grill** at the Silverton. At the Hard Rock Hotel, **Mr. Lucky's 24/7** is a particularly good diner, with particularly good people-watching. And then ask your server about the $7.77 steak, three grilled shrimp, and sides; it's not on the menu, so you have to know about it.

of the Mandarin Oriental hotel tower, facing the Strip. Although easy to spot, it can be a bit confusing to get there.

At CityCenter, 3750 Las Vegas Blvd. S. *(*) **702/598-0191**. www.bobbysburgerpalace.com. Main courses $10–$12. Open daily 10am–midnight.

Burger Bar ★ DINER   The brainchild of culinary genius Hubert Keller (see Fleur, p. 83), this burgers-done-your-way experience starts with various meats (from beef to buffalo), throws in a dizzying array of toppings (the usuals, such as bacon and avocado, but also adventurous options like truffles and lobster), plus choices of buns, sauces, and cheese. It adds up to a hilarious and, if you have a deft touch, delicious experience—albeit an expensive one, considering you are really just having a hamburger. Shakes are creamy, fries aren't bad (we like the skinny ones better than the fat ones), though if you haven't before, try the sweet-potato fries. One of the cleverest desserts in town lurks on this menu, a "sweet burger"—a slab of really fine Nutella mousse "burger" on a warm donut "bun," topped with cunningly crafted strawberry "tomato" slices. Skip the highfalutin' burger options—Kobe beef is too soft to use as burger meat, while foie gras is just wasted in this context. In other words, don't show off, but do have fun.

In Mandalay Place, 3930 Las Vegas Blvd. S. *(*) **702/632-9364.** www.burger-bar.com. Main courses $10–$60 (burgers start at $10, depending on kind of meat; toppings start at 45¢ and go way up). Sun–Thurs 11am–11pm; Fri–Sat 11am–1am.

MID-STRIP

Expensive

Bouchon ★★★ BISTRO   Thomas Keller made his name with his Napa Valley restaurant French Laundry, considered by many to be the best restaurant in the United States. Bouchon is a version of his Napa Valley bistro, which is not nearly as lauded, so imagine our surprise when we discovered that humble though these dishes sound, in nearly every case they are gold-standard versions of classics. Someone is certainly keeping a close eye on this kitchen, and that someone has learned the lessons well. Ever wondered why people get worked up over raw oysters? The sweet and supremely

Mid-Strip Restaurants

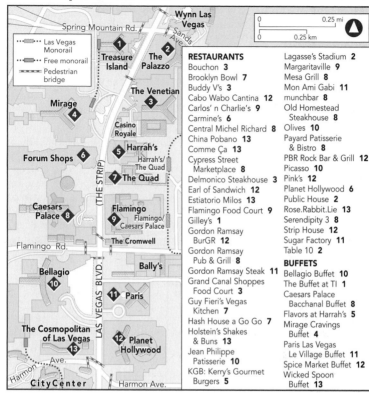

RESTAURANTS

Bouchon **3**
Brooklyn Bowl **7**
Buddy V's **3**
Cabo Wabo Cantina **12**
Carlos' n Charlie's **9**
Carmine's **6**
Central Michel Richard **8**
China Pobano **13**
Comme Ça **13**
Cypress Street
  Marketplace **8**
Delmonico Steakhouse **3**
Earl of Sandwich **12**
Estiatorio Milos **13**
Flamingo Food Court **9**
Gilley's **1**
Gordon Ramsay
  BurGR **12**
Gordon Ramsay
  Pub & Grill **8**
Gordon Ramsay Steak **11**
Grand Canal Shoppes
  Food Court **3**
Guy Fieri's Vegas
  Kitchen **7**
Hash House a Go Go **7**
Holstein's Shakes
  & Buns **13**
Jean Philippe
  Patisserie **10**
KGB: Kerry's Gourmet
  Burgers **5**

Lagasse's Stadium **2**
Margaritaville **9**
Mesa Grill **8**
Mon Ami Gabi **11**
munchbar **8**
Old Homestead
  Steakhouse **8**
Olives **10**
Payard Patisserie
  & Bistro **8**
PBR Rock Bar & Grill **12**
Picasso **10**
Pink's **12**
Planet Hollywood **6**
Public House **2**
Rose.Rabbit.Lie **13**
Serendipity 3 **8**
Strip House **12**
Sugar Factory **11**
Table 10 **2**

BUFFETS

Bellagio Buffet **10**
The Buffet at TI **1**
Caesars Palace
  Bacchanal Buffet **8**
Flavors at Harrah's **5**
Mirage Cravings
  Buffet **4**
Paris Las Vegas
  Le Village Buffet **11**
Spice Market Buffet **12**
Wicked Spoon
  Buffet **13**

fresh (kept in water until the moment they are served to you) Snow Creek oysters will enlighten you, as they seem to melt on contact with your tongue. The rest of the menu is delightfully seasonal, focusing on the freshest of ingredients in not-at-all-intimidating, French-influenced cuisine. This is a superlative Vegas restaurant, and while it may be hard to reconcile the prices with the apparent simplicity of the food, recall that it takes serious skill to make even the most humble of dishes correctly, as your palate will reassure you.

In The Venetian, 3355 Las Vegas Blvd. S. ⓒ **702/414-6200.** www.bouchonbistro.com. Reservations strongly recommended. Main courses $19–$48 dinner, $12–$34 brunch. Mon–Fri 7am–1pm and 5–10pm; Sat–Sun 8am–2pm (brunch) and 5–10pm. Oyster bar daily 3–10pm.

Comme Ça ★★ FRENCH Chef David Myers' resume reads like a culinary dream; he's worked for Charlie Trotter and Daniel Boulud and has been endorsed by *Wine Spectator* and Oprah. This version of his popular Los Angeles restaurant is his first venture in Sin City and he seems determined to give the other French bistros in town a run for their money. The space certainly deserves attention; it's a gorgeously bright room featuring floor-to-ceiling windows overlooking the Strip and a big outdoor dining patio pointed directly at the Eiffel Tower at Paris Las Vegas, just to put you in a Gallic mood. Dine out here if the weather is cooperating; the view is unbeatable. The

WHERE TO EAT

Mid-Strip

menu is traditional French but in a safe Julia Child way (coq au vin, *côte de bouef*, cassoulet, and so forth), so those usually intimidated by the cuisine can feel at ease. Kick things off with a selection of cheeses or meat from the charcuterie (think of it as a deli platter), and then be sure to ask about the soups and hope they have the sweet tomato and cream available. If not, the cheesy, gooey French onion is a good second choice. The beef Bourguignon is a fine main course choice, with tender braised beef, slow cooked and lightly seasoned; and the Wagyu steaks are worth their elevated cost (although we would've preferred a better side than fries and a bland garlic aioli).

In The Cosmopolitan of Las Vegas, 3708 Las Vegas Blvd. S. ℂ **702/698-7910.** www.commecarestaurant.com. Main courses lunch $16–$26; dinner $18–$34. Lunch Fri–Sun noon–5pm; dinner nightly 5–10pm.

Delmonico Steakhouse ★★ CREOLE/STEAK   You might well feel that Emeril Lagasse is omnipresent. This incarnation is a steakhouse version of his hard-core classic Creole restaurant; this ever-so-slight twist is just enough to make it a superior choice over the more disappointing New Orleans locale. Steak is obviously the centerpiece here, and our vote goes for the bone-in rib-eye for its full-bodied flavor and sterling presentation, but you'd be remiss for automatically choosing a steak when there are so many other interesting things on the menu. The apple-smoked pork chop and BBQ salmon with Andouille sausage hash are standouts. Too full for dessert? No, you aren't. Have the Emeril's trademark banana cream pie with caramel sauce and heaping mounds of whipped cream.

In The Venetian, 3355 Las Vegas Blvd. S. ℂ **702/414-3737.** www.emerils.com. Main courses lunch $14–$52; dinner $36–$55. Daily 11:30am–2pm; Sun–Thurs 5–10pm; Fri–Sat 5–10:30pm.

Estiatorio Milos ★★★ GREEK/SEAFOOD   As the waitstaff gives you a tour of the open fish market–style stands with dozens of fresh catches on ice, note the fact that it doesn't reek like a fish market. That should tell you how fresh the selections are— stunning if for no other reason than many of the options are regional specialties that you won't find too often outside the Mediterranean, such as fangri or skaros. Don't know what those are? That's okay; the server will describe them to you and give you a comparison that will help you understand. Selections are prepared whole, lightly dressed in olive oil and lemon juice, and not placed directly on the grill; instead the fish are sort of suspended above it so as not to lose any of their flavor before being deboned and served. It's all bursting with freshness and is the first time we have ever been able to say "it doesn't taste fishy" with a straight face. There are a few land-based options, including a finely tuned rib-eye served with Greek potatoes. As good as all the main courses are, we would be remiss if we didn't tell you to begin your meal with the Milos Special, a stack of thinly sliced zucchini and eggplant, gently fried and served with *kefalograviera* cheese and homemade yogurt dip. It's classic Greek and will have you longing for a vacation to a seaside cafe in Santorini.

In The Cosmopolitan of Las Vegas, 3708 Las Vegas Blvd. S. ℂ **702/698-7930.** www.milos.ca. Lunch 3-course prix fixe $22; dinner main courses $28–$68. Sun–Thurs noon–11pm; Fri–Sat noon–midnight.

Gordon Ramsay Steak ★ STEAK/SEAFOOD   The fiery British Ramsay, whose popular *Hell's Kitchen* and *Kitchen Nightmares* shows on Fox have turned him into a household name, was conspicuously absent from the crowded celebrity chef restaurant lineup in Vegas for a long time. That has been corrected, with not one but three new eateries opening within a year of each other including this, the flagship steakhouse. The cute concept design moves you from Paris (the host hotel) to London via a structure meant to evoke the Chunnel containing the often-crowded bar. Once inside, the two-story restaurant features English drawing-room furnishings and decor mixed with whimsical modern touches like a giant Union Jack painted on the ceiling. The food itself is fairly steakhouse basic (meat, seafood, and so on) but with a few British twists thrown in to keep it interesting (fish and chips, Beef Wellington). Cuts of beef are aged for 28 days in Pat La Freida's Himalayan salt room and then served with a variety of sauce options to dress it up. The traditional filet was fantastic without the need for accompaniments. Save your money and go for the standard cuts instead of upgrading to the Kobe—the quality gap isn't big enough to justify the price differential. Although it doesn't necessarily break new ground in the crowded steakhouse market, this one should allow fans of the Ramsay brand to feel as though they have gotten their money's worth.

In Paris Las Vegas, 3655 Las Vegas Blvd. S. ✆ **877/346-4642.** www.gordonramsay.com. Main courses $41–$78. Daily 5–10:30pm.

Mesa Grill ★★ SOUTHWESTERN Food Network darling Bobby Flay is building a mini-empire here in Vegas, with a new burger joint down the street in addition to this, his flagship Sin City restaurant. The flavors are subtly southwestern, with a bit of a Tex-Mex flair to the proceedings. Look for items like the blue-corn crusted halibut or the chicken quesadilla (made in a dedicated oven) that comes with garlic crème fraiche if you are looking for a spicy deep dive, or go for items like the pan-seared scallops or the chipotle glazed rib-eye if you want to just stick your toe in the spicy waters. Service is among the best we have ever experienced in Las Vegas, and that's saying a lot.

In Caesars Palace, 3570 Las Vegas Blvd. S. ✆ **877/346-4642.** www.mesagrill.com. Main courses $16–$24 brunch and lunch, $25–$52 dinner. Mon–Fri 11am–2:30pm and 5–11pm; Sat–Sun 10:30am–3pm and 5–11pm.

Javier's ★★ MEXICAN Mexican restaurants are omnipresent in Vegas these days, but most focus on middle-market traditional tastes; think tacos, burritos, and fajitas. You can get versions of those things at this southern California transplant, but even those basics are served with upscale twists and gourmet ingredients and sauces, plus a more authentic presentation. Pass those known items by, though, and go for the specials of the house, including a mind-blowing Chile Colorado pork chop in a sweet tomato sauce. It'll make you forget about drive-thru Mexican fast food forever. Granted, this is a lot more expensive than those drive-thru places, but the quality and scope make it worthwhile. Don't miss the fresh, hand-shaken margaritas; a couple of those and you won't care how much your meal costs.

In Aria Las Vegas, 3730 Las Vegas Blvd. S. ✆ **866/590-3637.** www.aria.com. Main courses lunch $16–$55; dinner $20–$60. Daily 11:30am–midnight.

Old Homestead Steakhouse ★★★ STEAK The original version of this classic American steakhouse debuted in New York City in 1868 and claims to have invented the doggy bag. This should tell you a lot about how good the food is (you don't stay in business for more than 150 years without doing something right) and how big the portions are. The menu is mostly steakhouse classic, with beef and seafood leading the charge, but there are a few twists thrown in just to keep things interesting. Don't miss the Kobe beef meatball appetizer, which is roughly the size of your head and drowning happily in a tangy tomato sauce. And if you never listen to anything we say, listen to this: The potato gnocchi, served in an insanely rich truffle-butter-cream sauce, will make the trip worth it all on its own. The steaks themselves are massive (we're talking pounds of meat here), and although you can get sauces and toppings to spice them up, they really don't need it. The prices are verging on insane, with the cheapest steak around $60 and the most expensive, a 10-ounce A5 Wagyu, over $300, but this is one of those rare instances where we endorse spending the money to get the quality. Whether Old Homestead can make it 150 years in Vegas is yet to be seen, but with food this good, they deserve to.

In Caesars Palace, 3570 Las Vegas Blvd. S. ℂ **877/346-4642.** www.theoldhomesteadsteakhouse. com. Main courses $31–$110. Sun–Thurs 5–10:30pm; Fri–Sat 5–11pm.

Olives ★★ ITALIAN/MEDITERRANEAN   If there was an Olives in our neighborhood, we would eat there regularly. A branch of Todd English's original Boston-based restaurant, Olives is a strong choice for a light lunch that need not be as expensive as you might think. Here's how to enjoy a moderately priced meal here: Munch on the focaccia bread, olives, and excellent tapenade they give you at the start, have a lovely salad (the Greek is noteworthy), and then split a flatbread topped with delicious combinations like ham and provolone or fig and prosciutto. They are rich and wonderful—split one between two people, and you have an affordable and terrific lunch. Pastas are a slightly more expensive option but worth the extra few bucks. The constructed, but not too fussy, food gets more complicated and costly at night, adding an array of meats and seafood, all with a Mediterranean influence.

In Bellagio, 3600 Las Vegas Blvd. S. ℂ **866/259-7111.** www.bellagio.com. Main courses $18–$32 lunch, $25–$55 dinner. Daily 11am–2:45pm and 5–10:30pm.

Picasso ★★★ FRENCH   A Spanish chef who cooks French cuisine in an Italian-themed hotel in Vegas? Trust us, it works. This is one of the best restaurants in Vegas, and given the serious competition for such a title, that says a lot. This is an extraordinary dining experience that includes the thrill of having millions of dollars worth of Picassos gaze down over your shoulders while you eat. Dining rooms like this are rare treats, even in Vegas where over-the-top is the standard. Serrano's cooking is a work of art that can proudly stand next to the masterpieces. The menu changes frequently and always offers a choice between a four- or five-course prix-fixe dinner or a tasting menu. The night we ate there, we were bowled over by roasted Maine lobster with a trio of corn—kernels, sauce, and a corn flan—that was like slightly solid sunshine. Hudson Valley foie gras was crusted in truffles and went down most smoothly. A filet of roasted sea bass came with a light saffron sauce and dots of cauliflower purée. Portions are dainty but so rich that you'll have plenty to eat without groaning and feeling heavy when you leave. Desserts are powerful yet prettily constructed. Everything is delivered by attentive staff that makes you feel pampered. Can we go back soon and try it all again?

In Bellagio, 3600 Las Vegas Blvd. S. ℂ **866/259-7111.** www.bellagio.com. Reservations required. Prix-fixe 4-course dinner $115; 5-course degustation $125. Wed–Mon 5:30–9:30pm.

Rose.Rabbit.Lie ★★★ CONTINENTAL   An unparalleled dining experience from both a culinary and atmosphere perspective, this wholly original reinvention of the Vegas supper club mixes an off-kilter ambience, live entertainment, and some of the best food you'll find anywhere. Performers from the show *Vegas Nocturne* (p. 191) filter through the dining areas in character, interacting with guests or just living in their own worlds (why is there a guy in the corner in an Admiral uniform playing chess by himself? Who knows?). You're doing yourself a disservice by not also seeing the full shows in the adjacent "ballroom," but even if you don't, dinner is worth the trip. It's mostly small plates of exquisitely prepared treats ranging from a simple yet

WHERE TO EAT | Mid-Strip

kid-friendly DINING STRATEGIES

Buffets Cheap meals for the whole family. The kids can choose what they like, and there are sometimes make-your-own sundae machines. See "Buffets & Brunches" (p. 124) for buffet reviews. Those with reduced prices for kids are noted.

Food Courts Yes, you can get a Subway sandwich at home, but there is something comforting about the safe array of choices that kids will recognize and probably not complain about. In addition to those listed in the Quick Bites box on p. 91, check out Cypress Street Marketplace (p. 104) at Caesars, which has few recognizable names but better quality.

Theme Restaurants Although the cuisine usually won't win any awards, theme restaurants are often great places to take kids for their wide-ranging menus and plenty of distractions to keep them entertained. See "You Gotta Have a Theme" (p. 89).

---

sublime snow pea salad with pancetta or Brussels sprouts with chicken skin all the way up to caviar "tacos" (Yukon Gold potato shells) and a deconstructed beef stroganoff hidden under a sheaf of herb pasta. If the braised pork with polenta and black truffle is still on the menu, order it and thank us later. Everything is perfectly balanced with seemingly disparate flavors and textures (sweetbreads with licorice and root beer jus) blending in surprising and endlessly delicious ways. For the food, for the atmosphere, for the service, and more, this one is a favorite.

At The Cosmopolitan of Las Vegas, 3708 Las Vegas Blvd. S. ℂ **877/667-0585**. www.roserabbitlie. com. Small plates $9–$36. Thurs–Sun 5:30pm until close.

Strip House ★★ STEAK What turns a pedestrian steakhouse visit, admittedly a dime-a-dozen experience in Vegas, into something truly special? Here it comes down to the two prime ingredients: the atmosphere and the steaks. The place is done in a cheeky bordello theme, with red-flocked walls adorned with black-and-white photos of peek-a-boo strippers from the bygone days when stripping seemed only slightly naughty as opposed to today's raunchiness. These Bettie Page–like works of art are endlessly entertaining to look at, not for the titillation but for the kitsch factor. It is worth noting that while most of the photos are safe for young eyes, there are a few in the mix that are decidedly PG-13, so parents with children may want to scan the walls before sitting to make sure there are no uncomfortable questions during the appetizer course. Speaking of which, there are the traditional (crab cakes and calamari), but head directly for the warm garlic bread served in a bed of Gorgonzola fondue, cholesterol numbers be darned. Or how about a plate of bacon with Russian dressing? Yep, they went there. Follow that up with any of the fine cuts of beef, all done in a black-pepper rub that might be overwhelming to some with the first few bites, but go with it and you'll be rewarded with one of the best and most flavorful steaks on the Strip.

In Planet Hollywood Resort & Casino, 3667 Las Vegas Blvd. S. ℂ **702/737-5200**. www.striphouse. com. Main courses $29–$54. Sun–Thurs 5–11pm; Fri–Sat 5–11:30pm.

Table 10 ★★ AMERICAN Emeril Lagasse's imprint is easy to spot on the menu here, from the subtle Louisiana influences on some dishes to the more obvious inclusions of things like his signature banana cream pie. That may a good or bad thing, depending on your feelings about the celebrity chef, but you really should forget about that entirely because this delightful restaurant stands on its own as a creation that, if

5

WHERE TO EAT

Mid-Strip

you didn't know better, was completely outside of Lagasse's world. The dining room is warmly lit, heavy on the rich woods, and supremely comfortable. Start with the candied bacon served with maple syrup or the fried Great Lakes smelt with lemon mayo, and work your way up to Colorado filet or, better yet, the Hawaiian snapper, simply dressed and steamed to perfection. The menu is seasonal so details may change, but it is also wide-ranging and eclectic from things like suckling pig to lobster spaghetti to sea scallops, so there should be something for just about every taste. And if you want to finish off with the banana cream pie, we certainly won't blame you, but do consider the malasadas, which are like cinnamon powdered donut holes stuffed with white chocolate. Bam, indeed.

In The Palazzo, 3327 Las Vegas Blvd. S. ℂ **702/607-6363.** www.emerils.com. Main courses $15–$38 lunch, $26–$48 dinner. Daily 11am–10pm.

Moderate

Brooklyn Bowl ★★ ECLECTIC Based on the popular NYC hangout, this megavenue has 32 lanes of bowling on two levels, a SRO-style concert venue, multiple bars, and a restaurant serving up big portions of hearty comfort food. The menu is eclectic; where else are you going to find appetizers that include hummus, potato, and onion knishes along with pork rinds with jalapeños and cheese? Keep searching through the French bread pizzas, fried chicken, and BBQ to get to the sandwiches and entrees, which include a zesty delight in the "Really" Sloppy Joe plus other favorites such as pulled pork, Cajun catfish, muffaletta, and more. The burgers are a bit of a disappointment, but you can get a burger anywhere, and those places probably don't have an oyster po' boy to distract you. Note the separate kids' menu, which has smaller portions of many signature items for around $10.

In The LINQ, 3545 Las Vegas Blvd. S., Suite 22. ℂ **702/862-2695.** www.brooklynbowl.com. Main courses $14–$28. Sun–Thurs 11am–2am; Fri–Sat 11am–4am.

Buddy V's Ristorante ★★ ITALIAN Most famous for his wild creations on TLC's *Cake Boss*, Buddy Valastro is about more than just pastries. Here he takes his family's traditional Italian recipes and serves them to the hungry Vegas hordes. All the favorites are here, from lasagna and spaghetti and meatballs to chicken "parm" and steak pizzaiolo. Of special note is the Sunday gravy: red sauce with hunks of succulent meatballs, pork, lamb, and sausage served with a side of rigatoni. If you come from an Italian family, this place will make you feel like you're home, and if you don't, you'll wish you had grown up with food this good. Desserts are, as you might expect, dreamy, including an insanely good spun pastry "lobster tail" stuffed with cream. Or you could skip dessert here and go across the hall to the branch of Carlo's Bakery, as seen on *Cake Boss*, and just crawl into one of the refrigerated display counters and live there. We know we want to. All of the portions are huge, the service is fantastic, and the prices, while not exactly cheap, are about average for a restaurant on the Strip.

In The Grand Canal Shoppes at The Palazzo, 3325 Las Vegas Blvd S. ℂ **702/607-2355**. www.buddyvlasvegas.com. Main courses lunch $14–26; dinner $14–44. Sun–Thurs 11:30am–10pm; Fri–Sat 11:30am–11pm.

Cabo Wabo Cantina ★ MEXICAN Should you really be taking culinary recommendations from Sammy Hagar? If it's at his Cabo Wabo Cantina, then the answer is a resounding "why not?" Part restaurant and part party pit, this Vegas version of his famous (or is it infamous?) Cabo San Lucas joint definitely tries to bring a spring-break-in-Mexico vibe to the Strip with loud music, bright colors, and a waitstaff that may burst into the Cha Cha Slide at any moment. If you don't know what that is and/or think it is idiotic, don't go here. The drink menu, featuring margaritas made with Hagar's Cabo Wabo Tequila, of course, is bigger than the food menu, but if you need something to soak up all that alcohol, the Mexican dishes are certainly up to the task. All the basics are covered—tacos, burritos, nachos (including a Cadillac variety where every chip is loaded separately), fajitas, and so forth—and it's all good, especially the cheesy quesadillas . . . although if you have enough of the tequila, you'll probably be too busy doing the Cha Cha Slide with the waitresses to care about how good the food is.

In Planet Hollywood Resort & Casino, 3663 Las Vegas Blvd. S. ℭ **702/385-2226.** www.cabowabo-cantina.com/vegas. Main courses $14–$35. Daily 8am–11pm.

Carlos 'n Charlie's ★ MEXICAN   There are a bunch of Mexican party bar/restaurants in Las Vegas these days, but this one is probably the most familiar owing to its multiple branches in Mexico and the U.S. The concept will also be familiar, with a bunch of wacky decor on the walls and ceilings (Is that a big plastic cow hanging over the bar? Of course it is) and a waitstaff forced to wear things like balloon hats. Ignore the silly and focus on the food, which comes in big, heaping mounds of traditional Mexican goodness. Look for anything marked as *Charlie's* (quesadilla, tacos, burrito, and the like) because those are the ones with the special blends of multiple meats like chicken, chorizo, and pork. Meat: good. It's all flavorful and filling and relatively affordable, which makes it all worth the forced zaniness that surrounds you. Bonus points for the outdoor patio overlooking the beautifully landscaped Flamingo pool.

In The Flamingo Las Vegas, 3555 Las Vegas Blvd. S. ℭ **702/522-9254.** www.carlosandcharlies. com. Main courses $12–$26. Daily 8am–2am.

Carmine's ★ ITALIAN   At first glance, the prices at this classic Italian eatery seem outrageous. $35 for lasagna? $38 for veal scaloppine?! But take those prices and divide by at least three, maybe four depending on who the four are, because that's how many each of the family-size serving portions will feed. This branch of the popular New York chain is housed in what is being called the largest restaurant in Vegas, and it certainly feels like it. The two-story space has multiple rooms (including some private ones for groups), a faux outdoor dining patio facing the Roman street scene of the Forum Shops, and a real outdoor one facing the Strip available to rent for special events. The menu is epic, with a host of Americanized Italian favorites from spaghetti and meatballs to porterhouse pizzaiola, all served in those massive, it-takes-a-village sizes. It's obviously not good for a single person or a couple, but it's a great option if you have a big, boisterous group looking to sample and share. While the food may not be groundbreaking, it is all stick-to-the-ribs heart,y and there's certainly enough of it.

In The Forum Shops at Caesars Palace, 3500 Las Vegas Blvd. S. ℭ **702/473-9700.** www. carminesnyc.com. Family-style main courses $28–$86. Sun–Thurs 11am–11pm; Fri–Sat 11am–midnight.

Central Michel Richard ★ ECLECTIC   Washington, D.C., Chef Richard is aiming to reinvent the 24-hour Las Vegas cafe with upscale bistro. The trappings are certainly more luxe; instead of vinyl booths and keno boards, you get a sleekly modern design, full bar, and big windows overlooking the plaza in front of Caesars Palace. The menu is eclectic, with hints of Chef's French cuisine background in the mussels and cheese plate, but options run the gamut from American classics like burgers and steaks to comfort food like spaghetti and meatloaf. Although there are occasional bum notes in the main courses (the meatloaf was a little overdone), delightful "lighter" options like the bacon-and-onion tart or the signature Faux Gras made with chicken liver, butter, and cream keep things moving briskly. Breakfasts include simple fare to full-on feasts (steak and eggs, anyone?), while the late-night dining offers a little bit of everything so you can nosh after a night of clubbing. There's even a "Late Risers" menu of breakfast items served from 11am until 6am, which seems highly apropos for Vegas.

In Caesars Palace, 3570 Las Vegas Blvd. S. © **702/650-5921.** www.centrallv.com. Main courses breakfast $16–$29; lunch $18–$39; dinner $18–$65. Daily 24 hrs.

China Poblano ★ CHINESE/MEXICAN   Mixing Chinese and Mexican cuisines may not seem like the most obvious choice. Chef José Andrés defends the concept with a history lesson about Spanish galleons sailing the Asian seas and bringing spices and fruit to Mexico. Okay, but it still takes a moment to reconcile a menu that has dim sum and tacos on the same page. Still, the place has won culinary awards for its inventiveness, so take the plunge if you trend toward adventure. They don't actually mix the two cuisines—no sweet and sour burritos, darn it—but instead offer small plates that can be mixed, matched, and shared. The success or failure of the concept totally depends on what you order, and the more you stick to similarly sweet or savory or spicy, the better off you'll be. For instance, the Chinese barbecue pork steamed buns have a sticky sweet flavor that goes well with the pork belly with pineapple, but not so much with the spicy *carnitas.* Sadly, mixing two cuisines that aren't famous for their desserts doesn't help here, so skip the flan and the sticky mango rice and go get a cupcake instead.

In The Cosmopolitan of Las Vegas, 3708 Las Vegas Blvd. S. © **702/698-7900.** www.chinapoblano. com. Small plates $5–$22. Daily 11:30am–11:30pm.

Gordon Ramsay Pub & Grill ★ PUB/BRITISH   This split-personality restaurant from the British firebrand chef (of *Hell's Kitchen* fame) takes some of the dishes from his upscale steakhouse at Paris and some of the more casual ones from his BurGR (p. 105) joint at Planet Hollywood and puts them together on one menu. It's probably more successful as the daytime, more affordably priced pub than the fancier, more expensive nighttime grill, but if you're looking for the broadest possible swath of offerings from the Ramsay kitchens, this is the place to go. The burgers are huge and mouthwatering, while the Cornish chicken with a light truffle stuffing is divine. Noteworthy are the anglophile favorites like Shepherd's Pie, Irish beef cheek stew, and traditional fish and chips. Prices are probably higher than they should be for a relatively casual restaurant but certainly cheaper than the sister steakhouse, so it's a good option if you want a Gordon Ramsay fix. Note that some of the seating is in an area open to the casino and a heavily trafficked hallway. Ask for something inside if you want a more peaceful meal.

In Caesars Palace, 3570 Las Vegas Blvd. S. © **877/346-4642.** www.gordonramsay.com. Main courses lunch $14–$27, dinner $21–$67. Sun–Thurs 11am–11pm, Fri–Sat 11am–midnight.

Gilley's ★★ BARBECUE   You don't have to be a cowboy to love this place. Located along the sidewalk with great people-watching, this bright and airy space is done like a roadhouse saloon, all rustic wood and metal, with two big bars. And, yes, they have a mechanical bull. His name is TIten (TI—Treasure Island—see what they did there?) and if you want to work off your lunch, you can ride him for $5 a pop. And you may just need to do that (or stick around for the line-dancing lessons at night) with the massive portions of down-home country cooking served here. Do not miss the award-winning pork-green chili, which is not green at all but filled with succulent, melt-in-your-mouth hunks of pork and not-too-spicy hatch and poblano chiles. The burgers are roughly the size of your head, made of deliciously smoky certified Black Angus beef and just waiting for one of the custom barbecue sauces (the roasted onion is our favorite). The rest of the menu is waistline-expanding, with really good BBQ, fried chicken, chicken-fried steak, ribs, and more—most of it served with two sides, including such favorites as molasses baked beans, white cheddar–and–green chili grits, and corn on the cob. It's all moderately priced, which is not to say exactly cheap, but the combination of tasty food, friendly service, and a great location make it worth putting on your ten-gallon hat and moseying on down.

At Treasure Island, 3300 Las Vegas Blvd. S. ✆ **702/894-7111.** www.gilleyslasvegas.com. Main courses $9–$35. Daily 11am–midnight.

Guy Fieri's Vegas Kitchen ★ AMERICAN   Pretty much everything you need to know about this place can be encapsulated by one of their signature dishes: a bacon mac and cheese burger. If that horrifies you, skip to the next restaurant. If that intrigues you, even if it's in a horrified kind of way, then read on. Food Network staple Fieri has brought his trademark high-calorie, crowd-pleasing cooking to Vegas with this sunny space that mixes loud music, a rustic rock-and-roll aesthetic (think tattoos and cowhide), and a down-home service that encourages alcohol-fueled frivolity (check out the long list of barrel aged, "frozen" shots). It's primarily a big burger, BBQ, and fried things menu, so you may want to consider skipping the outrageous appetizers like the pepperoni wrapped breadsticks with cheese fondue topped with tomatoes and olive oil. Or don't, they are really good. Portions are huge—if you can finish any of the main courses you deserve an award or perhaps a juice fast—and messy. The aforementioned mac and cheese burger is almost impossible to eat, but has a fascinating mix of flavors using a perfect beef patty done to charcoal perfection. Save room for dessert—or maybe take it to go.

In The Quad, 3535 Las Vegas Blvd. S. ✆ **702/731-3311.** www.guyfieri.com. Main courses $13–$18. Daily 10am–2am.

Hash House a Go Go ★★★ AMERICAN   Back when this place was located on the west side of town, we told you to go but we understood if it was too far to drive or cab. Now that there are multiple locations, including one at the Quad on the Strip, one at the Rio just off the Strip, and another at the Plaza Downtown, you only have yourself to blame if you miss it. Yes, you could go to a breakfast buffet and pay $15 for scrambled eggs warmed under a heat lamp, but why not experience the "twisted farm food" here instead? The brainchild of a couple of Midwest natives, breakfast (and dinner) go beyond the typical into realms of the almost unimaginable. Pancakes (traditional buttermilk to coconut mango) are the size of large pizzas, and waffles are the size of checkerboards (and some come with bacon baked right inside). The signature hashes come in varieties from corned beef to meatloaf, and "scrambles" throw everything but the kitchen sink into a frying pan and serve it hot to your table that way. Been out partying too late? Try the O'Hare of the Dog special, a 24-ounce Budweiser served in a paper bag with a side of bacon.

Lunch and dinner add salads, sandwiches, burgers, fried chicken, pot pie, and more, all with the same fun sensibility and a farm-fresh flavor that you can practically taste before you put it in your mouth. But it's breakfast that we dream about as we write this. *Note:* Check the website for contact info and directions for other locations.

In The Quad, 3535 Las Vegas Blvd. S. ✆ **702/254-4646.** www.hashhouseagogo.com. Main courses $10–$39. Daily 24 hrs.

5

WHERE TO EAT

Mid-Strip

Holstein's Shakes & Buns ★★ AMERICAN   We have to admit that we are getting a little tired of the gourmet burger trend. Don't get us wrong—we like burgers as much as the next guy, but we're usually just as happy with the ones that are ordered through a clown's mouth as we are with ones that are topped with foie gras and cost more than most fine meals. Sometimes, even more happy. But Holstein's has reaffirmed our faith in the concept by tempering the fancy with fun. They've got everything from classic burgers (love the sirloin with smoked bacon and garlic-chive aioli) to Kobe beef with tempura avocado, beef topped with brisket (beef on beef!), tandoori chicken with apricot-date chutney, and duck stuffed with, yes, foie gras. Not as good as those served at the famed L.A. restaurant Roscoe's, but still darned tasty. And, of course, don't forget the shake part of their name—gourmet-worthy ice-cream concoctions that can be ordered straight or spiked with various booze options. Note that the bar out front and its proximity to the Marquee nightclub mean that late-night dining can be a loud experience, so lunch might be a better option. Photo op: you and the colorfully painted cow sculptures they use as decor.

In The Cosmopolitan of Las Vegas, 3708 Las Vegas Blvd. S. ✆ **702/698-7940.** www.holsteinslv. com. Main courses $12–$30. Daily 11am–2am.

Lagasse's Stadium ★ AMERICAN   This is what you get when you mix Emeril Lagasse's cooking with sports of every conceivable variety. Whether it's a good thing probably depends on which of those ingredients you care more about. Emeril fans will find a mix of some of his trademark New Orleans–style dishes (shrimp po' boy, Creole sausage and peppers) but mostly it's fairly standard pub grub: soups, salads, pizza, burgers, sandwiches, barbecue, and the like. While everything we sampled was certainly good, it may be disappointing to those looking for a true Lagasse experience. Sports fans will find more than 100 HDTVs showing everything from the NFL to girls' high school basketball, and just about all of it can be bet on at the sports book conveniently located in the newly redecorated main dining room. They'll probably love it and not care a whit about the chef who designed the menu. Prices are affordable until you get to the table minimums ($25–$50 per person, depending on if you choose a table on the main floor, the upper mezzanine, or the big comfy couches in a stadium-like setting), and it's worth noting that sports fans and the games they watch are not terribly conducive to a quiet dining experience.

In The Palazzo, 3325 Las Vegas Blvd. S. ✆ **702/607-2665.** www.emerils.com. Main courses $14–$34. Daily 11am–10pm.

Mon Ami Gabi ★★★ BISTRO   Although dinner is certainly a good option, lunch is the primary reason we want to send you to this charming French bistro, especially if you can get a seat on the Strip-facing patio or in the sunny garden atrium. You may be tempted to just people-watch for an hour or so, interspersed with viewings of the Bellagio Fountains across the street. But pay attention to the plates coming to your table, filled with safely Americanized versions of Parisian cafe cuisine, including sandwiches (Croque Monsieur is really just a deliciously gooey ham sandwich), crepes, salads, quiche, hamburgers, steaks with French fries (sorry, *pommes frites*), and more. The baked goat cheese appetizer, served with a zesty tomato purée and garlic bread, is a must, and the ham-and-cheese crepe is a delightfully light lunch option. Dinner adds more substantial entrees (and higher prices), while breakfast serves up everything from omelets to made-from-scratch waffles with a variety of berries and even chocolate to accompany their fluffy goodness.

In Paris Las Vegas, 3655 Las Vegas Blvd. S. ✆ **702/944-4224.** www.monamigabi.com. Main courses $10–$26 lunch, $13–$40 dinner. Sun–Thurs 7am–11pm; Fri–Sat 7am–midnight.

Payard Patisserie & Bistro ★★★ BISTRO   Breakfast here offers one of the few real remaining bargains in Vegas, given quality-to-price ratio. Surely it can't last, considering the state of things in modern-day Vegas, but for now you can look forward to a continental breakfast like no other. Just $22 gets you two of their heavenly pastries (perhaps unsurprisingly, the chocolate croissant is our favorite), fruit or yogurt, coffee, and juice. Because the chef has his roots in Paris, these buttery bits of brioche and croissant are as good as any you could consume by the Seine. One can easily spend that much on a breakfast buffet or a lunch entree elsewhere in town, but there is no comparison for quality. Lunch is light and of the French variety and dinner is more substantial (steaks and the like), but it's the breakfast and the pastry counter that you most want to pay attention to.

In Caesars Palace, 3570 Las Vegas Blvd. S. ✆ **702/731-7972.** www.caesarspalace.com. Breakfast $16–$22; lunch $16–$28; dinner $16–$30. Daily 6:30–11:30am breakfast, 11:30am–2:30pm lunch. Dinner Wed–Sun 5–10pm. Pastry counter daily 6am–11pm.

Public House ★ GASTROPUB   The gastropub trend is already threatening to collapse in on itself, with waves of self-consciously hip eateries mixing beer lists that are longer than the walk from your hotel room to the casino and food that attempts to be epicurean fun but usually just ends up being twee and bland. This one, however, is a prime example of what can happen when the booze and the food have the creativity and execution to back up the bluster. At first glance, the epic beer list (four pages of really small print) and some of the "with the what now?" menu selections (poutine, pork rinds, duck rillettes) may make you groan, but dig past it for some true rewards. Ask their in-house cicerone (the beer version of a sommelier) to suggest a brew and then try the brilliant pork fillet, juicy and fork-cutting tender, or the roasted free-ranch chicken, which could challenge Zankou for "best chicken ever." Lamb pierogies are another interesting option, but if you can't handle the offbeat offerings, just go for the pub burger served with bacon marmalade and Gruyère cheese. Or just keep having the cicerone bring you beer—after a few of them, the grilled octopus, roasted bone marrow, or foie gras pâté may sound as everyday as a turkey sandwich. Try to get a table in the quieter side dining room unless you appreciate an "energetic" dining ambience.

In The Palazzo, 3327 Las Vegas Blvd. S. ✆ **702/407-5310.** www.publichouselv.com. Main courses $14–$44. Sun–Thurs 11am–11pm; Fri–Sat 11am–midnight.

Serendipity 3 ★ AMERICAN   Yes, it has the famous foot-long hot dogs from the New York City original, along with a full menu of quite good cafe food (including some very well-made hamburgers on freshly baked spiral buns), but it's really the frozen hot chocolate and other signature desserts that are bringing you here, right? That frozen hot chocolate, so beloved by generations of New Yorkers and tourists alike, is served in a giant overflowing glass with two straws. If that's not decadent enough for your sensibilities, perhaps you want to go for the Treasure Chest, made of chocolate and filled with cookies, cakes, ice cream, and more. It's $93, but it serves four! Still not hitting the over-the-top mark for you? How about the Golden Opulence dessert, recognized as the most expensive in the country? A cool $1,000 will get you a sundae made from rare ice creams and chocolate and topped with edible gold leaf. What else are you going to do with that slot-machine jackpot? A Strip-side dining patio provides some fantastic crowd-watching views on temperate days.

In Caesars Palace, 3570 Las Vegas Blvd. S. ✆ **877/346-4642.** www.caesarspalace.com. Reservations not accepted. Main courses $10–$20; desserts $10–$1,000. Sun–Thurs 8am–11pm; Fri–Sat 8am–midnight.

Sugar Factory ★★ AMERICAN Perhaps most famous for their celebrity-endorsed, over-the-top lollipops (Britney Spears and Nicole Scherzinger have signature versions), Sugar Factory has moved up in the world with this multifunction, full-service restaurant, bar, lounge, gift shop, and, yes, candy store. A fantastic location right on the Strip allows for an almost panoramic view of the throngs of people and the Bellagio Fountains across the street. There is a wide selection of menu choices, including signature crepes (try the ham and brie topped with apples as a brunch option) and other breakfast items, soups, salads, sandwiches, burgers, pizza, pastas, and even entrees like steak or pork chops. Start with the fried macaroni and cheese, served with a delicate tomato-herb sauce, and end with one of their deliriously iced cupcakes (because in Vegas there are no calories). Despite the gimmicky nature, the food is surprisingly good; it's one of the best theme joints in town. Afterward, visit the chocolate lounge, where the bar has built-in fondue heaters, and then blow all your casino winnings in the candy shop; Britney reportedly dropped three grand on one visit. To put it briefly, this place is sweet! (Sorry, it had to be done.) *Note:* There is a second outlet at the Town Square shopping center just south of the Strip at 6605 Las Vegas Blvd. S.

In Paris Las Vegas, 3655 Las Vegas Blvd. S. ℂ **702/331-5100.** www.sugarfactory.com. Main courses $10–$28. Daily 24 hrs.

Inexpensive

Cypress Street Marketplace ★★ FOOD COURT Often when we go to a Vegas buffet (and we are not alone in this), we sigh over all the choices, all those different kinds of pretty good, if not better, cuisines there for the taking, but of course we can't possibly try everything. And yet, in some of the higher-priced venues, we are charged as if we can. Here, in this modern version of the classic food court, it's sort of like being at a well-stocked buffet: There's darn fine barbecue (including North Carolina–influenced pulled pork), custom-made sandwiches, Asian favorites including sushi, decent New York pizza, plump Chicago hot dogs, peel-and-eat shrimp and lobster chowder, a bargain-priced salad bar, plus pastries and even wine. And with the range of food, an entire family with very different tastes will all find something satisfactory.

In Caesars Palace, 3570 Las Vegas Blvd. S. ℂ **702/731-7110.** www.caesarspalace.com. Most items under $15. Daily 11am–11pm.

Earl of Sandwich ★★ SANDWICHES It seems credulity-straining, but the sandwich was something that had to be invented, and thus someone got their simple yet ingenious idea named after them. At least, so the story goes, so sufficiently accepted as historical lore that it carries enough weight for the intrepid inventor's descendant, the 11th Earl of Sandwich, to lend his name to a chain of sandwich shops. It's a gimmick, but a good one, and so is the food. The eponymous, and largely excellent, sandwiches are served warm (wraps are cold) on bread made for the shop and include varieties such as grilled Swiss, blue, and brie with applewood-smoked bacon and roast beef with horseradish cream and cheddar cheese. There are also complex if unoriginal salads, smoothies, and breakfast sandwiches. Portions aren't huge, but it's not a problem if you are devoted to Vegas-size meals; the low prices make it possible to order two of everything if appetites demand. *Note:* There is a second location at The Palms Casino Resort, 4321 Flamingo Rd.

In Planet Hollywood Resort & Casino, 3667 Las Vegas Blvd. S. ℂ **702/463-0259.** www.earlof sandwichusa.com. Most items under $8. AE, MC, V. Daily 24 hrs.

Gordon Ramsay BurGR ★★ BURGERS   If you want to visit a Gordon Ramsay restaurant in Vegas but can't afford the high-end steakhouse or even the kind of pricey pub, try this casually cheeky burger joint instead. The *Hell's Kitchen* flame theme is cute, complete with a wall of fire, but it's the burgers that really make a statement. You can go traditional (with American cheese and red tomato) to extreme (fiery jalapeño and asadero cheese) or even embrace your inner anglophile with burgers topped with things like figgy-onion jam or English sharp cheddar and mango chutney, all juicy, generously proportioned, and relatively affordable. Don't miss the milkshakes, which feature multiple layers of sweet and creamy complementary flavors in one glass. Genius!

In Planet Hollywood Resort & Casino, 3667 Las Vegas Blvd. S. ℂ **702/785-5555.** www.gordon ramsay.com. Main courses $14–$20. Sun–Thurs 11am–midnight; Fri–Sat 11am–2am.

KGB: Kerry's Gourmet Burgers ★★★ BURGERS   Finding the best burger in a particular city is like a vision quest; a culinary rite of passage for gastronomes. That quest should start and end right here at rock-'n'-roll chef Kerry Simon's entry into the crowded gourmet burger market. You can build your own from dozens of meats (beef, chicken, turkey, lamb, and so on), bun, cheese, and topping choices, or you can put your faith in their signature concoctions like the barbecue burger (topped with smoky applewood bacon, Gouda, and crispy onion straws) or Sloppy Joe burger (topped with tangy short-rib meat—meat on meat!). The appetizers, like deep-fried macaroni and cheese with white-cheddar sauce or the insanely delicious waffle fry nachos (topped with that killer Sloppy Joe), are tempting, but the burgers are huge, so don't get filled up on the starters. A casually fun atmosphere with its own custom-designed music soundtrack and relatively moderate prices are great but will seem like icing on the cake once you take a bite of the best burgers in Vegas.

In Harrah's, 3475 Las Vegas Blvd. S. ℂ **702/369-5065.** www.kerrysimon.com. Main courses $13–$17. AE, DC, DISC, MC, V. Sun–Thurs 11am–11pm; Fri–Sat 11am–midnight.

munchbar ★★★ AMERICAN   This small eatery tucked into a corner near Caesars' race and sports book appears to be nothing more than a glorified snack bar. But don't judge a cafe by its cover. This casual diner serves up some of the most deliriously enjoyable food in town at prices that will leave you with plenty left over for other pursuits—or you could just order more food. With a nod to the name, it's mostly munchie-type stuff such as wings, sliders, and the like, with some additional "Big Munch" items including salads, burgers, and tacos. Start with the mini–grilled cheese sandwiches served with a creamy tomato dipping sauce (comfort-food heaven) or the Pizzadilla, which is basically a quesadilla stuffed with pizza fixings, then move on to one of their juicy hamburgers, so loaded with fixings atop sweet, soft buns that you will never want to eat at McDonald's again. Don't forget about dessert—huge soft-serve ice-cream cones and sundaes that are too big for normal human beings to consume, but so good you'll want to try. They also offer takeout service in case you want to grab and go.

In Caesars Palace, 3570 Las Vegas Blvd. S. ℂ **888/686-8624.** www.munchgroup.com. Main courses $9–$17. Sun–Thurs 11am–2am; Fri–Sat 11am–4am.

Pink's ★★★ DELI   The hot dogs served by Pink's are legendary in Los Angeles— almost mythic, in fact. In business at the same location for more than 70 years, the little shack draws hordes, with lines down the block turning peak dining times into waits of more than an hour. Why? Well, the all-beef dogs, cooked to "snapping" perfection, are certainly good, but it's the toppings that make it different: chili, bacon, guacamole, mushroom and Swiss, sauerkraut, pastrami, nacho cheese—you name it and they probably put it on the bun. This Vegas location at Planet Hollywood is Pink's second full outlet, and while the lines aren't as crazy (except for late at night when the post-nightclub crowds need a nosh), the dogs are just as good. All the traditional versions are on the menu—the bacon chili cheese, piled high with tomatoes and onions, is virtually impossible to pick up and a favorite of ours—but they also throw in some Vegas-only options like the Showgirl (relish, onions, bacon, tomato, sauerkraut, and sour cream), the Vegas Strip (two dogs in one bun with guacamole and jalapeños), and the Planet Hollywood (a Polish with grilled onions and mushrooms, bacon, and nacho cheese). There are also burgers, burritos, and some nonbeef varieties, but that's just background noise as far as we are concerned. Nothing on the menu is over $10, which only adds to the allure.

At Planet Hollywood Resort & Casino, 3663 Las Vegas Blvd. S. © **702/405-4711.** www.planet hollywoodresort.com. Main courses $6–$10. Sun–Thurs 10:30am–midnight; Fri–Sat 10:30am–3am.

NORTH STRIP

Expensive

Bartolotta Ristorante di Mare ★★★ ITALIAN/SEAFOOD James Beard Foundation Award–winning chef Paul Bartolotta's gorgeously designed, multilevel, indoor/outdoor space is proof that celebrity chefs are all very well and good, but it's not the same as having them on the premises. In this case, the result is as authentic Italian food as one can find outside Italy. The fish is flown in daily straight from the Mediterranean to his Vegas kitchen, and you can expect a wide array from the familiar to the virtually unknown; the server will walk you through the choices, all lovingly displayed in a tableside case. Most are prepared in light butter and/or olive oil and filleted at your table, allowing the rich, decidedly nonfishy taste to burst through. A Mediterranean sea bass seemed like a safe choice, but we were rewarded with a robust flavor that would convert all but the most vehement of anti-seafood campaigners. Langoustines are grilled to charred smoky rightness, and seared scallops with porcini mushrooms in browned butter are what scallops should be. Pastas are perfect, especially the *maccheroni,* a hand-rolled spaghetti in Tuscan meat sauce. And don't miss dessert (like we need to tell you that), especially the selection of house-made ice cream, gelato, and sorbet. Prices are palpitation-inducing, but this is one of those rare instances where it is totally worth it, especially if you can get a table alfresco alongside the reflecting pool. Heaven.

In Wynn Las Vegas, 3131 Las Vegas Blvd. S © **888/352-3463** or 702/248-3463. www.wynnlasvegas. com. Main courses $25–$110. Daily 5:30–10pm.

Sinatra ★★★ ITALIAN Old Blue Eyes is the theme here, with memorabilia (including an Oscar and a Grammy), giant pictures of Frank, and even a few of his favorite menu items to choose from. But this swank restaurant is so much more than its gimmick. The dining room is one of the most gorgeous in town, with giant windows facing a garden patio and plush, eclectic, vaguely retro furnishings encouraging the kind of laid-back dining experience that is rare in this rush-to-get-the-check town. Chef Theo Schoenegger was born and raised in Italy, gaining fame in the U.S. during his stint as the executive chef at Los Angeles–based Patina, and his short but satisfying selection of northern Italian dishes is bursting with fresh flavors. Start with the prosciutto appetizer, almost sweet with a fire-roasted pepper accompaniment, then move

North Strip Restaurants

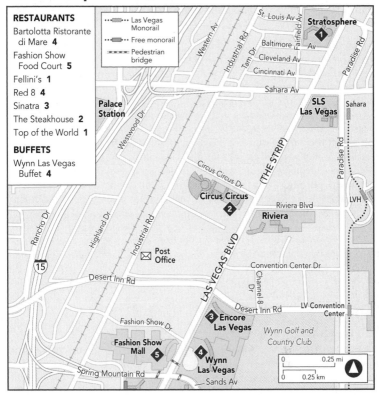

RESTAURANTS

Bartolotta Ristorante di Mare **4**

Fashion Show Food Court **5**

Fellini's **1**

Red 8 **4**

Sinatra **3**

The Steakhouse **2**

Top of the World **1**

BUFFETS

Wynn Las Vegas Buffet **4**

······ Las Vegas Monorail

······ Free monorail

▪▪▪▪▪ Pedestrian bridge

on to the *agnolotti*, a handmade ravioli pasta stuffed with ricotta cheese and drenched in a buttery asparagus sauce. Or go full-theme with Frank's beloved spaghetti and clams or osso buco "My Way," braised veal with risotto. Allow the expert sommelier to pair the perfect glass of *vino* with whatever you are having.

In Encore Las Vegas, 3121 Las Vegas Blvd. S. *©* **702/248-3463.** www.wynnlasvegas.com. Main courses $27–$55. Sun–Thurs 5:30–10pm; Fri–Sat 5:30-10:30pm.

The Steakhouse ★ STEAK Most of the steakhouses in Las Vegas have fallen prey to modernization, adding faux-elegant lounge-worthy design schemes, fancy extraneous dishes, cocktail menus, and prices that push into the stratosphere. What happened to the traditional meat–and-potatoes steakhouse? It's right here, my friends. In business for more three decades, the Steakhouse at Circus Circus does things the old-fashioned way, with a dark cigar club–style design (think high-backed booths and faux animal heads on the wall), familial but professional service, classic cuts cooked over a wood flame, and prices that won't make you dip into your gambling budget. Regarding the latter, it may seem like $50 is not exactly cheap, but unlike most Strip steakhouses, the price includes soup or salad and a side dish, things that will cost you extra just about everywhere else. Ask the server for off-menu specials that make things even more affordable. It's a retro delight in a town that currently seems ruthless about weeding out such things.

In Circus Circus, 2880 Las Vegas Blvd. S. © **702/794-3767.** www.circuscircus.com. Main courses $32–$77. Sun–Fri 4–10pm; Sat 4-11pm.

Top of the World ★★ CONTINENTAL   It really is impossible to beat the views from this revolving restaurant more than 800 feet up atop the Stratosphere Tower, but for a long time the food didn't live up to the surroundings. Good news: A revised menu is much more interesting, the prices are much more affordable (albeit still expensive), and the food is much better. Although there are shades of a steakhouse in the offerings, they go way beyond those borders with eye-catching options throughout the menu. The menu changes seasonally, but look for interesting items like a roasted pork belly appetizer served with an Argentinian chimichurri sauce, or maybe the grilled portobello mushroom with roasted red pepper and buffalo mozzarella. The steaks are tempting— the filet with a red wine–mushroom sauce is especially noteworthy—but consider the more unique offerings such as the pork tenderloin wrapped in bacon and served with apple-and-cranberry chutney or the rack of lamb with Moroccan couscous. Wine fans should put their faith in the very talented sommelier and extensive grape list. And did we mention that view?! It takes about an hour and 20 minutes to make the full rotation, and the best part is when you're under the Sky Jump platform so you see people dropping off the top of the building as you dine (and perhaps laugh at the level of their insanity).

In Stratosphere Casino Hotel, 2000 Las Vegas Blvd. S. © **702/380-7777.** www.topoftheworldlv. com. Main courses lunch $25–$34, dinner $40–$80. Daily 11am–3:30pm; Sun–Thurs 4:30–10pm; Fri–Sat 4:30–10:30pm.

Moderate

Fellini's ★ ITALIAN   A Vegas institution in its original but now-closed West Las Vegas location, much beloved by in-the-know locals, Fellini's is a classic Italian restaurant—you know, gloopy red sauce, garlicky cheesy bread—which isn't meant to be an insult at all. It might not be ambitious, but it is reliable and more than satisfying. Fellini's does a strong version of pasta (rigatoni, in this case) *amatriciana,* and they are generous with the pancetta. And while some Italian food purists would shudder at the gnocchi with tenderloin tips, topped with Gorgonzola and shallot cream sauce, they are just missing out, that's all. The well-proportioned menu offers a variety of options from osso buco to basic pizza, and, given the prices, that makes it a good option for families with a similar range of tastes and needs. Put on your hiking shoes to get to the place, which is located in the furthest back corner of the casino, practically in another county from the parking garage.

In Stratosphere Casino Hotel, 2000 Las Vegas Blvd S. © **702/383-4859.** www.fellinislv.com. Main courses $24–$33. Sun–Thurs 5–11pm; Fri–Sat 5–midnight.

Red 8 ★★ ASIAN   Such a relief, in the otherwise pricey Wynn, to find a dining spot that is both good and affordable. This visual standout is a small cafe—as you wander by, you think "Cool! Some of the tables overlook the casino!" Then you realize those are *all* of the tables—with a decor that screams the place's colorful name. It's popular, given the location, size, and pricing—not to mention the quality of the food. Covering a sort of Pan-Asiatic terrain, look for noodle dishes both wet (soup) and dry (pan-fried), rice, Korean barbecue, Mongolian beef, vegetarian options, and more. There are some "market price" specials that can quadruple a bill pretty fast, but

5

North Strip

WHERE TO EAT

otherwise, this is a pretty budget-friendly option unless you go crazy with the dim sum. And why wouldn't you?

In Wynn Las Vegas, 3131 Las Vegas Blvd. S. ℰ **702/770-3380.** www.wynnlasvegas.com. Main courses $15–$38. Sun–Thurs 11:30am–midnight; Fri–Sat 11:30am–1am.

DOWNTOWN

Expensive

Andiamo Steakhouse ★★ STEAK/SEAFOOD   Joe Vicari's small chain of Italian steakhouses have been a staple in the Detroit area for more than two decades, and if they are as good as this Las Vegas outpost, it's easy to understand why. The room has an old-school, upscale vibe, with a grotto-like entrance, gorgeously soft-lit booths and tables, and servers wearing white coats. Although it's all-new as of 2013, it feels like it has been around forever; the kind of place where you'd expect the Rat Pack to hang out. They would eat well, that's for sure. The menu is part steakhouse, with various chops and seafood, and part Italian, with several specialty pastas. The steaks from Pat LaFrieda and Stockyard Premium are downright fantastic on their own, but add the signature zip sauce—which is basically butter gravy—and it sends it into the stratosphere. The gnocchi is a highlight from the pasta side. Save room for desserts; all lovingly displayed on a serving cart that you will want to try to sneak out the front door.

In The D Las Vegas, 301 E. Fremont St. ℰ **702/388-2220.** www.thed.com. Main courses $20–$65. Nightly 5pm–11pm.

Hugo's Cellar ★ CONTINENTAL   Hugo's Cellar is indeed in a cellar, or at least below street level in the Four Queens hotel. No, they aren't ashamed of it—quite the opposite. This is their pride and joy, and highly regarded by the locals for more than two decades. This is Old School Vegas Classy Dining. Each female guest is given a red rose when she enters the restaurant—the first of a series of nice touches. The meal is full of ceremony as well, perfectly delivered by a well-trained and cordial waitstaff. Salads, included in the price, are prepared at your table, from a cart full of choices. In Vegas style, though, most choices are on the calorie-intensive side, ranging from chopped egg and blue cheese to pine nuts and bay shrimp. Unfortunately, the main courses are not all that novel (various cuts of meat, seafood, and chicken prepared in different ways), but satisfying in a classic Vegas dining experience kind of way. The fact that salad and a small dessert are included makes an initially hefty-seeming price tag appear a bit more reasonable, especially compared to Strip establishments that aren't much better and can cost the same for just the entree. Great retro fun.

In the Four Queens, 202 Fremont St. ℰ **702/385-4011.** www.hugoscellar.com. Main courses $36–$52. Daily 5:30–10:30pm.

Oscar's Beef Booze Broads ★★ STEAK   Located in the iconic dome at the Plaza Hotel in Downtown Las Vegas, this traditional steakhouse is the brainchild of flamboyant former Las Vegas Mayor Oscar Goodman. An unrepentant imbiber, the Mayor's quote on the menu reads, in part, "drink a few too many, and have some fun." All of that is easy to do here, even though the dining part of the offerings don't necessarily break any new ground. Steak and seafood rule the menu, but you can find some interesting options here and there like a bone-in veal chop billed as "Wiener" schnitzel and roasted corn brûlée as a side. Prices are downright reasonable compared to most Strip steakhouses and the service is fantastic, but it's really the ambience—with an unparalleled view of the Glitter Gulch light and sound show across the street—that makes this a one-of-a-kind Vegas experience.

In The Plaza, 1 Main St. ℂ **702/386-7227.** www.oscarslv.com. Main courses $25–$45. Daily 5pm–close.

Moderate

La Comida ★★ MEXICAN   Michael Morton, son of famed steakhouse impresario Arnie, had several restaurants and clubs in Las Vegas but now has refocused his empire on this foodie version of a Mexican joint in Downtown Las Vegas. You have to admire the space for a minute, with its flowery garden entrance, big windows overlooking an outdoor dining patio, and an eclectic, rustic casa adobe interior featuring roughhewn woods, unfinished walls, and a gorgeous dark-wood bar. Then when you are done appreciating that bar, order a margarita from it to get yourself started; they are packed with fresh flavors, including one with passion fruit. On the food front, you may be tempted to skip the appetizers and soups, but you'd be doing yourself a disservice by not trying the *tortilla con pollo* soup, done with a creamy tomato base and spiced just perfectly so. Let your server guide you to the best main courses, but be on the lookout for the *pollo al horno,* a half chicken breast done *mixiote* style with a sweet chocolate mole. And cross your fingers that they are serving the *tres leches,* a vanilla-bean cinnamon cake soaked in condensed, evaporated, and sweet milk. This will restore your faith in Mexican desserts after too much flan.

100 Sixth Ave. (btw. Fremont St. and Carson Ave.). ℂ **702/463-9900.** www.facebook.com/lacomidalv. Main courses $15–$25. Mon–Thurs 11:30am–11pm; Fri–Sat 11:30am–2am.

Lola's: A Louisiana Kitchen ★★★ CAJUN/CREOLE   Regional cuisine often inspires passionate arguments about authenticity, but you'll rarely find anyone more deeply protective of their food than those who love Cajun and Creole cooking. They will say, often with a fervor reserved for tent revivals, that you simply cannot get authentic Louisiana cooking outside of Louisiana. These folks have probably never been to Lola's. Run by a New Orleans native, this charming bistro would be right at home in the Garden District or French Quarter, with Big Easy favorites like jambalaya, po' boys, gumbo, red beans and rice, gulf shrimp, and blackened catfish, among others. Forget how genuine the food is for a moment (the po' boys are served on the revered Liedenheimer bread, flown in from NOLA) and just relish how flavorful and masterfully prepared the dishes are. The roast beef debris po' boy is a work of sweet-and-sour genius, while the traditional bread pudding will have you asking for seconds. *Laissez les bons temps rouler,* indeed! Note that a recent appearance on the Food Network's *Diners, Drive-Ins and Dives* has turned an already-popular place into a destination that sometimes involves long waits for a table. *Note:* A second, bigger location is now open in the Summerlin area near the JW Marriott at 1220 N. Town Center Drive.

201 W. Charleston Ave, no. 101 (at Grand Central Pkwy.). ℂ **702/227-5652.** www.lolaslasvegas.com. Main courses $8–$25. Mon–Thurs 11am–9pm; Fri 11am–10pm; Sat noon–10pm.

Stewart + Ogden ★★ AMERICAN   The garage-sale funky furnishings and casual ambience belie the creative menu here, which goes far beyond what you'd find at a typical breakfast-lunch-dinner restaurant. Sure, you've got eggs and pancakes at breakfast, but you can also get things like a Croque Madame, a French ham and cheese sandwich covered in a creamy white béchamel sauce, and cinnamon roll waffles (exactly what it sounds like). At lunch you can get a salad or traditional burger in

WHERE TO EAT | Downtown

Downtown Restaurants

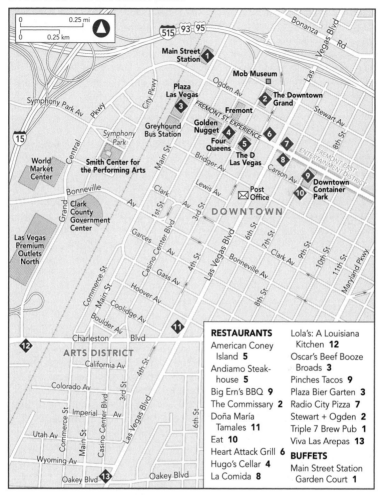

RESTAURANTS

American Coney Island **5**

Andiamo Steakhouse **5**

Big Ern's BBQ **9**

The Commissary **2**

Doña María Tamales **11**

Eat **10**

Heart Attack Grill **6**

Hugo's Cellar **4**

La Comida **8**

Lola's: A Louisiana Kitchen **12**

Oscar's Beef Booze Broads **3**

Pinches Tacos **9**

Plaza Bier Garten **3**

Radio City Pizza **7**

Stewart + Ogden **2**

Triple 7 Brew Pub **1**

Viva Las Arepas **13**

BUFFETS

Main Street Station Garden Court **1**

addition to "loco moco," a Hawaiian version of a burger topped with fried egg and brown rice. Dinner has roasted chicken and spaghetti and meatballs, but also a divine "Over the Top" mac and cheese made with bacon, caramelized onions, and five different cheeses. As if this wasn't interesting enough, check out the prices, which are a fraction of what you'd pay for lesser meals on the Strip. A Downtown must-visit.

At the Downtown Grand, 206 N. 3rd St. (at Ogden Ave.) ✆ **702/719-5100**. www.downtowngrand. com. Main courses breakfast $5–$12; lunch $5–$14; dinner $9–$29. Daily 7am–1am.

Inexpensive

American Coney Island ★ DELI/HOT DOGS   The original Detroit version of this all-American classic has been in business since 1917, started by a Greek immigrant whose grandchildren brought the simple but satisfying concept to Vegas. There

111

are only a few choices on the menu—a Coney Island dog, which comes with chili (no beans); gyros in a soft pita with homemade tzatziki; and Coney Loose Burger, which is basically ground-up hamburger meat with special seasonings served in a hot dog bun. It's the kind of seaside boardwalk or summer BBQ food of your youth (before we worried about things like cholesterol and calories), and it is the perfect antidote to the too-fancy-for-its-own-good cuisine on the Strip. The fact that you can fill up on a flavorful meal for under $10 is a nice bonus.

In The D Las Vegas, 301 E. Fremont St. 🕻 **702/388-2400.** www.thed.com. Main courses under $5. Daily 24 hrs.

Bier Garten ★★ AMERICAN   The indoors portion of this restaurant at the Plaza is uninteresting; basically a counter for orders and tables shared with fast-food outlets like McDonald's. But go outside and there's a beautiful backyard setting complete with real grass, picnic tables, trellises, and TVs. It's a completely anachronistic, and completely welcome, sight in the concrete and neon jungle that is Downtown Las Vegas. The food is delightful too, with a series of signature sausages and "wursts" that are named after famed Vegas casinos. Try the Stardust, a German bratwurst topped with caramelized onions and sauerkraut; or the Hacienda, a sweet Italian sausage with peppers, onions, and a spicy relish. You can also build your own with two dozen choices of meat (bratwurst, Louisiana hot link, Andouille, and more), toppings (jalapeños, onions, and more), add-ons (fried egg, Cheese Wiz, Cajun blue cheese), and buns. Don't forget the fries, mainly because you can add a variety of sauces for dipping, including German mustard, *chimichurri*, and *sriracha* ketchup.

At The Plaza Hotel & Casino, 1 S. Main St. (at Fremont St.). 🕻 **702/386-2110.** www.biergartenlv. com. Main courses all under $10. Daily 11am–midnight.

Big Ern's BBQ ★★ BARBECUE   BBQ snobs are justly suspicious of anything in the genre produced outside of the southern U.S., but a few bites of Big Ern's and the prejudices may start to fall away as easily as meat off the bone. Pure smoky goodness comes in the form of ribs, brisket, ham, pulled pork, chicken, and more, served with a sweet molasses sauce that vinegar lovers may not appreciate but everyone else will. Add in the traditional sides (baked beans, mac and cheese, corn bread, and the like) and this is as authentic an experience as you'll find west of Texas. The restaurant itself is microscopic; there's only room for about a dozen people inside, but you can eat at any of the tables outside, which is where real BBQ should be consumed anyway. Affordable prices are like a bonus with 'cue this good.

In the Downtown Container Park, 707 Fremont St. (at 7th St.). 🕻 **702/834-7845.** www.bigernsbbq. com. Main courses $7–14. Sun–Thurs 11am–11pm; Fri–Sat 11am–1am.

The Commissary ★★★ LATIN   A Latin kitchen done as a food court, the fun starts with the funky, mismatched decor that gives the sunny room a decidedly casual BoHo vibe. Order at a variety of stations and they'll bring the food to you, starting with a list of fantastic *tortas* (the Cubano with ham and *carnitas* is especially noteworthy). Rotisserie chicken and Latin brisket are perfect, with the latter a hot and spicy delight; both come in sizes that can feed an entire family. You can also make your own tacos, bowls, and burritos, or go in a completely different direction with burgers, hot dogs, or salads. Food this good shouldn't be this cheap, especially in Vegas, but check out those prices.

At the Downtown Grand, 206 N. 3rd St. (at Ogden Ave.). 🕻 **702/719-5100.** www.downtowngrand. com. Main courses $5–$12. Daily 6am–midnight.

Doña María Tamales ★ MEXICAN Decorated with Tijuana-style quilt work and calendars, this quintessential Mexican diner is convenient to both the north end of the Strip and Downtown. The cooks use lots of lard, lots of cheese, and lots of sauce. As a result, the food is really good—and really fattening. Yep, the folks who did those health reports showing how bad Mexican food can be for your heart probably did some research here. The fat just makes it all the better, in our opinion. Locals apparently agree; even at lunchtime, the place is crowded. You will start off with homemade chips and a spicy salsa served in a mortar. Meals are so large that it shouldn't be a problem getting full just ordering off the sides, which can make this even more of a budget-friendly option. Naturally, the specialty is the fantastic tamales, which come in red, green, cheese, or sweet. There are also excellent enchiladas, *chiles rellenos,* burritos, and fajitas. All dinners include rice, beans, tortillas, and soup or salad. Sauces are heavy but oh-so-good. A second outlet on the west side of town in Summerlin has the same great food but lacks some of the original's funky charm.

910 Las Vegas Blvd. S. (at Charleston Blvd.). (℃) **702/382-6538.** www.donamariatamales.com. Main courses $8–$15 breakfast and lunch, $9–$15 dinner. Daily 8am–10pm.

Eat ★★★ AMERICAN While the renaissance of Downtown Las Vegas has mostly been driven by bars and nightclubs, the dining scene has been struggling to keep up. There are a few bright outposts, though, if you know where to look, and you can start right here. The aptly named Eat is only a block off the main drag, but it is miles from the boring, processed casino food that has dominated this neighborhood forever. The funky space has an eclectic cafeteria style, with exposed ductwork, cement floors, and cozy banquette, table, and community seating, all wrapped up in brilliant shades of orange and green that have almost as much energy as the classic soul soundtrack that is often playing. The place is only open for breakfast and lunch, and which you go for is a tough choice. The sandwiches and salads are spectacular constructions of organic and locally sourced ingredients (the BLT with avocado and chipotle mayo is especially noteworthy), but if you have to make a choice, go for an early-riser special like the truffled egg sandwich, with thick-cut bacon, feta cheese, and mushrooms on soft ciabatta bread served with crispy/soft-roasted potatoes. Regardless of which path you take, start or end with the beignets, fluffy smooth and perfectly powdered with homemade jam and vanilla mascarpone; they rival Cafe du Monde's legendary version. Take note that the peak breakfast and lunch times bring out legions of fans, so either go at an off-hour or be prepared to wait a bit for a table.

707 Carson Ave. (at 7th Ave.). (℃) **702/534-1515.** www.eatdtlv.com. Main courses $6–$13. Mon–Fri 8am–3pm; Sat–Sun 8am–2pm.

Heart Attack Grill ★ BURGERS There's something pure, and purely ridiculous, about the concept here, which can be boiled down to this: Their food is hazardous to your health. The medical theme is kooky fun, with waitresses dressed as (naughty) nurses, bartenders in scrubs, and diners in hospital johnnies, but it's their artery-hardening burgers, fries, and shakes that will make you want to set up an appointment with your cardiologist. The fact that a couple of people, including their unofficial spokesperson, have died of heart attacks after eating here is purely coincidental, we're sure. Their signature Quadruple Bypass Burger is 8,000 calories of meat, bacon, and cheese, and if you finish it you get a wheelchair ride back to your car (or a waiting ambulance, perhaps). Shakes are billed as having the highest butterfat content in the world, and that's before they add a pat of butter on top. Fries cooked in pure lard, nonfilter cigarettes, and a full bar serving blended margaritas that are 50% alcohol round out the limited choices. The burgers are merely okay, but it's really the experience, and surviving it, that makes this place worth knowing about, especially if you weigh over 350 pounds. If you do and are willing to prove it by stepping on the scale in the center of the restaurant, you eat for free.

450 E. Fremont St. ✆ **702/254-0171.** www.heartattackgrill.com. Main courses $8–$15. Cash only. Daily 11am–2am.

Pinches Tacos ★★ MEXICAN   Popular in multiple locations around Los Angeles, this purveyor of traditional Mexican specialties almost didn't make it to Las Vegas after a particularly uptight city councilman objected to the name, which can be used as an obscenity in some Spanish-speaking areas. After the dust settled, what was left was a delightful little eatery serving up tacos, tostadas, burritos, enchiladas, tortas, quesadillas, *flautas,* and more in chicken, pork, shrimp, beef, fish, cactus, and veggie varieties. It all tastes homemade, which is a delight considering the typical processed Mexican fast food that is pretty standard in this country. Note that there are few indoor seats so outdoor dining at the Downtown Container Park is likely; watch the weather or be prepared to wait for an inside table.

In the Downtown Container Park, 707 Fremont St. (at 7th St.). ✆ **702/910-3100**. www.pinches tacos.com. Main courses $3–$9. Sun–Thurs 11am–11pm, Fri–Sat 11am–1am.

Radio City Pizza ★★★ PIZZA   This creative take on a pizza parlor should not only be welcomed as a great dining option in Downtown, but done so with open arms (and mouths). You can make your own pie from a choice of nearly two dozen toppings, but their specialty pizzas with inventive twists are where you should focus your energy. The Hawaiian comes with ham and pineapple, of course, but also jalapeños and cilantro, while the Chicken Club has grilled chicken, bacon, tomato, ranch dressing, and French fries. Or if you missed the breakfast buffet, you can get the Breakfast Pizza with ham, bacon, scrambled eggs, and omelet-style veggies. You can't get the specialties by the slice, but grab a few other people and you'll all have plenty to eat with the 18-inch monsters they serve. The prices per person are a true bargain at under $10 for everything on the menu, which also includes a couple of salads, sandwiches, and calzones.

508 E. Fremont St. (at Las Vegas Blvd.) ✆ **702/982-5055.** www.radiocitypizza.com. Main courses $7–$9, pizzas $16–$21. Sun–Thurs 11:30am–10pm; Fri–Sat 11:30–2am.

Triple 7 Brewpub ★ PUB FARE   The wide-ranging menu of pub grub includes everything from salads to sushi, but it's the almost shockingly affordable pizza and sandwiches that you should focus most of your attention on. The crispy-crust, simple pepperoni pie is "Mamma Mia!" worthy, and the cheesesteak, loaded with onions and peppers, is a victory by just about any measure. A huge selection of beers includes their own microbrews, which you can sample while you watch sports on one of the omnipresent TV screens or enjoy the frequent evening entertainment. Note the operating hours—perfect for a place to stop in at 4am to sample their late-night menu of breakfasts, burgers, and Bloody Mary Red Bulls after you've hit all the Fremont Street bars. Not that we would never do something like that.

In Main Street Station, 200 N. Main St. ✆ **702/387-1896.** www.mainstreetcasino.com. Main courses $7–$17. Daily 11am–7am.

Viva Las Arepas ★★ VENEZUELAN   Located in the no-man's land of pawn shops and no-tell motels in between the Strip and Downtown Las Vegas are some really interesting eateries, often serving up authentic ethnic foods like Viva Las Arepas does. Arepas, for those new to the fiesta, are grilled cornmeal patties that here are stuffed with tasty fillings such as wood-fired grilled chicken, shredded beef, shrimp, ham, and more. The flavors are bold and exciting, and we became instant fans of the roasted pork butt and the simple cheese versions. Other options include Venezuelan barbecue chicken, pork ribs, beef, and sausage in addition to empanadas and *tequeños* (deep-fried cheese sticks). Prices are a fraction of what you'd pay for inferior food elsewhere, so it's worth the cab ride. Get some to go and have a feast back in your room.

1616 Las Vegas Blvd. S. (at Oakey Blvd.). © **702/366-9696.** www.vivalasarepas.com. Main courses $4–$10. Sun–Thurs 9am–10pm; Fri–Sat 9am–midnight.

JUST OFF THE STRIP

Expensive

Alizé ★★★ FRENCH   Just a perfect restaurant, thanks to a combination of the most divine dining room and view in Vegas, not to mention one of the best chefs in Vegas. Situated at the top of the Palms hotel, three sides of full-length windows allow a panoramic view of the night lights of Vegas; obviously, window-side tables are best, but even seats in the center of the room have a good view. Many great chefs have restaurants locally but are rarely in their kitchens (we love Emeril and Wolfgang, but they can't be in 25 different places at once). This operation is carefully overseen by André Rochat, longtime Vegas restaurateur who started with the eponymous (and sadly, long-closed) Andre's in Downtown. The menu here changes seasonally, but this is a close-your-eyes-and-point kind of place; anything you order will be heavenly. If you can swing the $135, go for the tasting menu, which will give you the best broad view of the cuisine; if not, go a la carte and go home happy. A recent visit included a divine pork belly appetizer, served in a sweet apple–and-cream sauce; an insanely rich Maine lobster and tomato bisque; and two cuts of beef—a filet in a green-peppercorn crust and cognac cream sauce and a rib-eye with a smoky pinot noir glaze—that would shame the best of steakhouses in Vegas. Desserts are similarly outstanding and often of great frivolity, such as an inside-out raspberry cheesecake (cubes with graham cracker crust on the outside, raspberry compote inside) and mint chocolate mousse.

In Palms Resort & Casino, 4321 W. Flamingo Rd. © **702/951-7000.** www.alizelv.com. Reservations strongly recommended. Main courses $47–$57; 7-course tasting menu $135. Daily 5:30–10:30pm.

Pamplemousse ★ FRENCH   A little bit off the beaten path, this charming little bistro has been a Vegas institution for nearly 40 years. Evoking a cozy French-countryside inn (at least, on the interior), it's a catacomb of low-ceilinged rooms and intimate dining nooks with rough-hewn beams. It's all very charming and un-Vegasy. The restaurant's name, which means "grapefruit" in French, was suggested by the late singer Bobby Darin, one of the many celebrity pals of owner Georges La Forge. Your waiter recites the menu, which changes frequently. The meal always begins with a large complimentary basket of crudités (about 10 different crisp, fresh vegetables), a big bowl of olives, and, in a nice country touch, a basket of hard-boiled eggs. Recent menu offerings have included out-of-this-world soups (French onion and cream of asparagus, to name a couple) and appetizers such as shrimp in cognac cream sauce and Maryland crab cakes with macadamia-nut crust. Main courses are more steakhouse than traditional French but have enough Gallic influence to be forgiven. Leave room for the fabulous desserts.

CHEF ANDRÉ ROCHAT'S TOP 10 THINGS ONE SHOULD NEVER ASK A french chef

French-born chef André Rochat has been delighting Las Vegas audiences with his fine cuisine since 1973. His restaurants Alizé at the Palms and André's at Monte Carlo are among the most popular and best-reviewed French restaurants in the city, so who better to ask what you *shouldn't* ask him?

1. May I have my duck breast well done?
2. May I have A-1 sauce with steak au poivre?
3. I brought this from my garden; can you cook it for me?
4. I want the lobster Thermidor; but can you hold the cream?
5. Can I have the crème brûlée as an appetizer?
6. May I order a soufflé to go?
7. Can we do the seven-course chef's tasting menu in 45 minutes?
8. Can I have mint jelly with the rack of lamb?
9. Will you keep the food under the heat lamps in the kitchen while we go smoke?
10. May I have ketchup with the lobster Thermidor?

And yes . . . Chef André says he's actually been asked these questions. Welcome to Las Vegas!

5 400 E. Sahara Ave. (btw. Santa Paula and Santa Rita drives, just east of Paradise Rd.). ℂ **702/733-2066.** www.pamplemousserestaurant.com. Main courses $28–$38. Tues–Sun 5–10pm.

Moderate

Culinary Dropout ★★★ AMERICAN What if you took classic American comfort food and gave it a casual hipster spin? The result would be this terrific diner, where the servers all dress in whatever comes out of their closet on that particular day; the decor is shabby chic, with cement floors and mismatched furnishings; and the food is an affordable amalgam of coffee-shop classics given an indie spin. Start with the charcuterie, a do-it-yourself dim sum of butcher case meats, cheeses, and roasted veggies, or selections from the raw bar of mussels, oysters, shrimp, and more. If that's too adventurous, how about the house-made potato chips and onion dip? Sandwiches like an Italian grinder, salads like gorgonzola chicken, and entrees from meatloaf to mini-grilled cheese sandwiches on sourdough bread with bacon and tomato to fried chicken and chicken jambalaya provide a dizzying set of choices—and we couldn't find a bum note in any of them. Even before you get to the moderate prices and a gorgeous (on cooperative weather evenings) patio, this place passes with flying colors.

In the Hard Rock Hotel, 4455 Paradise Rd. (at Harmon Ave.). ℂ **702/522-8100.** www.culinarydropout.com. Main courses $12–$27. Mon–Thurs 11am–11pm; Fri 11am–midnight; Sat 10am–midnight; Sun 10am–11pm.

Fu ★★ ASIAN Most people's experience with Asian cuisine in Vegas is at the Chinese station at the buffet. Too bad, because they will miss out on wonderful, off-the-beaten-track experiences like this one. True, it's at a major hotel casino, but it's not on the Strip and it's tucked way back in the corner so it feels like a hidden gem of sorts. The pan-Asian menu includes Chinese, Japanese, Thai, and Korean dishes with an almost staggeringly long list of options that will require you to depend on the helpful wait staff for guidance. The beef tenderloin in a creamy soy-ginger sauce is incredible,

Restaurants Beyond the Strip

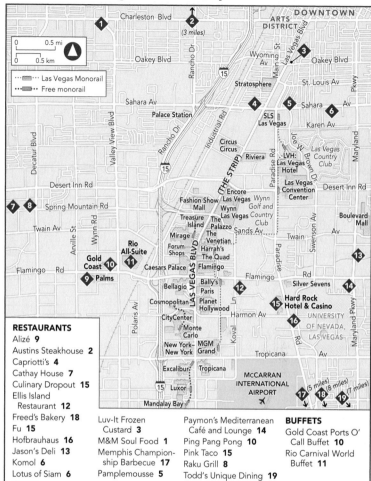

RESTAURANTS

Alizé **9**
Austins Steakhouse **2**
Capriotti's **4**
Cathay House **7**
Culinary Dropout **15**
Ellis Island
  Restaurant **12**
Freed's Bakery **18**
Fu **15**
Hofbrauhaus **16**
Jason's Deli **13**
Komol **6**
Lotus of Siam **6**

Luv-It Frozen
  Custard **3**
M&M Soul Food **1**
Memphis Champion-
  ship Barbecue **17**
Pamplemousse **5**

Paymon's Mediterranean
  Café and Lounge **14**
Ping Pang Pong **10**
Pink Taco **15**
Raku Grill **8**
Todd's Unique Dining **19**

BUFFETS

Gold Coast Ports O'
  Call Buffet **10**
Rio Carnival World
  Buffet **11**

and even the simple dishes like veggie fried rice are worth the stomach space. Beware of anything that has the word "spicy" in its title; they aren't kidding.

In the Hard Rock Hotel, 4455 Paradise Rd. (at Harmon Ave.). © **702/522-8188**. www.hardrock hotel.com. Main courses $16–$30. Sun–Thurs 11:30am–10:30pm; Fri–Sat 11:30am–midnight.

Hofbrauhaus ★ GERMAN Leave it to Las Vegas to bring an exact replica of a 400-year-old beer garden to the Nevada desert. Based on the Munich landmark in business since 1589, the beer brewed for the establishment was, according to legend, so good that Swedes called off their planned plundering of the city in 1614 in exchange for 344 buckets of the stuff. They fly it in to the Vegas location and re-create the schnitzel, strudel, and bratwurst specialties to give you something to wash down. Portions are huge and often drenched in butter or cream; if you're looking for a light lunch, you probably aren't going to find it here, but it's a good place to go to put a little oomph in your pah-pah. *Note:* Polka fans should check the website to see when they have their frequent live entertainment, and folks visiting during the fall should consider their spirited *Oktoberfest* celebrations.

4150 Paradise Rd. (at Harmon Ave.). © **702/853-2337.** www.hofbrauhauslasvegas.com. Main courses $10–$25. Sun–Thurs 11am–11pm; Fri–Sat 11am–midnight.

Ping Pang Pong ★★ CHINESE   This longtime local favorite has taken a step up to national acclaim, picked by *Travel + Leisure* as one of the "Top Chinese Restaurants in the U.S." It's hard to believe they found the place, tucked into the back of an off-Strip casino behind rows of slot machines and video poker, but it's easy to see why they put it on their list. Forget the P.F. Chang's–style orange chicken or sweet-and-sour pork—you won't find those kinds of dishes here. Instead you get a long menu of provincial Chinese specialties having an air (and a flavor) of authenticity missing in most regional cuisine–focused restaurants in Vegas. Start with the dim sum–style pot stickers, done in a lightly seared puff pastry and stuffed with delectable beef and pork, then move on to the crispy Cantonese chicken, usually done extra-hot with spicy chilies but customizable based on your taste buds. The more adventurous can try the salt-and-pepper frog legs or pork belly stew. Owned, managed, and frequented by the Asian community, this is one of the most "real" Chinese restaurants in the city.

In the Gold Coast Hotel & Casino, 4000 W. Flamingo Rd. © **702/367-7111.** www.goldcoastcasino.com. Main courses $10–$25. Daily 10am–3pm and 5pm–3am.

Pink Taco ★ MEXICAN   A megahip Mexican cantina, this folk art–bedecked spot is a scene just waiting to happen. There are no surprises in terms of the food; you know the drill—tacos, burritos, quesadillas—but it's all tasty and filling, and some of it comes with some surprising accompaniments, such as tapenade, along with the usual guacamole and sour cream. Despite it attempting to appear like a hole-in-the-wall, mom-and-pop joint, it's really a slick, hip operation, and so the food and overall experience feels much more processed than Mexican restaurants resembling this usually are. This is a popular place late weekend nights as people start trickling out of the hotel's jam-packed nightclubs.

In the Hard Rock Hotel & Casino, 4455 Paradise Rd. © **702/693-5525.** www.hardrockhotel.com. Main courses $13–$22. Sun–Thurs 11am–10pm; Fri–Sat 11am–2am.

Inexpensive

Capriotti's ★★★ SANDWICHES   Although certainly no Subway (in a lot of different ways), the Capriotti's sandwich empire is expanding, with outlets in 13 states and the District of Columbia as of this writing. Vegas wasn't first, but it was early in their expansion and we have been fans for more than 15 years, especially of the original location near the Strip. It looks like a dump, but Capriotti's is one of the great deals in town, for quality and price. It roasts its own beef and turkey on the premises and stuffs them (or Italian cold cuts, or whatever) into sandwiches mislabeled "small," "medium," and "large"—the latter clocks in at 20 inches, easily feeding two or three for what works out to a few bucks each. And deliciously so. The Bobby (turkey, dressing, and cranberry sauce, like Thanksgiving dinner in a sandwich) would be our favorite sandwich in the world had we not tried the Slaw B Joe: roast beef, coleslaw, and Russian dressing. But other combos, such as the Italian cold cuts, have their fans, too, and Capriotti's even has veggie varieties. There are outlets throughout the city, but this one is right off the Strip and right by the freeway. We never leave town without a stop here, and you shouldn't either.

322 W. Sahara Ave. (at Las Vegas Blvd. S.). © **702/474-0229.** www.capriottis.com. Most regular sandwiches under $10. Mon–Sat 10am–8pm; Sun 11am–7pm.

Ellis Island Restaurant ★ DINER   Believe it or not, this simple little 24-hour coffee shop–style restaurant is pretty famous in Las Vegas. Why? The most expensive thing on the menu is around $13, and that's a king cut of prime rib that comes with soup or salad, a baked potato, and a glass of beer. Yes, this is the epicenter of the much-beloved meal deal, with most items under $10. The surprising thing is that the food is pretty good in a coffee shop kind of way, the portions are huge, and the selections (burgers, sandwiches, salads, pasta, pizza, and so on) are epic. You can even get selections from a separate barbecue joint in this restaurant later in the afternoon. If budget is a concern, take a detour from the pricey Strip and find yourself a bargain here.

In Ellis Island Casino, 4178 Koval Lane (at Flamingo Rd.). © **702/733-8901.** www.ellisislandcasino. com. Main courses $5–$14. Daily 24 hrs.

Komol ★ THAI   Once you get past the rundown strip mall in which this local's favorite is found, the inside is surprisingly nice and has a large menu of poultry, beef, pork, vegetarian, rice, and noodle selections. They'll spice the food to your specifications, but unless you're a Thai expert, it might be best to play it on the safe side. Although we don't want things bland, too much heat can overwhelm all other flavors. The mild to medium packs enough of a kick for most people. Among the items we tried during a recent visit were a vegetarian green curry and the *pad kee mao* (flat rice noodles stir-fried with ground chicken, mint, garlic, and hot peppers). *Nam sod* is ground pork with a hot-and-sour sauce, ginger, and peanuts, all of which you wrap up in lettuce leaves—sort of an Asian burrito. The Thai iced tea was particularly good— just the right amount of sweetness and tea taste for a drink that is often served overly sweet.

In the Commercial Center, 953 E. Sahara Ave. © **702/731-6542.** www.komolrestaurant.com. Main courses $8–$21. Mon–Sat 11am–10pm; Sun noon–10pm.

Lotus of Siam ★★★ THAI   Much has been written about this out-of-the-way Thai joint (Jonathan Gold of *Gourmet* magazine called it the best Thai restaurant in North America), but what makes this place so darn special? First of all, in addition to all the usual beloved Thai favorites, there is a full menu featuring lesser-known dishes from northern Thailand. Second, the owner drives at least twice a week back to Los Angeles to pick up the freshest herbs and other ingredients needed for his dishes' authenticity. That's dedication that should be rewarded with superlatives. Be careful with the spice level, especially on the Northern dishes; let the servers guide you. Menu items change, of course, but look for standouts like the Issan sausage (a grilled sour pork number); the *nam kao tod* (that same sausage, ground up with lime, green onion, fresh chile, and ginger, served with crispy rice); *nam sod* (ground pork mixed with ginger, green onion, and lime juice, served with sticky rice); jackfruit *larb* (spicy ground meat); and *sua rong hai* ("weeping tiger"), a dish of soft, sliced, and grilled marinated beef. If you insist on more conventional Thai, that's okay, in that it's unlikely you are going to have better *mee krob* noodles or *tom kah kai*. The popular and inexpensive lunch buffet often requires arriving before they open to secure a table.

In the Commercial Center, 953 E. Sahara Ave. © **702/735-3033.** www.saipinchutima.com. Main courses $10–$29. Mon–Fri 11:30am–2:30pm and 5:30–10pm; Sat–Sun 5:30–10pm.

SOUTH & EAST OF THE STRIP

Expensive

Todd's Unique Dining ★★★ CONTINENTAL   Las Vegas is filled with some great dining options, most of which are located within steps of wherever you are staying. But true foodies know that to find the best culinary experiences you need to get away from the tourist areas, and that's most definitely true of Todd's Unique Dining. Located in a boring strip mall in Henderson, about 20 minutes from the Strip, this small bistro is the brainchild of Chef Todd Clore, former chef de cuisine for the Sterling Brunch at Bally's. It's intimate and friendly—a family restaurant where you'll often find the chef's wife waiting tables. The menu changes almost daily, focusing on the freshest ingredients Clore can get his hands on, which is most obvious in the seafood selections that rival—and in many cases, beat—the fish you'll find at much more expensive restaurants on the Strip. Genius items like the lobster-wrapped sole, dressed in a simple yet flavorful butter sauce, prove that you don't need the backing of a big hotel to get the best catches. Signature items include grilled skirt steak "on fire," so spicy delicious it'll make your eyes water (in a good way) and served with fun chili-cheese fries; and a boneless braised short rib, slow-cooked for days and served in a red-wine gravy atop a bed of jalapeño mashed potatoes. The latter is like the best, most tender, most mouth-watering pot roast you'll ever have and is the reason you should put down this book, get in a cab, and head here for dinner right this second. *Hint:* Join their mailing list on the website and you'll get frequent special offers and notices of events.

4350 E. Sunset Rd., Henderson (just east of Green Valley Pkwy.). ℂ **702/259-8633.** www.todds unique.com. Main courses $25–$35. Mon–Sat 4:30–10pm.

Moderate

Memphis Championship Barbecue ★★ BARBECUE   We simply refuse to get into the debate about Texas versus Kansas City versus Mississippi barbecue (and if you've got another place with the best dang barbecue, we really don't want to hear about it). But we can say that if you aren't physically in those places, you gotta take what you can get—and luckily for Vegas visitors, eating at Memphis Championship Barbecue is hardly settling. The restaurant's vinegar-based sauce is sweet but has a kick. Food is cooked over mesquite applewood, and the meat falls off the bone just the way you want it to. It offers hot links, baked beans, and everything you would want and hope for. Standouts include a pulled barbecue chicken sandwich, onion straws, and delicious mac and cheese. A $70 feast includes a rack of St. Louis or baby back ribs, a half-pound of pork, a half-pound of beef brisket, a half-pound of hot links, a whole chicken, baked beans, coleslaw, rolls, cream corn, and fries. It feeds four; we think even if two of those four are teenage boys, you might have leftovers. Note that there is a second location on the far north side of town near the Las Vegas Motor Speedway. The one listed below is closer to the Strip.

2250 E. Warm Springs Rd. (near I-215). ℂ **702/260-6909.** www.memphis-bbq.com. Main courses $8–$23; special barbecue dinner (serves 4) $70. Daily 11am–10pm.

Inexpensive

Jason's Deli ★ DELI   There are five (and counting) local outlets of this nationwide chain, but this one is convenient to those staying east of the Strip and popular with locals, especially kids from nearby UNLV. It's a bustling deli where all items are advertised as free of artificial trans fats and offering a selection of "slimwiches," so as multipurpose diner/delis go, this may be a fairly healthy option. Jason's also does a brisk takeout business, again useful for those staying in nearby chain hotels without much in the way of room service. There is the usual deli fare—at least a dozen soups, sandwiches, wraps, and junior meals. The wraps tip you off that this is not a Brooklyn-style pastrami deli, but fancy California-influenced versions of sandwiches. A wild card is the New Orleans–inspired muffalettas. The sandwiches are piled with meat, and the chicken pot pie is huge. Naturally, the salad bar contains pudding and vanilla wafers—wouldn't want to carry "healthy" too far.

3910 S. Maryland Pkwy. *C* **702/893-9799.** www.jasonsdeli.com. Most items under $10. Daily 10am–9pm.

Paymon's Mediterranean Café & Lounge ★ MEDITERRANEAN If you can get past the overwrought Mediterranean and Middle Eastern decor, you'll discover yet another interesting and authentic ethnic cuisine experience in a strip mall in Vegas. The menu skips around the region with stops in Greece (gyros, pitas, moussaka); Italy (lasagna, spaghetti, chicken parm); and the Middle East (kabobs, kibbe, *fesenjan*); plus a detour to India (tandoori and chicken curry), which is geographically questionable—but with food this good, we'll let it slide. As the menu warns, kabobs take 20 minutes, so order an appetizer plate with various dips to while away the time. The hummus here is too reminiscent of its chickpea origins, but the *baba ghanouj* is properly smoky and the falafel has the right crunch. Gyros may not be the most adventurous thing to order, but who cares about that when you've got a well-stuffed pita pocket, gloopy with yogurt sauce. *Fesenjan* is a dish of falling-apart chicken swimming in a tangy pomegranate sauce; ask them to ensure that the ratio of sauce to chicken is greater than 10:1. Bonus points for the honest-to-goodness hookah lounge, which features DJs and no cover charge on Saturday nights.

4147 S. Maryland Pkwy. (at Flamingo Rd., in the Tiffany Sq. strip mall). *C* **702/731-6030.** www.paymons.com. Main courses $8–$14; most sandwiches under $10. Daily 11am–1am.

NORTH & WEST OF THE STRIP

Expensive

Austins Steakhouse ★★ STEAK/SEAFOOD Now, understand that we don't send you out to nether regions such as Texas Station lightly. We do so here because, improbably, Austins Steakhouse has gained a reputation for serving what many consider to be the best steaks in town. Really. Even the snooty critics at the *Las Vegas Review-Journal* agree with the hubbub about this place. The filet is not only so tender and juicy that you can literally cut it with a fork, but it is one of the few filets in town that doesn't require some sort of accompaniment to make it interesting—it does that on its own in a smoky, woodhouse kind of way. The bone-in rib-eye is Texas epic, and the prime rib (which you can often get on special) competes with the gold standard Lawry's for best in class. The already-reasonable prices are even more so when the soup or salad and side vegetable that is included is factored in. A comparable meal on the Strip would cost $20 to $30 more per person and often not be as good.

In Texas Station, 2101 Texas Star Lane. *C* **702/631-1033.** www.texasstation.com. Main courses $16–$42. Sun–Thurs 5–10pm; Fri–Sat 5–11pm.

sweet SENSATIONS

Plenty of opportunities exist in Vegas for satisfying your sweet tooth, but for the discriminating, here are four spots you may have to make a detour for.

Jean-Philippe Patisserie ★★★ in Bellagio, 3600 Las Vegas Blvd. S. (𝄐 **702/693-8788;** www.jpchocolates. com), makes us swoon, not just because it has the world's largest chocolate fountain (20 feet high! Though only 11 feet are on view, and they won't let us drink from it. Darn), but perhaps, more to the point, it's the home of World Pastry champion Jean-Philippe Maury. (Yes, you can win gold medals for pastries.) Each visit causes us to spin around distractedly, trying to take in all the choices, both visually and gastronomically. From perfect gourmet chocolates to ice cream to diet-conscious sorbets to the eponymous pastries, each of which are little works of art, we hit greed overload. For us, this is true Vegas decadence—if only

"what happens in Vegas, stays in Vegas" applied to calories. The patisserie also serves some solidly good sandwiches, and some adequate savory crepes. It is open Monday through Thursday from 6am to 11pm and Friday through Sunday from 6am until midnight. There's a second location inside Aria Las Vegas, but they don't have the chocolate fountain.

A local favorite for more than 50 years is **Freed's Bakery,** 9815 S. Eastern Ave., at Silverado Ranch Blvd. (𝄐 **702/ 456-7762;** www.freedsbakery.com), open Monday through Thursday from 9am to 8pm, Friday and Saturday from 8am to 8pm, and Sunday from 9am to 6pm. If you've got a serious sugar craving, this is worth the 20-minute drive from the Strip. It's like walking into Grandma's kitchen, provided you had an old-fashioned granny who felt pastries should be gooey, chocolaty, and

Moderate

Cathay House ★ CHINESE   Ordering dim sum, for those of you who haven't experienced it, is sort of like being at a Chinese sushi bar, in that you order many individual, tasty little dishes. Of course, dim sum itself is nothing like sushi. Rather, it's a range of pot stickers, pan-fried dumplings, *baos* (soft, doughy buns filled with such meat as barbecued pork), translucent rice noodles wrapped around shrimp, sticky rice in lotus leaves, chicken feet, and so forth. Some of it is steamed; some is fried—for that extra-good grease! You can make your own dipping sauce by combining soy sauce, vinegar, and hot-pepper oil. The waitstaff pushes steam carts filled with little dishes; point, and they'll attempt to tell you what each one is. Better, just blindly order a bunch and dig in. Each dish is only a few bucks, the server makes a note of what you just received, and the total is tallied at the end. Dim sum is usually available only until midafternoon.

5300 W. Spring Mountain Rd. 𝄐 **702/876-3838.** Main courses $8–$22. Daily 10:30am–10pm.

M&M Soul Food ★★ SOUL FOOD   Though we've listed this in the North/West area, it's really not too far from the Strip. At first glance, the neighborhood seems intimidating, but only when compared to the sanitized Strip. Why come here? Because locals have voted this their favorite soul-food place year after year, and while the competition may not be all that high, the quality stands out regardless. Appropriately, it's a hole in the wall, with somewhat higher prices than you might expect, but the generous portions make up for it. Mini cornbread pancakes are served to every table.

buttery. Their signature wedding cakes will make you want to rush down the aisle, but you'll want to bring a basket for the fresh bread, napoleons, strawberry cheesecake, cream puffs, sweet rolls, danishes, and doughnuts, many of which are made with surprisingly fresh ingredients. Some may find the goodies too heavy and rich, but for those of us with a powerful sweet tooth, this place hits the spot. There is no dining area so everything is to go; do try to at least make it to your car before you start digging in.

Just down the street is the delightful **The Cupcakery ★★★**, 9680 S. Eastern Ave. (**(©** 702/207-2253**;** www.thecup cakery.com). The delectable cakes here aren't large, but they pack a wallop of moist cake and creamy frosting. Clever combinations include Boston cream pie (filled with custardy cream), but even the basic chocolate-on-chocolate is a

buttercream pleasure. There are even sugar-free cupcakes for those with such dietary needs. The Cupcakery is open Monday through Friday from 8am to 8pm, Saturday from 10am to 8pm, and Sunday from 10am to 6pm.

Hot Vegas days call for cool desserts, and frozen custard (softer than regular ice cream, but harder than soft serve) is a fine way to go. Head for **Luv-It Frozen Custard,** 505 E. Oakey (**(©** 702/384-6452;** www.luvitfrozencustard.com), open Sunday through Thursday from 1 to 10pm and Friday and Saturday from 1 to 11pm. Because custard has less fat and sugar than premium ice cream, you can even fool yourself into thinking this is somewhat healthful (ha!). Made every few hours using fresh cream and eggs, the custard is available in basic flavors for cup or cone, but more exotic flavors (maple walnut, apple spice, and others) come in tubs.

Smothered fried chicken is moist, slightly spicy, and topped with a robust gravy. The menu includes hot links, collard greens, and other typical options.

3923 W. Charleston. **(©** 702/453-7685.** www.mmsoulfoodcafe.com. Main courses $9–$19. Daily 7am–8pm.

Raku Grill ★★★ JAPANESE   Look at the rundown strip mall location and you would not expect that this is the kind of place that would garner rave notices in *GQ* and *New York Magazine*, nor that master chefs like Paul Bartolotta leave their 5-star kitchens on the Strip to come here to eat. Not only is all of that true, but this is one of the most interesting, unique, and purely divine restaurants in all of Las Vegas. It's tiny, with seats for fewer than three dozen, and what with all the deserved attention it has gotten, those seats are hard to come by (make reservations at least a week in advance, if not more). But if you get one, you'll be treated to a litany of taste bud–popping flavors from the *robata* grill.

Everything is small plates, most served on skewers. It's the esoteric items that have gotten most of the press—pork ear, pork cheek, Kobe beef liver—but the long list includes perfectly moist chicken breast, Kobe with milder-than-expected wasabi, a miniature lamb chop, seared foie gras, grilled duck, asparagus or tomato wrapped in bacon (both joy-inducing in their freshness), ground chicken, and much more. Daily specials include seafood flown in from Japan, and there is also an *odin* (broth pot) section and rice, noodle, and soup dishes. But it is that *robata* grill that should dominate your choices—the smoky charcoal-grill flavor brings everything to life but allows each dish to have its own distinct flavors. Even the somewhat-less-than-mainstream options are heavenly, with the pork cheek tasting basically like a hunk of bacon lard, and we mean that in a good way. Although most of the selections are only a few bucks (most under $5), it is easy to rack up a big bill here because after the first bite you'll be tempted to just have them bring you everything on the menu. And we would not blame you for doing so.

5030 W. Spring Mountain Rd., no. 2 (at Decatur). © **702/367-3511.** www.raku-grill.com. Reservations required. *Robata* grill items $3–$16. Mon–Sat 6pm–3am.

BUFFETS & BRUNCHES

Like so much else that was Vegas tradition, the buffets have evolved. Gone, mostly, are the days of trays and cafeteria-style lines serving heaping mounds of warmed-over blandness at bargain-basement prices. The modern buffet uses come-and-go serving areas, live-action cooking stations, multiple ethnic and regional cuisines, and a general rise in quality that puts many on par with traditional restaurants. Of course, as the quality has gone up so, too, have the prices, which now make them less of a bargain. But consider it this way: You would pay much more, per person, at one of the fancier restaurants in town, where you would order just one, potentially disappointing, item. At a buffet there's more variety and more chance to find something you love. More variety per person means less likelihood for disappointment, so if you hate what you picked you can simply dump your plate and start all over. They are, generally speaking, not nearly as atmospheric as a proper restaurant, but how else can you combine good barbecue with excellent Chinese and a cupcake or 10?

There is a lot of variety within the buffet genre. Some are still buffet-basic with the perfunctory steam-table displays and salad bars that are heavy on the iceberg lettuce, while others are unbelievably opulent spreads with caviar and free-flowing champagne. Some are quite beautifully presented as well. Some of the food is awful, some of it is decent, and some of it is memorable.

Buffets are extremely popular, and reservations are not taken, so be prepared for a long line at peak times. Eating at offbeat hours (lunch at 2pm, for example) will mean a shorter wait to get in, as will some hotel/casino players' club cards, which can get you line cuts.

Note: At press time, several hotels were offering all-you-can-eat all-day-long packages where you could pay one flat fee and come back to the buffets as many times as you like in a given day. Caesars Entertainment (Harrah's, Flamingo, Rio, and so on) is even offering a full-day pass to most of their buffets for as low as $50 so you can mix and match. Details and pricing on these change often, so visit the hotel's website or call ahead to see if they are offering any special deals when you're in town.

South Strip

EXPENSIVE

The Buffet at Aria ★ BUFFET   While the food here may not be the pinnacle of all-you-can-eat delights, it is certainly a cut above standard buffet fare. Various regional and ethnic food stations serve up enough variety to keep your stomach confused for days (pizza, pot stickers, and hummus on one plate?) and the quality is evident with every bite, although very little of it is so good that it makes you want to go back for seconds. Well, maybe the full rack of bacon at the carving station during the weekend brunches is worth another helping. The dining room got a makeover that reduced the school cafeteria look but is still not a postcard-worthy locale.

At Aria Las Vegas, 3730 Las Vegas Blvd. S. © **702/590-7111.** www.arialasvegas.com. Breakfast $20; lunch $24; dinner $35–$40; Sat–Sun brunch $30 (not including cocktails). Daily 7am–10pm.

MODERATE

Excalibur's Buffet ★ BUFFET   This one strikes the perfect balance of moderate prices, forgettable decor, and adequate food. It's what you want in a cheap Vegas buffet—except it's just not that cheap anymore—until you start comparing it places like the Bacchanal at Caesars, and then it looks like a bargain. You can combine this with the buffet at Luxor in one day-long, all-you-can-eat package that knocks a few bucks off the total.

In Excalibur, 3850 Las Vegas Blvd. S. ℂ **702/597-7777.** www.excalibur.com. Breakfast $17; lunch $18; dinner $23. Daily 7am–10pm.

Mandalay Bay's Bayside Buffet ★ BUFFET   This is a particularly pretty, not overly large buffet. Floor-to-ceiling windows overlooking the beach part of the elaborate pool area make it less stuffy and eliminate the closed-in feeling that so many of the other buffets in town have. The buffet itself is adequately arranged but features nothing particularly special, though there are some nice salads, hearty meats, and a larger- and better-than-average dessert bar. Considering that prices have remained relatively low (if you can call $22 for lunch low), it has become more forgivable that the food is relatively forgettable.

In Mandalay Bay, 3950 Las Vegas Blvd. S. ℂ **702/632-7402.** www.mandalaybay.com. Breakfast $18; lunch $22; dinner $33; Sun brunch $26. Reduced prices for children 5–12; free for children 4 and under. Daily 7am–2:30pm and 4:30–9:45pm.

MORE, The Buffet at Luxor ★ BUFFET   Once one of our favorite buffets not just for the excellent price-to-quality ratio, but also because of its Indiana Jones–invoking decor, the Luxor buffet has been redesigned and renamed as part of the ongoing de-Egypt-ing of the hotel. Dang. We are sick of neato modern classy, already, and want our mummies back. That said, the food is the best in its price range, and it is one of the top buffets in town. There's a Mexican station with some genuinely spicy food, a Chinese stir-fry station, and different Italian pastas. Desserts were disappointing, though they do offer a pretty large selection of diabetic-friendly options. The quality-to-price ratio is no secret, and, as a result, the lines are always enormous. As noted above, you can combine this with the buffet at Excalibur and save some dough.

In Luxor, 3900 Las Vegas Blvd. S. ℂ **702/262-4000.** www.luxor.com. Breakfast $17; lunch $18; dinner $23; free for children 4 and under. Daily 7am–10pm.

Mid-Strip

EXPENSIVE

Bellagio Buffet ★★ BUFFET   Though one of the priciest of the buffets, the Bellagio still gets high marks from visitors. The array of food is fabulous, with one ethnic cuisine after another (Japanese, Chinese that includes dim sum, build-it-yourself Mexican items, and so on). There are elaborate pastas and semitraditional Italian-style pizza from a wood-fired oven. The cold fish appetizers at each end of the line are not to be missed—scallops, smoked salmon, crab claws, shrimp, oysters, and assorted condiments. Other specialties include breast of duck and game hens. There is no carving station, but you can get the meat precarved. The salad bar is more ordinary, though prepared salads have some fine surprises, such as the eggplant-tofu salad and an exceptional Chinese chicken salad. All this and a gorgeous dining room to boot? Hard to beat that.

In Bellagio, 3600 Las Vegas Blvd. S. ℂ **877/234-6358.** www.bellagio.com. Breakfast $19, lunch $23; dinner $34–$40; weekend brunch $30 ($42 with champagne). Daily 7am–10pm.

A SEAT AT THE table

Opportunities to sample cuisines from master chefs in interesting surroundings abound in Las Vegas, but if you want to expand your horizons beyond the four walls of the traditional restaurants, **Project Dinner Table** offers some of the most truly unique dining experiences in town. Some of the city's top culinary geniuses design lavish, multicourse meals that are served at one long, family-dining-style table in interesting locations to raise money for various local charities. Past events have included cuisine from Fleur's Hubert Keller, Central's Michel Richard, and Sensi's Roy Ellmar at once-in-a-lifetime spots like on the baseball diamond at Cashman Field, in the middle of an orchard, in the courtyard of the World Market Center, and in the park at the Town Square shopping center. Dinners are once a month from April to November and the $140 tickets include the meal, drinks, and entertainment, with proceeds going to local charities. For more information, visit www.project dinnertable.com.

Caesars Palace Bacchanal Buffet ★★ BUFFET   Back in the day, Caesars had a legendary restaurant called the Bacchanal Room, a modern food orgy complete with toga-clad waitresses and free-flowing wine. This being a whole new millennium, the new Bacchanal comes in the form of a 500-plus item, all-you-can-eat buffet that takes the crown for not only conspicuous consumption but also for the cost of living this large (both literally and metaphorically). Because we have a page limit on this book we can't possibly list every dish offered, but if you can eat it, they probably serve it. Although everything we sampled was fresh, flavorful, and well-prepared, there was nothing that made us want to head back to the food stations for seconds. While it is true that traditional sit-down restaurants charge these kinds of prices and more, this is (as of this writing) the most expensive buffet in town, and for that kind of coin we want mind-blowing, memorable food.

In Caesars Palace, 3570 Las Vegas Blvd. S. ✆ **702/731-7928.** www.caesarspalace.com. Breakfast $26; lunch $36; dinner $51; weekend brunch $45 (includes champagne). Mon–Fri 7am–10pm; Sat–Sun 8am–10pm.

Mirage Cravings Buffet ★ BUFFET   This buffet features a gleaming, streamlined look, all shining steel and up-to-the-minute high-design concept. Gone are the heaping mounds of shrimp and other symbols of Vegas excess and bargain. In its place are plenty of live-action stations, with noteworthy items such as an excellent pizza, pot stickers and Chinese barbecue pork, quite good barbecue, tangy Japanese cucumber salad, and slightly dry but flavorful Mexican slow-roasted pork (at least it was when we visited). Some of the live-action cooking stations, where a chef makes something to order (like an omelet), are interesting, but often have time-consuming lines that make them less so. The hand-scooped gelato is yummy, but the rest of the desserts are generally disappointing. Despite the drawbacks, this remains popular with buffet connoisseurs.

In The Mirage, 3400 Las Vegas Blvd. S. ✆ **702/791-7111.** www.mirage.com. Breakfast $17; lunch $22; dinner $31; Sat–Sun brunch $28. Reduced prices for children 5–10; free for children 4 and under. Daily 7am–9pm.

Paris Las Vegas Le Village Buffet ★★★ BUFFET   One of the more ambitious buffets, with a price to match—still, you do get a fine assortment of food and more value for the dollar than you are likely to find anywhere else. The Paris buffet is housed in a Disneyland-esque replica of a French village that is either a charming respite from Vegas lights or sickening, depending on your perspective. Buffet stations are grouped according to French regions, and though in theory entrees change daily, there do seem to be some constants, like their famous made-to-order crepes and bananas Foster. Although there are some French spins on dishes, most of it is good old-fashioned American grub, so don't let the Parisian flair scare you away. Despite increased competition, this is still a very popular buffet. As such, expect a long line during peak weekend meal times.

In Paris Las Vegas, 3655 Las Vegas Blvd. S. **ⓒ 702/946-7000.** www.parislasvegas.com. Mon–Fri breakfast $22–$24, lunch $25, dinner $31–$34; Sat–Sun brunch $31. Reduced prices for children 4–10 and for Total Rewards Players Club members; free for children 3 and under. Daily 7am–10pm.

Wicked Spoon Buffet ★ BUFFET   Although the bulk of this buffet is pretty standard (food in trays that you spoon onto a plate), they twist things up a bit by doing lots of "small plate" offerings—eggs Benedict served in a miniature copper pan, for instance. It's interesting, although it does make carting your food back to your table a little more challenging. They have the full range of cuisines (American to Chinese, Mexican to seafood, and beyond) plus some live-action cooking stations that you'd expect of a modern buffet. That said, there's really nothing here that makes it stand out as a must-visit all-you-can-eat experience. By the way, don't wander around looking for this place near the other restaurants; it is located at the back of the property on the second floor.

In The Cosmopolitan of Las Vegas, 3708 Las Vegas Blvd. S. **ⓒ 877/551-7772.** www.cosmopolitan lasvegas.com. Weekday brunch $26; weekend brunch $34; dinner $38–$41. Brunch Mon–Fri 8am–2pm, Sat–Sun 8am–3pm; dinner Sun–Thurs 5–9pm, Fri–Sat 5–10pm.

MODERATE

The Buffet at TI ★ BUFFET   This handsome buffet space is done as sort of con-temporary diner, all dark gleaming wood, mirrors, and geometric lines. We feel mixed on the food choices; this is a smaller buffet than one might expect for such a big hotel, and while there is a reasonable range of cuisines (Italian; Japanese, with sushi chefs who will make up fresh plates for you; Southern, including unexpected spoon bread; deli), and much of it is good to very good, there isn't the overwhelming bounty and stunning quality we've come to consider our right when it comes to Vegas buffets. The biggest draw here has to be the relatively affordable prices.

In Treasure Island, 3300 Las Vegas Blvd. S. **ⓒ 702/894-7111.** www.treasureisland.com. Breakfast $18; lunch $21; dinner Mon–Thurs $26, Fri–Sun $29; Sat–Sun champagne brunch $24. Reduced prices for children 4–10; free for children 3 and under. Daily 7am–10pm.

Flavors at Harrah's ★ BUFFET   A casually comfortable room may not be all that special, but the food at least approaches it. Oddly, here it's the carving station that stands out, with simultaneous servings of turkey, ham, prime rib, chicken, game hen, sausage, roast vegetables, and lamb. The other stations are typical—Mexican, Italian, seafood, Chinese. A particularly good dessert area is heavy on the cookies, cakes, and little pastries, such as Oreo mousse tarts and mini crème brûlées. Oh, and then there's the chocolate fountain. We can't forget about that!

In Harrah's, 3475 Las Vegas Blvd. S. **ⓒ 702/369-5000.** www.harrahslv.com. Breakfast $20; lunch $21; dinner $25–$27; brunch Sat–Sun $24. Reduced prices for children 4–10; free for children 3 and under. Daily 7am–10pm.

Spice Market Buffet ★★ BUFFET   This is one of the better choices in the city, thanks to unexpected and unexpectedly good Middle Eastern specialties (a leftover from when the hotel was the Aladdin, with an *Arabian Nights* theme), including the occasional Moroccan entrees. Look for tandoori chicken, hummus, couscous, stuffed tomatoes with ground lamb, and, at dinner, lamb skewers. The Mexican station is particularly good as well, even if it confuses the palate to go from guacamole to hummus. The dim sum also gets a vote of confidence. We still wish it were a bit cheaper; at these prices, it's edging toward the high end.

3667 Las Vegas Blvd. S. ℃ **702/785-5555.** www.planethollywoodresort.com. Breakfast $25; lunch $27; dinner $33–$38; Sat–Sun brunch $32. Daily 7am–11pm.

North Strip
EXPENSIVE

Wynn Las Vegas Buffet ★★★ BUFFET   Goodness, we do love a nice buffet, and this one is particularly nice (if notably super-expensive). It's thoughtful and artful, starting with the *Alice in Wonderland*–evoking atrium styled with towers of fruit flowers and foliage and even some natural light. Don't worry if you don't score one of the few tables set there; it's a bit far from the food lines, and you want to be close to the action, after all. Look for such items as jerk chicken, wood-fired pizza, honey-glazed pork, nice little salmon rolls, five kinds of *ceviche,* sweet Kansas City–style barbecue, and tandoori chicken among the stations, which include Mexican, Southern, seafood, and Italian. Desserts are superior to those at probably all the other buffets, in construction and in taste, giving the impression that a pastry chef is active on the premises. Don't miss the mini floating islands, the unusual tiramisu, the excellent chocolate mousse and ice creams, and even a plate full of madeleines.

In Wynn Las Vegas, 3131 Las Vegas Blvd. S. ℃ **702/248-3463.** www.wynnlasvegas.com. Breakfast $21; lunch $26; dinner $39–$40; Sat–Sun brunch $33 (not including cocktails). Daily 8am–10pm.

Downtown
INEXPENSIVE

Main Street Station Garden Court Buffet ★★★ BUFFET   Set in what is truly one of the prettiest buffet spaces in town (and certainly in Downtown), with very high ceilings and tall windows bringing in much-needed natural light, the Main Street Station Garden Court buffet is one of the best in town, let alone Downtown. It features nine live-action stations where you can watch your food being prepared, including a wood-fired brick-oven pizza (delicious); many fresh salsas at the Mexican station; a barbecue rotisserie; fresh sausage at the carving station; Chinese, Hawaiian, and Southern specialties (soul food and the like); and so many more we lost count. On Friday night, it has all this and nearly infinite varieties of seafood, all the way up to lobster. We ate ourselves into a stupor and didn't regret it. Try to visit at non-peak times to avoid the long lines.

At Main Street Station, 200 N. Main St. ℃ **702/387-1896.** www.mainstreetcasino.com. Breakfast $8; lunch $9; dinner $12–$23; Sat–Sun champagne brunch $12. Free for children 3 and under. Daily 7–10:30am breakfast; 11am–3pm lunch; Mon–Thurs 4–9pm dinner; Fri–Sun dinner 4–10pm.

Just Off the Strip
EXPENSIVE

Rio's Carnival World Buffet ★★ BUFFET   This buffet has long been voted by locals as the best in Vegas, and for good reason. It's laid out as a food court of sorts

Online Restaurant Inspections

The Southern Nevada Health District is the organization responsible for inspecting restaurants. Each is visited at least twice a year and then graded (A, B, or C), given demerits for infractions (improper food storage and handling, and the like), and in extreme cases, shut down. You can now read the inspections online for every restaurant in town, although you may not want to if you ever feel like eating in Las Vegas again. If you think you and your stomach can handle it, visit www.southernnevada healthdistrict.org.

with "South American" cooked-to-order stir-fries, Mexican taco fixings and accompaniments, Chinese fare, a Japanese sushi bar and *teppanyaki* grill, a Brazilian mixed grill, Italian pasta and antipasto, and fish and chips. There's even a diner setup for hot dogs, burgers, fries, and milkshakes. All this is in addition to the usual offerings of most Las Vegas buffets. Best of all, a dessert station features at least 70 kinds of pies, cakes, and pastries from an award-winning pastry chef, plus a large selection of gelatos and sorbets. A separate seafood-only buffet located at the other end of the hotel is also worth your attention.

In Rio All-Suite Hotel & Casino, 3700 W. Flamingo Rd. © **702/252-7777.** www.riolasvegas.com. Breakfast $23; lunch $26; dinner $36–$41; Sat–Sun champagne brunch $35. Reduced prices for children 4–8; free for children 3 and under. Daily 8am–10pm.

INEXPENSIVE

Gold Coast Ports O' Call ★ BUFFET   As formerly bargain buffet prices skyrocket—and we aren't helping matters by highly recommending $40-and-up places such as the Bacchanal at Caesars—it's getting harder and harder to find anything budget-minded on the Strip. Well, anywhere worth eating, certainly. This isn't on the Strip, but it is nearby, and the prices are cheaper than at any buffet within a 5-mile radius. Plus, you are less likely to find tremendous lines here. Having said that, don't expect anything miraculous, though they get points for keeping the food at the correct temperature (many a buffet's hot food suffers from a cooling effect as it sits out). Options run the usual gamut: Asian (decent pot stickers), Mexican (fine beef fajitas), and a carving station (with full rotisserie chickens). Heaping piles of crab legs are a noteworthy favorite.

In Gold Coast, 4000 W. Flamingo Rd. © **702/367-7111.** www.goldcoastcasino.com. Breakfast $7; lunch $9; dinner $13–$25; Sun brunch $13. Reduced prices for children 4–9; free for children 3 and under. Mon–Sat 7–10am, 11am–3pm, and 4–9pm; Sun 8am–3pm and 4–9pm.

EXPLORING LAS VEGAS

You aren't going to lack for things to do in Las Vegas. More than likely, you've come here for the gambling, which should keep you pretty busy. But you can't sit at a slot machine forever. After all, you're going to have to get up to go to the bathroom at some point! When you do, maybe you should look around at some of the other things here that can keep you entertained.

Just walking on the Strip and gazing at the gaudy, garish, absurd wonder of it all can occupy quite a lot of time. This is the number-one activity we recommend in Vegas; at night, it is a mind-boggling sight. Beyond that there are options galore, from popular bits of Vegas silliness like volcanoes and pirate battles to museums, thrill rides, spas, recreation, and beyond. And, of course, you can engage in those most iconic Vegas traditions, getting married and gambling. All of that and more is covered in this chapter. Don't forget there are shows and plenty of other nighttime entertainment, which you can read more about in chapter 8. There are also out-of-town sightseeing options, such as **Hoover Dam** (a major tourist destination), **Red Rock Canyon,** and excursions to the **Grand Canyon.** We've listed the best of these in chapter 9.

LAS VEGAS ICONIC SIGHTS

ENTERTAINMENT COMPLEXES

KISS by Monster Mini Golf ★★, p. 144
Pole Position Raceway ★, p. 147
SkyZone ★, p. 146

EXHIBITS

Bodies . . . The Exhibition ★★, p. 132
Score! ★★, p. 134
Titantic: The Exhibition ★, p. 134

MUSEUMS & GALLERIES

The Arts Factory ★, p. 138
Bellagio Gallery of Fine Art ★★, p. 134
CityCenter Fine Art Collection ★★, p. 132
Clark County Museum ★★, p. 144
Discovery Children's Museum ★★★, p. 138
Emergency Arts ★★, p. 139
Las Vegas Natural History Museum ★, p. 140
Madame Tussauds Las Vegas ★★, p. 135
The Mob Museum ★★★, p. 140
National Atomic Testing Museum ★★★, p. 144
The Neon Museum ★★★, p. 141
Nevada State Museum ★, p. 147
Pinball Hall of Fame & Museum ★★★, p. 145
Shelby American Heritage Center ★, p. 146

THEME PARKS & RIDES

Adventuredome ★★, p. 136
Big Apple Coaster & Arcade ★★, p. 132
Eiffel Tower Experience ★, p. 135
High Roller Observation Wheel ★★, p. 135
SlotZilla ★★, p. 141
Stratosphere Tower & Thrill Rides ★★, p. 137
Wet 'n Wild ★, p. 148

ZOOS

Lion Habitat Ranch ★★★, p. 145
Siegfried & Roy's Secret Garden & Dolphin Habitat ★★★, p. 136
Shark Reef at Mandalay Bay ★, p. 134

OTHER ATTRACTIONS

Downtown Container Park ★★★, p. 172
Ethel M Chocolates ★, p. 145
Fremont Street Experience ★★★, p. 140
The Smith Center for the Performing Arts ★★★, p. 141
Springs Preserve ★★★, p. 148

SOUTH STRIP

Big Apple Coaster & Arcade ★★ THRILL RIDE   As if the outside of New York-New York wasn't busy enough, someone decided to knock it up a few notches by having a roller coaster wind around the whole thing. The whimsically designed cars evoke Manhattan taxi cabs and run at speeds up to 67 mph while going through drops of as much as 144 feet, a full loop, and the "heartline" twist, which simulates a jet-fighter barrel roll. Adrenaline junkies may find it too tame, but the average fun-seeker will do a lot of screaming. If that's too much for you, try the tamer amusements in the arcade that features carnival and video games.

In New York–New York, 3790 Las Vegas Blvd. S. ⓒ **702/740-6969.** www.newyorknewyork.com. Single rides $14 adults; all-day pass $25. Must be 54 in. tall to ride. Sun–Thurs 11am–11pm; Fri–Sat 10:30am–midnight. Closed during inclement weather.

Bodies . . . The Exhibition ★★ EXHIBIT   A stunning and controversial exhibit featuring what can be best described as real live dead bodies (over 200 full and partial specimens donated by their former inhabitants, though that's where some controversy comes in). Utilizing a patented freeze-dry operation, full bodies, artfully dissected body parts, and stripped cadavers are on display not for sensationalism—though it is pretty sensational in nearly all senses of the word—but for visitors to fully appreciate the wonder and mechanics that go into our transient flesh. When a body is positioned in an athletic pose, you can see how the muscles work, and when a cross section of a lung afflicted with cancer is right in front of you, you may be glad Vegas has passed stricter smoking laws. It's educational and bizarre and not something you're likely to forget soon. Surprisingly, not grotesque, but not for the ultrasqueamish.

In the Luxor, 3900 Las Vegas Blvd. S. ⓒ **702/262-4000.** www.bodiestheexhibition.com/lasvegas. Admission $32 adults, $30 seniors 65 and over, $24 ages 4–12, free 3 and under, $29 Nevada residents. Daily 10am–10pm; last admission 9pm.

CityCenter Fine Art Collection ★★ ART MUSEUM   Previous attempts at displaying fine art have met with mixed success in Las Vegas. Of the four major galleries/museums to open over the last couple of decades, only the one at Bellagio remains. But CityCenter has gone a different route, choosing to integrate its fine art collection throughout the resort, turning the entire place into one big gallery of sorts. There's a sculpture from Maya Lin, designer of the Vietnam War Memorial, over the check-in desk; the iconic *Reclining Connected Forms* sculpture by Henry Moore; a massive installation of canoes and rowboats in a valet area by Nancy Rubins; a mural from artist and filmmaker Julian Schnabel; and a 250-foot-long LED display from street artist Jenny Holzer, to name a few. You can pick up a brochure and map at the concierge desk at Aria Las Vegas that will guide you to the major works, or there's even "an app for that"—download it for free to your iPhone and it will guide you to the works and give you in-depth background. Wear comfortable shoes; there is a lot of walking involved.

At CityCenter, 3730 Las Vegas Blvd. S. ⓒ **702/590-7111.** www.citycenter.com. Free admission. Most artworks are outdoors or in 24-hour public spaces.

CSI: The Experience ★★ ENTERTAINMENT COMPLEX   Although spinoffs have moved the sleuthing to Miami and New York, the original *CSI* television show takes place in Las Vegas, so how apropos is this major attraction, which allows you to work a crime scene right here on the Strip. Three different crimes have occurred—a car has crashed into a house, a woman has been murdered behind a motel, and a

Las Vegas Attractions

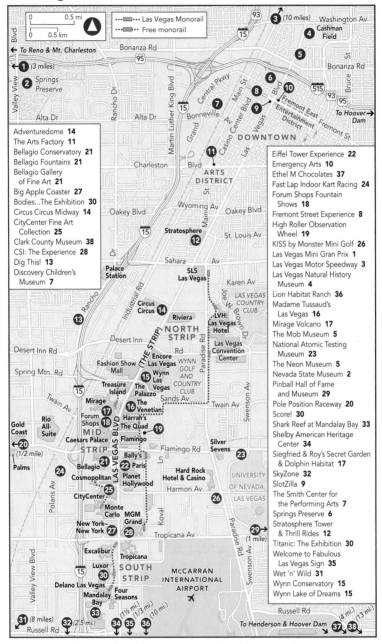

Adventuredome **14**
The Arts Factory **11**
Bellagio Conservatory **21**
Bellagio Fountains **21**
Bellagio Gallery
  of Fine Art **21**
Big Apple Coaster **27**
Bodies...The Exhibition **30**
Circus Circus Midway **14**
CityCenter Fine Art
  Collection **25**
Clark County Museum **38**
CSI: The Experience **28**
Dig This! **13**
Discovery Children's
  Museum **7**

Eiffel Tower Experience **22**
Emergency Arts **10**
Ethel M Chocolates **37**
Fast Lap Indoor Kart Racing **24**
Forum Shops Fountain
  Shows **18**
Fremont Street Experience **8**
High Roller Observation
  Wheel **19**
KISS by Monster Mini Golf **26**
Las Vegas Mini Gran Prix **1**
Las Vegas Motor Speedway **3**
Las Vegas Natural History
  Museum **4**
Lion Habitat Ranch **36**
Madame Tussaud's
  Las Vegas **16**
Mirage Volcano **17**
The Mob Museum **5**
National Atomic Testing
  Museum **23**
The Neon Museum **5**
Nevada State Museum **2**
Pinball Hall of Fame
  and Museum **29**
Pole Position Raceway **20**
Score! **30**
Shark Reef at Mandalay Bay **33**
Shelby American Heritage
  Center **34**
Siegfried & Roy's Secret Garden
  & Dolphin Habitat **17**
SkyZone **32**
SlotZilla **9**
The Smith Center for
  the Performing Arts **7**
Springs Preserve **6**
Stratosphere Tower
  & Thrill Rides **12**
Titanic: The Exhibition **30**
Welcome to Fabulous
  Las Vegas Sign **35**
Wet 'n' Wild **31**
Wynn Conservatory **15**
Wynn Lake of Dreams **15**

skeleton has been found in the desert—and it's up to you to examine the crime scene, look for clues, take notes, and then run it all through an interactive lab of sorts with help from videos of various stars of the show (we miss you, Gil Grissom!) and real-life CSI technicians. It's silly, gory fun and highly engrossing if you have an analytical mind (all but the most sullen of teenagers will love this).

In MGM Grand, 3799 Las Vegas Blvd. S. ✆ **877/660-0660** or 702/891-5738. http://lasvegas.csi exhibit.com. Admission $28 adults; $21 children 4–11. Daily 9am–9pm (last admission 7:30pm).

Score! ★★ EXHIBIT   Most people watch sports in Vegas because they have wagers on the outcome of the game. But true sports fanatics should step away from the betting window and check out this cool facility that gives you a chance to become a sports star by conquering various challenges. Navigate a puck through a hockey obstacle course; test your hand-eye coordination as a football player; clock your arm with a measured baseball pitch; become a pit crew member on a NASCAR racing team; and more. In between are various bits of memorabilia including signed jerseys, winning game balls, trophies, photos, and the like. At the end you are awarded your pro-sports "contract" complete with your name and face on the cover of a virtual sports magazine before being sent into the sports-obsessive's dream of a gift shop.

In the Luxor, 3900 Las Vegas Blvd. S. ✆ **702/262-4200.** www.scorelv.com. Admission $28 adults; $20 locals; $15 children under 12. Daily 10am–10pm.

Shark Reef at Mandalay Bay ★ ZOO   Given that watching fish can lower your blood pressure, it's practically a public service for Mandalay Bay to provide this facility in a city where craps tables and other gaming areas can bring your excitement level to dangerous heights. Although we admire the style (it's built to look like a sunken temple), and standing in the all-glass tunnel surrounded by sharks is cool, it's just a giant aquarium, which we like, but not at these prices. *Note:* It is *waaay* off in a remote part of Mandalay Bay, which might be a hassle for those with limited mobility.

In Mandalay Bay, 3950 Las Vegas Blvd. S. ✆ **702/632-4555.** www.sharkreef.com. Admission $18 adults, $12 children 5–12, free for children 4 and under, $15 Nevada residents. Sun–Thurs 10am–8pm; Fri–Sat 10am–10pm. Last admission 1 hr. before closing. Hours vary seasonally.

Titanic: The Exhibition ★ EXHIBIT   It's too easy to say "you've seen the movie, now see the exhibit." But that is sort of the case; if you were captivated by the Oscar-winning epic, you will definitely want to take in this exhibit on the unsinkable luxury liner that sank on its maiden voyage. While it's a can't-miss for buffs, it might still be of some interest for those with only marginal feelings about the massive 1912 disaster. It's a strangely somber subject for Vegas. It features displays explaining the ship's ill-fated maiden voyage; relics salvaged from the sunken liner; and even re-creations of sample cabins from first, second, and third class, including atmospheric conditions, giving you a sense of how it felt to travel aboard what was an incredible vessel. There is even a large chunk of real ice standing in for the culprit berg.

In the Luxor, 3900 Las Vegas Blvd. S. ✆ **702/262-4400.** www.luxor.com. Admission $32 adults, $30 seniors 65 and over, $24 children 4–12, free for children 3 and under, $29 Nevada residents with ID. Daily 10am–10pm (last admission 9pm).

MID-STRIP

Bellagio Gallery of Fine Art ★★ ART MUSEUM   This small but effective gallery is one of the few remaining places on the Strip where you can see fine art, if you are so inclined. Works by brand-name artists (like Monet, Picasso, and Ansel

Adams) give it legitimacy, and shows from more unexpected choices (actor/comedian Steve Martin, for instance) give it cachet. Will there be as interesting a show when you go? Beats us. (When we wrote this, it was a collection of works by Andy Warhol, so in this instance, yes.) Then there's that ticket price. Do let us point out that admission to the Louvre—needless to say, quite a bit larger and with, one can safely say, some notable works—is about the same price as this gallery.

In Bellagio, 3600 Las Vegas Blvd. S. © **702/693-7871.** www.bellagio.com. Admission $16 adults, $13 seniors and Nevada residents, $11 teachers, students with ID, military. Daily 10am–7pm (last admission 5:30pm).

Eiffel Tower Experience ★ OBSERVATION TOWER   Whether this is worth the dough depends on how much you like views. The "ride" portion is a glass-enclosed elevator to the top as a guide delivers a few facts—this is a half-size exact replica, down to the paint color of the original. Once you reach the uppermost platform, you are welcome to stand around and look out for as long as you want, which probably isn't 2 hours, the length of the average movie, which costs about what this does. Nice view, though.

In Paris Las Vegas, 3655 Las Vegas Blvd. S. © **702/946-7000.** www.parislv.com. Admission $11.50 adults 9:30am–7:15pm, $16.50 7:15pm–close; $7.50 seniors 60 and over and children 12 and under 9:30am–7:15pm, $11.50 7:15–close. Mon–Fri 9:30am–12:30am; Sat–Sun 9:30am–1am; weather permitting.

High Roller Observation Wheel ★★ THRILL RIDE   The *if bigger is better, then biggest is best* ethos that Las Vegas loves so much continues here with the world's tallest observation wheel. Standing at nearly 550 feet high, the massive structure has fundamentally changed the skyline and provides some of the best views of the Strip (and much of southern Nevada) you'll find. There are 28 fully enclosed, air-conditioned cabs, each capable of holding up to 40 people, although if you get stuck in one that full you will need to fight your way to good snapshot-worthy window space. One full revolution takes about 30 minutes, so it's less of a thrill ride than a leisurely, albeit really high up, walk in the park. Even those with height phobias may find this tolerable. Go at night for the best photo opportunities of the city in its fully lit-up glory—it's worth the extra few bucks you have to pay for the privilege. Prices are high for this relatively short experience—a pass to the top of the even taller Stratosphere Tower (see below) is significantly less expensive. Maybe it's because the tower doesn't go around in a circle? The good news is that they not only allow drinks on board, they practically encourage it, with a bar on your way to the boarding area. Of course, there are no bathrooms on the ride, so drink at your own peril. Note that lines can be long during peak periods both to get tickets and to queue up for the cabs, so it's best to buy online beforehand and budget some extra time for standing in line.

3545 Las Vegas Blvd. S. © **800/CAESARS.** www.thelinq.com. High Roller admission $25 day, $35 night. Daily 10am–2am.

Madame Tussauds Las Vegas ★★ MUSEUM   Madame Tussauds's waxworks exhibition has been a top London attraction for nearly 2 centuries, so even if you aren't a fan of wax museums, this is probably worth a stop. Figures here are state of the art, painstakingly constructed to perfectly match the real person. Truth be told, while some are nearly identical to their living counterparts—Brad Pitt gave us a start—others look about as much like the celebrity in question as a department-store mannequin. All the waxworks are free-standing, allowing—and indeed encouraging—guests to get up close and personal. Go ahead, lay your cheek next to Elvis's or Sinatra's and have your photo taken. Or put on a wedding dress and get "married" to George Clooney (you know you want to). Or fondle J. Lo's butt (she won't mind). Recent additions include Sofia Vergara and Whitney Houston. Newer additions include a section of Marvel superheroes and a 4-D theater featuring animated versions of Iron Man, the Hulk, and others.

In The Venetian, 3355 Las Vegas Blvd. S. ✆ **702/862-7800.** www.madametussauds.com/lasvegas. Admission $30 adults, $20 children 4–12, free for children 3 and under. Discounts for booking online. Sun–Thurs 10am–9pm; Fri–Sat 10am–10pm; hours vary seasonally.

Siegfried & Roy's Secret Garden & Dolphin Habitat ★★★ ZOO   After more than 20 years, this engaging animal habitat remains one of the best antidotes to Las Vegas stress. Spend an hour watching dolphins and tigers and you won't care how much money you lost on the slots. The bulk of your time will most likely be spent in the well-regarded dolphin habitat, a 2.5-million-gallon home for a family of bottlenose dolphins that were either rescued or born here. This is more than just a Sea World–style, sit in bleachers and watch the animals cavort kind of place (although they have that, too). Here you can get up close to the pools and sometimes interact with them (splashing is involved), which is a treat, especially for kids. Pay extra and you can go VIP, behind-the-scenes tours; spend an entire day as a trainer, complete with time in the pool; and even "paint" with them as you hold a canvas and the dolphin holds a special brush in its mouth. The latter is an unmitigated thrill that allows you to connect with these amazing animals, or at least pretend you are.

The Secret Garden part is a small zoo, originally designed as an on-site home for the animals used in Siegfried & Roy's magic show, which ended in 2003 after a disagreement between Roy and a tiger. The animals that remain are mostly of the big cat variety, including some of the illusionists' famed white tigers. It's fine, but don't expect a lot of excitement. On hot Vegas days they mostly (and wisely) just lay around in the shade or shallow pools in their habitats, so don't expect them to be hunting elk or playing with big balls of yarn.

While it's easy to have a pang of environmentally conscious guilt over animals in captivity, the entire facility is well run and scrupulously maintained, the trainers are obviously passionate, and the animals seem to thrive here. Several of the dolphins are more than 30 years old, which is more than double their life expectancy in the wild.

In The Mirage, 3400 Las Vegas Blvd. S. ✆ **702/791-7111.** www.miragehabitat.com. Admission $20 adults, $15 children 4–10, free for children 3 and under. Mon–Fri 11am–5:30pm; Sat–Sun 10am–5:30pm; hours vary seasonally.

NORTH STRIP

Adventuredome ★★ AMUSEMENT PARK   This is an okay place to spend a hot afternoon, especially since it's one of the few family-friendly attractions in town. Plus, unlike most theme parks, it's indoors! The glass dome that towers overhead lets in natural light so you get the best of both worlds—sunlight and air-conditioning. A double-loop roller coaster careens around the simulated Grand Canyon, and there's a laser-tag area, some bouncy/twirly/stomach-churning rides, and a modest number of other, tamer rides for kids of all ages. Video games and a carnival-style arcade are separate from the attractions, though it all still feels pretty hectic. The log-flume ride closed in 2013 to make way for a cutting-edge roller coaster, El Loco, which is one of only six of its kind in the world. Although it's a short ride (a little longer than a minute), it's a scary one, with negative-g drops, reverse barrel rolls, and open cars that seem ready to tip you off of them.

2880 Las Vegas Blvd. S. (behind Circus Circus). © **702/794-3939.** www.adventuredome.com. Free admission; $5–$10 per ride; daily pass $29.95 adults, $16.95 children 33–47 in. tall. Mon–Thurs 10am–6pm; Fri–Sat 10am–midnight; Sun 10am–9pm; hours vary seasonally.

Circus Circus Midway ★ ENTERTAINMENT COMPLEX   First inaugurated in 1968, the big-top action at this family-friendly hotel is billed as the largest permanent circus in the world. High-wire, trapeze, juggling, acrobatics, and more fill the top of the "tent" daily from 11am until late at night, while more than 200 carnival-style midway games get the young ones inured to the joys (and heartache) of risking money for questionable odds of a reward. Note that while the attractions here are definitely kid-friendly, you have to go through the casino to get to them.

In Circus Circus, 2880 Las Vegas Blvd. S. © **702/734-0410.** www.circuscircus.com. Free admission. Daily 11am–midnight.

Stratosphere Tower & Thrill Rides ★★ THRILL RIDE   Whether you come for the views or the scary rides, the Stratosphere Tower is a uniquely Vegas experience. Indoor and outdoor decks provide some pretty remarkable views of the city, southern Nevada, and perhaps even California on a clear day from this, the tallest observation tower west of the Mississippi (more than 1,100 feet). Obviously, acrophobics should avoid this at all costs.

Atop the tower are four marvelous thrill rides that will test your mettle and perhaps how strong your stomach is. The **Big Shot** is a breathtaking free-fall ride that thrusts you 160 feet in the air along a 228-foot spire at the top of the tower, and then plummets back down again. Sitting in an open car, you seem to be dangling in space over Las Vegas. Amping up the terror factor is **X-Scream,** a giant teeter-totter–style device that propels you in an open car off the side of the 100-story tower and lets you dangle there weightlessly before returning you to relative safety. Then there's the aptly named **Insanity,** a spinning whirligig of a contraption that straps you into a seat and twirls you around 1,000 feet or so above terra firma. Insanity is right.

Finally, if whirling and twirling and spinning around at the top of the tower is just not good enough for you, there's **SkyJump,** in which you get to leap off the top of the thing. Although we kind of wish we were kidding, we're really not. Jumpers are put into flight suits and harnesses, then taken up to the 108th floor where they get connected to a big cable/winch contraption. Then, they jump. It's a "controlled" descent, meaning that you don't just drop the roughly 830 feet to the landing pad, but you are flying down at speeds of up to 40 mph with nothing but a couple of metal wires keeping you in place. There are lots of safety features that they tout and the three other SkyJumps around the world (in New Zealand, China, and South Korea) have sterling safety records. Nevertheless, they may call the other ride Insanity, but we think this one is the truly insane option. *Note:* The rides are shut down in inclement weather and high winds.

Atop Stratosphere Las Vegas, 2000 Las Vegas Blvd. S. © **702/380-7777.** www.stratospherehotel. com. Tower: Admission $18 adults; $12 seniors, Nevada residents and hotel guests; $10 children 4–12; free for children 3 and under. Rides: Big Shot $15, X-Scream $15, Insanity $15, SkyJump $110. Tower admission waived with SkyJump. Multi-ride and all-day packages available. Sun–Thurs 10am–1am; Fri–Sat 10am–2am; hours vary seasonally. Minimum height 48 in. for Big Shot, 52 in. for X-Scream and Insanity. Maximum weight 275 lbs. for SkyJump.

free **VEGAS**

Vegas used to be the land of freebies—or at least, stuff so cheap it seemed free. Those days are an increasingly dim memory, but some hotels still offer free attractions designed to lure you into their casinos, where you might well then drop far more than the cost of a day ticket to Disney World. Here's a handy list of the best of the free bait—er, sights:

Bellagio Conservatory (in Bellagio) ★★★ PARK/GARDEN   A totally preposterous idea, a larger-than-life greenhouse atrium, filled with seasonal living foliage in riotous colors and styles, changed with meticulous regularity. From Easter to Chinese New Year, events are celebrated with carefully designed splashes of flowers, plants, and remarkable decorations—it's an incredible amount of labor for absolutely no immediate financial payoff. No wonder it's one of the most popular sights in Vegas. Open 24 hours.

Bellagio Fountains (outside Bellagio) ★★★ ICON   Giant spouts of water shoot up and down and sideways, and dance their little aquatic hearts out to music ranging from show tunes to

Chopin. When we tell people about this, they roll their eyes when they think we aren't looking, and then they go see it for themselves . . . and end up staying for several numbers. Shows are daily every half-hour, starting early afternoon, then every 15 minutes 7pm to midnight. Closed when it's windy; hours vary seasonally.

The Forum Shops Fountain Shows (in the Forum Shops at Caesars) ★ ICON   The first established of the free shows and easily the stupidest. We love it—in theory, at least—as giant "marble" Greco-Roman statues come to creaky animatronic life and deliver a largely unintelligible speech, mostly exhorting the crowds to eat, drink, and get so merry they will think nothing of dropping a bundle at the slots. A second show in another part of the mall adds fire, so that's cool. It's great silly fun in the way that Vegas should be. Daily every hour, starting at 10am.

Mirage Volcano (outside The Mirage) ★★ ICON   When it first opened with the hotel in 1989, this erupting "volcano" literally stopped

DOWNTOWN

The Arts Factory ★ COMMERCIAL ART GALLERY   Believe it or not, Las Vegas has a pretty decent art scene (what some would consider soul-crushing is what others consider inspirational), and this complex, located in the 18b Arts District, is the place to find proof. It features several galleries, boutiques, and a number of work spaces for local artists plus a bistro and bar.

107 E. Charleston Blvd. ✆ **702/383-3133.** www.theartsfactory.com. Free admission. Hours vary by gallery.

Discovery Children's Museum ★★★ MUSEUM   This stunning $55-million facility opened in 2013 on the campus of the Smith Center for the Performing Arts, and is hands down the best thing to do in Vegas with your small children (and not just because it's one of the only things to do in Vegas with your small children). Three floors of hands-on exhibits and interactive displays use engaging play activities to subtly teach kids about nutrition, problem solving, physics, environmental sustainability, art, the power of imagination, and much more. Everything is cool, but the Water traffic on the Strip. The fact that it's not quite as spectacular these days—even after a 2008 makeover amped up the fire, lights, sound, and effects to a much more entertaining level—says more about how jaded we've become than how cool it is. Get up close to feel the heat of the "lava" blasts and the rumble of the sound system. Eruptions are daily on the hour after dark until 11pm.

Welcome to Fabulous Las Vegas Sign ★★★ ICON   Erected in 1959, this colorfully lit neon sign is probably the most iconic and most photographed attraction in Las Vegas. Located in the median of Las Vegas Boulevard about a mile south of Mandalay Bay, visiting was made easier a few years back with the addition of a parking lot, which means you no longer need to play chicken with oncoming traffic to get to it. It has no formal address, but GPS users should use 5200 Las Vegas Blvd. S. to get in the vicinity. The lot is open 24 hours, but go at night when it's all lit up for the best photo opportunities.

Wynn Conservatory (in Wynn Las Vegas) ★ PARK/GARDEN   Although not as jaw-dropping as its spiritual cousin, the Bellagio Conservatory (see above), this indoor atrium of floral displays is still worth a gander, if for no other reason than it's on your way from the front door to the casino. The arrangements change regularly, though they may reflect the striking floral mosaics on the floor below. It's open 24 hours.

Wynn Lake of Dreams (in Wynn Las Vegas) ★ ICON   Masked as it is from the street by a 150-foot-tall "mountain," this light, laser, fog, and special-effect show can only be seen from select areas inside the hotel, mostly in bars requiring you to buy expensive drinks. Should you bother? Maybe. Basically, twice an hour, a lake lights up with pretty colors, cued to tunes ranging from classical to Louis Armstrong for "interludes." At the top of the hour are bigger extravaganzas of weird hologram erotic-psychedelic images projected on the wall waterfall, while shapes and puppets pop out for even more weird action, with some rather adult imagery at times. Shows are every 30 minutes, from 6pm to midnight.

World, with its replica of Hoover Dam, and the Summit, a three-story jungle-gym of science education, are especially noteworthy.

360 Promenade Place (at The Smith Center for the Performing Arts). © **702/382-5437.** www. discoverykidslv.com. Admission $12 ages 1–99. Tue–Fri 9am–4pm; Sat 10m–5pm, Sun noon–5pm.

Emergency Arts ★★ COMMERCIAL ART GALLERY   The artists in residence here rescued a derelict downtown building that was once a medical clinic and turned it into a funky, fun, bohemian space dedicated to the creation and conservation of all things art. The first floor has a small cafe (perfect for having a coffee while discussing Sartre, we think), a used record store, and the temporary home of the Burlesque Hall of Fame and Museum. The latter is a small couple of rooms with what is said to be a tiny fraction of photos and memorabilia honoring the peek-a-boo art form. The rest of the first and all of the second floor of the space are taken up by small boutiques where local artists show and sell their wares. There are paintings, sculpture, jewelry, clothing, and much more, and while the quality obviously varies from artist to artist, it's all totally unique and a much better way to spend your souvenir dollars than on a Las Vegas snow globe.

520 E. Fremont St. ✆ **702/686-3164.** www.emergencyartslv.com. Free admission. Hours vary by gallery.

Fremont Street Experience ★★★ ICON The Fremont Street Experience is a 5-block, open-air, landscaped strip of outdoor snack shops, vendor carts, and colorful kiosks purveying food and merchandise. Overhead is a 90-foot-high steel-mesh "celestial vault" that at night becomes **Viva Vision,** a high-tech video-and-sound show (the canopy is equipped with more than 12.5 million lights), enhanced by a concert hall–quality sound system. There are a number of different shows, and there's music between the light performances as well. It's really cool, in that Vegas over-the-top way that we love so much. The addition of several hotel bars open to the pedestrian street has upped the "party" quotient and frequent concerts and events have made it even more popular than it was. Oh, and look up to see people zooming by on a zip line! It's a great place where you can stroll, eat, or even dance to the music under the lights.

Fremont St. (btw. Main St. and Las Vegas Blvd.), Downtown. www.vegasexperience.com. Free admission. Shows nightly on the hour.

Las Vegas Natural History Museum ★ MUSEUM This humble temple of taxidermy harkens back to elementary-school field trips, around 1965, when stuffed elk and brown bears forever protecting their kill were as close as most of us got to exotic animals. Worn around the edges but very sweet and relaxed, the museum is enlivened by a hands-on activity room and two life-size dinosaurs that roar at one another intermittently. A small boy was observed leaping toward his dad upon watching this display, so you might want to warn any sensitive little ones that the big tyrannosaurs aren't going anywhere. The former King Tut's Tomb exhibit that used to be at Luxor is now here, which feels a bit out of place amidst the "natural" history exhibits (as opposed to a man-made one) but it's still cool that it isn't sitting in a warehouse somewhere. Surprisingly, the gift shop here is particularly well stocked with neat items you won't too terribly mind buying for the kids.

900 Las Vegas Blvd. N. (at Washington Ave.). ✆ **702/384-3466.** www.lvnhm.org. Admission $10 adults; $8 seniors, students, and military; $5 children 3–11; free for children 2 and under. Daily 9am–4pm. Closed Thanksgiving and Dec 25.

The Mob Museum ★★★ MUSEUM Vegas has a long and complicated history with the Mafia. Most of the classic hotels—the ones that helped define the city like the Flamingo, the Dunes, the Sands, and the Stardust—were built, in part or in whole, with mob money, and organized crime virtually ran Sin City for decades. When Senator Estes Kefauver headed an early 1950s committee to investigate the mob and its power, hearings were held in cities around the country, including in a courthouse in Las Vegas. That courthouse is now the Mob Museum.

The three-story facility has been lovingly restored and features 17,000 square feet of exhibit space examining the Mafia in America, from its beginnings in New York and Chicago through Prohibition, its expansion to Las Vegas, and its influence on everything from law enforcement to popular culture. Although the topic is deadly serious, the museum itself is dynamic and engaging, using the latest state-of-the-art tricks to bring the stories it is telling to life. A video about the St. Valentine's Massacre is broadcast on the actual wall against which seven mob associates were gunned down in Chicago; touch-screen displays allow visitors to try to identify mug shots; a Tommy gun bucks and makes gunshot noises when you pull the trigger; old slot machines have modern interfaces that explain casino cheats; and so much more. Each exhibit is a highlight of its own, including the actual Kefauver hearing courtroom, which now has video and 3-D displays that evoke the feeling that you are watching the real thing happening in the room in which it did.

Officially known as the National Museum of Organized Crime and Law Enforcement, this endlessly fascinating, brilliantly executed facility deserves to become a Las Vegas icon—the kind of must-see attraction that should be on everyone's list when visiting the city and a reason to come here all by itself. Be sure to check the website for frequent special events like a celebration of Repeal Day and lectures from former mobsters and G-men.

300 Stewart Ave. © **702/229-2734.** www.themobmuseum.org. Admission $20 adults; $14 children 5–17 and students with ID; $16 seniors, military, law enforcement, and teachers; $10 NV residents with ID. Sun–Thurs 10am–7pm; Fri–Sat 10am–8pm.

The Neon Museum ★★★ MUSEUM   No other attraction is more archetypically Las Vegas than this, the "boneyard" where retired neon signs from casinos, hotels, stores, and more go when their jobs are done. Several of the signs have been fully restored to their former glory, including a camel-covered advertisement for the Sahara and a giant horseshoe-shaped beauty that used to sit atop Binion's. Most of the signs, however, are faded, dented, and dusty, which in a way almost makes them more beautiful. They are relics of Las Vegas's history, when names like Stardust, Aladdin, Dunes, and Moulin Rouge meant something. Incredibly knowledgeable guides give a tour of the lot, which lasts for roughly an hour and includes colorful stories about the signs, their designers, and the city itself. Nighttime tours are a special treat, with the working signs lit up and others bathed in colored lights that help evoke their former beauty. Note that tour group size is limited and sell out early, so you must book in advance—walk-ups are discouraged and will usually not be accommodated. Also note that the bulk of the tour is outside, so check the weather schedule and dress accordingly.

770 Las Vegas Blvd. N. (at McWilliams Ave.). © **702/387-6366.** www.neonmuseum.org. Admission $18 daytime tours adults; $12 seniors., students, military, NV residents; $25 nighttime tours adults; $22 seniors, students, military, NV residents; children 6 and under free. No kids under 13 allowed on nighttime tours. Daily 9am until 9pm, hours vary seasonally.

SlotZilla ★★ THRILL RIDE   Here it is, the newest Vegas attraction that deserves to take a place in the Pantheon of iconic Sin City silliness alongside the Bellagio Fountains and the Welcome to Fabulous Las Vegas sign. Billed as, and shaped like, the world's tallest slot machine, it's really a launching platform for two sets of zip lines that run down Fremont Street. The lower four are traditional, seated lines running from about 6 stories up by Neonopolis about three blocks to Binion's. The top "zoom" lines feature an opportunity to fly superhero-style, face down, from 12 stories up all the way to a platform next to Main Street some five blocks away. Compared to some zip lines in more adventurous settings, this one is pretty tame, but it's still not for the faint of heart, especially as you step out over the edge and then come in for the unexpectedly jerky landing. Go at night for the full effect of all the Glitter Gulch neon lights. This thing started out popular and there is no reason to believe it will be anything but that in the future, so plan way ahead—rides may be sold out and/or wait times could be epic.

425 Fremont St. © **702/ZIPVEGAS.** www.vegasexperience.org. Admission $20–$30. Must be over 60 pounds and under 300 pounds to ride. Sun–Thurs noon to midnight; Fri–Sat noon–2am.

The Smith Center for the Performing Arts ★★★ PERFORMING ARTS VENUE   Although Las Vegas has been synonymous with entertainment for decades, filled with showrooms and theaters galore, the one thing the city never had was a true

THE RESURGENCE OF downtown LAS VEGAS

For decades, the bulk of the attention, and development dollars, in Las Vegas has been paid to the Strip, while the original part of Sin City, the Downtown area, languished and seemed on the verge of extinction.

Credit, at least in part, online retailer Zappos.com for changing all that. Its plan to move its headquarters and a couple thousand employees into the former city hall building spurred a resurgence in Downtown Las Vegas, with major revamps to old hotels, new restaurants, fun and funky bars, attractions, street festivals, and more all lending a new sense of life to the area.

The bulk of the action happens on the **Fremont Street Experience,** the pedestrian-only mall on Fremont Street between Main Street and Las Vegas Boulevard. That's where you'll find most of the casinos, shopping, and restaurants.

The **Fremont East Entertainment District** takes up several blocks of Fremont Street just east of Las Vegas Boulevard and has several bars, lounges, and clubs all within a few feet of each other, so no matter how much you may be stumbling, you can probably still make it to the next one in your all-night pub crawl.

This is the area where you'll find the **Downtown Container Park** (p. 172), a shopping and dining complex made out of recycled shipping containers and prefabricated metal cubes. In addition to the retail and food options, there are a giant treehouse-style jungle gym inside for the kids and a fire-breathing praying mantis sculpture out front for kids of all ages.

The **18b Arts District** is a few blocks south of Fremont Street, bounded, more or less, by Las Vegas Boulevard to the east, Commerce Street to the west, Hoover Avenue on the north, and Colorado Avenue on the south. Art galleries, antique and collectible stores, and more

performing arts venue—the kind of place where symphonies and true Broadway shows (not the cut-down versions that happen on the Strip) could spread their wings. The Smith Center changes all that and should firmly establish Sin City as a cultural center to be reckoned with.

The buildings are stunning, designed with a timeless Art Deco style inspired by Hoover Dam—notice the chandeliers, which look like an inverted version of the water intake towers. The whole thing is bright, modern, and dramatic, yet comfortable, familiar, and built to last. While many Vegas buildings attempt scope and grandeur, they feel impermanent somehow—as if they are just waiting to be imploded so the next big thing can be built. The Smith Center feels like the kind of place that will be here for centuries.

The main space, Reynolds Hall, is a finely tuned, Carnegie Hall–worthy, 2,050-seat concert venue that hosts philharmonics, headliners, and touring versions of Broadway shows like *The Book of Mormon*. The 300-seat Cabaret Theater is a classic nightclub-style space with big windows, giving it a sense of airiness missing in most theaters. It features a jazz series, more intimate concerts, and a can't-miss, once-a-month set from former Strip headliner Clint Holmes. A third, 200-seat "black box"–style theater holds smaller theater and dance productions. Outside is a beautiful park that can also be used for performances or just as place to sit and enjoy the view.

361 Symphony Park Ave. (at Grand Central Pkwy.). ℂ **702/749-2000.** www.thesmithcenter.com. Prices and times vary by show.

than a few pawn shops and bail bonds offices (to give it color, we suppose) are scattered about the neighborhood, giving it a refreshingly bohemian feeling as it sits in the shadow of the overprocessed Strip.

The monthly **First Friday Las Vegas** street festival happens in the heart of the 18b Arts District on the blocks surrounding the intersection of Casino Center Drive and Colorado Avenue. Local artists hawk their wares while live bands and DJs keep the crowds moving, play areas (complete with a video game truck) keep the kids entertained, and a sea of food vendors and food trucks keep everyone fat and happy. It's one of the few places where there is a true sense of community in Vegas. It happens, appropriately enough, on the first Friday of every month from 5 until 11pm. For more information, visit www.first fridaylasvegas.com.

Las Vegas StrEATS is another street festival occurring on the second Saturday of every month on the Jackie Gaughan Plaza near the El Cortez Hotel in the Fremont East District. This one is a little more urban in feeling, with the vendors focusing on street art and streetwear and the entertainment leaning toward indie rock, but it's the parking lot full of the city's best food trucks that really brings out the crowds. For more information, visit www.vegasstreats.com.

The area has even qualified for its own big-time music, arts, and food event with the **Life is Beautiful Festival,** held each October. The inaugural event in 2013 drew more than 65,000 people and featured stages with Beck, the Killers, Kings of Leon, Imagine Dragons, and more while food tents had eats from Cat Cora, Hubert Keller, Todd English, and Paul Bartolotta, among others. For more information, visit www.lifeisbeautifulfestival.com.

JUST OFF THE STRIP

Dig This! ★★ ENTERTAINMENT COMPLEX   Did you have a sandbox that you used to play in when you were a kid? Well, then you're going to love this: a big kid's sandbox where you get to play with real bulldozers and excavators. The program starts with classroom instruction where you get the overview on how to operate the big machines. It's a lot more complicated than you'd think, requiring a level of hand-eye coordination far beyond that of piloting your family-sized SUV. Next, you get to climb into the machine out in a big dirt lot and get used to the controls. Then the real fun starts, with a series of games and challenges that include digging holes, moving rocks, and even playing a version of excavator basketball. It isn't cheap, but fantasy fulfillment rarely is.

3012 Rancho Dr. (between Meade and Sirius aves.). © **888/344-8447** or 702/222-4344. www. digthisvegas.com. Admission $249 and up. Open daily; hours vary seasonally.

Fast Lap Indoor Kart Racing ★★ ENTERTAINMENT COMPLEX   When NASCAR pro Kurt Busch is in Las Vegas, this is the place he comes to play. Tucked away on a dead-end street in a mostly industrial part of town near the Strip, this is a no-frills go-kart experience, with a short track filling a former warehouse space that still looks like a warehouse. The gasoline-powered karts are equipped with 200cc Honda motors, allowing you to push the little monsters up to 50 mph (if you dare) as you battle in 10-minute-long races (as many laps as you can get) against other drivers.

While bumping and other unsportsman-like contact is officially frowned upon, in reality this is a grown-up (mostly testosterone-driven) sport. So put your foot on the gas and see if you can be first to the checkered flag! *Note:* You must be at least 5 feet tall to participate, and children 17 and under must be accompanied by a parent or guardian.

4288 Polaris Ave. ☏ **702/736-8113.** www.fastlaplv.com. $25 per race or $65 for 3 races. Mon–Sat 10am–11pm; Sun 10am–10pm.

KISS by Monster Mini Golf ★★ ENTERTAINMENT COMPLEX   If they had stopped at the indoor, glow-in-the-dark, 18-hole miniature golf course themed to the classic rock band KISS, it probably would've been just mildly amusing. But then they went and added a gift shop, a cafe, a wedding chapel (where KISS impersonators will marry you), arcade games, a DJ playing nonstop KISS tunes, and more KISS memorabilia than the members of the band probably have in their garages. The entire package reaches an almost epic level of giddy, grin-worthy silliness. And yes, there is a hole where you have to putt the ball up a giant replica of Gene Simmons's tongue.

4503 Paradise Rd. (at Harmon Ave.). ☏ **702/558-6256.** www.monsterminigolf.com/kiss. Free admission; 18 holes of mini-golf $12 ages 7 and up; free for children 6 and under. Daily 10am–midnight.

National Atomic Testing Museum ★★★ MUSEUM   From 1951 until 1992, the Nevada Test Site was this country's primary location for testing nuclear weapons. Aboveground blasts in the early days were visible to the tourists and residents of Las Vegas, becoming not only a tourist attraction (viewing parties were held on the roofs of casinos and bars along Fremont Street) but helped usher in the atomic age. This well-executed museum, library, and gallery space (a Smithsonian affiliate) offers visitors a fascinating glance at the test site from ancient days through modern times, with memorabilia, displays, official documents, videos, interactive displays, motion-simulator theaters (such as sitting in a bunker watching a blast), and emotional testimony from the people who worked there. It respectfully treads that tricky line between honoring the work done at the site and understanding its terrible implications. Not to be missed, even if it's only because of the Albert Einstein action figure in the gift shop. Visitors should plan on spending at least an hour.

755 E. Flamingo Rd. ☏ **702/794-5151.** www.nationalatomictestingmuseum.org. Admission $14 adults; $12 kids 7–17, seniors, military, students with ID, and Nevada residents; free for children 6 and under. Mon–Sat 10am–5pm; Sun noon–5pm.

SOUTH & EAST OF THE STRIP

Clark County Museum ★★ MUSEUM   Someday, one of these casino moguls (paging Mr. Wynn) is going to take just some of those megamillions he is pouring into yet another Strip hotel and put it into the museum that this bizarre town, and its ridiculously rich 100-year history, deserves. Until then, this dear little place will have to do its best—and that best is actually pretty good. With everything from dioramas of dinosaurs to a small street filled with original buildings, including the 1932 Boulder City train depot and the original Candlelight Wedding Chapel, this is a throwback to ghost towns and other low-tech diversions—sweet, informative, and you can't beat the price. *Note:* Hot days will make the outdoor portions less than bearable.

1830 S. Boulder Hwy., Henderson. ☏ **702/455-7955.** www.clarkcountynv.gov. Admission $2 adults, $1 seniors and children 3–15, free for children 2 and under. Daily 9am–4:30pm. Closed Thanksgiving, Dec 25, and Jan 1.

Ethel M Chocolates ★ FACTORY TOUR   Ethel Mars began making fine chocolates in a little candy kitchen in the early 20th century. Her small enterprise evolved to produce not only dozens of varieties of superb boxed chocolates, but also some of the world's most famous candies: M&Ms, Milky Way, 3 Musketeers, Snickers, and Mars bars. Alas, the tour lasts only about 10 minutes and consists entirely of viewing stations with an audiotape explaining the chocolate-baking process. Even more sadly, you get only one small chocolate as a sample—delicious, but hardly satisfying. Of course, there is a fully-stocked gift shop if you want to buy more. *Note:* Come before 2:30pm, which is when the workers start to pack up and go home.

What's really worth seeing is outside: a lovely and extensive **4-acre garden ★** displaying over 300 species of rare and exotic cacti with signs provided for self-guided tours. It's best appreciated in spring when the cacti are in full bloom, or in December when the entire garden is bedecked with holiday lights.

2 Cactus Garden Dr. (just off Mountain Vista and Sunset Way, in the Green Valley Business Park). ✆ **702/435-2655** or 702/435-2608. www.ethelschocolate.com. Free admission. Daily 8:30am–6pm. Self-guided chocolate factory tours Mon–Thurs 8:30am–4:30pm. Holiday hours may vary.

Lion Habitat Ranch ★★★ ZOO   Longtime Vegas visitors roared with displeasure when the MGM Grand closed their signature lion habitat after nearly 20 years of amusing tourists. The big secret, however, was that populating those casino-facing digs was merely the lions' day job, and their "main office" is now open for tours that are significantly more satisfying to visit. More than two dozen lions, from infant to ancient, are in residence at the facility run by Keith and Bev Evans for more than 20 years. All of the animals are either rescues or born here, and while it always gives one pause to see these kinds of majestic creatures in captivity instead of running wild, the digs are plush, they are obviously well taken care of, and seem like very happy kitties indeed. And, of course, if you do see them running wild, they may be running after you, so perhaps this is best after all. Visitation programs vary from simple do-it-yourself tours to "Trainer for a Day" options that will put you in direct contact with the lions. *Note:* Finding the place can be challenging; it is in the middle of a bunch of scrub brush desert, close to the M Resort on the southernmost edge of Las Vegas. Consult a map or GPS before you go.

382 Bruner Ave. (near St. Rose Pkwy.). ✆ **702/595-6666.** www.lionhabitatranch.com. Admission $20 and up adults; one child per adult free. Fri–Mon 10am–4pm; hours vary seasonally.

Pinball Hall of Fame & Museum ★★★ MUSEUM   Picture this: You walk into the Louvre in Paris and instead of gazing at the art on the walls from a safe distance, you are able to take it down, examine it from different angles, and even paint some strokes on top of the canvases. Of course, you'd never do that in a museum elsewhere, but this is Las Vegas and that is what you get to do with the pieces of art here at the Pinball Hall of Fame. More than 100 lovingly restored pinball machines from the 1940s through modern times are lined up and waiting for you to play. Try your hand at getting a ball into a dinosaur's mouth in the mid-1990s *Jurassic Park* machine, or giggle at the Elton John costumes on the artwork while you're playing the 1975 *Captain Fantastic* machine. Or go really old school with a football-themed game dating to 1949. They also have a big section of classic arcade games from *Donkey Kong* to *Super Mario Brothers* if you feel like going back to the '80s for a while. Note that many of the machines have QR bar codes on them, so you can use your smartphone to surf for additional info about these masterpieces.

1610 E. Tropicana Ave. ✆ **702/597-2627.** www.pinballmuseum.org. Free admission; game costs vary. Sun–Thurs 11am–11pm; Fri–Sat 11am–midnight.

Shelby American Heritage Center ★ MUSEUM   Automotive legend Carroll Shelby started what would become his empire in the 1960s with a series of racing victories leading to the creation of his iconic Cobra roadster and a decades-long partnership with Ford to create powerful versions of its Mustang and other vehicles. The facility here includes a full shop where they do the modifications, but you only get to see that part through a series of windows. A museum area features about two dozen cars, including the first one Shelby ever built, some classic Mustangs, and a few examples from the ridiculous few years where he created vehicles for Chrysler, such as a pickup with racing stripes. You can tour the small space on your own, but there's scant contextual information on the vehicles or photos that line the wall. Instead, try taking one of the guided tours that provide exhaustive behind-the-scenes stories and anecdotes about the man and his mission. They don't require reservations, but tours can get very crowded on weekends; consider a weekday visit for a more personal experience. Tours and admission are free, but the center does ask for donations to the Carroll Shelby Foundation which provides education, outreach, and support for organ donation (Shelby, who died in 2012, got a heart transplant in 1990).

6405 Ensworth St. (at Sunset Rd.) (✆) **702/942-7325.** www.shelbyamerican.com. Free admission. Mon–Sat 9am–6pm; guided tours Mon–Fri 10:30am and 1:30pm and Sat 10:30am.

SkyZone ★ ENTERTAINMENT COMPLEX   So you brought the kids to Vegas and they're bouncing off the walls with boredom. How about giving them a chance to bounce off the walls with glee instead? This indoor facility features several trampoline arenas; some are used for organized games and activities such as dodgeball and others are open for random bouncing about. There are other amusements here as well, including a foam-block pit that kids can jump into, games, and a small snack shop, plus some much-needed quiet areas for parents. Adults are allowed, but this is mainly a place for children, so if you're hoping to practice your Cirque du Soleil skills you may want to find someplace else to do it.

7440 Dean Martin Dr. (at Warm Springs Rd.) (✆) **702/560-5900.** www.skyzone.com/lasvegas. Admission $13–$26. Mon–Thurs 2pm–8pm; Fri 2pm–10pm; Sat 10am–11pm; Sun 11am–8pm.

NORTH & WEST OF THE STRIP

Las Vegas Mini Gran Prix ★★ ENTERTAINMENT COMPLEX   Finally, after all our yammering about how Vegas isn't for families and how most of the kid-friendly options are really overpriced tourist traps, we can wholeheartedly recommend an actual family-appropriate entertainment option. Part arcade, part go-kart racetrack, this is exactly what you want to help your kids (and maybe yourselves) work their ya-yas out. The arcade is well stocked, with a better quality of prizes than one often finds, but we suggest not spending too much time in there and instead hustling outside to the slide, the little roller coaster, and best of all, the four go-kart tracks. Each offers a different thrill, from the longest track in Vegas, full of twists and turns as you try to out-race other drivers (be a sport, let the little kids win occasionally), to a high-banked oval built just so you can try to make other drivers take spills onto the grass, to, best of all, a timed course. The last requires a driver's license, so it's for you rather than your kids (but the wee ones will find the fourth course is just for them), and here you can live out your Le Mans or police-chase fantasies as you blast through twisting runs one kart at a time, trying to beat your personal best. The staff is utterly friendly, and the pizzas at the food court are triple the size and half the price of those found in your hotel. The one drawback: It's far away from main Strip action, so you'll need that rental car. *Note:* Kids have to be at least 36 inches tall to ride any of the attractions.

1401 N. Rainbow Rd. (just off U.S. 95 N.). 🕐 **702/259-7000.** www.lvmgp.com. Ride tickets $7.50 each, $7 each for 5 or more; ride wristbands $21.50 per hr. Mon–Fri 11am–9pm; Sat–Sun 10am–9pm; hours vary seasonally.

Las Vegas Motor Speedway ★★ RACECOURSE   This impressive facility is widely considered to be the premiere racing venue in the southwest United States and rivals fabled speedways in Talladega, Charlotte, and Daytona for its scope and the deep catalogue of year-round events. The main oval hosts a major NASCAR race weekend in March, packing pretty much every one of the 135,000 seats, but there are happenings on it and the other tracks more than 260 days a year. There is an NHRA-sanctioned drag strip that runs high-octane funny cars and motorcycles, two road courses, a dirt track, a short oval "bullring," and more.

Of the many unique features (how many raceways have a view of the Strip?), one of the most interesting for race fans is the Neon Garage, an infield facility where the drivers and their teams set up camp for the major races. Big windows and overhead galleries allow people to watch the cars being worked on and give up-close access to the men and women behind the wheel. You pay a premium, obviously, but true speed freaks should get their tickets early.

If watching the action is not enough for you, there are several programs available to put you behind the wheel for some adrenaline junkie action. **The Richard Petty Driving Experience** (🕐 800/237-3889; www.drivepetty.com) offers both NASCAR-style vehicles and new American muscle cars (Camaro, Mustang, Challenger, and the like) that are raced on the superspeedway; **Dream Racing** (🕐 702/605-3000; www.dream racing.com) has specially modified Ferrari race cars running the inside road track; and **Exotics Racing** (🕐 702/405-7223; www.exoticsracing.com) has a full fleet of Ferraris, Porsches, Lamborghinis, McLarens, and more that run on their proprietary 1.2-mile course. All give you classroom instruction and time behind the wheel, and while they are not cheap, there are few things more thrilling than going down the back straightaway in a race car doing 140 miles per hour or trying to find the perfect path out of tight curve you are taking in a 430 Scuderia at stupid grin-worthy speeds.

7000 Las Vegas Blvd. N. (directly across from Nellis Air Force Base). 🕐 **702/644-4443.** www.lvms. com. Tickets $10–$75 (higher for major events). Race days vary. Take I-15 north to exit 54.

Nevada State Museum ★ MUSEUM   The home to the history of the Silver State has only about 13,000 square feet of exhibit space in which they try to cram several millennia worth of the flora, fauna, people, and events that shaped Nevada. The result is a disappointingly cursory glance at the topics, most of which are presented in a fairly dry manner with very little of the hands-on interactivity that is fashionable in museums these days. But in what other museum would you find a mammoth skeleton near a wall of showgirl costumes? That alone might make it worth visiting, but if not, consider the fact that it is free with your admission to the endlessly fascinating Springs Preserve next door (see below). A small but well-stocked gift shop might be the right place to find an "edutainment" gift for the history buff in your family.

309 S. Valley View Blvd. (at Meadows Lane). 🕐 **702/486-5205.** http://museums.nevadaculture.org. Tickets $19 ($10 for NV residents), free for children 17 and under. Admission includes neighboring Springs Preserve. Thurs–Mon 10am–6pm.

Pole Position Raceway ★ ENTERTAINMENT COMPLEX   Similar in concept to the Fast Lap facility (p. 143), Pole Position is a more polished go-kart racing venue owing to its sleek, modern facility and electric-powered racers. The indoor course is short but satisfying, and the lack of gas-powered engines doesn't mean you sacrifice any of the speed. You may retain your hearing for longer, which is definitely a good thing. It's worth noting that the karts are small and the mandatory helmets are tight, so claustrophobics may want to seek alternative fun. The facility also has a small video and virtual-reality game arcade and a gift shop.

4175 S. Arville Rd. ⓒ **702/227-7223.** www.polepositionraceway.com. Adults 56 in. or taller $25.50, kids 17 and under or 48 in. and taller $22; multi-race packages available. Sun–Thurs 11am–11pm; Fri–Sat 11am–midnight.

Springs Preserve ★★★ NATURAL RESERVE   By now, perhaps you've learned that *Las Vegas* is Spanish for "the meadows." This facility is set on the 180-acre site of the original springs that fed Las Vegas until it dried in the 1960s (told you that Hoover Dam comes in handy). These days, Las Vegas is an environmental nightmare, along with much of the rest of this planet, and this remarkable recreational attraction is here to educate us about the possibilities to reverse some of the damage.

Set amid nature and hiking trails, plus man-made wetlands, which is an interesting concept, the focal point is a large interpretive center that gives the history of Las Vegas from a land- and water-use perspective. The displays are creative and interactive, including a room with a reproduction flash flood that uses 5,000 gallons of water and one with a simulation of the experience of working on Hoover Dam. The other buildings are all built according to standards that have the least environmental impact, using modern construction versions of adobe and other green concepts. Each building tackles an aspect of desert living and the environment, including one that instructs kids on the glories of recycling, complete with a compost tunnel to crawl through! Other displays focus on environmentally friendly kitchens and bathrooms, while the gardens demonstrate environmentally friendly gardening, including a section instructing seniors and those with disabilities on how to garden despite physical limitations.

The outdoor kids' play area is made from recycled materials and has big fake animals to climb on and real live ones to look at, in case the kiddies have grown tired of learning responsible stuff. Given the care, knowledge, and urgency of the issues addressed, this is an extraordinary facility for any town, but particularly for this one.

Note: Admission includes entrance to the adjacent Nevada State Museum reviewed above.

333 S. Valley View Blvd. ⓒ **702/822-8344.** www.springspreserve.org. Admission $19 adults, $17 seniors and students with ID, $11 children 5–17, free for children 4 and under, $10 Nevada residents. Free admission to trails and gardens. Daily 10am–6pm.

Wet 'n Wild ★ AMUSEMENT PARK   Las Vegas—or at least the tourist parts of it—is not exactly family-friendly. In order to find something to do that will keep your kids from taking out their bored frustration on you, travel away from the glittering casinos to places like this, the city's only (for now) water amusement park. A descendant of the Wet 'n Wild that was on the Strip for 2 decades, this state-of-the-art facility is located on the far west side of town at the foothills of the famous Red Rock National Conservancy Area. It has more than 20 slides, rides, and attractions from scary dropping, looping things to lazy, play-around-in-the-water–type features. Adrenaline junkies should note the Constrictor, featuring what are billed as the tightest, highest banked curves in the world, and the Tornado, a multi-person raft ride that shoots you 36 feet in the air before blasting you through a tunnel and into a whirlpool funnel. Shade is at a premium and the crowds make the lines long, but if you want something fun to do with your kids, this is one of your few good Vegas options.

7055 S. Fort Apache Rd. (at Arby Ave.). ℂ **702/800-7474.** www.wetnwildlasvegas.com. Admission $40 adults; $30 kids under 42″ tall. Season passes available. Sun–Thurs 10am–6pm, Fri–Sat 10am–10pm.

CASINO GAMBLING

Las Vegas is no longer the gambling capital of the world. That title belongs to Macau, China, where casinos with familiar names like MGM Grand, the Venetian, and Wynn pull in more money in 2 months than the casinos on the Strip generate all year. Even in the United States, the proliferation of legal gambling in other areas is eclipsing Las Vegas in terms of revenue and scope. As of this writing, there are more than two dozen states that have Indian or riverboat casinos, and nearly that many that have commercial casinos, with more on the way. And in Las Vegas, gambling is no longer the biggest revenue generator, earning less than half of most resorts' revenue (the rest comes from hotel rates, dining, nightclubs, and the like).

But strip away all the facts and figures, and what you are left with is the undeniable lure of Las Vegas as a gambling mecca. It is, in no small part, what built this city and what continues to drive it, as evidenced by the fact that you can find gaming almost everywhere. There are slot machines at the airport, waiting for you to get off the plane or giving you something to do while you wait for your baggage. Convenience stores and gas stations have video poker so you can play a few hands while filling up. And the average Strip casino has literally dozens of blackjack, craps, roulette, and other gaming tables.

People come here to play, and although they may lose more often than they win, it doesn't stop anyone from trying to win the Big One. You know, like that woman in 2010 who won $2.9 million on a "Wizard of Oz" penny slot (whose name was Dorothy, by the way). That only a few ever do win big doesn't stop people from trying again and again and again. That's how the casinos make their money.

As you walk through the labyrinthine twists and turns of a casino floor, your attention will likely be dragged to the various games and, your interest piqued, your fingers may begin to twitch in anticipation of hitting it big. Before you put your money on the line, it's imperative to know the rules of the game you want to play. Most casinos offer free gambling lessons at scheduled times on weekdays and occasionally on weekends. This provides a risk-free environment for you to learn the games that tickle your fancy. Some casinos follow their lessons with low-stakes game play, enabling you to put your newfound knowledge to the test at small risk. During those instructional sessions, and even when playing on your own, dealers in most casinos will be more than happy to answer any questions you might have. Remember, the casino doesn't need to trick you into losing your money . . . the odds are already in their favor across the board; that's why it's called gambling. Another rule of thumb: Take a few minutes to watch a game being played in order to familiarize yourself with the motions and lingo.

And of course, the Internet has revolutionized gambling in more ways than one, not the least of which is that you can find a free, online version of just about every casino game imaginable. Spend a few hours online betting virtual bucks before you haul out your wallet to try the real deal.

If you are planning on gambling at all, it pays to join a players' club. These so-called clubs are designed to attract and keep customers in a given casino by providing incentives: meals, shows, discounts on rooms, gifts, tournament invitations, discounts at hotel shops, VIP treatment, and (more and more) cash rebates. Join a players' club (it doesn't cost a cent to sign up), and soon you too will be getting those great hotel-rate offers—$20-a-night rooms, affordable rooms at the luxury resorts, and even free rooms.

These days, players' clubs go beyond the casino as well. Many of them track your overall spending at participating casinos, including what you pay for meals, shopping, rooms, spa treatments, and more. This means you can earn points toward rewards pretty much anytime you pull out your wallet.

Baccarat

The ancient game of baccarat, or *chemin de fer*, is played with eight decks of cards. Firm rules apply, and there is no skill involved other than deciding whether to bet on the bank or the player. No, really—that's all you have to do. The dealer does all the other work. You can essentially stop reading here. Oh, all right, carry on.

Any beginner can play, but check the betting minimum before you sit down, as baccarat tends to be a high-stakes game. The cards are shuffled by the croupier and then placed in a box called the "shoe." Players may wager on "bank" or "player" at any time. Two cards are dealt from the shoe and given to the player who has the largest wager against the bank, and two cards are dealt to the croupier, acting as banker. If the rules call for a third card, the player or banker, or both, must take the third card. In the event of a tie, the hand is dealt over. *Note:* The guidelines that determine whether a third card must be drawn (by the player or banker) are provided at the baccarat table upon request.

The object of the game is to come as close as possible to the number 9. To score the hands, the cards of each hand are totaled and the *last digit* is used. All cards have face value. For example: 10 plus 5 equals 15 (score is 5); 10 plus 4 plus 9 equals 23 (score is 3); 4 plus 3 plus 3 equals 10 (score is 0); and 4 plus 3 plus 2 equals 9 (score is 9). The closest hand to 9 wins.

Each player has a chance to deal the cards. The shoe passes to the player on the right each time the bank loses. If the player wishes, he may pass the shoe at any time.

Note: When you bet on the bank and the bank wins, you're charged a 5% commission. This must be paid at the start of a new game or when you leave the table.

Blackjack

In this, the most popular casino card game, the dealer starts by dealing each player two cards. In some casinos, they're dealt to the player face up, in others face down, but the dealer always gets one card up and one card down. Everybody plays against the dealer. The object is to get a total that is higher than that of the dealer without exceeding 21. All face cards count as 10; all other number cards, except aces, are counted at their face value. An ace may be counted as 1 or 11, whichever you choose it to be.

Starting at her left, the dealer gives additional cards to the players who wish to draw (be "hit") or none to a player who wishes to "stand" or "hold." If your count is nearer to 21 than the dealer's, you win. If it's under the dealer's, you lose. Ties are a "push" (standoff) and nobody wins. After all the players are satisfied with their counts, the dealer exposes her face-down card. If her two cards total 16 or less, the dealer must hit until reaching 17 or over. If the dealer's total exceeds 21, she must pay all the players whose hands have not gone "bust." It is important to note here that the blackjack dealer has no choice as to whether she should stay or draw. A dealer's decisions are predetermined and known to all the players at the table.

If you're a novice or just rusty, do yourself a favor and buy one of the small laminated cards available in shops all over town that illustrate proper play for every possible hand in blackjack. Even longtime players have been known to pull them out every now and then, and they can save you from making costly errors.

Craps

The most exciting casino action is usually found at the craps tables. Betting is frenetic, play is fast-paced, and groups quickly bond while yelling and screaming in response to the action.

While it can be intimidating, it's very easy to play a basic game of craps, but figuring out the various bets and the odds associated with the advanced bets is sort of like learning rocket science, only with dice. Entire books are written about the game and so it would be impossible to explain it all in a couple of paragraphs, but here is enough to at least get you started.

The table is divided into marked areas (Pass, Come, Field, Big Six, Big Eight, and so on), where you place your chips to bet. Novices should stick with the "Pass Line" or "Come" bets until they get used to the rhythm of the game.

PASS LINE A "Pass Line" bet pays even money. If the first roll of the dice adds up to 7 or 11, you win your bet; if the first roll adds up to 2, 3, or 12, you lose your bet. If any other number comes up, it becomes your "point." If you roll your point again, you win, but if a 7 comes up again before your point is rolled, you lose.

DON'T PASS LINE Betting on the "Don't Pass Line" is the opposite of betting on the Pass Line. This time, you lose if a 7 or an 11 is thrown on the first roll, and you win if a 2 or a 3 is thrown on the first roll.

If the first roll is 12, however, it's a "push" (standoff), and nobody wins. If none of these numbers is thrown and you have a point instead, in order to win, a 7 will have to be thrown before the point comes up again. A Don't Pass bet also pays even money.

COME Betting on "Come" is the same as betting on the Pass Line, but you must bet after the first roll or on any following roll. Again, you'll win on 7 or 11 and lose on 2, 3, or 12. Any other number is your point, and you win if your point comes up again before a 7.

DON'T COME This is the opposite of a Come bet. Again, you wait until after the first roll to bet. A 7 or an 11 means you lose; a 2 or a 3 means you win; 12 is a push, and nobody wins. You win if 7 comes up before the point. (The point, you'll recall, was the first number rolled if it was none of the above.)

Poker

Poker is the game of the Old West (there seems to be at least one sequence in every Western where the hero faces off against the villain over a poker hand). For most of the new millennium, poker was just about the biggest thing going, thanks to the popularity of celebrity poker TV shows, poker tours, books, and magazines. Just about every casino had a poker room and those that didn't wanted one.

That popularity has waned a bit in the last few years with several of the poker rooms getting smaller, offering fewer games, or closing altogether. What's behind the trend? Nothing more than the cooling of a hot fad, really. The game is still played by lots of people and you can easily find a table, but these days you probably won't have to wait as long to get a seat.

There are lots of variations on the basic game, but one of the most popular is **Texas Hold 'Em.** Two cards are dealt, face down, to the players. After a betting round, five community cards (everyone can use them) are dealt face up on the table. Players make the best five-card hand, using their own cards and the "board" (the community cards), and the best hand wins. The house dealer takes care of the shuffling and the dealing, and moves a marker around the table to alternate the start of the deal. The house usually rakes around 10% (it depends on the casino) from each pot. Most casinos also provide tables for playing Seven-Card Stud, Omaha High, and Omaha Hi-Lo. A few even have Seven-Card Stud Hi-Lo split. To learn how these variations are played, either read a book or take lessons.

PAI GOW

Pai Gow is a variation on poker that has become popular. The game is played with a traditional deck plus one joker. The joker is a wild card that can be used as an ace or to complete a straight, a flush, a straight flush, or a royal flush. Each player is dealt seven cards to arrange into two hands: a two-card hand and a five-card hand. As in standard poker, the highest two-card hand is two aces, and the highest five-card hand is a royal flush. The five-card hand *must* be higher than the two-card hand (if the two-card hand is a pair of 6s, for example, the five-card hand must be a pair of 7s or better). Any player's hand that is set incorrectly is an automatic loser. The object of the game is for both of the players' hands to rank higher than both of the banker's hands. Should one hand rank exactly the same as the banker's hand, this is a tie (called a "copy"), *and the banker wins all tie hands.* If the player wins one hand but loses the other, this is a "push," and no money changes hands. The house dealer or any player may be the banker. The bank is offered to each player, and each player may accept or pass. Winning hands are paid even money, less a 5% commission.

LET IT RIDE

Let It Ride is another popular game that involves poker hands. You place three bets at the outset and are dealt three cards. The dealer is dealt two cards that act as community cards (you're not playing against the dealer). Once you've seen your cards, you can choose to pull the first of your three bets back or "let it ride." The object of this game is to get a pair of 10s or better by combining your cards with the community cards. If you're holding a pair of 10s or better in your first three cards (called a "no-brainer"), you want to let your bets ride the entire way through. Once you've decided whether or not to let your first bet ride, the dealer exposes one of his two cards. Once again, you must make a decision to take back your middle bet or keep on going. Then the dealer exposes the last of his cards; your third bet must stay. The dealer then turns over the hands of the players and determines whether you've won. Winning bets are paid on a scale, ranging from even money for a single pair up to 1,000 to 1 for a royal flush. These payouts are for each bet you have in play. Similar to Caribbean Stud, Let It Ride has a bonus that you can win for high hands if you cough up an additional $1 per hand, but be advised that the house advantage on that $1 is obscene. But hey, that's why it's called gambling.

THREE-CARD POKER

Three-Card Poker has become one of the most popular table games in Las Vegas, with gamblers appreciating the relatively low mental input requirements and relatively high payout possibilities. It's actually more difficult to explain than to play. For this reason, we recommend watching a table for a while. You should grasp it pretty quickly.

Basically, players are dealt three cards with no draw and have to make the best poker hand out of those three cards. Possible combinations include a straight flush (three sequential cards of the same suit), three of a kind (three queens, for example), a straight (three sequential cards of any suit), a flush (three cards of the same suit), and a pair (two queens, for example). Even if you don't have one of the favored combinations, you can still win if you have cards higher than the dealer's.

On the table are three betting areas—Ante, Play, and Pair Plus. There are actually two games in one on a Three-Card Poker table—"Pair Plus" and "Ante and Play." You can play only Pair Plus or only Ante, or both. You place your chips in the areas in which you want to bet.

In Pair Plus, you are betting only on your hand, not competing against anyone else at the table or the dealer. If you get a pair or better, depending on your hand, the payoff can be pretty fab—straight flush: 40 to 1; three of a kind: 30 to 1; straight: 6 to 1; flush: 3 to 1; and pair: 1 to 1.

In Ante and Play, you are betting that your hand will be better than the dealer's, but you're not competing against anyone else at the table. You place an Ante bet, view your cards, and then, if you decide you like your hand, you place a bet in the Play area equal to your Ante bet. If you get lousy cards and don't want to go forward, you can fold, losing only your Ante bet and your Pair Plus bet, if you made one. Once all bets are made, the dealer's hand is revealed—he must have at least a single queen for the bet to count; if not, your Ante and Play bets are returned. If you beat the dealer's hand, you get a 1 to 1 payoff, but there is a bonus for a particularly good winning hand: straight flush, 5 to 1; three of a kind, 4 to 1; straight, 1 to 1.

Your three cards are dealt. If you play only Pair Plus, it doesn't matter what the dealer has—you get paid if you have a pair or better. If you don't, you lose your bet. If you play the Ante bet, you must then either fold and lose the Ante bet or match the Ante bet by placing the same amount on the Play area. The dealer's hand is revealed, and payouts happen accordingly. Each hand consists of one fresh 52-card deck.

There are several variants to this game, including a bonus bet that can win a progressive jackpot (usually $1) and a six-card version where your cards are combined with the dealer's cards to come up with the best five- or six-card hand. Caesars Entertainment casinos are even offering a million-dollar top prize in their six-card games if, between you and the dealer, you come up with the 9-10-J-Q-K-A of diamonds. Don't scoff—several people have actually won it already!

OTHER POKER VARIANTS

Meanwhile, as if all this weren't enough, new variations on poker games keep popping up. There's Crazy 4 Poker, similar to Three-Card Poker, only with five cards dealt, no draw, and make your best four-card poker hand out of it; a version of Texas Hold 'Em, where you are not competing against other players; several riffs on Three-Card poker that include secondary bonus bets, progressive jackpots, and multiple betting strategies; and more. All of them follow the basic tenets of poker (highest hand wins), but each has its own set of rules, betting strategies, and payouts; if you see one of these games, look for an instructional pamphlet at the table or ask the dealer for a quick lesson before you sit down.

Roulette

Roulette is an extremely easy game to play, and it's really quite colorful and exciting to watch. The wheel spins and the little ball bounces around, finally dropping into one of the slots, numbered 1 to 36, plus 0 and 00. You can place bets "Inside" the table and

"Outside" the table. Inside bets are bets placed on a particular number or a set of numbers. Outside bets are those placed in the boxes surrounding the number table. If you bet on a specific number and it comes up, you are paid 35 to 1 on your bet. Bear in mind, however, that the odds of a particular number coming up are actually 38 to 1 (don't forget the 0 and 00!), so the house has an advantage the moment you place an inside bet. The methods of placing single-number bets, column bets, and others are fairly obvious. The dealer will be happy to show you how to make many interesting betting combinations, such as betting on six numbers at once. Each player is given different-colored chips so that it's easy to follow the numbers you've bet on.

Slots

You put the coin in the slot and pull the handle. What, you thought there was a trick to this?

Actually, there is a bit more to it. But first, some background. Old-timers will tell you slots were invented to give wives something to do while their husbands gambled. Slots used to be stuck at the edges of the casino and could be counted on one hand, maybe two. But now they *are* the casino. The casinos make more from slots than from craps, blackjack, and roulette combined. There are more than 150,000 slot machines (not including video poker) in the county. Some of these are at the airport, steps from you as you deplane. It's just a matter of time before the planes flying into Vegas feature slots that pop up as soon as you cross the state line.

But to keep up with the increasing competition, the plain old machine, where reels just spin, has become nearly obsolete. Now they are all computerized and have buttons to push so you can avoid getting carpal tunnel syndrome from yanking the handle all night (though the handles are still there on some of them). Many don't even have reels anymore but are entirely video screens, which offer a number of little extras that have nothing to do with actual play. The idea is still simple: Get 3 (or 4, or 10) cherries (clowns, sevens, dinosaurs, whatever) in a row, and you win something. Each machine has its own combination. Some will pay you something with just one symbol showing; on most, the more combinations there are, the more opportunities for loot. Some will even pay if you get three blanks. Study each machine to learn what it does. ***Note:*** The **payback** goes up considerably if you bet the limit (from 2 to hundreds of coins on penny slots, for instance).

Progressive slots are groups of linked machines (sometimes spread over several casinos) where the jackpot gets bigger every few moments (just as lottery jackpots build up). Some machines have their own progressive jackpot, which can be slightly less stressful because you're not competing with other players to win the top prize.

Themes and interactivity are the watchwords these days. Pick a pop culture reference and there's probably a slot machine dedicated to it. **Wizard of Oz, The Amazing Race, Airplane!** ("Don't call me Shirley!"), **Jaws, Michael Jackson,** and **The Game of Life** are just a few of the familiar titles you'll see on casino floors. Each of them features bonus rounds and side games that have animations, video clips, music, competitions between other players, and, in some cases, even motion-activated seats.

Penny and nickel slots, which for a long time had been overlooked, relegated to a lonely spot somewhere by a back wall because they were not as profitable for the casinos as quarter and dollar slots, have made a comeback. You can bet just a penny or nickel, but maximum bets for the bigger jackpots are usually in the $2 to $3 range, sometimes even more. As a result, more cash is pocketed by the casino (which keeps a higher percentage of cash off of lower-denomination slots than it does off of higher ones), which is happy to accommodate this trend by offering up more and more cheaper slots. See how this all works? Are you paying attention?

Cashless machines are the standard in Vegas these days. Now when gambling, players insert their money, they play, and when they cash out, they get—instead of the clanging sound of coins cascading out into the tray—a little paper ticket with their total winnings on it. Hand in your ticket at a cashier's window (or use the omnipresent ATM-style redemption machines), and you get your winnings. Purists howl, bemoaning the loss of the auditory and tactile thrill of dealing with coins, but most of them are the type of people who would put $5 in a machine, lose it, and then be done with gambling for the rest of the trip. Those who are more than just casual players love the convenience and simplicity of the tickets and wouldn't go back to the days of having to lug big buckets of change around if you promised them better payoff odds.

Are there surefire ways to win on a slot machine? No. But you can lose more slowly. The slot machines use minicomputers known as random number generators (RNGs) to determine the winning combinations on a machine, and though each spin may indeed be random, individual machines are programmed to pay back different percentages over the long haul. As a result, a machine programmed to return a higher percentage might be "looser" than others. A bank of empty slots probably (but not certainly) means the machines are tight. Go find a line where lots of people are sitting around with lots of credits on their meters. A good rule of thumb is that if your slot doesn't hit something in four or five pulls, leave it and go find another. Also, each casino has a bank of slots that they advertise as more loose or with a bigger payback. Try these. It's what they want you to do, but what the heck.

Video Poker

Video poker works the same way as regular poker, except you play against the machine. You are dealt a hand, you pick which cards to keep and which to discard, and then you get your new hand. And, it is hoped, you collect your winnings. This is somewhat more of a challenge and more active than slots because you have some control (or at least the illusion of control) over your fate, and it's easier than playing actual poker with a table full of serious poker players.

There are a number of varieties of video poker machines, including **Jacks or Better, Deuces Wild,** and so forth. Be sure to study your machine before you play. (The best returns are offered on the **Bonus Poker** machines; the payback for a pair of jacks or better is two times your bet, and three times for three of a kind.) The Holy Grail of video-poker machines is the 9/6 (it pays nine coins for a full house, six coins for a flush), but you'll need to pray a lot before you find one in town. Some machines offer **double down:** After you have won, you get a chance to draw cards against the machine, with the higher card the winner. If you win, your money is doubled, and you are offered a chance to go again. Your money can increase nicely during this time, and you can also lose it all very quickly, which is most annoying.

Other options include multi-hand video poker, where you play anywhere from 3 to 100 hands at the same time; bonus spin poker, allowing you to spin a wheel for extra credits when you get certain hands; and progressive jackpots for things like royal flushes or four aces.

Sports Books

Most of the larger hotels in Las Vegas have sports-book operations, which look a lot like commodities-futures trading boards. In some, almost as large as theaters,

CASINO royale

When it comes right down to it, all casinos are basically the same—they all have slot machines, table games, too many people (often), lots of cigarette smoke (usually), and a general sense of hullaballoo that is completely unlike anyplace else on Earth.

But not all casinos are created equally. Some are big and feel like it, some are big and don't feel like it, some are loud, some are bright, some are light, some are cheap, some are overwhelming, and on and on it goes. Where you decide to gamble away little Billy's college fund really is a matter of taste, budget, and timing, but here are a few of our favorites, and not just because we have won money in them. Well, not *entirely* because we have won money in them.

If you are looking for a classic Las Vegas casino, go no further than **Caesars Palace** (3570 Las Vegas Blvd. S.;

② **702/731-7110;** www.caesarspalace. com). The domed ceiling over the main pit just off the lobby dates all the way back to 1966 but has been kept up-to-date and sparkling. Plus, you might still see a toga-clad wench or an armor-plated gladiator wandering around posing for pictures.

If you prefer modern, try either **Aria Las Vegas** (3730 Las Vegas Blvd. S.; *②* **702/590-7111;** www.arialasvegas. com) or the **Cosmopolitan of Las Vegas** (3708 Las Vegas Blvd. S.; *②* **702/698-7000;** www.cosmopolitanlasvegas.com). Both offer dramatic, art-inspired rooms bursting with eye-candy, with Aria's dramatic sculptures and natural lighting and the Cosmo's three-story chandelier and evocative decor.

The themed madness has been toned down at most casinos, but you can still get a geo-location giggle with the Big

you can sit comfortably, occasionally in recliners, and sometimes with your own video screen, and watch ball games, fights, and, at some casinos, horse races on huge TV screens. To add to your enjoyment, there's usually a deli/bar nearby that serves sandwiches, hot dogs, soft drinks, and beer. As a matter of fact, some of the best sandwiches in Las Vegas are served next to the sports books. Sports books take bets on virtually every sport (and not just who'll win, but what the final score will be, who'll be first to hit a home run, who'll be MVP, who'll wear red shoes, you name it). They are best during important playoff games or big horse races, when everyone in the place is watching the same event—shrieking, shouting, and moaning, sometimes in unison. Joining in with a cheap bet (so you feel like you, too, have a personal stake in the matter) makes for bargain entertainment.

Speaking of the future, in early 2010, the Nevada Gaming Commission approved rules that would allow casino sports books to take wagers on the outcomes of nonsporting events such as the Academy Awards, *American Idol,* and even presidential elections. In the past, you couldn't bet on these types of events because in many of them the outcome is known by someone before the results are announced (those Oscar accountants get all the luck!) or there was too high a risk that the outcomes could be influenced. At press time, no major casino in Vegas was offering these types of wagers because of all of the restrictions the commission put on them to guard against the concerns that made them illegal before, but it is only a matter of time—the casinos smell big money here and they'll figure out a way to make it work. So who do you think is going to win *Dancing With the Stars?* Wanna bet?

Apple silliness at New York-New York (3790 Las Vegas Blvd. S.; (*) **702/740-6969;** www.newyorknewyork.com), complete with the facades of famous Gotham landmarks looming around you; the walk-like-an-Egyptian madness of Luxor Las Vegas (3900 Las Vegas Blvd. S.; (*) **702/262-4444;** www.luxor.com), which is still there if you look hard enough for it; or the Gallic-inspired romance of Paris Las Vegas (3655 Las Vegas Blvd. S.; (*) **702/946-7000;** www.parislasvegas.com), including legs of the Eiffel Tower replica sticking down into the casino.

If luxury and high limits are your thing, go to the fraternal twin casinos at **Wynn Las Vegas/Encore Las Vegas** (3131 Las Vegas Blvd. S.; (*) **800/320-7125;** www.wynnlasvegas.com). The former is a large garden-inspired space with luxurious seating and fabrics, while the latter is a

more intimate, European-gambling-parlor–style room infused with natural light.

If you prefer your gambling more down-to-earth and affordable, check out one of the Downtown or locals' casinos. Our personal favorites are the lovely earth-toned space at **The Golden Nugget** (129 Fremont St.; (*) **702/385-7111;** www.goldennugget.com); the retro-modern industrial chic at **The Downtown Grand** (206 N. 3rd St.; (*) **702/719-5100;** www.downtowngrand.com); the richly textured stunner at **Red Rock Resort** (10973 W. Charleston Ave.; (*) **702/767-7773;** www.redrocklasvegas.com); and the warm Mediterranean-inspired space at **Green Valley Ranch** (2300 Paseo Verde Dr., Henderson; (*) **702/617-7777;** www.greenvalleyranchresort.com).

GETTING MARRIED

Getting hitched is one of the most popular things to do in Las Vegas. Just ask Britney Spears—as she rather infamously revealed, it's all too easy to get married here. See that total stranger/childhood friend standing next to you? Grab him or her and head down to the **Clark County Marriage License Bureau,** 201 Clark Ave. ((*) **702/761-0600;** daily, including holidays, 8am–midnight), to get your license. Find a wedding chapel (not hard, as there are about 50 of them in town; they line the north end of the Strip, and most hotels have them) and tie the knot. Just like that. No blood test, no waiting period—heck, not even an awkward dating period . . . though you may have a potentially very awkward time explaining it afterward to your mother, your manager, and the press.

Even if you have actually known your intended for some time, Las Vegas is a great place to get married. The ease is the primary attraction, but there are a number of other appealing reasons. You can have any kind of wedding you want, from a big, traditional production number to a small, intimate affair; from a spur-of-the-moment "just-the-happy-couple-in-blue-jeans" kind of thing to an "Elvis-in-a-pink-Cadillac-at-a-drive-thru-window" kind of thing (see the box "Vows with a Wow," below). The wedding chapels take care of everything; usually they'll even provide a limo to take you to the license bureau and back. Most offer all the accessories, from rings to flowers to a videotaped record of the event.

More than 100,000 couples who yearly take advantage of all this can't be wrong. If you want to follow in the footsteps of Elvis and Priscilla (at the first incarnation of the

AN ELVIS IMPERSONATOR'S TOP 10 REASONS TO get married IN LAS VEGAS

Jesse Garon has appeared in numerous Las Vegas productions as "Young Elvis." He arrives at any special event in a 1955 pink, neon-lit Cadillac, and does weddings, receptions, birthdays, conventions, grand openings, and so on. For all your Elvis impersonator needs, call ℂ **702/588-8188,** or visit his website at www.vegaselvis.com.

1. It's the only place in the world where Elvis will marry you, at a drive-up window, in a pink Cadillac—24 hours a day.
2. Chances are, you'll never forget your anniversary.
3. Where else can you treat all your guests to a wedding buffet for only 99¢ a head?
4. Four words: One helluva bachelor party.
5. On your wedding night, show your spouse that new "watch me disappear" act you learned from Siegfried & Roy.
6. Show your parents who's boss—have your wedding your way.
7. Wedding bells ring for you everywhere you go. They just sound like slot machines.
8. You can throw dice instead of rice.
9. It's easy to lie about your age on the marriage certificate—just like Joan Collins did!
10. With all the money you save, it's dice clocks for everyone!

Aladdin Hotel); Michael Jordan; Jon Bon Jovi; Richard Gere and Cindy Crawford; Pamela Anderson and ill-fated husband no. 3; Angelina Jolie and Billy Bob; and, of course, Britney and What's-His-Name; you'll want to peruse the following list of the most notable wedding chapels on or near the Strip.

You can also call **Las Vegas Weddings** (ℂ **800/322-8697;** www.lasvegasweddings.com), which offers one-stop shopping for wedding services.

Weddings can be very inexpensive in Vegas: A license is $60 and a basic service not much more. Even a full-blown shebang package—photos, music, flowers, video, cake, and other doodads—will run only about $500 total. We haven't quoted any prices here because the ultimate cost depends entirely on how much you want to spend. Go cheap, and the whole thing will set you back maybe $150, including the license; go elaborate, and the price is still reasonable by today's wedding-price standards. Be sure to remember that there are often hidden charges, such as expected gratuities for the minister (about $25 should do; no real need to tip anyone else), and so forth. If you're penny-pinching, you'll want to keep those in mind.

Same-sex marriage is not legal in Nevada as of this writing but many chapels will perform commitment ceremonies. The best bet for gay and lesbian couples is to go with one of the facilities in the hotels as opposed to dealing with the smaller, independent shops.

Be aware that Valentine's Day is a very popular day to get married in Vegas. Some of the chapels perform as many as 80 services on February 14. But remember, you also don't have to plan ahead. Just show up, get your paperwork, close your eyes, and pick a chapel. And above all, have fun. Good luck and best wishes to you both.

Chapel of the Bells ★ Sporting perhaps the largest and gaudiest wedding chapel sign on the Strip, this is also one of the longest-running chapels, operating since 1957. This combination of classic Vegas "style" and "tradition" is most of what this place has going for it. The chapel is pretty, garnished with swaths of white material and light green accents, seating 25 to 35, but nothing dazzling. It's not particularly distinctive, but Kelly Ripa got married here, so there is that. The chapel prefers advance booking but can do same-day ceremonies.

2233 Las Vegas Blvd. S. (at Sahara Ave.). ✆ **800/233-2391** or 702/735-6803. www.chapelofthe bellslasvegas.com. Sun–Thurs 9am–9pm; Fri–Sat 9am–midnight.

Chapel of the Flowers ★★   This chapel's claim to fame is that Dennis Rodman and Carmen Electra exchanged their deathless vows here—but don't hold it against the place. They offer full services from photos to flowers, and more, with three chapels to choose from. The La Capella Chapel fits 50 and has a rustic Tuscan feel, with wood pews and frosted-glass sconces. The Victorian chapel, which holds only 30, has white walls and dark-wood pews and doesn't look very Victorian at all—but as the plainest, it's also the nicest. The smallest is the Magnolia Chapel, done in simple white marble with a free-standing arch. If you want an outdoor vow exchange, you might choose the gazebo by a running stream and waterfall that nearly drowns out the Strip noise. There's also a medium-size reception room and live organ music upon request, plus Internet streaming of services is available for those of you who have second thoughts about not inviting the family to your vows. It's a pretty, friendly place (owned by the same family for more than 50 years) that seems to keep an eye on its bustling business. It does not allow rice or confetti throwing.

1717 Las Vegas Blvd. S. (at E. Oakey Blvd.). ✆ **800/843-2410** or 702/735-4331. www.littlechapel. com. Mon–Thurs 7am–8pm; Fri–Sat 7am–9pm.

Graceland Wedding Chapel ★   Housed in a landmark building that's one of the oldest wedding chapels in Vegas, the Graceland bills itself as "the proverbial mom and pop outfit." No, Elvis never slept here, but one of the owners was friends with Elvis and asked his permission to use the name. This is a tiny New England church building with a small bridge and white picket fence out front. Inside is a 30-seat chapel; the walls are off-white, with a large, modern, stained-glass window of doves and roses behind the pulpit. It's not the nicest of the chapels, but Jon Bon Jovi and Billy Ray Cyrus got married here (though not to each other). Naturally, an Elvis package is available.

619 Las Vegas Blvd. S. (at E. Bonneville Ave.). ✆ **800/824-5732** or 702/382-0091. www.graceland chapel.com. Daily 9am–11pm.

Little Church of the West ★★   Built in 1942 on the grounds of the Frontier, this gorgeous traditional chapel has been moved three times in its history and has hosted weddings for everyone from Judy Garland to Angelina Jolie. Elvis even got married here, at least on film—the building played the backdrop for his nuptials to Ann-Margret in *Viva Las Vegas*. There are rich wood walls, ceiling, and pews; stained-glass windows; and a traditional steeple amongst the well-landscaped grounds, making it a really lovely option for those looking to walk down the aisle.

4617 Las Vegas Blvd. S. (at Russell Rd.). ✆ **800/821-2452** or 702/739-7971. www.littlechurchlv.com. Daily 8am–11pm.

Little White Wedding Chapel ★   This is arguably the most famous of the chapels on the Strip, maybe because there is a big sign saying Michael Jordan and Joan Collins were married here (again, not to each other), maybe because they were the first to do the drive-up window, or maybe because this is where Britney and that guy who isn't the guy from *Seinfeld* began their 51 hours of wedded bliss (no, we will never,

Simply getting married is not a big enough deal for some people. No, they can't trust that the exchange of vows with the person they love will create memories that will last forever, they have to make sure it is truly memorable by throwing in a volcano, a giant fountain, or maybe even a roller coaster. If you are such a person, Las Vegas has plenty of places to put a little wow into your vows.

If you want to have the iconic dancing waters as a backdrop, you can get married on a balcony overlooking the Bellagio Fountains at **Bellagio**, 3600 Las Vegas Blvd. S. (© 702/693-7700; www.bellagio.com/weddings). As you might expect, it ain't cheap, but you can even time your "I do" to the fountains' big climax.

An almost aerial view of the fountains is available across the street from the Eiffel Tower at **Paris Las Vegas**, 3655 Las Vegas Blvd. S. (© 877/650-5021; www.parislv.com). You can get married on the observation deck at the top of the tower replica. Similar wow-worthy vistas are available at the world's tallest observation wheel, **High Roller**, 3545 Las Vegas Blvd. S. (© 800/CAESARS).

An even higher view is available at the top of the **Stratosphere Las Vegas**, 2000 Las Vegas Blvd. S. (© 800/789-9436; www.chapelintheclouds.com). Their chapels overlook the entire city from more than 100 stories up, or you can get married on the indoor or outdoor observation decks. They even have packages that will include the thrill rides, so you can take the plunge both metaphorically and literally.

Adrenaline junkies can also join in holy matrimony while zooming along at nearly 70 mph on the Roller Coaster at **New York-New York**, 3790 Las Vegas Blvd. S. (© 702/740-6616; www.newyorknewyork.com).

If you want to add a little fire to the festivities, try getting married in front of the volcano at **The Mirage**, 3400 Las Vegas Blvd. S. (© 702/791-7155; www.mirage.com). You can have the ceremony during the day or at night when the thing is all lava-riffic.

Finally, several of the city's most popular museums offer themed wedding packages with very interesting backdrops, including the **Mob Museum** (p. 140) and the **Neon Museum** (p. 141).

ever get tired of mocking that bit of bad decision making). There are four separate chapels plus a drive-thru (allegedly the first of its kind), and an outdoor gazebo. It's all fine, but it has a factory-line atmosphere, processing wedding after wedding all day. Move 'em in and move 'em out. If you want something special, there are probably better choices.

1301 Las Vegas Blvd. S. (btw. E. Oakey and Charleston blvds). © **800/545-8111** or 702/382-5943. www.alittlewhitechapel.com. Daily 8am–midnight.

A Special Memory Wedding Chapel ★ This is a very nice wedding chapel, particularly compared to the rather tired facades of the classics on the Strip. This is absolutely the place to go if you want a traditional, big-production wedding; you won't feel it the least bit tacky. It's a New England church–style building, complete with steeple. The interior looks like a proper church (well, a plain one—don't think ornate Gothic cathedral), with a peaked roof, pews with padded red seats, modern stained-glass windows of doves and flowers, and lots of dark wood. It's all very clean and new and seats about 87 comfortably. There is a short staircase leading to an actual bride's room; she can make an entrance coming down it or through the double doors at the back. The area outside the chapel is like a mini-mall of bridal paraphernalia stores. Should all this just be too darned nice and proper for you, they also offer a drive-up window. They have a photo studio on-site and will do receptions featuring a small cake, cold cuts, and champagne. There is a gazebo for outside weddings, and they sell T-shirts!

800 S. 4th St. (at Gass Ave.). © **800/962-7798** or 702/384-2211. www.aspecialmemory.com. Sun–Thurs 8am–10pm; Fri–Sat 8am–midnight.

Viva Las Vegas Weddings ★★★   Yes, you could come to Las Vegas and have a traditional wedding in a tasteful chapel where you walk down the aisle to a kindly minister. But wouldn't you rather literally ride into the chapel in the back of a pink Cadillac and get married by Elvis? Or wade in through dry ice fog while Dracula performs your ceremony? This is the mecca of the wacky themed Vegas wedding, complete with indoor and outdoor spaces, tux and costume rentals, florists, theme rooms for receptions, and a staff of former stage performers who love to put on a show. *This* is what a Vegas wedding should be like.

1205 Las Vegas Blvd. S. (btw. Charleston and Oakey blvds.). © **800/574-4450** or 702/384-0771. www.vivalasvegasweddings.com. Sun–Thurs 9am–9pm; Fri–Sat 8am–10pm.

Wee Kirk O' the Heather ★★   This is the oldest wedding chapel in Las Vegas (it's been here since 1940; ah, Vegas, and its mixed-up view of age) and the one at the very end of the Strip, right before Downtown (and thus close to the license bureau). It was originally built as a house in 1925 for a local minister, but marriage bureau officials kept sending couples there to get married and they eventually just gave up and turned it into a chapel. The decor is entirely fresh, and while that means gold-satin-patterned wallpaper in the chapel, we like it a great deal. Just the right balance between kitsch and classic, and that's what you want in a Vegas wedding chapel. Plus, if there were a competition for the friendliest chapel in town, this one would win hands down.

231 Las Vegas Blvd. S. (btw. Bridger and Carson aves.). © **800/843-5266** or 702/382-9830. www. weekirk.com. Daily 10am–8pm.

OUTDOOR ACTIVITIES

Biking

Bicycle rentals can be arranged through the concierge at most of the major hotels in town. If you'd prefer to do it on your own, check out **Las Vegas Cyclery** (© **702/596-2953;** www.lasvegascyclery.com), a rental and tour operator offering everything from street to mountain to tandem bikes and the necessary safety equipment and accessories. Guided tours of Red Rock Canyon, Mount Charleston, and more are also offered. Prices for mountain bike rentals start at around $40 for a half-day and guided tours at around $130.

Boating & Fishing

The bulk of the water-based activities in the area take place at the **Lake Mead National Recreation Area,** located about 20 miles east of Las Vegas. Several harbors offer rentals of power, fishing, and house boats and personal watercraft. They can also help you with fishing licenses and equipment. For more information, see chapter 9.

Golf

See "Fore! Great Desert Golf" (below).

Gyms

All of the major hotels (and many of the minor ones) have fully stocked gyms on the premises. The size and quality varies, of course, but the bigger resorts have facilities that would make most commercial fitness centers green with envy. Entrance to most is covered by the nightly resort fee, but if the hotel you are staying in doesn't have one, expect a charge of anywhere from $15 to $35 per day. Several national chains, including **24 Hour Fitness,** have outlets in Las Vegas, and your membership may allow you to use the local branch.

Hiking

We consider the length you have to walk between hotels on the Strip or from your room to the front door enough of a hike, but if you are looking for something more traditional, the **Red Rock Canyon** and **Mount Charleston** areas have numerous hiking trails. For more information, see chapter 9.

Horseback Riding

Looking to indulge your inner cowboy/girl? There are several stables and horseback-tour companies in town, most of which are located near **Red Rock Canyon** and **Mount Charleston.** For more information, see chapter 9.

Ice Skating

The **SoBe Ice Arena** at the Fiesta Rancho, 2400 N. Rancho Rd. (© **702/631-7000;** www.fiestarancholasvegas.com), features an NHL regulation–size rink and offers daily open skating hours, lessons, and equipment rental. Public skating times vary from week to week based on the schedules of the various hockey leagues that use the facility; usually the rink is open for at least a couple of hours every afternoon and after 8pm on Friday and Saturday nights, when a DJ and nightclub-worthy lighting may help mask the sound and sight of you falling down a lot.

Skiing & Snowboarding

See information about the **Las Vegas Ski and Snowboard Resort** in the Mt. Charleston section of chapter 9.

Swimming

Part of the delight of the Vegas resort complexes is the gorgeous pools—what could be better for beating the summer heat? But there are pools and there are pools, so you'll need to keep several things in mind when searching for the right one for you.

During the winter, it's often too cold or windy to do much lounging, and even if the weather is amenable, the hotels often close part of their pool areas during winter and early spring. The pools also are not heated, for the most part, but in fairness, they largely don't need to be.

Most hotel pools are shallow, chest-high at best, only about 3 feet deep in many spots (the hotels want you gambling, not swimming). Diving is impossible—not that a single pool allows it anyway.

And finally, during those hot days, be warned that sitting by pools next to heavily windowed buildings such as the Mirage and Treasure Island allows you to experience the same thing a bug does under a magnifying glass with a sun ray directed on it. Regardless of time of year, be sure to slather on the sunscreen; there's a reason you see

ORGANIZED TOURS

Just about every hotel in town has a tour desk offering a seemingly infinite number of sightseeing opportunities in and around Las Vegas. You're sure to find a tour company that will take you where you want to go. For example, **Gray Line** (*℗* **800/634-6579;** www.grayline.com) offers a rather comprehensive roster, including the following:

o A pair of 5- to 6-hour **city tours** (day or night) with various itineraries, including visits to **Ethel M**

Chocolates and the **Fremont Street Experience**

o Half-day excursions to **Hoover Dam** and **Red Rock Canyon**

o A half-day tour to **Lake Mead** and **Hoover Dam**

o Several full-day **Grand Canyon** excursions

Call for details or inquire at your hotel's tour desk, where you'll also find free magazines with coupons for discounts on these tours.

---

so many unhappy lobster-red people roaming the streets. Many pool areas don't offer much in the way of shade.

At any of the pools, you can rent a cabana (which often includes a TV, special lounge chairs, and even better poolside service), but these should be reserved as far in advance as possible, and, with the exception of the Four Seasons' complimentary shaded lounging area, most cost a hefty fee. If you are staying at a chain hotel, you will most likely find an average pool, but if you want to spend some time at a better one, be aware that most of the casino-hotel pool attendants will ask to see your room key. If they are busy, you might be able to sneak in, or at least blend in with a group ahead of you.

Tennis

Tennis used to be a popular pastime in Vegas, but these days, buffs only have a couple of choices at hotels in town that have courts. **Bally's** (*℗* **702/967-4598**) has eight night-lit hard courts. Fees start at $20 per hour per court for guests of Bally's or Paris Las Vegas and $25 per hour for nonguests, with rackets available for rental. Facilities include a pro shop. Hours vary seasonally. Reservations are advised. The **Las Vegas Hotel** (*℗* **702/732-5009**) has six outdoor hard courts (four night-lit) and a pro shop. It's open to the public but hours vary seasonally. Rates are $20 per hour for guests and $25 per hour for nonguests. Lessons are available. Reservations are required.

FORE! GREAT DESERT GOLF

In addition to the listings below, there are dozens of local courses, including some very challenging ones that have hosted PGA tournaments. *Note:* Greens fees vary radically depending on time of day and year. Also, call for opening and closing times, because these change frequently. Because of the heat, you will want to take advantage of the cart that in most cases is included in the greens fee.

Angel Park Golf Club ★★ This 36-hole, par-70/71 public course is a local favorite. Arnold Palmer originally designed the Mountain and Palm courses (the Palm Course was redesigned several years later by Bob Cupp). Players call this a great escape from the casinos, claiming that no matter how many times they play it, they

striking **OUT**

Las Vegas is one of the favorite cities in the world for bowlers of all levels, with several huge alleys offering everything from regular bowling to rock-'n'-roll style action.

- The Strip got its first serious bowling alley in 2014 at **Brooklyn Bowl,** 3545 Las Vegas Blvd. S. (at the LINQ; © **702/862-2695**). The 32-lane facility has two floors of state-of-the-art scoring from Brunswick, swank couches at the lanes instead of hard plastic seats, and high-definition projection screens over the alleys. Be warned that the nice surroundings come with a high price ($25 and up per lane per hour). It's open Sunday through Thursday from 11am until 2am and Friday and Saturday until 4am.

- **Gold Coast Bowling Center,** 4000 W. Flamingo Rd. (at Valley View; © **702/367-7111**), has a

70-lane bowling center; open daily 24 hours.

- The **Orleans Bowling Center,** 4500 W. Tropicana Ave. (© **702/ 365-7400**), has 70 lanes, a pro shop, lockers, meeting rooms, and more; open daily 24 hours.

- **Red Rock Lanes,** 11011 W. Charleston Ave. (© **702/797- 7467**), is a luxury bowling center with 72 lanes, plasma TVs, and VIP suites where you can pick your own music and get bottle service. It's open Monday through Thursday from 8am until 2am and 24 hours on Fridays and Saturdays.

- **Santa Fe Station Bowling Center,** 4949 N. Rancho Rd. (© **702/ 658-4995**), has a 60-lane alley with the most modern scoring equipment, new furnishings, a fun and funky bar, a small cafe, and much more. Open Sunday

never get tired of it. The Palm Course has gently rolling fairways that offer golfers of all abilities a challenging yet forgiving layout. The Mountain Course has rolling natural terrain and gorgeous panoramic views. Facilities include a pro shop, night-lit driving range, 18-hole putting course, restaurant, cocktail bar, snack bar, and more.

100 S. Rampart Blvd. (btw. Summerlin Pkwy. and Alta St., 20 min. NW of the Strip). © **888/446-5358** or 702/254-4653. www.angelpark.com. Greens fees $30–$155. Internet specials available.

Arroyo Golf Club ★ Also designed by Arnold Palmer, this 18-hole, par-72 course is one of the more scenic in town owing to its location nestled along Red Rock Canyon. Stunning mountains on one side and Las Vegas in the distance on the other side; what more could you want? Well, you get a challenging (but not insanity-inducing) course that will keep all but the most competitive of golfers entertained. Facilities include a pro shop, night-lit driving range, 18-hole putting course, restaurant, cocktail bar, snack bar, and more.

2250 C Red Springs Dr. (just west of the 215, 25 min. NW of the Strip). © **866/934-4653** or 702/258-3200. www.thearroyogolfclub.com. Greens fees $69–$189.

Bali Hai Golf Club ★★★ One of the most exclusive golf addresses belongs to this multimillion-dollar course on the Strip, just south of Mandalay Bay. Done in a wild South Seas theme, the par-72 course has over 7 acres of water features, including an island green, palm trees, and tropical foliage everywhere you look. Not impressed yet? How about the fact that all their golf carts are equipped with GPS? Okay, if that through Thursday 7am until midnight and Friday and Saturday 7am until 1am.

o **Sam's Town Bowling Center,** 5111 Boulder Hwy. (© **702/456-7777**), offers 56 lanes plus a snack shop, cocktail lounge, video arcade, day-care center, pro shop, and more. It's open daily 24 hours.

o **South Point Bowling Center,** 9777 Las Vegas Blvd. (© **702/797-8080**), has a 64-lane facility with a similar divided layout to its sister at Suncoast (see below). It has all the latest gee-whiz scoring and automation, plus the usual facilities, and is open 24 hours. A separate $30-million, 60-lane facility designed to host pro-bowling tournaments should be open by the time you read this.

o **Strike Zone** at Sunset Station, 1301 W. Sunset Rd., in

Henderson (© **702/547-7467**), has a high-tech, 72-lane facility with all the latest automated scoring gizmos, giant video screens, a full bar, a snack shop, a pro shop, a video arcade, and more. It's open daily 24 hours.

o **Suncoast Bowling Center,** 9090 Alta Dr., in Summerlin (© **702/636-7111**), offers 64 lanes divided by a center aisle. The high-tech center with touch-screen scoring has become a regular stop on the Pro Bowlers tours. It's open daily 24 hours.

o **Texas Star Lanes,** 2101 Texas Star Lane (© **702/631-8128**), offers a 60-lane alley, video arcade, billiards, a snack bar and lounge, and more. It's open daily 24 hours.

doesn't convince you of the upscale nature of the joint, check out the greens fees. Even at those prices, premium tee times are often booked months in advance. Among the many facilities are a pro shop, putting green, gourmet restaurant, grill, and lounge.

5150 Las Vegas Blvd. S. © **888/427-6678.** www.balihaigolfclub.com. Greens fees $99–$395.

Bear's Best Las Vegas ★★★   Golf legend Jack Nicklaus has designed hundreds of courses around the world, but here he has taken 18 of his favorite holes and put them all together in one delightfully challenging package. From courses in Mexico to Montana and back again, the bunkers, water features, and traps have all been faithfully re-created, giving you an opportunity to try the best of "The Bear." Facilities include a pro shop, putting green, restaurant (with Nicklaus memorabilia), and club house.

11111 W. Flamingo Rd. © **702/804-8500.** www.clubcorp.com. Greens fees $69–$229.

Las Vegas National Golf Club ★   This 18-hole, par-71 public course is one of the most historic in town. Built in 1961, it was at various times associated with or run by the Stardust, Sahara, and the Las Vegas Hilton. Yes, the Rat Pack played here, and you can, too. The course itself is classically designed (not the desert layout that most in Vegas have), and although it's not the most challenging in town, it will keep you entertained. Facilities include a pro shop, driving range, restaurant, cocktail lounge, and golf school.

1911 Desert Inn Rd. (btw. Maryland Pkwy. and Eastern Ave.). © **866/695-1961.** www.lasvegas national.com. Greens fees $39–$129.

Rio Secco Golf Club ★★   You don't have to be staying at the Rio Suites (or another Caesars Entertainment property) to play this gorgeous 18-hole course, but you get preferred tee times and discounts if you do. Set in the foothills of the mountains overlooking Las Vegas, the views are incredible and the course, designed by Rees Jones, is one of the most in demand in town. Facilities include a pro shop, driving range, restaurant, and bar.

2851 Grand Hills Dr., Henderson. ✆ **702/777-2400.** www.riosecco.net. Greens fees $79–$219.

TPC Las Vegas ★★   Justin Timberlake has held his charity golf tournament at this course, so if it's good enough for him, it should be good enough for you, right? Luckily the sexy-back guy has good taste, as this scenic course, which follows the arroyos and plateaus of the terrain, is also a favorite of the PGA. That should tell you there are no windmills or clown's mouths here. It's a very challenging course, so bring your A game. Facilities include a pro shop, driving range, restaurant, clubhouse, and golf school.

9851 Canyon Run Dr. ✆ **702/256-2500.** www.tpc.com. Greens fees $69–$249.

Wynn Las Vegas Golf Club ★★   Before Mr. Wynn came along and bulldozed the legendary Desert Inn Golf Club, he rescued a bunch of the landscaping and then reinstalled it here on his elegant 18-hole, par-70 course behind Wynn Las Vegas. The facility is as gorgeous as you would expect it to be, with waterfalls, lush foliage, and stunning greens designed by the acclaimed Thomas Fazio. It ain't cheap, but many golfers say it is totally worth it. Note that it is only open to guests of Wynn or Encore. Facilities include a pro shop, driving range, putting green, and food service.

At Wynn Las Vegas, 3131 Las Vegas Blvd. S. ✆ **888/320-7122.** www.wynnlasvegas.com. Greens fees $300 and up.

SPAS

Most of the major resorts in Las Vegas have spa facilities that range from pretty basic (sauna, Jacuzzi, some treatment rooms for massages) to extravagant (is that a rock climbing wall?), but many are only available to guests of the hotels in which they are located.

The spas that follow all have hours during which they are open to the general public. Those hours change seasonally and sometimes even weekly based on hotel guest demand, so call ahead or visit the websites for more details.

Aquae Sulis Spa ★★   The centerpiece here is the "Ritual," a series of dunks and soaks in cold, warm, hydrotherapy, and floating pools, some of which are outside in a gorgeously landscaped grotto. It's totally unique and worth the 20-minute drive from the Strip.

At the JW Marriott, 221 N. Rampart Blvd. (at Summerlin Pkwy.). ✆ **877/869-8777.** www.jwlas vegasresort.com. Massage and treatments $70–$215.

Canyon Ranch SpaClub ★   The largest spa in Las Vegas has more than 130,000 square feet worth of treatment rooms, workout facilities, and even a rock climbing wall. Although they do a good job of keeping things relatively peaceful, the sheer size of the place and the number of people who visit may inhibit your relaxation efforts. Note that prices are more expensive on the weekends, so go on a weekday if you can.

At The Venetian, 3355 Las Vegas Blvd. S. ✆ **877/220-2688.** www.canyonranch.com/lasvegas. Massage and treatments $50–$355.

Qua Baths & Spa ★★   Check out the Environment rooms at this lavishly designed spa, which include the Arctic Ice room complete with snow showers and a Roman Baths section that would make Caesar proud. Treatments and massages are not cheap, but the spa faithful say this is one of the best in town.

At Caesars Palace, 3570 Las Vegas Blvd. S. © **866/782-0655.** www.caesarspalace.com. Massage and treatments $140–$400.

Red Rock Resort Adventure Spa ★★★   The facility has the requisite spa accoutrement—a Zen-like space, massages, facials, sauna, and so on—but it's the "Adventure" part of the program that makes it truly unique. Capitalizing on the hotel's location on the edge of the Red Rock Canyon National Conservancy Area, the spa offers horseback riding, river rafting, kayaking, hiking, rock climbing, biking, and more. Go get a great outdoors workout and then come back for a massage to soothe your aches and pains.

At Red Rock Resort, 11011 W. Charleston Ave. (at I-215). © **866/328-9270.** www.redrocklasvegas. com. Massage and treatments $90–$285.

Spa at Bellagio ★★   The surroundings are luxe and the staff is so soothingly attentive that you just know it's going to cost you a fortune to get worked on here—but it's totally worth it. Few other spas in town will make you feel so richly pampered.

At Bellagio, 3600 Las Vegas Blvd. S. © **702/693-7472.** www.bellagio.com. Massage and treatments $95–$350.

Spa at Encore ★★★   By far the most beautifully designed spa in Las Vegas, the Moroccan garden decor is at once breathtaking and calming. Your bill can get shocking really fast, but one walk down the lantern-lit treatment room hallway will make all your cares melt away.

At Encore Las Vegas, 3121 Las Vegas Blvd. S. © **702/770-4772.** www.encorelasvegas.com. Massage and treatments $80–$425.

SHOPPING

Las Vegas is one of the top shopping destinations in the world, and many visitors list the malls, stores, outlets, and boutiques as one of their primary reasons for coming to the city. Several top-grossing retail outlets are in Las Vegas, including the Forum Shops at Caesars Palace, which makes more money per square foot than any other mall in the United States. But in between the big malls and high-end luxury stores are lots of fun and offbeat boutiques that help to make Vegas a shopper's paradise, no matter your taste or budget.

Because they are as much tourist attractions as shopping destinations, the malls, stores, and boutiques on the Strip are open longer than you may expect, generally from 10am until 11pm on weekdays and until midnight on weekends. Once you get off the Strip, things become more normal, with typical operating hours between 9am and 6 or 7pm. Some of the smaller independent stores are closed on Sundays.

Generally speaking, the further away you get from the Strip, the cheaper the prices. This applies to just about all categories of merchandise, even at name-brand chain stores where they will bump up prices by a few bucks just because they can. So if you're planning on getting a pair of shoes or jeans at a familiar chain store, check to see if they have an outlet elsewhere in the city and you can often save yourself some dough.

This also holds true for sundry items like toothpaste, shampoo, and deodorant. If you buy these at the hotel gift shops, expect to pay significantly more than you would if you go off the Strip to a regular retailer like Target or Wal-Mart.

SOUTH STRIP

Crystals ★ Architecturally speaking, Crystals is as evocative a building as you'll find in Vegas. All sharp angles jutting into the sky, the shape is meant to evoke a pile of crystals (get it?), and it is nothing if not dramatic. Inside, the soaring ceilings and plenty of windows give it an airy feeling, but too much white space makes it a little bland once you get past the structure. Stores are all almost exclusively the highest of high-end, including a 10,000-square-foot Tiffany & Co., a flagship outlet from designer Tom Ford, Harry Winston jewelers, Louis Vuitton, Prada, Porsche Design (in case you can't actually afford to own the vehicle but want to look like you do), and Dolce & Gabbana men's and women's outlets. Restaurants include the fantastic **Todd English P.U.B.** (p. 90), a Wolfgang Puck pizzeria, Mastro's Ocean Club, a popular sushi restaurant/nightclub Social House, and even a Pinkberry for fans of fancy frozen yogurt. Don't miss the two water features by the same folks who did the Bellagio Fountains. These are smaller and not as "wow," but still cool. The mall is open Sunday

Las Vegas Shopping

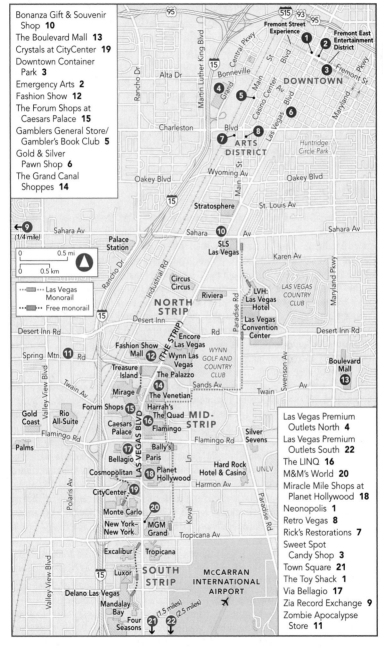

Bonanza Gift & Souvenir Shop **10**
The Boulevard Mall **13**
Crystals at CityCenter **19**
Downtown Container Park **3**
Emergency Arts **2**
Fashion Show **12**
The Forum Shops at Caesars Palace **15**
Gamblers General Store/ Gambler's Book Club **5**
Gold & Silver Pawn Shop **6**
The Grand Canal Shoppes **14**

Las Vegas Premium Outlets North **4**
Las Vegas Premium Outlets South **22**
The LINQ **16**
M&M's World **20**
Miracle Mile Shops at Planet Hollywood **18**
Neonopolis **1**
Retro Vegas **8**
Rick's Restorations **7**
Sweet Spot Candy Shop **3**
Town Square **21**
The Toy Shack **1**
Via Bellagio **17**
Zia Record Exchange **9**
Zombie Apocalypse Store **11**

through Thursday 10am until 11pm and Friday and Saturday 10am to midnight, but individual store and restaurant hours may vary. 3720 Las Vegas Blvd. S. (at CityCenter). www.crystalsatcitycenter.com. © **702/590-9299.**

M&M's World ★★ What can one do when faced with a wall of M&Ms in colors never before seen by man or woman (purple! teal! lime green!)? Overpriced? Yeah! Who cares? There are doodads galore, replete with the M&M's logo, and a surprisingly enjoyable short film and comedy routine, ostensibly about the "history" of the candy but really just a cute little adventure with a decent budget behind it. A "sweet" feature is a machine that will print your personal messages on the candies (although you can't get too verbose; there's only so much room). If this isn't enough chocolate for you, there should be a Hershey's Chocolate World open right across the street at New York-New York by the time you read this. It's open daily from 9am until midnight. In the Showcase Mall, 3785 Las Vegas Blvd. S. (just north of the MGM Grand Hotel). www.mymms.com. © **702/740-2504.**

MID-STRIP

The Forum Shops at Caesars Palace ★★★ This Rodeo-Drive-meets-the-Roman-Empire affair comes complete with a 48-foot triumphal arch entranceway, a painted Mediterranean sky, acres of marble, lofty Corinthian columns with gold capitals, and a welcoming goddess of fortune under a central dome. Then there is the Festival Fountain, where some seemingly immovable "marble" animatronic statues of Bacchus (slightly in his cups), a lyre-playing Apollo, Plutus, and Venus come to life for a 7-minute revel with dancing waters and high-tech laser-light effects. The shows take place every hour on the hour. Other nonretail highlights include a 50,000-gallon aquarium with another fountain show involving fire (don't stand too close; it gets really hot) and a circular escalator, said to be one of only two in the world. The entire thing is pretty incredible, but also very Vegas. Even if you don't like shopping, it's worth the stroll just to giggle.

Oh, right, the stores. With all the gawking opportunities, it may be easy to forget that you can shop and buy things here. Tenants are mostly of the exclusive variety, although there are a few more Average Joe kind of stores (yes, of course there's a Gap). Some examples: Jimmy Choo, Burberry, Christians Dior *and* Louboutin, A|X Armani Exchange, Gucci, Versace, Brooks Brothers, Juicy Couture, cosmetics giants Kiehl's and Sephora, and Vosges Haut Chocolat—makeup and sweets, that sounds like shopping nirvana to us! If that's not enough, they now have the largest H&M in the United States, with three stories of affordable fashion bliss.

If you are feeling peckish, the mall features more than a dozen restaurants, including Wolfgang Puck's seemingly immortal Spago, a branch of the popular NYC eatery Carmine's, and a massive Planet Hollywood theme restaurant (which recently moved to a bigger space).

The majority of the shops are open Sunday through Thursday from 10am to 11pm and Friday and Saturday from 10am to midnight. In Caesars Palace, 3500 Las Vegas Blvd. S. www.forumshops.com. © **702/893-4800.**

The Grand Canal Shoppes ★★ The Venetian half of this megamall is a re-created Italian village, complete with a painted, cloud-studded blue sky overhead and a canal right down the center on which gondoliers float and sing. Pay them ($19 to $76), and you can take a lazy float down and back, serenaded by your faux-Italian boatman. The stroll (or float) ends at a miniature version of St. Mark's Square, the central landmark of Venice. Here, you'll find opera singers, strolling musicians, glass blowers, and other bustling marketplace activity. It's all most ambitious and beats the heck out of animatronic statues.

The stores on this side feature more selections that at least approach affordability, including Cache, Davidoff, Kenneth Cole, Ann Taylor, BCBG, bebe, Banana Republic, Victoria's Secret, and Sephora.

The newer half of the Shoppes at sister resort Palazzo don't have a canal or the hyper-reality Venetian theme, but up the ante with the kind of high-end retail experiences that this town is famous for. Look for marquee names like Barney's New York, Cartier, Jimmy Choo, Burberry, and Ralph Lauren, to name a few.

And if all that shopping gets you hungry, a veritable piazza's worth of celebrity-chef restaurants can be found in and around the retail offerings, including ones from Mario Batali, Emeril Lagasse, Wolfgang Puck, and *Cake Boss* Buddy Valastro. The shops are open Sunday through Thursday from 10am to 11pm and Friday and Saturday from 10am to midnight. In The Venetian/Palazzo, 3327-3377 Las Vegas Blvd. S. www.thegrand canalshoppes.com. ☎ 702/414-4500.

The LINQ ★★ The biggest draw here is the High Roller, the world's tallest observation wheel (p. 135), but pay attention while you're making your way to ride because the LINQ is a nice little diversion from the typical Vegas hullabaloo. The pedestrian mall between the Quad and the Flamingo has only a couple of dozen stores and restaurants, but they are hipper than the norm with a Kitson "lifestyle boutique," a Koto knickknack store, Goorin Brothers hat shop (hats are in again!), Yard House restaurant, and a branch of the Brooklyn Bowl concert venue and restaurant (p. 98). Worth a stop is the Polaroid photo bar and museum, where you can print out your selfies as classic Polaroids and see photo-inspired art and history (an exhibit of Andy Warhol's photos opened the museum). They even recreated the luck 'o the Irish–themed O'Sheas, torn down in the process of making this place, with a new bar and mini-casino. Especially sweet treats can be found at the Ghirardelli Ice Cream and Chocolate Store and at Vegas' first branch of LA's popular Sprinkles cupcakes. They even installed that company's world-famous cupcake ATM. Yes, it's a machine that dispenses cupcakes. That alone is reason to visit as far as we are concerned. Hours vary by store. 3454 Las Vegas Blvd. S. (between The Quad and The Flamingo). www.thelinq.com. ☎ 800/CAESARS.

Miracle Mile Shops at Planet Hollywood ★ Though not without some eye-catching details, these shops aren't all that glamorous: It's pretty much a new-Vegas, whiz-bang version of every nice upper-end mall in America, a letdown made all the worse because the original version was so charming. Although some of the original *Arabian Nights* details from when this mall was known as the Desert Passage still exist, most of the mall is pretty generic. At least some of the shops stand out, with notables including Frederick's of Hollywood, True Religion Jeans, a giant Urban Outfitters, Steve Madden footwear, American Apparel, bebe, BCBG, Sephora, and a branch of the insanely popular H&M clothing store. At the center of it all is the AXIS Theater, where pop princess Britney Spears is headlining through 2015. The shops are open Sunday through Thursday from 10am to 11pm and Friday and Saturday from 10am to midnight. In Planet Hollywood Resort & Casino, 3663 Las Vegas Blvd. S. www.miracle mileshopslv.com. ☎ 702/866-0703.

Via Bellagio ★★ This collection of stores isn't as big as some of the other mega-hotel shopping arcades, but here it's definitely quality over quantity. It's a veritable roll call of glossy magazine ads: Prada, Chanel, Tiffany & Co., Gucci, Louis Vuitton, Dior,

Giorgio Armani, Fendi, and Hermès. The newest I-can't-afford-this boutique is from watchmaker Breguet, creator of bejeweled timepieces for those in the know since 1775. You need anything else? Well, yes—money. If you can afford this stuff, good for you, you lucky dog. Hours vary by store. In Bellagio, 3600 Las Vegas Blvd. S. www.bellagio. com. ✆ **702/693-7111.**

NORTH STRIP

Bonanza Gift and Souvenir Shop ★★   If you prefer your souvenirs to be a little less class and a little more kitsch, head here to the self-proclaimed "World's Largest Gift Shop." It certainly is big. T-shirts; Native American "handicrafts"; all kinds of playing cards, both new and used (casinos have to change decks frequently, so this is where used packs go); dice; things covered in rhinestones; snow globes—in short, something for everyone, provided "everyone" has a certain sensibility. We looked, and we felt the tackiest item available was the pair of earrings made out of poker chips. But don't worry about sullying your reputation by coming in here; even celebrities pay a visit. Angelina Jolie and Brad Pitt brought four of their kids in for a mini-shopping spree in 2013! If it's good enough for Brangelina . . . . It's open daily from 8am until midnight. 2440 Las Vegas Blvd. S. (at Sahara Ave.). www.worldslargestgiftshop.com. ✆ **702/385-7359.**

Fashion Show ★★   What was once a nondescript, if large, mall now has a *yowsa*! exterior much more fitting for Las Vegas. It's capped by a giant . . . well . . . they call it a "cloud," but we call it "that weird thingy that looks like a spaceport for UFOs." Inside, it's still, more or less, a basic mall, including Nevada's only Nordstrom, Saks Fifth Avenue, a Neiman Marcus, and other high-end retailers. Wear comfortable shoes so you can explore the other 250 shops, restaurants, and services the mall offers. And the cloud/alien spaceport thingy has giant LED screens, music, and other distractions—again, much more fitting for Vegas, where even the malls have to light up. Fashion Show is open Monday through Saturday from 10am to 9pm and Sunday from 11am to 7pm. 3200 Las Vegas Blvd. S. (at the corner of Spring Mountain Rd.). www.thefashion show.com. ✆ **702/369-8382.**

DOWNTOWN

Downtown Container Park ★★★   It seems like every day Downtown Las Vegas gets a little more interesting, and it's because of places like this. Even though shopping and dining are the primary reasons for this place to exist, it also has to be featured in the Things to Do chapter because its construction, features, and unique sense of place turn it into a "destination" all on its own. Built out of recycled shipping containers and pre-manufactured steel cubes, the complex feels arty (in a good way), and that's before you get to the galleries, independent eateries, handmade clothing stores, barbershop, and more lining the perimeter. Of course, before you get to that, you have to pay homage to the fire-breathing praying mantis sculpture out front (originally created for Burning Man and active after dark nightly). Kids will love the giant treehouse play area in the middle of the complex. A stage offers frequent live entertainment, and an "immersion dome" serves up special events like shows and screenings. The center is open Sunday through Thursday from 11am to 11pm and Friday and Saturday from 11am to 1am, although store hours vary. 707 Fremont St. (at 7th St.) www. downtowncontainerpark.com. ✆ **702/637-4244.**

Emergency Arts ★★   Located in a former medical clinic, this gallery and boutique collective has a decidedly boho flavor, with funky finds on everything from clothes to jewelry to classic vinyl. It's all created or curated by local talent, so it has a one-of-a-kind feeling that you won't get at the slick shops on the Strip. There's also a fun coffee shop on the first floor that feels like the perfect place to sit and discuss Nietzsche; a yoga studio upstairs; a tech library; and a mini-museum acting as the Burlesque Hall of Fame. Gallery and boutique hours vary, but are generally 10am until 6pm. 520 E. Fremont St. www.emergencyartslv.com. ✆ **702/409-5663.**

Gamblers General Store/Gambler's Book Club ★   The two best gambling-related shopping experiences in Vegas have merged to become one big megastore devoted to all things lady luck. This is a gambler's paradise stocked with over 3,000 book titles, antique and modern slot machines, gaming tables (blackjack, craps, and so on), roulette wheels, collectible chips, casino dice, classic Vegas photos, and truckloads of gaming-related souvenirs. They will even make custom cards and chips for your own (perfectly legal, we're sure) in-home casino. Looking for a book on how to beat casino odds? They have all of them, although it's probably important to note that the casinos would be out of business if they worked reliably. The store is open Monday through Saturday from 9am to 6pm and Sunday from 9am to 5pm. 800 S. Main St. (Downtown). www.gamblersgeneralstore.com. ✆ **800/522-1777** or 702/382-9903.

Las Vegas Premium Outlets North ★   This open-air mall near Downtown Las Vegas has several strikes against it. While it's fine on a regular day, it's an open oven of misery on typically hot Vegas summer days. You'll roast away while shopping among disappointingly dull stores, some of which are "outlets" only because they aren't in regular malls and offer discounts that you have to search for with a microscope. Having said all that, it's insanely popular and can at least give you the illusion that you are saving money while shopping at stores like Burberry, Calvin Klein, Polo Ralph Lauren, TAG Heuer, Ferragamo, Dolce & Gabbana, Coach, True Religion, and Ann Taylor. An upcoming expansion will add dozens of new stores and some much-needed new parking by 2015. The mall is open Monday through Saturday from 9am to 9pm and Sunday from 9am to 8pm. 875 S. Grand Central Pkwy. (at I-15). www.premium outlets.com. ✆ **702/474-7500.**

Neonopolis ★   When this $100-million shopping complex opened on Fremont Street in 2002, it had movie theaters, stores, and restaurants; but a series of ownership missteps led to the place becoming mostly abandoned. There is new life here with the addition of terrific stores like **The Toy Shack** (p. 174) and restaurants like **Heart Attack Grill** (p. 113) and Downtown Las Vegas' first Denny's (complete with its own wedding chapel). The restored neon signs throughout the complex are worth a gander. Hours vary by store. 450 Fremont St. www.neonopolislv.com. ✆ **702/868-9138.**

Retro Vegas ★★   This fun and funky antiques and collectibles boutique is not entirely about Sin City—the large selection of midcentury and Danish modern furnishings is definitely worth drooling over—but it is the Vegas history on display that will probably offer the biggest thrill. Go small with a '60s-era ashtray from the Sands or go big with a '70s-era smoked-glass chandelier from the Desert Inn, with lots of bric-a-brac from across the eras in between. It's open Monday through Saturday from 11am to 6pm and Sunday from noon to 5pm. 1131 S. Main St. (at Charleston Ave.). www.retro-vegas.com. ✆ **702/384-2700.**

Sweet Spot Candy Shop ★★   Part of the genius of the design of this retro/modern candy store are the white walls and furniture and plain floors—a blank canvas

SHOPPING gets real

The proliferation of reality TV shows has turned an island's worth of Average Joes, from ice road truck drivers to overly tanned Jersey boys, into pop-culture stars. Although you can't go trawling on a fishing boat (for instance) with your favorite demi-celebrities, in Las Vegas you can visit a couple of the places that made them famous by way of two of the History Channel's most popular series.

Pawn Stars is sort of like the more desperate version of PBS' *Antiques Roadshow*, where people bring in their treasures and trash to the **Gold & Silver Pawn Shop,** 713 Las Vegas Blvd. S. (www.gspawn.com; *(C)* **702/385-7912**), hoping to make a mint (or at least enough to keep them gambling in the casinos). Operated by the colorful Harrison family, the store is heavy on the hocked jewelry—but there are lots of other odds and ends worth a quick browse. The bad news is that the Harrisons themselves are rarely on-site anymore, which can be a disappointment to the hordes of people waiting in line (seriously!) at all times of the day to get inside. And you can just imagine what the crowds were like when Lynyrd Skynyrd, who did the show's new theme song, held a concert in the parking lot in 2013. The store is open daily from 9am until 9pm.

You'll have a much better chance of seeing people you've seen on TV at **Rick's Restorations,** 1112 S. Commerce St.(www.ricksrestorations.com;*(C)***702/366-7030**), where *American Restoration* is filmed. Owner Rick Dale, his wife Kelly, and a crew of lovable oddballs restore classic Americana (soda machines, gas pumps, bicycles, slot machines, and more) in a rambling facility that offers tours, a showroom, a gift shop, and more. Big windows in the public areas give you a glimpse into the working facility, and people from the show, including Rick, will often pop out to say hi and sign autographs. The restorations themselves are stunning accomplishments, but you're going to need a high credit limit to afford any of it. Recently offered gas pumps, for instance, started at around $7,000 and went up from there. The store is open Monday through Friday from 9am until 5pm.

that allows the literally candy-colored treats to pop out and amuse. The childhood favorites like Goo Goo Clusters and Mary Janes are fun, but it's their incredible selection of premium chocolates and gummies, displayed in old-fashioned candy jars, that will make you want to find extra room in your suitcase so you can take some home. The store is open Monday through Saturday from 10am until 9pm and Sunday from 10am until 8pm. At Downtown Container Park, 707 Fremont St. www.sweetspotcandylasvegas. com. *(C)* **702/324-2777.**

The Toy Shack ★★★   Fans of the History Channel's *Pawn Stars* may recognize the name Jimmy Jiminez, who acts as the toy expert on the show. He's the brains behind this blast-from-the-past (and present) store that celebrates all things play with new and collectible toys of all stripes, from action figures and dolls to model cars and trucks (and one of the biggest selections of Hot Wheels in the country). If you had a favorite from your childhood, you'll probably find three of them here, and if you don't, they can probably get it for you. Regular events like superhero costume gatherings and custom car shows turn the toys into life-size "realities." The Toy Shack is open Sunday through Thursday from 10am until 10pm and Friday and Saturday from 10am until midnight. In Neonopolis, 450 E. Fremont St. www.lasvegastoyshack.com. *(C)* **702/538-8600.**

JUST OFF THE STRIP

The Boulevard ★ There is absolutely nothing ground-breaking about this suburban mall—it is filled with the same Sears, JCPenney, Foot Locker, and Lane Bryant archetypes that you'll find in the mall near your home—but that's exactly why we are including it here. Window-shopping at the malls on the Strip with their Nordstrom and Dolce & Gabbana stores can be fun, but if you actually need a pair of moderately priced shoes or sensible clothing, this is where you should come. A makeover for the center is planned to go into 2015 and will add more stores, a farmer's market, and a generally spiffed-up experience. The mall is open Monday through Saturday from 10am to 9pm and Sunday from noon to 7pm. 3528 S. Maryland Pkwy. (btw. Twain Ave. and Desert Inn Rd.). www.boulevardmall.com. © **702/735-8268.**

Zia Record Exchange ★★ A sign that individual Vegas culture might not be dead after all, these fairly large shops mix new and used records. The emphasis is on CDs, but there is a big vinyl section, and both show a varied selection of music styles (rock, punk, jazz, soundtracks, and so on). Cleverly, the stores spotlight bands coming to Vegas, both large and small, with special displays, plus there are always bins of music from local acts. They also feature occasional in-store CD signings, concerts, and events, many of which have an offbeat, indie vibe. Visitors with hair on their upper lip got $1 off any regular purchase during Mustache May in 2013. And the mustache didn't even need to be real! Both locations are open daily from 10am to midnight. 4503 W. Sahara Ave. www.ziarecords.com. © **702/233-4942.** 4225 S. Eastern Ave., STE 17. © **702/735-4942.**

Zombie Apocalypse Store ★★ Although you can stock your bunker with enough supplies to survive any type of apocalypse from the selections at this store, we classify this place under "Gifts & Souvenirs" for the delightfully silly zombie paraphernalia in which they wrap their end-of-the-world fear feeding. In addition to the survivalist store staples like knives, stun guns, and food rations, they have bumper stickers with sayings like "My Zombie Ate Your Honor Student," T-shirts that read "Zombies should get a life," helpful posters with zombie killing and survival tips, zombie-shaped target practice sheets, books, DVDs, and even a bunker-style den where you can sit and watch zombie movies. Perhaps Brad Pitt's character in *World War Z* should have shopped here. The store is open daily from 10am to 7pm (hours vary seasonally). 3420 Spring Mountain Rd. (at Polaris Ave.). www.zombieapocalypsestore.com. © **702/320-0703**.

SOUTH & EAST OF THE STRIP

Las Vegas Premium Outlets South ★ Your neighbors may be a little bit more impressed with the lineup of stores you can name-drop at the sister **Outlets North** (see above), but you'll probably be more satisfied with the genuine bargains from mainstream retailers you can find here. There are a couple of higher-end stores with nameplates like DKNY and Brooks Brothers, but the rest of the lineup is from middle-America mall outlets like Gap, Hot Topic, Levi's, Lane Bryant, Nike, Dressbarn, Burlington, and Calvin Klein. The plus side is, unlike its counterpart, this one is enclosed and air-conditioned; the downside is they got rid of their really sweet indoor carousel. Boooo! The mall is open Monday through Saturday from 9am to 9pm and Sunday from 9am to 8pm. 7400 Las Vegas Blvd. S. (at Warm Springs Rd.). www.premiumoutlets.com. © **702/896-5599.**

Town Square ★   Instead of an enclosed mall or boring box store shopping center, Town Square is designed to look like, well, a town. Tree-lined streets bisect the 117-acre property, and if you're lucky, you can grab a parking space right in front of whatever store you're visiting (or park in one of the huge lots or garages nearby). The facades of the buildings resemble small-town America, only cleaner and more crowded than most. It's a great place to stroll and window-shop, at least on the roughly 27 days a year when it isn't either insanely hot or blustery and chilly. More than 150 shops and boutiques include plenty of typical mall favorites, such as Gap, American Eagle, Old Navy, Juicy Couture, Abercrombie & Fitch, and Banana Republic—plus some unique outlets, such as a Whole Foods market. Former Strip favorite GameWorks made a comeback here in 2014 with a 37,000 square-foot venue featuring bowling, laser tag, video games, a restaurant, and more. Over a dozen restaurants (among them Claim Jumper, Yard House, and local favorite Capriotti's) provide sustenance, while bars, movie theaters, parks, and playgrounds offer entertainment. Hours vary by store. 6605 Las Vegas Blvd. S. (at I-215). www.mytownsquarelasvegas.com. ✆ **702/269-5000.**

ENTERTAINMENT & NIGHTLIFE

According to an advertising slogan, Hollywood is the "Entertainment Capital of the World." But consider for a moment the sheer number of shows, headliners, bars, nightclubs, lounges, and other forms of entertainment and nightlife in Las Vegas. Your options are almost limitless: Cirque du Soleil has more than a half-dozen permanent shows here; virtually every hotel has at least one showroom, if not four; Céline Dion, Elton John, and Shania Twain are among the big names who perform regularly, and sometimes exclusively, in Vegas; most bars are open 24 hours a day; 12 of the top 25 grossing nightclubs in the U.S. are in Vegas, accounting for over half a billion dollars in revenue in 2013; and yes, there are even a few showgirls left. Hollywood may have the slogan, but Las Vegas is the real capital.

You certainly won't be lacking in things to do; in fact, the opposite may be true in that there are simply not enough hours in your vacation to do all the things you may want to do. The key is to cover the basics—a Cirque show if you've never seen one; a headliner if one is in town; a fun bar; a high-energy nightclub—and then start layering in the off-the-beaten-track, the one-of-a-kind, and the less-high-profile shows, clubs, and entertainment offerings that will make your trip more memorable.

What follows are the things you should not miss—and some that are not worth your time no matter what you may have heard—in the categories of performing arts, which includes shows both big, small, and in between; the bar scene, including lounges, piano bars, and pubs; the club and music scene, which covers the big dance clubs, ultralounges, comedy clubs, and more; and, of course, the strip clubs, which are big business in Vegas. There's also a section for gay and lesbian visitors showcasing the best and brightest bars and clubs around town.

THE PERFORMING ARTS

This category covers all the major Las Vegas production shows, and a few of the minor ones as well. Note that shows can close without warning, even ones that have been running just shy of forever, so please call first. You might also want to double-check on days and times of performances; schedules can change without notice. *Note:* Most ticket prices do not include taxes, fees, or drinks, so you might also check for those potential hidden costs.

Absinthe ★★★ Like the supposedly hallucinatory drink it is named after, this Cirque du Soleil–style revue may leave you reeling, but, boy, will that hangover be worth it. The show is performed in the round in a small tentlike structure in front of Caesars Palace, with a tiny circular stage and only a few rows of seating. This gives new meaning to the phrase "death-defying stunts," with acrobats, trapeze artists, high-wire walkers, and even high-speed roller skaters literally feet—and in some cases inches—from your face. Adding to the thrills are the raunchy host, The Gazillionaire, and his faithfully dimwitted sidekick assistant, who introduce the acts with a dirty glee and X-rated humor that will leave you laughing so hard you'll forget to be offended or shocked. The cast rotates so the show differs from performance to performance, but cross your fingers that you'll get a sock-puppet segment so deliriously over the top that it transcends its inherent vulgarity to become virtually awe-inspiring—it's worth the price of admission alone. Definitely not for kids or prudes! Shows are Wednesday through Sunday at 8 and 10pm only. In Caesars Palace, 3570 Las Vegas Blvd. S. ☎ **800/745-3000**. www.absinthevegas.com. Tickets $99–$159.

Blue Man Group ★   Are they blue? Indeed they are—three bald, nonspeaking men dipped in azure paint, doing decidedly odd stunts with marshmallows, art supplies, smoke-ring blowing cannons, giant inflatable balls, and an amazing array of percussion instruments fashioned fancifully from PVC piping. The show was revamped for its move to its third hotel showroom in Vegas, and if some of the magic has been lost, it's probably only because what was essentially a high-budget obscure performance art piece has now become a mainstream crowd-pleaser. Moments of silly genius are still there—a routine with a Twinkie and a hapless audience member is classic, and those giant smoke rings are oddly compelling—but an extended robotics sequence, where the blue guys interact with a pair of auto-assembly machines, was probably more interesting on paper. In the end, the show that used to be unique in Vegas is now uniquely Vegas, as much a part of the entertainment landscape as Cirque du Soleil, and for that alone it is worth a visit. *Note:* A procession of props, lights, and music from the show meanders through the casino daily at 6:15pm. Shows are nightly at 7 and 9:30pm. At Monte Carlo Resort & Casino, 3770 Las Vegas Blvd. S. ☎ **866/641-7469**. www.blueman.com. Tickets $65–$140; VIP and backstage tour packages available.

Cirque du Soleil's KÀ ★★★   *KÀ* subverts expectations by largely eschewing the usual Cirque format—acrobatic-style acts and ethereal performance art trappings with a tenuous-at-best connective tissue—in favor of an actual plot, as a brother and sister

Las Vegas Shows

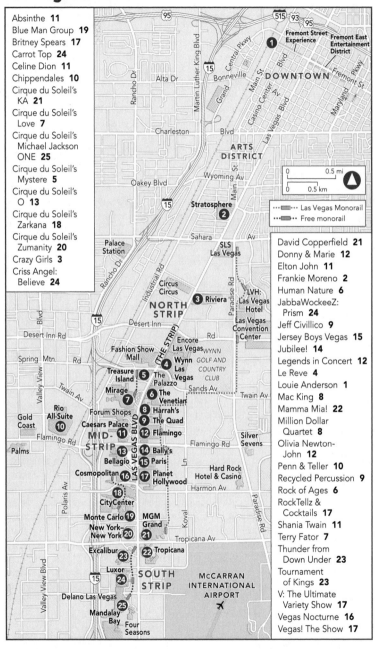

Absinthe **11**
Blue Man Group **19**
Britney Spears **17**
Carrot Top **24**
Celine Dion **11**
Chippendales **10**
Cirque du Soleil's KA **21**
Cirque du Soleil's Love **7**
Cirque du Soleil's Michael Jackson ONE **25**
Cirque du Soleil's Mystere **5**
Cirque du Soleil's O **13**
Cirque du Soleil's Zarkana **18**
Cirque du Soleil's Zumanity **20**
Crazy Girls **3**
Criss Angel: Believe **24**

David Copperfield **21**
Donny & Marie **12**
Elton John **11**
Frankie Moreno **2**
Human Nature **6**
JabbaWockeeZ: Prism **24**
Jeff Civillico **9**
Jersey Boys Vegas **15**
Jubilee! **14**
Legends in Concert **12**
Le Reve **4**
Louie Anderson **1**
Mac King **8**
Mamma Mia! **22**
Million Dollar Quartet **8**
Olivia Newton-John **12**
Penn & Teller **10**
Recycled Percussion **9**
Rock of Ages **6**
RockTellz & Cocktails **17**
Shania Twain **11**
Terry Fator **7**
Thunder from Down Under **23**
Tournament of Kings **23**
V: The Ultimate Variety Show **17**
Vegas Nocturne **16**
Vegas! The Show **17**

8

ENTERTAINMENT & NIGHTLIFE | The Performing Arts

BIG NAMES, bigger shows

During its fallow days in the 1970s and '80s, Las Vegas was the place where an entertainer's act went to die. The headliner showrooms were the refuge for singers whose careers' best days were years, and sometimes decades, behind them.

That all changed when Céline Dion came to town in 2003. Her 5-year engagement at Caesars Palace shattered box office records and made it safe for big-name headliners to call Vegas their home. In the last decade we have seen marquee-topping extended runs from Elton John, Cher, Bette Midler, Prince, Garth Brooks, Tim McGraw & Faith Hill, Shania Twain, Rod Stewart, and more.

Tickets are expensive, with the best seats going for upward of $300, and the concerts are not performed every week, so if you want to see one you have to plan your vacation around their schedule rather than yours. But many of the shows are exclusive engagements, meaning if you want to see the stars, you have to come to Vegas.

Céline Dion is deep into her second headlining run at Caesars Palace, 3570 Las Vegas Blvd. S. (© **877/423-5463;** www.celinedion.com; show times vary; tickets $55–$250). Backed by a 31-piece orchestra, this is a more dignified affair than her dance-heavy 2003–2008 show, which showcases her voice in a way that proves she is probably one of the most naturally gifted singers in the world. On signature ballads like "Because You Loved Me" and the inevitable "My Heart Will Go On," it's easy to understand how she can sell out a 4,000-seat theater on a regular basis. We would've liked to hear more of her hits rather than her covers of other's music that take up big chunks of the show, and we longed for more up-tempo moments, but fans will likely be rapt.

Sharing the same stage (but not at the same time, sadly), **Elton John,** at Caesars Palace, 3570 Las Vegas Blvd. S. (© **888/435-8665;** www.eltonjohn.com; show times vary; tickets $55–$250), is

from some mythical Asian kingdom are separated by enemy raiders and have to endure various trials and tribulations before being reunited. Gleefully borrowing imagery from magical realist martial-arts movies such as *Crouching Tiger, Hidden Dragon,* the production makes use of a technically extraordinary set that shifts the stage not just horizontally but vertically, as the action moves from under the sea to the side of a steep cliff and beyond. The circus elements—acrobats and clowns—are for once incorporated into the show in a way that makes some loose narrative sense, instead of a series of acts strung together just because they could.

The story is by turns funny, pulse-pounding, and whimsical, with moments that are nothing less than exquisitely perfect bits of theater. It might be too long and intense for younger children, but older ones will be enthralled—and so will you.

The tragic death of one of the show's performers during a show in 2013 has had only minor impacts on the fundamentals of this specific production but should have profound impact on the audience's interpretation of what Cirque does, reminding us that these are real human beings performing dangerous stunts for our amusement. Stand up at the end of the show and applaud that.

Performances are held Tuesday through Saturday at 7 and 9:30pm. In the MGM Grand, 3799 Las Vegas Blvd. S. © 866/740-7711. www.cirquedusoleil.com/ka. Tickets $69–$180.

Cirque du Soleil's LOVE ★ A collaboration between the Beatles (by way of Sir George Martin's son, who remixed and reconfigured the music with a free hand that also back for a second run of shows entitled *The Million Dollar Piano*. Sir Elton's canon of work is irreproachable: "Benny and the Jets," "Rocket Man," "Don't Let the Sun Go Down on Me." We could be here all day just listing his 5 decades' worth of hits. He's also a master showman; king of the bling and the tricked-out pianos like the one used in this production, complete with LED video panels built into it. Downsides (depending on your viewpoint) include a ballad-heavy playlist and some deep album cuts that only the most rabid of fans will recognize, along with less-energetic staging than we've seen in the past, but musically speaking, Elton John is a genius and this production proves why.

Country icon **Shania Twain** is also at Caesars Palace, 3570 Las Vegas Blvd. S. (© **800/745-3000;** www.shaniatwain.com; show times vary; tickets $55–$250), returning to the stage after more than a decade. The show is a crowd-pleasing mix of barn-burning foot-stompers like

"That Don't Impress Me Much" and "Man! I Feel Like a Woman!" alongside smartphone-waving ballads like "You're Still the One" and "From this Moment On," with a horse or two thrown in for good measure.

Finally, pop princess **Britney Spears** has taken up residency at Planet Hollywood, 3667 Las Vegas Blvd. S. (© **866/919-7472;** www.britneyspears.com; show times vary; tickets $65–$255), making the revamped Theater for the Performing Arts, now the Axis Theater, her home until at least the end of 2015. The show is heavy on the type of special-effects staging and energetic choreography that Brit's concerts have been famous for and lean heavily on her roster of hits like "Oops, I Did it Again," "Toxic," and "Scream and Shout." That she lip-syncs her way through most of the show (sorry, "sings to track") should not be a surprise to anyone who has been paying attention.

may distress purists) and Cirque du Soleil, this is the usual Cirque triumph of imaginative design, but it also feels surprisingly hollow. In one sense, it's an inspired pairing in that the Beatles' music provides an apt vehicle for Cirque's joyous spectacle. But while Cirque shows have never been big on plot, the particular aimlessness of this production means that the show too quickly dissolves into simply the introduction of one novel staging element after another. In other words, its visual fabulousness ends up repetitious rather than thrilling. Still, the familiar music provides an aura of accessibility to the sometimes dense world of Cirque du Soleil that other Vegas productions don't, so it could be good for both Cirque and Beatles newbies alike. Shows are held Thursday through Monday at 7 and 9:30pm. At The Mirage, 3400 Las Vegas Blvd. S. © **800/963-9634** or 702/792-7777. www.cirquedusoleil.com/love. Tickets $79–$180.

Cirque du Soleil's *Michael Jackson ONE* ★★★ Take the brilliantly conceived pop music and pop culture created by Michael Jackson and present it through the pop-art interpretive lens of Cirque du Soleil, and you have a perfect union of subject matter and subject matter experts. Massive walls of video seem to envelop the audience while speakers, built into the seats, pump the timeless soundtrack of Jackson classics, remixed and remastered, directly into your brain. Each is presented with a set piece that ranges from evocative to stunning to giddy glee-inducing. "Bad" features a gang zooming in on zip lines and bouncing around on what amounts to a giant rubber band stretched across the stage; "Wanna Be Starting Something" showcases an acrobatic troupe using Jackson's iconic fedoras as twirling and twisting props; a mashup of "Human Nature" and "Never Can Say Goodbye" has a solo dancer doing expert human animation; "Billie Jean" evokes the lighted sidewalk in the music video with lighted suits on dancers performing in an otherwise darkened theater. By the time they get to the part where it "snows" on the audience or the "Thriller" homage with zombies on trampolines, you'll want to stand up and cheer. When they bust out the gravity-defying "lean" from "Smooth Criminal" or any of the other instantly recognizable choreography from Jackson's videos, you will want to get up and dance with them. And when the company dances with a so-realistic-it-hurts hologram of Jackson during "Man in the Mirror," you may have a lump in your throat. It's okay if you do. You need to be at least an appreciator of the music and also willing to overlook the subtle hagiography of the guy who created it to properly enjoy the show, but anyone who owns a copy of "Thriller"—which is pretty much everybody—will be, in a word, thrilled. Shows are held Saturday through Wednesday at 7 and 9:30pm. At Mandalay Bay, 3950 Las Vegas Blvd. S. ℂ **877/632-7400** or 800/745-3000. www.cirquedusoleil.com/one. Tickets $69–$180.

Cirque du Soleil's Mystère ★★★ 2013 marked the 20th anniversary of the first (and many would still say the best) of the multiple Las Vegas Cirque du Soleil productions. Although there have been some tweaks here and there and a few new acts were added in 2012, the show is pretty much the same as it always has been, which, in a word, is *stunning*. It is the closest to the original ethos of the Montréal-based company's unique circus experience, which focuses on gorgeous feats of human strength and agility all wrapped up in performance art elements both surreal and absurd. The show features one simply unbelievable act after another (seemingly boneless contortionists and acrobats, breathtakingly beautiful aerial maneuvers), interspersed with Dadaist/*Commedia dell'arte* clowns. All this and a giant snail! The thesaurus runs dry trying to describe it: dreamlike, suspenseful, funny, erotic, mesmerizing, and just lovely. At times, you might even find yourself moved to tears. We're not ashamed to admit we were. Catch it Saturday through Wednesday at 7 and 9:30pm. In Treasure Island, 3300 Las Vegas Blvd. S. ℂ **800/392-1999** or 702/894-7722. www.cirquedusoleil.com/mystere. Tickets $69–$119, discounts for children under 12 based on availability.

Cirque du Soleil's O ★★★ How to describe the seemingly indescribable wonder and artistry of Cirque du Soleil's still utterly dazzling display? An Esther Williams–Busby Berkeley spectacular on peyote? A Salvador Dalí painting come to life? A stage show by Fellini? The French-Canadian troupe topped itself with this production and kind of made it impossible for subsequent shows to be as groundbreaking—and not simply because it's situated its breathtaking acrobatics in, on, around, and above a 1.5-million-gallon pool (*eau*—pronounced *O*—is French for "water"). Even without those impossible feats, this might be worth the price just to see the

adults-only SHOWS

Las Vegas gained its Sin City reputation for gambling, free-flowing alcohol, and entertainment that often involved big, feathered headdresses and bare breasts. Those showgirl revues are mostly gone, and even the shows that came after them, featuring topless hotties and hunks in various fantasy fulfillment–type sketches, are waning. Blame it on the Internet perhaps, where you can see a lot more than a pair of pasties and a G-string.

In addition to **Zumanity** and **Jubilee!** listed separately in this chapter, there are a few titillating entertainment options worth knowing about, although in some cases primarily just to stay away from them.

The most famous (or infamous, depending on your point of view) topless revue is the long-running **Crazy Girls** ★ at the Riviera, 2901 Las Vegas Blvd. S. (*C* **800/634-3420**; www.riviera hotel.com; nightly except Tuesday at 9:30pm; tickets $45–$71). It's basically a bunch of bare-breasted women contorting themselves on stage in come-hither poses and dance routines. For the same amount of money you could get as many as three lap dances at a strip club; we'll leave it up to you to decide what's the better bargain.

Ladies, we haven't forgotten about you. Of the several beefcake revues in town, **Chippendales** ★ at The Rio, 3700 W. Flamingo (*C* **855/234-7469**; www. chippendales.com; nightly 9pm with an additional 11pm show Fri–Sat; tickets $55–$80) gets the most attention simply because of its well-known brand name. The show ticks all of the boxes: inhumanly handsome and fit men; fantasy fulfillment sketches featuring the guys as cowboys and firemen and the like; and an audience of (mostly) women who go quite, quite crazy. Check the website for frequent guest appearances by "famous" hunks like Jeff Timmons or Ian Ziering (it's okay if you don't know who they are).

But if we were the ones screaming for more skin, we'd probably do so for the hunks of **Thunder from Down Under** ★★ at Excalibur, 3850 Las Vegas Blvd. S. Flamingo (*C* **702/597-7600**; www. thunderfromdownunder.com; Mon–Wed at 9pm; Thurs & Sat–Sun at 9 and 11pm; and Fri at 7, 9, and 11pm; tickets $51–$61). It's not that the guys are any hotter or the dancing any better, but this production has an edgier, anything-could-happen vibe that amps up the energy and the fun. Plus, the guys here are all Australian. Oh, those accents.

presentation, a constantly shifting dreamscape that's a marvel of imagination and staging. If you've seen *Mystère* at Treasure Island or other Cirque productions, you'll be amazed that they've once again raised the bar to new heights without losing any of the stylistic or humorous trademarks, including the hobo-esque clowns whose shenanigans are at turns funny and unexpectedly touching. Performances are held Wednesday through Sunday at 7:30 and 10pm. In Bellagio, 3600 Las Vegas Blvd. S. *C* **888/488-7111** or 702/796-9999. www.cirquedusoleil.com/o. Tickets $109–$180.

Cirque du Soleil's *Zarkana* ★   Replacing the underperforming but crowd-pleasing Elvis-themed show that played here at Aria Las Vegas with this more generic production may have made good business sense for Cirque du Soleil, but it is disappointing to loyalists looking for something fresh and new from the group. Perhaps that's why it was revamped in 2014, stripping out the nonsensical rock opera trappings and adding in a few new acts like twin brothers doing a dramatic aerial *pas de deux*. Did it make it better? Yes, definitely, but it still falls toward the bottom of the must-see rankings for Cirque shows in Las Vegas. There are a few noteworthy acts including a dramatic contemporary dancer performing a solo enhanced by light and shadow, but most of the production feels like it has been borrowed from other shows (acrobatics, high-wire, and trapeze acts). If you can only see one Cirque show in Vegas, there are better options. Shows are held Friday through Tuesday at 7 and 9:30pm. At Aria Las Vegas, 3730 Las Vegas Blvd. S. ✆ **855/927-5262.** www.cirquedusoleil.com/zarkana. Tickets $69–$180.

Cirque du Soleil's *Zumanity* ★ This adult show, dedicated to celebrating human sexuality, features a bevy of acts meant to be lewd or alluring or both, if you pay attention. They are mostly just basic Cirque acts (and worse, just basic striptease acts, which you can see anywhere in town for a great deal less money), though instead of giving the illusion of near-nakedness, they give the illusion of total nakedness (an illusion that works better the farther you sit from the stage). As they contort and writhe and feign pleasure or apathy, we feel sympathy for all the parents who spent money on gymnastics and ballet lessons over the years, only to have their poor kids end up in this. See, Cirque is naturally sexy and erotic, so all this is gilding the lily until it chokes from lack of oxygen and dies. There are some visually stunning moments (two women splashing about in a large glass, two men in a dramatic tango) and the drag queen emcee Edie is a fun hostess, but there are better ways to get your thrills in this town. Shows are held Friday through Tuesday at 7:30 and 10pm (show times vary seasonally). In New York–New York, 3790 Las Vegas Blvd. S. ✆ **866/606-7111** or 702/740-6815. www.zumanity.com. Tickets $69–$125. Only ages 18 and over admitted.

Criss Angel: *Believe* ★★ Forget what you may have heard about early versions of illusionist Criss Angel's show and hear this: *Believe* is probably the best traditional (and in many ways untraditional) magic show in Vegas. Angel has always been a compelling showman, astounding audiences with his bigger-than-life stunts that are mixed with a kind of rock-'n'-roll aesthetic. Although he can't do stuff in this showroom like float above the Luxor pyramid or walk on water as he has on his popular *Mindfreak* TV show, he still manages to bring out the "wow" factor with tricks both big (a gruesomely awesome sawing-a-woman-in-half bit) and small (is he really swallowing those razor blades?). Although this is technically still a Cirque du Soleil–related production, there is very little (if any) Cirque-style theatrics in it anymore, which is ultimately a good thing, considering that was the weakest part when the show first debuted. Shows are held Tuesday through Saturday at 7pm, with an additional show at 9:30pm on Tuesday, Friday, and Saturday. In the Luxor, 3900 Las Vegas Blvd. S. ✆ **877/826-0255.** www.crissangel.com. Tickets $59–$130.

David Copperfield ★ Illusionists don't come any more illustrious than David Copperfield, who has been in the business for decades and has done everything from making the Statue of Liberty disappear to walking through the Great Wall of China. He has played semi-regular sets at the MGM Grand for years, but now is making the hotel his home with his name on the showroom. He mixes small, up-close magic like popping balloons "with his mind" and making a small piece of tissue dance up someone's arm with larger stunts like making a car appear out of nowhere and causing an entire group from the audience to disappear (from the stage, not their seats). His laconic, "I'm so good at this I don't need to make a big deal about it" stage presence is a welcome relief from the hyper-dramatic theatrics that other magicians of his caliber often embrace, and Copperfield's ever-evolving act means that even if you have seen one of his TV specials, you'll witness new acts here. Shows are held nightly at 7 and 9:30pm with an additional 4pm show on Saturday. In the MGM Grand, 3555 Las Vegas Blvd. S. ✆ **877/880-0880.** www.davidcopperfield.com. Tickets $70–$110.

Divas Las Vegas ★   Star impersonator Frank Marino hosted the similar *La Cage* for more than 2 decades up the street at the Riviera. This show at the Quad isn't really all that different, in that it still features Marino as Joan Rivers in a series of Bob Mackie–esque gowns telling groan-worthy jokes and introducing a lineup of female impersonators. The "ladies" vary in quality and illusion: "Beyoncé" is done more for laughs and "Madonna" and "Dolly" are good, but "Céline Dion" is dead-on and "Lady Gaga" is frighteningly accurate (but hey, she kind of looks like a drag queen anyway). They lip-sync their way through hits, often accompanied by scantily clad male dancers, which gives you something to look at if the impersonator isn't up to snuff. Interesting side note: Marino's partner proposed on stage in 2013 on the couple's 20th anniversary. Shows are held Saturday through Thursday at 9:30pm. In The Quad, 3535 Las Vegas Blvd. S. ℭ **888/777-7664.** www.thequadlv.com. Tickets $55–$108.

Donny and Marie ★   Proving that a good fainting spell on *Dancing with the Stars* is worth a lot more than you'd expect, the wholesome brother-sister duo of Donny and Marie has made a comeback on the stages of Las Vegas, performing their personal blend of music, comedy, and variety at the Flamingo. The show is a lot more fun than it has any right to be as long as you go in with your tongue placed firmly in cheek and aren't flabbergasted by the $152 top-end ticket price. The duo is doing fewer shows each year here to give them room to perform elsewhere, but this is still their home base. Shows are held Tuesday through Saturday at 7:30pm. In the Flamingo, 3555 Las Vegas Blvd. S. ℭ **855/234-7469.** www.flamingolasvegas.com. Tickets $116–$152.

Frankie Moreno ★   Singer and pianist Moreno got his first big break as a kid on the talent show *Star Search*. That he never reached "stardom" levels of fame shouldn't deter you from catching his high-energy show that mostly features original tunes. It's a little bit Elvis and Jerry Lee–era rock and rockabilly plus some Michael Bublé–style cool swing all mixed together in a package that is undeniably entertaining. Bonus points for the staging by *Dancing with the Stars* vet Lacey Schwimmer, who puts both the headliner and the band through their paces with fun choreography and audience interaction. Shows are Wednesday through Saturday at 8pm. At The Stratosphere Hotel & Casino, 2000 Las Vegas Blvd. S. ℭ **800/99-TOWER.** Tickets $40–$50.

Human Nature ★★   If you roll your eyes at the thought of four white Australian guys doing Motown songs, you won't be the first; skepticism is justifiably high. But within minutes of the curtain going up, you'll understand why this group is "presented by" no less than Motown legend Smokey Robinson. Their tight harmonies are delightful throwbacks to the era when the Miracles, the Supremes, the Four Tops, and the Jackson 5 ruled the charts as they take the audience on a blast-from-the-past journey, which includes about two dozen classics like "Get Ready," "Stop in the Name of Love," "Dancing in the Streets," and "Uptight (Everything's Alright)," to name a few, all delivered with an infectious, unflagging energy. Having said that, it is the quieter moments that really stand out, with a cappella versions of "People Get Ready" and "Ooo Baby Baby" showcasing their perfectly blended voices. Shows are Monday through Friday at 7pm. At The Venetian/Palazzo, 3355 Las Vegas Blvd. S. ℭ **866/641-7469** or 702/414-9000. www.venetian.com. Tickets $73–$117.

Jabbawockeez: PRiSM ★★   The shtick here is that each of the crew of hip-hop dancers is totally covered with clothes and serene blank masks, so issues of race, gender, and physical perfection are left at the door. It's interesting and sporadically amusing as they use their bodies to communicate everything from lust to disgust, but the real benefit is that it allows the group to function as a single unit; almost like

BROADWAY & beyond

The opening of the Smith Center for the Performing Arts (p. 141) in 2012 changed the scope of entertainment for Las Vegas in dramatic ways. Despite the numerous showrooms, arenas, and theaters in this town, the closest thing to a performing arts stage was a 40-year-old concert hall in the middle of a shopping mall, adjacent to a casino that occasionally hosted a third-string Broadway touring show.

Now that the Smith Center has arrived, there is a legitimate home for cultural pursuits of all types, including the Las Vegas Philharmonic; in-demand Broadway touring companies like *Book of Mormon* and *Once;* a New York

Stage series with concerts from Broadway luminaries like Patty Lupone and Audra McDonald; a monthly jazz-tinged set from longtime Vegas showman Clint Holmes (which is one of the best shows and best values in town); a speaker series that has hosted legends like Carol Burnett to Alan Alda; and a host of other concerts from classical to contemporary to choral and more. This is all in a multi-venue facility that has become the envy of cities around the globe.

Visit the Smith Center website at www.thesmithcenter.com or call ℂ **702/ 749-2000** for information on shows that will be playing when you are in town.

a multicell organism, only one that pops and locks. The move to their own custom theater at Luxor has brought a more grown-up version of the show, which means you get a little less of the cutting-edge, hard-hitting artistry and a little more crowd-pleasing, "gangham-style" theatrics. While the genius-level stuff they did in their previous show in Vegas is missed, there's still enough stunning dance on display here to recommend the only totally dance-focused show in town. Shows are Sunday, Monday, and Thursday at 7pm and Friday and Saturday at 7 and 9:30pm. In Luxor, 3900 Las Vegas Blvd. S. ℂ **877/386-4658.** www.jbwkz.com. Tickets $60–$90.

Jeff Civillico: Comedy in Action ★★ Family-friendly shows are few and far between in Vegas, especially ones that can be as entertaining for adults as they are for children. This one hits both of those targets with kids wowed by the manic energy juggling of everything from bowling balls to chainsaws, and grown-ups appreciating that it is all presented with Civillico's lightning-quick wit and subtly sardonic patter. Some of the stunts are wow-worthy—he was a world-champion juggler by the time he was 15, after all—and some of his jokes are so sly that it'll take you a moment to fully appreciate how funny they are. Lots of audience participation gives the show a fun, off-the-cuff vibe and will keep it fresh for repeat viewings. With tickets starting at just over $30, this is a great entertainment value even before you add in all the discounts and bonus offers on other show tickets and meals that come with admission. Shows are Saturday through Monday, Wednesday, and Thursday at 4pm. In The Quad, 3535 Las Vegas Blvd. S. ℂ **855/234-7469.** www.thequadlv.com. Tickets $33–$50.

Jersey Boys Vegas ★★ Between 1962 and 1975, Frankie Valli and the Four Seasons racked up an astonishingly long string of catchy, well-crafted pop hits that are as beloved as any in pop music. These time-tested songs are the central draw of the massively popular, Tony Award–winning (for Best Musical) *Jersey Boys*. But this is far more than a rote musical revue, or just another re-creation of a popular oldies act. It's a real musical play, with a compelling street-to-suite storyline, a fair share of drama, and enough humor and uplift to satisfy both the theater veteran and the vacationing family (with a mild warning for some salty, Jersey-esque language). A dazzlingly visual production that crackles with energy and shines with precision stagecraft, *Jersey Boys* has already had an enthusiastic post-Broadway life, including here with its second incarnation in Vegas at Paris Las Vegas after several years of sold-out performances at the Palazzo up the street. Performances are Wednesday through Friday and Sunday at 7pm, Tuesday at 6:30 and 9:30pm, and Saturday at 5 and 8:15pm. In Paris Las Vegas, 3655 Las Vegas Blvd. S. © **702/777-7776.** www.jerseyboysinfo.com/vegas. Tickets $60–$200.

Jubilee! ★   This showgirl classic had become a bit of a relic, with silly 1970s-era variety show songs and choreography, goofy revue acts, and big set pieces involving the legend of Samson and Delilah and the sinking of the Titanic told with pretty girls and the occasional bare breast. In an attempt to reinvent the show for modern audiences, it has gotten a makeover that has turned it into an even sillier, schizophrenic experience that tries to blend new and old but just comes off as weird. Some of the parades of topless beauties and the variety acts have been jettisoned in favor of a truly bizarre "storyline" involving a showgirl named Catherine Jubilee who has to go on a journey through time and space, guided by silver aliens with giant glowing light sticks, to find, well, something. Love, maybe? Edification? Her top? There are some new numbers, mostly involving more modern and edgy choreography that are an undeniable improvement on the walk-and-pose showgirl action of yore, but it is all staged with sparse backdrops and what is attempting to be moody lighting that comes off as gloomy instead and sucks all the energy right out of the proceedings. The new character is randomly inserted into some of the bigger, iconic numbers (Samson and the Titanic are still there) before the whole storyline (and the aliens) mysteriously vanish about two-thirds of the way through and everyone starts dancing to random disco and '80s songs. This was the last showgirl extravaganza in Vegas, and although it was long-in-the-tooth, it had a certain unique Sin City charm. Too bad then that this revamp has effectively killed the genre. Much more entertaining and historically enlightening is the backstage walking tour Monday, Wednesday, and Saturday at 11am (tickets are $20, with $5 off if you buy a ticket to see the show). Shows are held Saturday through Thursday at 7 and 10pm. In Bally's Las Vegas, 3645 Las Vegas Blvd. S. © **855/234-7469.** www. ballyslv.com. Tickets $63–$123. Ages 18 and over.

Legends in Concert ★   After more than 25 years as a nighttime show at hotels like the Imperial Palace and Harrah's, this parade of faux celebrities made the move to afternoons at the Flamingo in 2013. The only real difference is that it is daylight when you walk out of the showroom. Performers vary depending on when you see the show; you may catch "Janet Jackson" and "Diana Ross," or you could get "Dolly Parton" and "Cher," but you will almost always get "Elvis." Unlike other impersonator shows, the singing is live (no lip-syncing, even when "Britney" is performing), which can enhance the illusion or destroy it. Some performers succeed more in appearance and others do better with vocal mimicry, and while most are at least passable, there are a few that will leave you wondering if he or she is the real thing playing a joke on the audience. Don't scoff; Ellen DeGeneres did that very thing during at 2008 show and captured the audience reactions ("didn't look anything like her") for her daytime talkfest. Shows are Saturday through Thursday at 4pm with occasional second shows at 7:30pm or 10pm; check the website for details. In the Flamingo Las Vegas, 3555 Las Vegas Blvd. S. © **855/234-7469.** www.flamingolasvegas.com. Tickets $50–$82.

Le Rêve ★★★   Challenged from the get-go, thanks to a decision to base this Cirque-like show around a stage of water, thus prompting inevitable comparisons with *O* down the street, this production has received major revamps, both in staging and choreography.

JUST FOR laughs

Depressed over all the money you lost in the casino? A surefire way to get cheered up is to check out one of the shows from stand-up comics currently playing in Las Vegas.

Louie Anderson has bounced around from showroom to showroom in Vegas over the last few years, most recently landing at the Plaza, 1 Main St. (© **702/386-2507;** www.plazahotelcasino.com; Wed–Sat 7pm; tickets $60–$110), where he does his laid-back riffs on whatever happens to be amusing him that day.

Or, if you're feeling absurdist, you can try the outrageous, stream-of-consciousness prop comedy of **Carrot Top,** at Luxor Las Vegas, 3900 Las Vegas Blvd. S. (© **800/557-7428;** www.luxor.com; Mon and Wed–Sun 8:30pm; tickets $50–$65).

Also be sure to see who is playing at the comedy clubs in Vegas; a couple of which are listed later in this chapter.

By and large, the choices—particularly to get revered avant-garde choreographer and MOMIX-genius Moses Pendleton to take over the choreography (thus increasing the presence of dance)—have been good ones, and this production is now not only a worthy rival to its competition, but in some ways better. Set in a dramatic theater in the round, the "stage" at the center of the bowl-shaped room can be solid, a shallow pool, or deep enough to dive into from what seem like insane heights, which is proven in a gasp-inducing moment. Certainly the acrobatic, diving, aerial work, and ballroom dance is as good as what you'll see in any Cirque show, but it is the moody atmospherics and visually arresting staging that really set the show apart. The wordless storyline concerns a woman considering love but needing to face her own demons and past as she wanders through a dreamscape of betrayal, passion, fear, and ultimately salvation. Provocative moments include a sultry tango performed in ankle deep water, an aerial ballet involving a giant puppet, and a set piece involving performers descending from the rafters, limp and motionless until they hit the water and then springing to life as they are repeatedly dipped in and dive into the pool. The latter ends with some of them being jerked back up into the smoky ceiling, screaming as they go. It, like much of the rest of the show, is dark and a bit disconcerting at times, but in a good way, remaining with you long after you leave the showroom. A backstage tour package is available that will take you from the deep pools to the towering dive platform, giving a deeper appreciation for the work. Shows are held Friday through Tuesday at 7 and 9:30pm. In Wynn Las Vegas, 3131 Las Vegas Blvd. S. © **888/320-7110.** www.wynnlasvegas.com. Tickets $105–$195. Only ages 13 and over admitted.

Mac King ★★★ One of the best entertainment values in Vegas, this is an afternoon comedy-magic show—and note the order of precedence in that introduction. King does magic, thankfully, emphasizing the only kind that's really mind-blowing these days—those close-up tricks that defy your eyes and mind. But he surrounds his tricks with whimsy and wit, and sometimes gut-busting guffaws, which all serve to make you wonder how someone else can still perform stunts with a straight face. Check out his "cloak of invisibility" (a rain poncho used to great comic effect) or how he takes a $100 bill and—wait, we don't want to give it away, but suffice to say it involves an old shoe, a Fig Newton, and several other unexpected props. Perfect for the kids, perfect for the budget, perfect timing if you need something in the afternoon before an evening of gambling, dining, and cavorting. Simply perfect. Shows are held Tuesday through Saturday at 1 and 3pm. In Harrah's, 3475 Las Vegas Blvd. S. www.mackingshow.com. © **800/427-7247** or 702/369-5222. Tickets $30–$50.

Mamma Mia! ★   Well, thank goodness! Vegas without the premiere ABBA musical just wasn't the same. After playing for more than five years at Mandalay Bay, the hit show took a hiatus, but is back in a new incarnation at the Trop. The recently redone showroom is nice enough, but you don't care about that—you came for the songs from the disco-era super group like "SOS," "Take a Chance on Me," and "Dancing Queen," all of which and more are woven into a fairly silly story about a woman reuniting with three of her long-lost loves on a Greek island. It's a lightweight romp in all of the best and worst ways; completely enjoyable if you're willing to go with it but also completely forgettable the second you leave the theater. Shows are Sunday through Thursday at 7:30pm and Saturday at 5:30 and 9pm. In The Tropicana of Las Vegas, 3801 Las Vegas Blvd. S. www.mackingshow.com. ⓒ **800/829-9034.** Tickets $49–$135.

Million Dollar Quartet ★★   Musical history was made on a chilly night in 1956 in Nashville when Elvis Presley, Johnny Cash, Jerry Lee Lewis, and Carl Perkins wandered into a studio at the famed Sun Records and had an impromptu jam session. This pared-down version of the hit Broadway musical imagines what that night might have been like with rock-'n'-roll classics like "Hound Dog," "Whole Lotta Shakin' Goin' On," and "I Walk the Line" driving the barely there storyline. The actors are excellent stewards of both the sounds and affectations of the legends they are embodying and bring down the house with their top-quality musicianship. Shows are held Sunday, Tuesday, Wednesday, and Friday at 7pm and Monday and Thursday at 5:30 and 8pm. ⓒ **888/746-7784** or 702/369-5111. At Harrah's Las Vegas, 3475 Las Vegas Blvd. S. www.mdqvegas.com. Tickets $63–87.

Olivia Newton-John ★★   From her "I Honestly Love You" beginnings through her "You're the One That I Want" and "Physical" superstardom and beyond, pop singer Olivia Newton-John puts on a terrific show that is more than just a retrospective of her career, it's a soundtrack to a lot of people's lives. She still sounds and looks great and could teach some of today's pop stars a thing or two about showmanship. The show is not performed every week, but when it is, show times are usually Tuesday through Saturday at 7:30pm. In the Flamingo, 3555 Las Vegas Blvd. S. ⓒ **855/234-7469.** www.flamingolasvegas.com. Tickets $69–$159.

Penn & Teller ★★★   The most intelligent show in Vegas, as these two—magicians? illusionists? truth-tellers? BS artists? geniuses?—put on 90 minutes of, yes, magic and juggling, but also acerbic comedy, mean stunts, and quiet beauty. Looking like two characters out of Dr. Seuss, big, loud Penn and smaller, silent Teller (to reduce them to their basic characteristics) perform magic, reveal the secrets behind a few major magic tricks, discuss why magic is nothing but a bunch of lies, and then turn around and show why magic is as lovely an art form as any other. We won't tell you much about the various tricks and acts for fear of ruining punch lines, but watching Teller fish money out of an empty glass aquarium or play with shadows is to belie Penn's earlier caveats about learning how tricks are done—it doesn't ruin the wonder of it, not at all, nor the serenity that settles in your Vegas-sensory-overloaded brain. Hang around the lobby after the show for a free meet-and-greet, something other Vegas headliners charge a hefty fee for. Shows are held Saturday through Wednesday at 9pm. In the Rio All-Suite Hotel & Casino, 3700 W. Flamingo Rd. ⓒ **888/746-7784.** www.riolasvegas.com. Tickets $75–$95. Only ages 5 and over admitted.

Recycled Percussion ★   If, for whatever reason, you are averse to loud noises and you think going to a show with the word "percussion" in the title is a good idea, we are here to counsel you otherwise. This quartet of cacophony-makers will bust out a beat

PENN & TELLER'S TOP 10 THINGS ONE SHOULD NEVER DO IN A VEGAS magic show

Penn & Teller have been exercising their acerbic wit and magical talents in numerous forums together for more than 25 years, and their show at the Rio is one of Vegas's best and most intelligent. We must confess that we couldn't get the quieter half of the duo, Teller, to cough up a few words, but the more verbose Penn Jillette was happy to share.

1. Costume yourself in gray business suits totally lacking in rhinestones, animal patterns, Mylar, capes, bell-bottoms, shoulder pads, and top hats.

2. Wear your hair in any style that could not be described as "feathered" or "spiked."

3. Use really good live jazz music instead of canned sound-alike cheesy rip-off fake pop "music."

4. Cruelly (but truthfully) make fun of your siblings in the magic brotherhood.

5. Do the dangerous tricks on each other instead of anonymous show women with aftermarket breasts and/or endangered species.

6. Toss a cute little magic bunny into a cute little chipper-shredder.

7. Open your show by explaining and demonstrating how other magicians on the Strip do their most amazing tricks, and then do that venerable classic of magic, "the Cups and Balls," with transparent plastic cups.

8. Treat the audience as if they have a brain in their collective head.

9. Allow audience members to sign real bullets, load them into real guns, and fire those bullets into your face.

10. Bleed.

(You will find many of these "don'ts" in the Penn & Teller show at the Rio All-Suite Hotel & Casino.)

on anything they can get their hands on, from real drum sets to improvised ones made from plastic buckets or, in one stunning set-piece, their own bodies. As if that's not enough, they also pass out metal pots and drumsticks to the audience before the show and encourage sonic mayhem throughout. It's a bit loud, is what we're saying. But the four lads are insanely talented, and their cheeky, oddball sense of humor plays well. Be on the lookout for a "totally random cookie break," which lives up to the random part of its name in a delightful way. Shows are held Saturday through Thursday at 7pm. In The Quad, 3535 Las Vegas Blvd. S. ℭ **855/234-7469.** www.thequadlv.com. Tickets $60–$90.

Rock of Ages ★ If you ever wondered what you'd get if you crossed a corny, over-the-top movie musical from the '40s with a heavy metal music video from the '80s, it would look a lot like this silly confection of a jukebox revue. The plot, about the lives and loves of a group of people affiliated with an imperiled Sunset Strip rock club, is kind of stupid (and knows it) and the music, from Journey, Bon Jovi, Pat Benatar, and other hair band icons is often bastardized to the point where it is unrecognizable as the "classic rock" it occasionally is. But there is something undeniably infectious about its throw-everything-at-the-wall energy and gamely talented cast. Plus they have people selling beer, shots, and wine coolers in the aisles before the show, so dude, let's rock! Shows are Sunday and Tuesday through Friday at 8pm and Saturday at 7 and 10pm. At The Venetian/Palazzo, 3355 Las Vegas Blvd. S. ℭ **866/641-7469** or 702/414-9000. www.venetian.com. Tickets $69–$167.

RockTellz & Cocktails ★★ This live stage show invites various performers (Meat Loaf, the Jacksons) on stage to do their hits and tell stories about their lives, careers, and music. Your mileage will vary depending on who is doing the singing and the storytelling, but the acts they have booked so far have both rich histories and more than enough talent to be more than just nostalgia acts. The Jacksons, for instance, danced, sang, and offered remembrances better than men half their age, turning what felt like an audience of grown-up fans into screaming teenagers. Hearing their classic hits and then hearing the stories of their unorthodox childhood was a delight. The production values are high and if they can keep drawing artists like the Jacksons, this is a show you may want to see every time you're in Vegas. Show times and days vary depending on the performer. At Planet Hollywood, 3667 Las Vegas Blvd. S., ✆ **800/745-3000**. www.rocktellz.com. Tickets $65 and up.

Terry Fator ★ *America's Got Talent* winner Fator is no Susan Boyle, that's for sure, but his shtick—ventriloquism meets impersonation—is downright entertaining. The format of the 80-minute show is fairly standard: A series of puppets joins Fator on stage, and they proceed to do a song or three impersonating a famous voice. Winston the Turtle does a serviceable Justin Bieber and a very good Kermit the Frog (which is weird if you think too long about it—turtle, frog, felt), while Walter the Cowboy kills on a Brooks & Dunn song—or rather Fator does, of course. Even the less-than-perfect impressions are still impressive considering the fact that he's doing it all with his mouth closed. Fator's overall demeanor is a little too laconic, especially when he doesn't have a piece of felt on his hand, but the show mostly hits its middle-of-the-road target on the bull's-eye, offering up some decent chuckles and a nice night of music. Try to get a seat in the center section, otherwise you'll spend most of your time watching the giant TV screens instead of the guy (and his friends) on stage. Shows are Monday through Thursday, with select Fridays at 7:30pm. At The Mirage, 3400 Las Vegas Blvd. S. ✆ **800/963-9634** or 702/792-7777. www.mirage.com. Tickets $60–$150.

Tournament of Kings ★ "Lords and Ladies, Wizards and Wenches, hasten thee to thy throne, for the battle is about to commence." Yes, that's how they talk at this dinner show—like a Renaissance fair, only with better production values. There's nothing different here than you'll find at one of those Medieval Times chain restaurants, with a decent dinner and lots of knights-in-shining-armor–style theatrics. It's not *Game of Thrones* (now THAT would be an interesting Vegas show), so it's one of the few family-friendly options in town; younger kids will like it, teenagers will be too jaded, and adults will probably be bored. Shows are Monday and Friday at 6pm and Wednesday, Thursday, Saturday, and Sunday at 6 and 8:30pm. In Excalibur, 3850 Las Vegas Blvd. S. ✆ **800/933-1334** or 702/597-7600. www.excalibur.com. Tickets $45–$59.

V: The Ultimate Variety Show ★ Although not as big budget as the Cirque productions, V can still offer some big thrills if you happen to see it on the right night. It's a collection of variety acts that could include acrobats, magicians, musicians, dancers, and more, but since the acts vary, so does the quality. Check to see if the thrilling roller-skating couple Vittorio and Jenny Aratas are on the roster. They only do 5 minutes of a 70-minute show, but their hold-your-breath stunts performed mere inches from the audience will make whatever you have to watch in the other 65 minutes totally worth it. Shows are nightly at 7 and 8:30pm. In the Miracle Mile Shops at Planet Hollywood Resort, 3667 Las Vegas Blvd. S. ✆ **866/932-1818** or 702/260-7200. www.vtheshow.com. Tickets $70–$90.

Vegas Nocturne ★★★ Created by the same folks who do the outrageous and outrageously entertaining Absinthe, this show follows a similar pattern with a series of variety acts strung together in a loose narrative. Here it's a soiree thrown by the boozy and snobby rich brother and sister Alfonso and Beverly, who act as hosts of a party featuring their family, friends, employees, and others doing everything from

headliner VENUES

Pretty much every singer worth their Twitter followings makes a stop in Vegas on their national tour. While the big acts usually play the big arenas, some go for the more intimate rooms so you may get a chance to see your favorites up close and in person. Major headliner show-rooms in Vegas include the following:

o The Cosmopolitan of Las Vegas, 3708 Las Vegas Blvd. S. (℃ 877/551-7778; www.cosmopolitan lasvegas.com) has two venues, the laid-back, open air **Boulevard Pool** overlooking the Las Vegas Strip, and the new **Chelsea,** which is a surprisingly intimate venue considering the fact that it can accommodate more than 3,000 people. This converted ballroom feels less like that and more like an industrial-chic play space complete with reclaimed wood accents, subway tile, and a cheeky attitude perfect for the hotel in which it is located. Both draw big names including Lorde, Adele, and a recurring stint by Bruno Mars.

o The 4,000-seat **Colosseum** (in Caesars Palace, 3570 Las Vegas Blvd. S. (℃ 866/227-5938; www.

caesarspalace.com) has been home to extended runs for big-name artists like Céline Dion, Elton John, Shania Twain, Rod Stewart, and more, with shorter stands by big-name singing and comedy acts like Janet Jackson and Jerry Seinfeld.

o Hard Rock Hotel's (4455 Paradise Rd.; ℃ 800/693-7625 or 702/693-5000; www.hardrockhotel. com) **The Joint** was rebuilt in 2009 and now holds 4,000 people for rock concerts and special events. The smaller **Vinyl** club is like a rock-'n'-roll haven on the Sunset Strip.

o The **House of Blues** can hold several hundred people for smaller rock and blues concerts and their weekly gospel brunch (in Mandalay Bay, 3950 Las Vegas Blvd. S.; ℃ 877/632-7400 or 702/632-7600; www.hob.com).

o **Brooklyn Bowl** opened in 2014 and has cornered the market on the indy-rock market for Vegas. The concert venue is intimate and relaxed; a perfect place to catch the general-admission shows from artists both edgy

tap dancing to magic to contortionism to Cirque-style acrobatics. It's all deliciously off-kilter, with gleefully inappropriate humor and a wild cast of characters who are impossible not to adore. The show is presented in three different "cantos," or acts, with the early show setting up the premise and transitioning people from the restaurant **Rose.Rabbit.Lie** (p. 96); the late show pushing the boundaries with more adult-themed acts and humor; and the short midnight show setting up the space's transition to the **Rose.Rabbit.Lie** nightclub experience (p. 204). The action is not limited to the main stage; other acts, including totally unique ones or continuations of others, happen in various rooms throughout the venue. For instance, pay attention for the announcement of a funeral for a fish happening in the nearby cloakroom and then run so you can be one of the handful who get to witness it. Do yourself a favor and experience it all, but if you want to see just one of the shows, the 9:30pm is probably the one to go for as long as you aren't easily offended. Shows are Thursday through Sunday at 7:30pm, 9:30pm, and midnight (each show is different). At The Cosmopolitan of Las Vegas, 3708 Las Vegas Blvd. S. ℃ 877/667-0585. www.roserabbitlie.com. Tickets $30–$135.

(Jane's Addiction, Fishbone, etc.) and safe (hey, where have you been, Steve Winwood?) (at the LINQ, 3545 Las Vegas Blvd. S., Suite 22; ☎ 702/862-2695; www.brooklynbowl.com).

o **Mandalay Bay Events Center** seats 12,000 people for arena-style concert tours and indoor sporting events (in Mandalay Bay, 3950 Las Vegas Blvd. S.; ☎ 877/632-7400 or 702/632-7580; www.mandalaybay.com).

o **MGM Grand Garden Events Arena** can hold over 17,000 people and is home to big-name concert tours and events (in the MGM Grand, 3799 Las Vegas Blvd. S.; ☎ 800/929-1111 or 702/891-7777; www.mgmgrand.com).

o **The Orleans Showroom** seats 9,500 people and often has concerts, ice hockey, traveling circuses, and other events (in the Orleans, 4500 W. Tropicana Ave.; ☎ 800/675-3267; www.orleans casino.com).

o **The Pearl Theater** is a three-level venue that seats up to 2,500 people for pop, rock, R&B,

and comedy concerts (in the Palms, 4321 W. Flamingo Rd.; ☎ 866/942-7770; www.palms.com).

o **Sam Boyd Stadium** is a 36,800-seat stadium that features big concerts and sporting events (7000 E. Russell Rd.; ☎ 800/745-3000; www.ticketmaster.com).

o **The Smith Center for the Performing Arts** has a 2,000 seat concert hall for big stage shows (including a Broadways series), a 300-seat Cabaret Jazz theater, and a 200-seat theater for smaller productions. See p. 141 for more details (361 Symphony Park Ave.; ☎ 702/614-0109; www.thesmithcenter.com).

o **The Thomas and Mack Center** is a 19,522-seat arena that hosts concerts and sporting events (UNLV Campus; ☎ 800/745-3000; www.ticketmaster.com).

o **The Fremont Country Club** is Downtown Las Vegas' only real concert venue, hosting rock shows and other special events. (601 E. Fremont St.; ☎ 702/382-6601; www.fremontcountryclub vegas.com).

Vegas! The Show ★★★   What would happen if you took the best bits of classic Las Vegas entertainment from the last 70 years or so and put it in one package? That's the basic question behind this loving look back at the ghosts of the Sin City stages, and the answer is this: It would be a heck of a lot of fun. A version of the Neon Boneyard provides the gateway to the days of Vegas gone by, with beautiful showgirls in skimpy costumes and big headdresses; headliners like the Rat Pack and Elvis; variety acts (tap dancing! magic!); dancing; singing; even Elton John and implosions. The show plays like a history channel special done by Busby Berkeley as the talented troupe leads the audience from the tuxedo and showgirl 1940s, the rock and roll '50s, the Frank and Dino '60s, the disco '70s, and beyond with performances that are more homages than impersonations. The singing and dancing are among the best you'll find in Vegas, which may very well make you long for the days before those French acrobats took over the showrooms. Shows are nightly at 7 and 9pm. In the Miracle Mile Shops at Planet Hollywood Resort, 3667 Las Vegas Blvd. S. ☎ 866/932-1818 or 702/260-7200. www.vegastheshow.com. Tickets $80–$100.

THE BAR SCENE

In addition to the venues listed below, you might check out the incredible nighttime view at the bars and lounges atop the **Stratosphere Casino Hotel & Tower** (p. 58) or midway up on the **Eiffel Tower Ride** (p. 135)—nothing beats them, except for maybe the more up-close view of the bar adjacent to the 23rd-floor lobby at the **Mandarin Oriental** (p. 41). The floor-to-ceiling windows make you feel like you're floating in the middle of the Strip, especially at night.

Bars & Cocktail Lounges

Atomic Liquors ★   Las Vegas history is on glorious display in this reinvention of a classic watering hole. The building dates back to 1945 and is the oldest freestanding bar in the city. It got its name in 1952 when people used to go up on the roof to watch the aboveground nuclear blasts from the Atomic Test Site north of Las Vegas and became a go-to spot for everyone from the Rat Pack to Barbra Streisand, who has her own memorial stool at the bar. Now fully restored after years of decline, there's a classic neon sign out front and a big bar and plenty of comfy seating inside, plus nearly two dozen microbrews, a craft cocktail menu (featuring some classic "Atomic" concoctions), and a variety of events to keep things interesting. As of this writing, there are about three blocks of nothing between it and the main action of the Fremont East Entertainment District (with El Cortez casino and bars like the Commonwealth), but it's a well-lit, dramatically nicer neighborhood than it used to be. For a bar as cool as this one, it's worth taking the stroll. Atomic Liquors is open Monday through Wednesday from 4pm until midnight; Thursday and Friday from 4pm until 4am; Saturday from 11am until 4am; and Sunday from 11am until midnight. 917 Fremont St. (at 9th St.) ✆ **702/349-2283.** www.atomiclasvegas.com. No cover except for special events.

Backstage Bar & Billiards ★   Originally conceived as a literal backstage area for the adjacent Fremont Country Club performance venue, this rock-'n'-roll bar stands on its own as a worthy destination for the tattooed and pierced set (and those who appreciate them). The bar and furnishings are made out of the cases in which roadies transport band equipment, and there is rock memorabilia, pool tables, a DJ and/or live music acts, and a big private VIP room. The atmosphere is a lot less polished than some of the other verging-on-trendy East Fremont bars, but that's part of its appeal. It's open nightly from 7pm until late. 601 E. Fremont St. (at 6th St.) ✆ **702/382-2227.** www.backstagebarandbilliards.com. No cover except for special events.

Beauty Bar ★   Popular with the young hipster set in Los Angeles and New York, the Vegas outpost of this bar done as a retro beauty salon draws a more diverse crowd, owing to its location near the businesses and tourists of Downtown Las Vegas. Although competition from other bars on Fremont Street has diminished its star a bit, it's still a hit with the cool-kids set. It's open nightly from 9pm until 2am. 517 E. Fremont St. ✆ **702/598-1965.** www.thebeautybar.com. No cover except for special events.

The Commonwealth ★★   Key to the revitalization of the Fremont East District are bars like this, a speakeasy-themed space that manages to appeal to a variety of different crowds without losing its sense of purpose. Early evenings and weeknights, it's a haven for the local post-business hours set and tourists from nearby Glitter Gulch. Late nights, especially on weekends, it becomes party central, with hordes of mostly younger locals drinking hard and grooving to the house beats. The space encourages interaction, with one big room downstairs done in prohibition-era industrial chic and a gorgeous outdoor patio upstairs. There's even a "hidden" room called the Laundry that

Las Vegas Nightlife

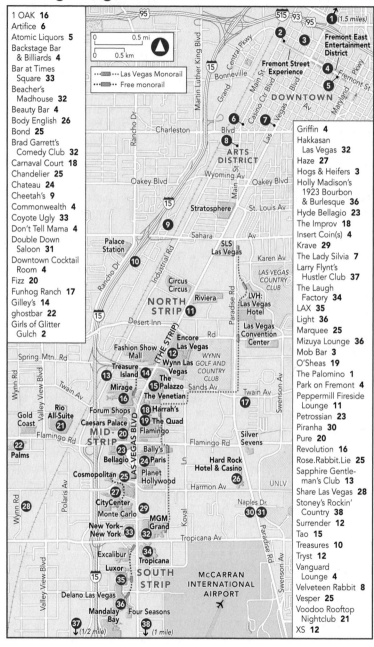

is only available to those in the know with advance reservations. Open Wednesday through Friday from 6pm until 2am and Saturday and Sunday from 8pm until 2am. 525 E. Fremont St. (at 6th St.) © **702/798-7000.** www.commonwealthlv.com. No cover except for special events.

Double Down Saloon ★★ "House rule: You puke, you clean." It seems a lot more intimidating than it really is, although there isn't a lot of pretense here so leave notions of entitlement back at the fancy cocktail lounges on the Strip. Popular with locals and adventurous tourists alike, the place features trippy hallucinogenic graffiti on the walls, the ceiling, and the tables, while decor includes thrift-store battered armchairs and sofas, a couple of pool tables, and a jukebox that holds everything from the Germs to Link Wray, Dick Dale, and Reverend Horton Heat. Oddly, the Double Down swears it invented the bacon martini here. Live bands perform on many nights (from punk to alt to blues). There's no cover unless an out-of-town band is playing that actually has a label. The Double Down is open daily 24 hours. 4640 Paradise Rd. (at Naples Dr.). © **702/791-5775.** www.doubledownsaloon.com. No cover except for special events.

Fizz ★★★ Created by filmmaker David Furnish, this delightfully grown-up champagne bar is located next to the theater where his husband, Elton John, performs regularly. The intimate space is decorated with photos from their personal collection, which go great with the vaguely retro decor meant to evoke the Caesars Palace of the '60s. Champagne and sparkling wines are the stars, with all tastes and price points represented and an expert staff to guide even those with no knowledge of bubbly. Champagne cocktails with exotic ingredients (hibiscus flower liqueur, for instance) and intricate construction are as close to perfect as you can get, and a big wine list, full bar, and small menu of tastes and bites created by Sir Elton's personal chef round out a fantastic package. See if you can sneak a peek into the singer's private VIP suite overlooking the club. The bar is open Sunday through Thursday from 5pm until 2am and Friday and Saturday from noon until 4am. At Caesars Palace, 3570 Las Vegas Blvd. S., © **702/776-3200.** www.fizzlv.com. No cover.

Griffin ★★ Part of the delightful revitalization of the Fremont East District (just a couple of blocks from the Fremont Street Experience), the fun starts with the old stone facade and eponymous sign and continues inside with the stone pillars, arched cave ceiling, and two fire pits. Just what you want in a stylish bar that revels in its history, but at the same time doesn't try too hard. Given its proximity to other top-notch downtown hangouts such as Downtown Cocktail Lounge, this is a must-stop on the anti–Strip and hotel bar tour. There are DJs on the weekends and it often draws a late-night crowd of entertainers from the Strip after their shows are done. It's open Monday through Wednesday from 5pm until 4am; Thursday and Friday from 5pm until 6am; Saturday from 7pm until 6am; and Sunday from 8pm until 4am. 511 E. Fremont St. © **702/382-0577.** www.facebook.com/griffin. No cover except for special events.

Hogs & Heifers Saloon ★ While there is a chain of Coyote Ugly nightclubs (including one here in Vegas), the movie of the same name was based on the hijinks that happened at the New York version of this rowdy roadhouse saloon. In Sin City since 2005, the hogs here are of the motorcycle variety, and the place definitely draws a crowd that can look intimidating but is usually a friendly (and boisterous) bunch. Saucy bar maidens and outdoor barbecues on select weekends make this a fun spot for a beer. The new Downtown Grand hotel across the street could change the atmosphere a little, but probably not enough to worry about. It's open daily, usually 1pm to 6am (call to check, as hours vary by month). 201 N. 3rd St. (btw. Ogden and Stewart aves., 1 block from the Fremont Street Experience). © **702/676-1457.** www.hogsandheifers.com. No cover.

Insert Coin(s) ★★★   The pinnacle of Fremont East entertainment district has to be this wildly original bar and nightclub that features dozens of restored classic video games right alongside the drinking and dancing. Grab a moderately priced beer and start chewing your way through *Ms. Pac Man*, or sidle up to the main bar, where you can play Nintendo and X-Box games (among others) on the giant overhead monitors. Or you can even get a semiprivate booth with bottle service and your own gaming station. The crowd skews toward the young, but gamers of all ages will feel at home here. Check the website for their frequent video game tournaments on titles like *Street Fighter* and *Call of Duty*. It's open Wednesday through Sunday from 8pm until late. Hours vary seasonally. 512 E. Fremont St. ✆ **702/477-2525.** www.insertcoinslv.com. No cover.

The Lady Silvia ★★   The speakeasy concept has been gaining traction lately, and this fantastic little craft cocktail bar embraces it to an almost detrimental degree. Finding the place is not easy, but making the effort is worth it. The unmarked door to the bar, located on the ground floor of a residential apartment building, faces the side street Hoover Avenue. A short hallway leads to another unmarked door, and behind that is the cute English library–themed space, done with cozy mismatched furnishings, bookshelves, thrift-shop chandeliers, and a checkerboard tile floor. The libations focus on the mixology end of the cocktail scale, but even the fanciest of drinks are affordably priced. Check the events schedule for their frequent art shows and guest DJs. Open daily from 4am until late. 900 Las Vegas Blvd. S. (at Hoover Ave.) ✆ **702/405-0816.** www. theladysilvia.com. No cover except for special events.

Mob Bar ★   Formerly located in a tiny slip of a joint, this prohibition speakeasy–themed place moved to a premiere location directly across the street from the Mob Museum in Downtown Las Vegas. The new space is bigger, fancier, and brighter thanks to large windows and a lighter design scheme, but still manages to retain its charm. The specialty cocktails have 1930s-era style and names, including a favorite with vermouth, rum, strawberry, lemon, and sparkling wine called the Volstead Act (which, for the history challenged, is the name of the law that created prohibition). A small menu of Italian bites and nibbles, including a signature spaghetti and meatball appetizer, will help soak up the booze, and frequent entertainment (including dueling pianos) keeps things lively. The bar is open Sunday through Thursday from 4pm until midnight and Friday and Saturday from 4pm until 2am. In the Downtown Grand, 206 N. 3rd St. (at Ogden Ave.), ✆ **702/719-5100.** www.mobbarlv.com. No cover.

O'Sheas ★   The original O'Sheas was a small casino with several raucous bars located between the Flamingo and what was known then as Imperial Palace (now the Quad), most famous for its cheap drinks, cheap gambling, and "mayor" Mr. Lucky (a little person wearing a leprechaun costume). It was removed to make way for the LINQ pedestrian mall, but has been reinvented as miniature version of itself inside the Quad. There are a couple of bars, several gaming tables, beer pong, and Mr. Lucky is back, but something has been lost in the translation. This may be a good thing for many people since the new place is miles better in terms of atmosphere and general sheen, but those looking for the wild, anything-goes party-bar atmosphere of the past are likely to be somewhat disappointed. Although still affordable, especially compared to other bars on the Strip, it's not quite the bargain-basement deal it used to be, either. The bar is open 24 hours a day. In The Quad, 3535 Las Vegas Blvd. S., ✆ **702/697-2711.** www. thequadlv.com. No cover.

Park on Fremont ★   Every one of the bars that has opened along the Fremont East Entertainment District has its own personality. There's the craft cocktail bliss of

Vanguard Lounge, the laid-back coziness of the Griffin, the speakeasy party vibe of the Commonwealth, and now this new-as-of-2013 establishment that is like a Vegas version of a beer garden. Outdoor patios in both the front and rear offer some great people-watching opportunities, and an extensive beer list could turn you into one of those people worth watching. A small menu of pub-grub food is interesting, but more as an afterthought than as a main intent. A good mix of ages and types provides an all-are-welcome atmosphere. Open Tuesday through Sunday from 11am until 3am. 506 Fremont St. (at Las Vegas Blvd.). ✆ **702/834-3160.** www.parkonfremont.com. No cover.

Peppermill Fireside Lounge ★   Walk through the classic Peppermill coffee shop (not a bad place to eat, by the way) on the Strip, and you land in this fabulously dated bar. It has low, circular banquette seats, fake floral foliage, a whole bunch of pink neon, and electric candles. But best of all is the water and fire pit as the room's centerpiece—a piece of kitsch thought to be long vanished from Earth and attracting nostalgia buffs like moths to a flame. It's a time-capsule straight out of the '80s—you'd almost expect Crockett and/or Tubbs to walk in with their pastel jacket sleeves rolled up. The enormous, froufrou tropical drinks (including the signature bathtub-size margaritas) will ensure that you sink into a comfortable stupor. The Peppermill is open daily 24 hours. 2985 Las Vegas Blvd. S. ✆ **702/735-4177.** www.peppermilllasvegas.com. No cover.

Vanguard Lounge ★★   The space itself is not much to look at—a small, narrow room of polished concrete, a long bar, and a couple of couches—but one that allows the cocktails to create all the noise and fury necessary to keep you entertained. A staff of professional mixologists create avant-garde concoctions using a lot of house-made, seasonal ingredients (jams, bitters, and the like) that are bursting with flavor and freshness. That they are better than, and half the price of, drinks like this on the Strip is a miracle. Come early to get a coveted seat on the small street-side patio. Vanguard is open Monday through Friday from 4pm until 2am and Saturday from 6pm until 2am. 516 E. Fremont St. ✆ **702/868-7800.** www.vanguardlv.com. No cover.

Velveteen Rabbit ★★   The Arts District of Las Vegas has been "on the verge" for years, always seemingly close to being a full-fledged destination but not quite getting there. Bars like this one are helping to establish the neighborhood's bona fides, with a casual, funky vibe not unlike the bars found in the booming Fremont East Entertainment District. It has a decidedly hipster aesthetic: kind of bohemian arts scene with fun touches like mannequin hands for beer taps. The latter is a specialty, with a wide variety of brews both on tap and in bottles, plus hand-crafted cocktails that are well made and almost shockingly cheap when you compare them to what you'll pay on the Strip. Live music, art shows, DJs playing things like classic soul, and a mostly local, mostly young crowd solidifies this as a "cool" place to hang. It's open daily from 5pm until 2am. 1218 Main St. (near Colorado Ave.). ✆ **702/685-9645.** www.facebook.com/velveteenrabbitlv. No cover.

Hotel Bars

Bond ★★   In any other building this would probably just be another hotel bar, but because it's at the boldly visual Cosmopolitan, they had to amp it up a few thousand notches. The relatively small space is covered with LED and LCD screens that broadcast eye-popping visuals alongside the window boxes looking out toward the Strip, where you'll find everything from street performers to artists. Get your groove on, have a drink, and enjoy the spectacle. Wednesday is their gay-friendly night "Confidential." Bond is open daily from 3pm until 4am. In The Cosmopolitan of Las Vegas, 3708 Las Vegas Blvd. S. ✆ **702/698-7979.** www.cosmopolitanlasvegas.com. Cover varies.

The Chandelier ★★★　One of the most dramatic elements of the very dramatic Cosmopolitan of Las Vegas hotel is the massive, three-stories-tall chandelier, but it is not just for decoration. Inside are three separate bars, including a casual casino lounge on the main floor, a mixology-focused space on the second level serving high-end cocktails, and an ultralounge space on the top floor that acts as an adjunct of sorts to the nearby Marquee nightclub. It's all sleek and modern and cool looking, yet somehow manages to be a lot less intimidating than most of the other nightlife spaces in the hotel. Finding a seat isn't always easy, especially in the evenings. The Chandelier is open 24 hours. In The Cosmopolitan of Las Vegas, 3708 Las Vegas Blvd. S. ✆ **702/698-7979.** www.cosmopolitanlasvegas.com. No cover.

Petrossian ★★★　Those despairing of a grown-up place to drink, a place for people who want a real cocktail made by people who know that martinis really do require vermouth (none of this "just wave the bottle in the general direction of the glass" nonsense and that "shaken not stirred" is a silly debate), rejoice and come here. Located just off the Bellagio lobby, this is one of the prettiest places to imbibe in the city as the glorious Dale Chihuly glass flowers "bloom" near your head. The bartenders are required to attend ongoing cocktail education, so they really know their stuff. Said stuff is made with the finest ingredients, which means none of the drinks come cheap. But the extra is worth it if you want it done right. They also have a good selection of high-end snacks and a delightful afternoon tea service. It's open daily 24 hours. In Bellagio, 3600 Las Vegas Blvd. S. ✆ **702/693-7111.** www.bellagio.com. No cover.

Vesper ★★　Yes, another bar at the Cosmo, but only because they do bars so well. This one, located just off the lobby, is a retro throwback that focuses on classic craft cocktails and a casual (and sometimes very loud) atmosphere. Go for modern interpretations of legendary drinks like a Manhattan, a gin fizz, or a daiquiri, or try one of their custom concoctions, made with fresh ingredients and an attention to detail that is noticeable in both taste and presentation. Vesper is open daily 24 hours. In The Cosmopolitan of Las Vegas, 3708 Las Vegas Blvd. S. ✆ **702/698-7000.** www.cosmopolitanlasvegas.com. No cover.

Piano Bars

The Bar at Times Square ★　If you're looking for a quiet piano bar, this is not the place for you. Two pianos are going strong every night, and the cigar-smoking crowd overflows out the doors. It always seems to be packed with a singing, swaying throng full of camaraderie and good cheer—or at least, full of booze. Hugely fun, provided you can get a foot in the door. The bar is open daily from 11am until 2:30am and shows are daily from 8pm to 2am, although you may want to skip the music and check out their happy-hour deals weekdays from 3pm to 7pm. In New York–New York, 3790 Las Vegas Blvd. S. ✆ **702/740-6969.** www.newyorknewyork.com. Cover $10 after 7pm.

Don't Tell Mama ★　The famed original Mama in NYC is a favorite of singers from Broadway to karaoke and everything in between. While the Vegas version may not have the same celebrities-might-show-up-to-sing energy that the Gotham version does, it's still a fun place to either listen to some good singers or belt out a tune or two yourself. The crowd is very hit-and-miss—packed with boisterous partiers one night and pretty much you and the staff on others—but there is no better place in town in which to live out your cabaret dreams. It's also a good change of pace on your bar-hopping tour of the Fremont East District when you need a break from the dance floor–style tunes played everywhere else. Hours are Tuesday through Sunday from 8pm until late. 517 E. Fremont St. ⓒ **702/207-0788.** www.donttellmama.com. No cover; one drink minimum.

THE CLUB & MUSIC SCENE

Most of the clubs in town have DJs, often famous ones, and on those rare occasions when you do have live entertainment, it's usually a pop or cover band. If you prefer alternative or real rock music, your choices used to be limited, but that's all changed. Most touring rock bands make at least one stop in the city. But otherwise, the alternative club scene in town is no great shakes. If you want to know what's playing during your stay, consult the local free alternative papers: the *Las Vegas Weekly* (with great club and bar descriptions in its listings; www.lasvegasweekly. com), and *City Life* (weekly, with no descriptions, but comprehensive listings of what's playing where all over town; www.lasvegascitylife.com). Both can be picked up at restaurants, bars, record and music stores, and hip retail stores. If you're looking for good alt-culture tips, try asking the cool staff at **Zia Records** (ⓒ **702/735-4942**); not only does it have bins dedicated to local artists, but local acts also play live in stores on the weekend.

Dance Clubs

In many ways, especially monetarily, the nightclub scene in Vegas has eclipsed famous party spots like Ibiza, New York, and Los Angeles. Almost every hotel has at least one club and almost all of them are packed whenever their doors are open.

Many of the following have insanely high cover charges ($30 and up), outrageously priced drinks ($10 for a domestic beer), and seating that is reserved for patrons willing to pay hundreds or even thousands of dollars to get bottle service. For the uninitiated it sounds crazy, and is, but the hordes of people willing to pay those kinds of costs seem to be having a good time, so maybe they know something we don't.

One bright note: Women are usually charged less for admission than men (sometimes even allowed in free), and any guest can get a comped ticket to even the hottest clubs, if you play it right. If you are gambling for any length of time, ask the pit boss for comps.

1 OAK ★ This Big Apple transplant is a favorite for celebrities and the impossibly hip alike. Fergie, Pitbull, and Katy Perry are among the big names who have made appearances, and the VIP booths are often filled with other famous folk drawn to the multiroom club. It's a cool space, with two beat-pounding dance floors, lots of dramatic black-and-white visuals, a dark and moody vibe, and an undeniable energy. All of this is great fun *if* you can get inside. It's a snap if you're rich, famous, or connected, but everyone else will be stuck with the uncontrolled hordes that are often clamoring for access outside the velvet ropes. BTW and FYI, 1 OAK = One of a Kind. It's open Tuesday and Thursday through Saturday from 10:30pm until dawn. In The Mirage, 3400 Las Vegas Blvd. S. ⓒ **702/588-5656.** www.1oaklasvegas.com. Cover $30 and up.

Artifice ★ The focus here is on the "art" part of the club's name, with a funky mix of a gallery space, a casual craft-cocktail bar, and a dance floor. Located in the Arts District, not too far from the Stratosphere Hotel, it's got a distinctly BoHo vibe and is mostly favored by locals, but the all-types-are-welcome spirit is refreshing. Grab a cocktail, check out the art on the wall, and maybe get your groove on to the DJ-spun tunes that will most likely veer more toward Bowie than Guetta. Check their website for the frequent special events and shows. Open daily from 4pm until 1:30am. 1025 First

St. #3 (at Charleston Blvd.). ℂ **702/489-6339.** www.artificebar.com. No cover except for special events.

Beacher's Madhouse ★★   Part high-energy nightclub, part swank ultralounge, and part carnival freak show, this party spot takes the prize for most unique concept and most outrageous atmosphere. Celebrity impersonators wander around for no good reason other than background; dancers in Elmo and Barney costumes bump and grind on platforms next to the go-go girls; little people are sent "flying" across the room to deliver bottle service to VIP booths; and periodically the DJ takes a break and random sideshow acts take the small stage. Depending on the night, you might see midget wrestling, contortionists, transvestite strippers, and other oddities designed to appeal to the same people to whom Miley Cyrus makes sense. It's weird, but provides lots of guilty pleasure entertainment and is certainly different. The crowd is young and party-ready, but noticeably more laid back than you'll find at most clubs, so that's a bonus. It's open Wednesday, Friday, and Saturday from 10pm until the party is over, which is often around dawn. At the MGM Grand, 3799 Las Vegas Blvd. S. ℂ **702/891-3577.** www.beachers madhouse.com. Cover $75 and up.

Body English ★★★   In some ways, the first incarnation of Body English helped draft the blueprint from which many of the clubs that followed it were created. Dark and moody (it's in a basement, after all) and infectiously high-energy, the club was one of the most popular in Vegas until it was shuttered in 2010 in favor of its upstairs sister Vanity. The club's 2013 reopening is a triumph, with all of the things that made it popular in the first place (a smaller, more intimate space; gothic decor; a slamming multilevel dance floor) upgraded to include the latest light and sound systems. While most clubs are going big, bigger, and biggest, Body English feels more manageable and less intimidating without losing any of the fun that a nightclub experience is meant to have. Body English is open Thursday through Saturday from 10pm until dawn. In the Hard Rock Hotel, 4455 Paradise Rd. ℂ **702/693-5555.** www.bodyenglish.com. Cover varies, usually $20 and up.

Chateau ★   This hot-spot entry from Paris Las Vegas holds a unique position—literally. It's the only major nightclub in town that offers direct access to the Strip; you don't have to walk through the casino to get there. That's kind of cool, but really it's the high-energy, high-gloss, high-price digs that you care about, and Chateau has them in spades. It's a long, narrow room, but the high ceiling provides some much-needed vertical relief, especially with the throngs packed in so tightly on the horizontal. If you need air, head outside to the beer garden overlooking the Strip and the Bellagio Fountains. Need more options? Try the 22,000-square-foot gardens at the base of the Eiffel Tower, with its own bars, cabanas, and dance floor. Crowds are young and a bit on the aggressive side in both demeanor and dress, but that's par for the course at most Vegas nightclubs. Chateau is open Wednesday, Friday, and Saturday from 10:30pm until dawn. In Paris Las Vegas, 3655 Las Vegas Blvd. S. ℂ **702/776-7770.** www.chateaunights.com. Cover varies, usually $20 and up.

Coyote Ugly ★   You've seen the movie, now go have some of that prepackaged fun for yourself. Oh, come on—you don't think those bartender girls really dance on the bar and hose down the crowd just because they are so full of spontaneous rowdy high spirits, now do you? Not when the original locale built a reputation (and inspired a bad movie) on just such behavior, creating a success strong enough to start an entire chain of such frat-boy fun places? By the way, sarcastic and cynical as we are, can we say it's a totally fun place? Rumors of its demise were greatly exaggerated—despite

crowd CONTROL

Huge lines outside are a point of pride for Vegas clubs. So if you're into dancing, you may spend a good chunk of the night single-file, double-file, or in an enormous, unwieldy cluster out in front of a club—particularly on Friday or Saturday. We're not kidding: Lines can be hours long (see below), and once you get to the front, you'll find that there's no actual order. You're at the mercy of a power-wielding, eye-contact-avoiding "executive doorman"—bouncer—who gives attractive women priority. To minimize your time in line, try the following strategies:

Arrive before 11pm. You'll have a harder time getting in if you show up between 12:30 and 1am, the busiest period at clubs.

Group yourself smartly. The larger the group, the longer the wait—especially a large group of mostly (or all) guys. Split up if you have to, but always keep some women with each part of your group (it's much harder for unaccompanied men to get into the clubs).

If you're trying to tip your way in, don't make it obvious. It's a negotiation. Don't wave cash above your head (the IRS has recently been clamping down on unreported tip income, so that tactic will make you very unpopular). Discreetly and respectfully hand the doorman $20 and ask if he can take care of you.

Don't buy a VIP Pass. Can you say "scam"? Many passes require you get there before midnight (a time when there'd normally be no line), and with others you're paying big bucks just to have someone make the call ahead that you could have made yourself. Again: Don't fall for this scam.

Do check the websites. Many clubs will offer front-of-line passes, cover discounts, and drink specials via text alerts and/or if you check-in via a social networking site like Facebook or Twitter. Details change often, so check the club's website for the latest offer.

Dress to impress. For women: Antediluvian but true—showing more cleavage is a line-skipping tactic. If that's not an option, stick with a little black dress or nice jeans and a sexy or club-wear–style top. For men: Look good. Avoid baggy jeans, shorts, tennis shoes, or work boots. Nice jeans or pants and a collared shirt work well.

Look confident. While cockiness never helps, assertiveness never hurts.

word that it was going to close, it's still open daily from 6pm until "late." In New York–New York, 3790 Las Vegas Blvd. S. (at Tropicana Ave.). ✆ **702/740-6969.** www.coyoteuglysaloon.com. Cover varies, usually $10 and up after 9pm.

Hakkasan Las Vegas ★★ The biggest nightclub in the world has landed with a bang in Las Vegas and it changes everything and nothing at the same time. An outgrowth of a boutique Asian restaurant chain with branches around the world, Hakkasan is a five-level facility with dining on the first two floors, a casual ultralounge space on the third, and a massive two-level dance club on the top that is so big it's almost hard to see the ends of it. Superstar DJs like Calvin Harris and Tiesto have had regular gigs here, and people are turning out en masse to see them—long lines and wall-to-wall people (despite those walls being really far from each other) are regular occurrences even with the sky-high cover and drink prices. The crowd is young and aggressive, so be sure to dress to impress and be ready to scream "wooooo" a lot. Open Thursday through Sunday from 10pm until dawn. In the MGM Grand, 3799 Las Vegas Blvd. S. ✆ **702/212-8804.** www.hakkasanlv.com. Cover varies, usually $40 and up.

Haze ★ From the same people who brought you Light at Mandalay Bay comes this place that has all the ingredients that seem to make Las Vegas nightclubs popular these days. It's crowded, dark, insanely expensive, loud, attitudinal, at times downright obnoxious, and yet somehow it all works. If you manage to make it past the crazy long lines, the dimly lit interior of the club features multiple levels, several bars, a big dance floor, lots of VIP bottle-service booths and tables, and a killer light-and-sound system, plus strange little exhibition rooms where costumed models pose in various states of repose. Are those wood nymphs? Okay. It's like a fever dream with a bass beat. Haze! Got it. *Jersey Shore* fans should note that DJ Pauly D is frequently behind the turntable here. It's open Thursday through Saturday from 10:30pm until 4am. In Aria Las Vegas, 3730 Las Vegas Blvd. S. ✆ **702/693-8300.** www.hazelv.com. Cover varies, usually $30 and up.

LAX ★ This is the second club to try this space, replacing the groundbreaking RA nightclub a few years ago. It was the top dog in town for about a minute, but then other bigger, and quite frankly better, clubs came along and stole the title away. Dimly lit to the point of needing a flashlight at times, the decor (when you can see it) is swank supper club gone mad; deep-red padded vinyl walls, richly textured curtains in red and purple, and plenty of high-gloss black marble lend an air of sophistication. Too bad the crowds aren't as high-class. LAX is open Wednesday through Saturday 10pm until dawn. In Luxor Las Vegas, 3900 Las Vegas Blvd. S. ✆ **702/242-4529.** www.laxthenightclub.com. Cover varies, usually $30 and up.

Light ★★★ Further expanding their dominance over Las Vegas, Cirque du Soleil moves into the nightlife realm with this dreamscape of a nightclub. It successfully integrates the best aspects of a high-energy club experience—a big dance floor, a cutting-edge light-and-sound system, big-name DJs like Skrillex and Zedd, lots of party people—with the kind of moody atmospherics and eye-popping visuals that Cirque is famous for. A three-story video wall displays ambient backgrounds that occasionally cue special effects (a model smokes and dry ice fog floods the room) and Cirque acrobats, dancers, and performance artists periodically pop up around (and above) the space. The overall effect is more sophisticated than your average club-going experience, a welcome change of pace from the almost nihilistic "the party is all that matters" vibe you'll find elsewhere. Open Wednesday from 10:30pm until 4am and Friday and Saturday from 10pm until 4am. In Mandalay Bay, 3950 Las Vegas Blvd. S. ✆ **702/632-7777.** www.thelightvegas.com. Cover varies, usually $30 and up.

Marquee ★★★ Speaking of "the party is all that matters," this is the place where they should have that written on the walls. Even though other big clubs have come after it, Marquee still reigns as one of *the* places to see and be seen. The multilevel space is a stunner, with no fewer than four separate clubs. Marquee is the main space with a huge dance floor, lots of table-service booths (some tucked into more private spaces), multiple bars, and a high-energy vibe. It also has a giant outdoor space with a pool, cabanas, another bar, and gaming tables if you prefer to party alfresco. Boombox is more of an ultralounge space with a DJ spinning different music (hip-hop, for example, if the main club is dance). Most appealing, at least to our sensibilities, is the Library, a cozy den of a space with a fireplace, pool table, and actual books on shelves (although the chances of anyone spending a lot of time reading here are minimal). Prices are high and lines are long, but would you expect anything different? Marquee is open Monday, Friday, and Saturday from 10pm until 5am. The pool club is open seasonally on weekend afternoons. In The Cosmopolitan of Las Vegas, 3708 Las Vegas Blvd. S. ✆ **702/333-9000.** www.marqueelasvegas.com. Cover varies, usually $30 and up.

ENTERTAINMENT & NIGHTLIFE

The Club & Music Scene

Rose.Rabbit.Lie ★★★   You really should experience this as a full package, from dinner through the show *Vegas Nocturne* (p. 191) to the part where the whole facility transforms before your eyes into a high-energy nightclub, but if you'd prefer to just show up for that—or to sit at the bar and enjoy the spectacle happening around you during the evening—you are welcome in any case. Get there by midnight to catch the final "canto" (act) of Vegas Nocturne, which includes jaw-dropping variety acts and over-the-top humor that ramps up the energy, so that by the time the DJ takes over, you're ready to party. Multiple bars include a quieter library and a chill lounge space; but the main club, with a dance floor where the show's stage is, is the primary party spot. Be sure to take some time to explore the specially crafted cocktail list, which features a level of mixology science almost unheard of in the Vegas nightclub world. The bars open at 5:30pm Thursday through Sunday and the nightclub portion gets going after the midnight canto. In The Cosmopolitan of Las Vegas, 3708 Las Vegas Blvd. S. ✆ **877/667-0585.** www.roserabbitlie.com. Cover varies.

Tao Nightclub ★   Although it used to be the must-see club in town, it has never been one of our favorites, especially now that newer competition has stolen some of its status. Don't get us wrong, this is still one of the hottest of the Vegas hot spots. Done as a Buddhist temple run amok, this multilevel club has all the boxes ticked: long lines and high cover charges, wall-to-wall crowds, flashing lights, pounding music, and general chaos. We find it overwhelming in ways that other nightclubs with the same ticked boxes aren't, but those lines mean our opinion is in the minority. It's open Thursday through Saturday from 10pm until dawn. In The Venetian, 3355 Las Vegas Blvd. S. ✆ **702/388-8588.** www.taolasvegas.com. Cover varies.

Tryst ★★   The clubs at Wynn Las Vegas and Encore are, generally speaking, more grown up and refined than the competition, not necessarily in age but in attitude. This is good because there are fewer instances of unruly 22-year-old drunken behavior, although if you are an unruly 22-year-old, maybe you should go somewhere else. The bad news is that grown-up and refined attitudes bring grown-up and refined prices, meaning higher-than-average covers and drinks. If you can afford it, you'll be rewarded with a gorgeous, semicircular club complete with a dance floor that opens up onto a 90-foot waterfall. If that's not doing it for you, try sister club XS (see below), which is just a short walk (or stumble) away. Tryst is open Thursday through Saturday from 10:30pm to 4am. In Wynn Las Vegas, 3131 Las Vegas Blvd. S. ✆ **702/770-3375.** www.trystlasvegas.com. Cover varies, usually $30 and up.

XS ★★★   If you've been to the other Wynn club, Tryst (see above), you'll definitely recognize the relationship when you walk into sister property Encore's version. The aptly named XS has the same basic floor plan as Tryst, only bigger and, well, more of just about everything. Done in an eye-catching gold, pink, and purple color scheme, the semicircular rings of booths and tables cascade down to a center dance floor that opens up onto a giant outdoor patio complete with its own pool, fireplaces, and lounge spaces. More grown up than most Vegas nightclubs, XS offers the same kind of high-energy vibe with a bit more sophistication and lighting—you can actually see who you're bumping into as you try to navigate the crowds. Warning: Cover and drink prices are high. Unsurprising, then, that this is the top-grossing nightclub in the United States, having pulled in about $100 million in 2013. XS is open Friday and Saturday from 9:30pm until 4am and Sunday and Monday from 10:30pm to 4am. In Encore Las Vegas, 3121 Las Vegas Blvd. S. ✆ **702/770-0097.** www.xslasvegas.com. Cover varies, usually $30 and up.

Ultralounges

What, you may be asking, is an ultralounge? That's an excellent question, since it is loosely defined at best. Generally speaking, ultralounges are smaller than traditional nightclubs, offering a more intimate vibe. Some have dance floors and some don't, although even the ones that don't usually have DJs and people will dance wherever they can find the room to do so. You'll also usually find a lot more seating at an ultralounge, but most of it will probably be reserved for people willing to pay for bottle service. Drink and cover prices may be a bit less than the big nightclubs. The type of crowd they draw depends on the location and theme, with the most popular bringing in the same young and pretty crowd that goes to the hot dance clubs (they'll often come to an ultralounge first, and then head to the dance floor elsewhere).

Downtown Cocktail Room ★★ Right around the corner from the bustling Fremont East bars is this den of cool; an oasis of laid-back energy that feels more authentic than the prefab (not to mention costly) Strip-side hotel bars. Once you find the door (it's hidden behind an industrial metal sheet on the left), you enter an Asian *moderne* space, complete with lounges that invite posing. It feels a little more young-executive–friendly than some of the rowdier neighbors on the main drag. The cocktail menu is as substantial as it ought to be. It's open Monday through Friday from 4pm until 2am and Saturday from 7pm until 2am. 111 Las Vegas Blvd. ✆ **702/880-3696.** www. thedowntownlv.com. No cover.

ghostbar ★ Although others may have come before it, ghostbar pretty much perfected the ultralounge concept. Newly redesigned as of 2013, the place still has the signature fantastic views from the top of a hotel tower at the Palms, but inside is now all sleek white, black, and fuchsia with plush couches and intricate crystal chandeliers giving it a more grown-up feel. The outdoor patio is a must-visit for its unparalleled views of the Strip. Go early in the evening if you want to be able to sit without paying for bottle service, although be prepared to get kicked out when the real party starts with a DJ and all the cool kids showing up. ghostbar is open daily from 8pm until late. In the Palms, 4321 W. Flamingo Rd. ✆ **702/942-6832.** www.palms.com. Cover varies, usually $20 and up.

Holly Madison's 1923 Bourbon & Burlesque ★★★ Taking over the space (and the general concept) from the long-closed Ivan Kane's Forty Deuce, this prohibition-style speakeasy features more than just great cocktails, a kick-back vibe, and some terrific retro/new music (sampling artists like Gloria Estefan and C+C Music Factory with EDM and hip-hop beats). It has actual entertainment in the form of frequent stage presentations from a small jazz ensemble and a bevy of beauties doing peek-a-boo striptease acts. It's not a strip club—don't expect a lap dance or even an actual topless woman (look closely to see the flesh-colored bras they end with)—but in many ways it's even more sexy than the bump-and-grind monotony you often find in those places. Other acts include some fun singers who play up the Roaring '20s theme and reality star and former Playboy playmate Holly Madison, who not only has her name on the place, but also appears often as part of the entertainment. Treat yourself at the bar to their barrel-aged bourbons or one of their signature, retro-themed cocktails like a gin fizz or a pisco sour. One downside for those sensitive to it: The bar offers hand-rolled cigars. and lots of people come here to smoke them. It's open Wednesday through Saturday from 10pm until dawn. In Mandalay Bay, 3950 Las Vegas Blvd. S. ✆ **702/632-7777.** www.1923lv.com. Cover varies.

Hyde Bellagio ★★   It's hard to figure out how to categorize this place. Early evenings it's a cocktail lounge focusing on mixology and small-plate appetizers; some late nights it's more of an ultralounge, all sleek and sexy with DJs keeping the make-shift dance floor moving; and late on weekends it becomes a full-fledged nightclub with the requisite pretty people standing in long lines to get in and getting next to no personal space in the jammed room once they do. Regardless of which version you experience, the multilevel, multiroom club done as an Italian villa has the best views of the Bellagio Fountains you'll find anywhere. It's open nightly at 5pm until they close, which is usually after midnight on most nights and 4am on Tuesday, Friday, and Saturday. In Bellagio, 3600 Las Vegas Blvd. S. ℂ **702/693-8700.** www.hydebellagio.com. Cover varies, usually $20 and up.

Revolution ★   This place is tied to the Beatles-themed Cirque *LOVE* show, so think *White Album*, not Chairman Mao. While we dig the Union Jack–miniskirt-clad greeters, we wish the somewhat sterile interior was more shagadelic. Apart from some random Beatles-esque elements, the furnishings are pretty much beanbag chairs, silver mirrors, and a whiff of Austin Powers. The music varies wildly from night to night and from song to song, and while you won't hear a lot of Beatles tunes, you'll hear a lot of rock and pop that was influenced by them. A Sunday-night party for the LGBT crowd is very popular. Note that an *Abbey Road*–themed bar at the front is open daily starting at noon, while the nightclub portion is open Thursday through Tuesday 10pm to 4am. In The Mirage, 3400 Las Vegas Blvd. S. ℂ **702/693-8300.** www.mirage.com.

Surrender ★★   Although it's a sexy space all by itself, with low-slung couches, a decent-size dance floor, and the requisite stripper poles for the go-go dancers to hold onto, the coolest thing about this ultralounge space is the big wall of windows that opens up onto the Encore Beach Club (p. 208). It acts as an extension of that space when the main party is outside, and things reverse themselves late at night when things move indoors. Big-name DJs occasionally spin here, including the likes of David Guetta and Avicii. Surrender is open Wednesday, Friday, and Saturday from 10:30pm until dawn. In Encore Las Vegas, 3121 Las Vegas Blvd. S. ℂ **702/770-7300.** www.surrendernightclub.com. Cover varies, usually $30 and up.

VooDoo Rooftop Nightclub ★   Occupying, along with a restaurant, two floors atop the Rio, the VooDoo almost successfully combines Haitian voodoo and New Orleans creole in its decor and theme. There are two main rooms: one with a large dance floor and stage for live music, and a disco room, which is filled with large video screens and serious light action. Big club chairs in groups form conversation pits, where you might actually be able to have a conversation. And if you don't suffer from paralyzing vertigo, be sure to check out the dramatic outdoor, multilevel patio, which offers some amazing views of the Strip and the new zip-line style attraction running between the two hotel towers. The lounge portion is open nightly 5pm to 3am and the nightclub operates Monday through Wednesday from 9pm until 3am and Thursday through Sunday until 4am. In the Rio All-Suite Hotel & Casino, 3700 Las Vegas Blvd. S. ℂ **702/777-6875.** www.riolasvegas.com. Cover varies, usually $20 and up.

Hotel Lounges

Most of the nightclubs in town are ruled by the young and pretty types—you know who we mean: the 23-year-olds with impossibly short dresses, tiny waists, and an attitude that can be seen from space. Not that there's anything wrong with that. If we were thin and pretty, we'd want to hang out at these nightclubs, too.

But what about the rest of us? What about older people who may not have a tiny waist anymore but still want to go out, dance, and have a good time?

For them we offer what some consider to be a dinosaur of a bygone age: the hotel lounge. Don't roll your eyes, because many of the hotel lounges offer entertainment, dance floors, low or no cover charge, cheaper drink prices, and an almost total absence of the kind of "hey, look at me" posing that comes along with the trendy nightclubs. These are great places to go to simply have a night out of fun that doesn't involve a slot machine or blackjack table. All of the major hotels have at least one, so you can just wander by to see if it strikes your fancy, but here are a couple that might be worth the extra effort to visit.

Carnaval Court ★ Flair bartenders work the crowd into a frenzy almost as well as the frequent live entertainment that plays here. Although certainly not cheap, it's a relatively affordable place to party the night away, provided the weather cooperates. The bar is located outside, so you may want to find somewhere else to play on extremely warm or cool evenings. The recent renovations to the neighboring the Quad (formerly Imperial Palace) have made the space even more appealing. It's open daily from 11am until 3am. At Harrah's Las Vegas, 3475 Las Vegas Blvd. S. ℰ **702/731-7778.** www. harrahslv.com. Cover varies.

Mizuya Lounge ★★ In addition to some darned good sushi, Mizuya's nightly entertainment makes it noteworthy in this category. It usually features no-name cover bands, but they are usually really good no-name cover bands who do a great job of whipping the crowd into a party-all-the-time lather. The lack of a cover, lower-than-nightclub drink prices, and more casual atmosphere make this one a must. If you don't want sushi, go to dinner at neighboring Citizens Kitchen (p. 86) and then party here afterward. It's open Monday through Thursday from 11am until 3am, Friday from 11am until 4am, Saturday from 9am until 4am, and Sunday from 9am until 3am, but the party part doesn't usually start until evening. In Mandalay Bay, 3950 Las Vegas Blvd. S. ℰ **702/632-4760.** www.mandalaybay.com.

Country/Western Clubs

Gilley's ★★ Yeehaw! When Gilley's former location at the Frontier closed, it was a sad day for the boot-scootin' boogie crowd in Las Vegas, but this institution, made famous in the movie *Urban Cowboy*, is back at Treasure Island and significantly upgraded. The dance floor is small, but there is still room for line dancing (with lessons on select nights), a mud-wrestling pit (it's actually pudding, but the concept is the same), and the mechanical bull is ready to embarrass all of you tenderfoots. DJs or live bands provide the country-music accompaniment, and there is even Cowboy Karaoke if you feel like emulating Garth or Gretchen. The nightclub portion of the facility gets going around 7 or 8pm and stays open until 2am weeknights and later on weekends. In Treasure Island, 3300 Las Vegas Blvd. S. ℰ **702/894-7111.** www.gilleyslasvegas.com. Cover varies.

Stoney's Rockin' Country ★ Even though it has moved to a bigger, more high-profile location, Stoney's still feels like the bad boy of country music clubs in Vegas, at least when compared to the more tourist-centric (and therefore "safer") Gilley's. It's a friendly enough place, but it definitely draws more locals than visitors, which may or may not be a plus depending on your point of view. There's a big dance floor, nightly dance lessons, a mechanical bull, and frequent drink specials that keep it affordable. It's open nightly from 7pm until late. 6611 Las Vegas Blvd S., #160. ℰ **702/435-2855.** www.stoneysrockincountry.com. Cover varies.

cool BY THE POOL

A critical part of the nightclub scene is that it takes place at night. Maybe that's why they call them "night" clubs. But you don't have to wait until the sun goes down to start partying, especially in Vegas, where a host of daytime pool clubs gives you an opportunity to boogie down while working on your tan.

Most of the major hotels have some form of a poolside day club that usually operates on weekends and only in season (Mar–Oct mostly). They all feature DJs or live music, bars, private cabanas, and lots of opportunity to splash around in pools that are separated from the main recreational facilities for people over 21 years of age only. All charge a cover (although they vary as much as nightclub covers do) and some offer table games (like blackjack) and topless sunbathing. All are open to the general public (you don't have to be staying at the host hotel).

It should go without saying that these usually draw a younger, fit crowd

who aren't embarrassed about how they look in a bikini or board shorts. If that isn't you, you may want to consider alternate afternoon entertainment.

Here are the most noteworthy of the current pool clubs:

○ **Bare** At the Mirage, 3400 Las Vegas Blvd. S. (🕐 **702/696-8300;** www.barepool.com). Small pool, cabanas, DJ, and bar. Topless sunbathing allowed. Open daily 11am–6pm. Cover $20 and up.

○ **Daylight** At Mandalay Bay, 3950 Las Vegas Blvd. S. (🕐 **702/693-8300;** www.daylightvegas.com). 50,000-square-foot beach area with pool, three wet decks, private cabanas, DJ, bars, and food service. No topless sunbathing. Open Wed 11am–3am and Fri–Sun 11am–6pm. Cover $25 and up.

○ **Encore Beach Club** At Encore Las Vegas, 3121 Las Vegas Blvd.

Comedy Clubs

Brad Garrett's Comedy Club ★ Best known for his role as long-suffering brother Robert on the hit sitcom *Everybody Loves Raymond*, Brad Garrett is a stand-up comedy veteran who has created what he says is a life-long dream: his own comedy club. The fact that it's in the basement of a Vegas casino creates a great opportunity for some self-deprecating humor from both Garrett and the rotating roster of talent who take the stage. The club itself is warm and cozy, with a nice specialty cocktail list (the Bill Cosmopolitan—cute) and fancy flavored popcorn. Your mileage may vary depending on who is performing (look them up on YouTube to see if they are to your taste) but if you can swing it, try to get a date when Garrett is hosting (he's not there all the time). His humor is decidedly R-rated and boundary-pushing, but he is a master of comic timing. Besides, if you're looking for a "clean" comic you probably shouldn't be in Vegas in the first place. Shows are Sunday through Thursday at 8pm and Friday and Saturday at 8 and 10pm. In MGM Grand, 3799 Las Vegas Blvd. S. (🕐 **866/740-7711.** www.bradgarrettcomedy.com. Tickets $43–$87.

The Improv ★ This offshoot of Budd Friedman's famed comedy club (the first one opened in 1963 in New York City) presents two or three comedians per show in a relatively plain 400-seat showroom (don't worry, the brick wall is there). Only stand-up junkies will have heard of most of the people who perform here, and whether or not it's worth the ticket price totally depends on the comics of the evening, but in general

S. (© **702/770-7300**; www.encorebeachclub.com). 60,000-square-foot facility, three pools, cabanas, DJ, gaming, bar, grill. No topless sunbathing. Open Fri 12–6pm and Sat–Sun from 11am–6pm. Cover $25 and up.

o **Liquid** At Aria Las Vegas, 3730 Las Vegas Blvd. S. (© **702/693-8300**; www.arialasvegas.com). Three pools, cabanas, DJ, bar, restaurant. No topless sunbathing. Open daily 11am–6pm. Cover $20 and up.

o **Marquee Dayclub** At the Cosmopolitan of Las Vegas, 3801 Las Vegas Blvd. S. (© **702/333-9000**; www.marqueelasvegas.com). Two pools, cabanas with private pools, DJ, gaming, bar, food service. No topless sunbathing. Open daily 10am–sunset. Cover $25 and up.

o **Rehab** At the Hard Rock Hotel, 4455 Paradise Rd. (© **800/473-7625**; www.rehablv.com). Several pools, sandy beaches, cabanas, DJ, gaming, bar, food service. No topless sunbathing. Open daily 10am–sunset. Cover $25 and up.

o **Tao Beach** At the Venetian, 3355 Las Vegas Blvd. S. (© **702/388-8588**; www.taobeach.com). One pool, cabanas, DJ, bar, food service. Topless sunbathing allowed. Open daily 10am–sunset. Cover $20 and up.

o **Wet Republic** At MGM Grand, 3799 Las Vegas Blvd. S. (© **800/851-1703**; www.wetrepublic.com). Two pools, cabanas, DJ, bar, food service. No topless sunbathing. Open Thurs–Mon 11am–6pm. Cover $20 and up.

there are more hits than misses. Shows are Tuesday through Sunday at 8:30 and 10pm. In Harrah's Las Vegas, 3475 Las Vegas Blvd. S. © **800/392-9002** or 702/369-5000. www.harrahslv.com. Tickets $30–$65.

The Laugh Factory ★ The original outlet of this chuckle hut opened on the Sunset Strip in Los Angeles in 1979 and has hosted everyone from George Carlin to Ellen DeGeneres. This Vegas version may not be as storied (yet), but you'll get a relatively dependable roster of journeymen (and women) comics all doing their best to make you laugh. Shows are nightly at 8:30 and 10:30pm. In The Tropicana Las Vegas, 3801 Las Vegas Blvd. S. © **800/462-8767**. www.troplv.com. Tickets $29–$45.

THE GAY & LESBIAN SCENE

Hip and happening Vegas locals know that some of the best scenes and dance action can be found in the city's gay bars. And no, they don't ask for sexuality ID at the door. All are welcome at any of the following establishments—as long as you don't have a problem with the people inside, they aren't going to have a problem with you. For women, this can be a fun way to dance and not get hassled by overeager Lotharios.

In addition to the dedicated clubs and bars listed below, a growing number of straight clubs are having nights dedicated to the gay and lesbian crowds, like

"RevoSundays" at the **Revolution Lounge** in the Mirage (p. 54) and "Confidential" at **Bond** lounge at the Cosmopolitan (p. 59).

If you want to know what's going on in gay Las Vegas during your visit, pick up a copy of *Q Vegas*, which is also available at any of the places described below. You can also call ℂ **702/650-0636** or check out the online edition at www.qvegas.com.

Funhog Ranch ★ You know those trendy nightclubs where you stand in line for hours, pay outrageously high cover charges and drink prices, and are surrounded by opulence and beauty everywhere you turn once you finally get inside? This isn't one of them. As down-home as it gets, Funhog Ranch is just a bar, a few booths, some video poker, a jukebox, and an electronic dartboard. Drinks are rock-bottom cheap, and the clientele, which skews a bit older and is more of the leather/Levi's crowd, is enormously friendly. Leave your pretensions at those fancy clubs on the Strip. Funhog is open daily 24 hours. 495 E. Twain Ave. (just east of Paradise Rd.). ℂ **702/791-7001.** www.funhogranchlv.com. No cover.

Krave ★ What a long, strange trip it's been for this, the premiere gay nightclub in Vegas now finally back on the Strip after an unfortunate detour into Downtown. After years as a mainstay at Planet Hollywood, the club tried to take over a former movie theater complex on Fremont Street to become the world's largest gay nightclub. It barely lasted two months. Now it's operating out of the Empire Ballroom facility, a venue that was hosting nightclubs in Vegas before nightclubs were cool. The space has a small, laid-back ultralounge up front and a theater-style dance club in back with multiple bars, VIP booths, and lots of impossibly beautiful men as go-go dancers and wait-staff. The crowd is mostly tourists (locals hate this place) and mostly young, but it does have a more come-as-you-are vibe than most gay clubs do. Finding it can be a challenge; look for the Walgreen's across the street from the Monte Carlo and head down the driveway toward the back of the shopping center. Krave is open Friday and Saturday from 10:30pm until late. 3765 Las Vegas Blvd. S. ℂ **702/677-1740.** www.kravelasvegas.com. Cover varies.

Piranha Las Vegas ★★ The premiere club on the so-called "Fruit Loop" has two distinct experiences—a high-energy nightclub done in lush colors and fabrics complete with lounge area on the second floor overlooking the dance floor, and a comfy ultralounge space with seating, a big bar, and a stage for frequent entertainment. Of note here is the outdoor patio, complete with fireplaces and comfortable seating. This is one of the most popular gay clubs in town; consequently lines are often long, and both cover and drink prices are high. By the way, the aquariums that used to hold the signature piranhas now have other less intimidating fishies, a victim of city regulations that apparently govern things like killer fish in a gay bar. Open nightly 9pm to dawn. 4633 Paradise Rd. (at Naples Dr.). ℂ **702/791-0100.** www. piranhavegas.com. Cover varies, usually $20.

Share Las Vegas ★★ A high-energy nightclub downstairs, a laid-back ultralounge upstairs, and a cavalcade of Chippendales-worthy go-go dancers make this one of the most interesting and sexy gay clubs in town. The location west of the Strip near the Orleans is a bit of a bummer—there are no other clubs (or anything else, for that matter) nearby, so it definitely draws more locals than tourists—but with a vibe as intriguing as this one, you won't mind making the trek. Be sure to check their website for specials and discounts on drinks and cover charges. Open daily at 6pm until 2am Sunday through Wednesday and 4am Thursday through Saturday. 4636 Wynn Rd. ℂ **702/258-2681.** www.sharenightclub.com. Cover varies.

STRIP CLUBS

No, we don't mean entertainment establishments on Las Vegas Boulevard South. We mean the other kind of "strip." Yes, people come to town for the gambling and the wedding chapels, but the lure of Vegas doesn't stop there. Though prostitution is not legal within the city, the sex industry is an active and obvious force in town. Every other cab carries a placard for a strip club, and a walk down the Strip at night will have dozens of men thrusting fliers at you for clubs, escort services, phone-sex lines, and more. And some of you are going to want to check it out.

And why not? An essential part of the Vegas allure is decadence, and naked flesh would certainly qualify, as does the thrill of trying something new and daring. Of course, by and large, the nicer bars aren't particularly daring, and if you go to more than one in an evening, the thrill wears off, and the breasts don't look quite so bare.

In the finest of Vegas traditions, the "something for everyone" mentality extends to strip clubs. Here is a guide to the most prominent and heavily advertised; there are plenty more, of increasing seediness, out there. You don't have to look too hard. The most crowded and zoo-like times are after midnight, especially on Friday and Saturday nights. Should you want a "meaningful" experience, you might wish to avoid the rush and choose an off hour for a visit.

Cheetah's ★ This is the strip club used as the set in the movie *Showgirls*, but thanks to renovations by the club, only the main stage will look vaguely familiar to those looking for Nomi Malone. There are also five smaller stages and VIP rooms so you can really get close to (and give much money to) the woman of your choice. Lap dances are $20. Cheetah's is open daily 24 hours. 2112 Western Ave. ✆ **702/384-0074.** www.cheetahslasvegas.com. Topless. Cover $30.

Glitter Gulch ★ Right there in the middle of the Fremont Street Experience, Glitter Gulch is either an eyesore or the last bastion of Old Las Vegas, depending on your point of view. One of the most venerable strip clubs in town, it has a contemporary bordello theme with lots of red decor and lighting. Check out the retro catwalk stage in the middle of the bar! Given its convenient location and lack of cover (you can pound the two-drink minimum in no time), this is the perfect place for the merely curious—you can easily pop in, check things out, goggle and ogle, and then hit the road. Lap dances are $20 and up. Glitter Gulch is open Sunday through Thursday from 1pm to 4am and Friday and Saturday from 1pm to 5am. 20 Fremont St. ✆ **702/385-4774.** Topless. No cover; 2-drink minimum.

Larry Flynt's Hustler Club ★ Leave it to the founder of *Hustler* magazine to take the concept of a strip club and turn it into something tacky. We aren't talking about the dancers or what they are doing, we're talking about the building itself, a 70,000-square-foot facility that is lit up on the outside like a piece of space junk on re-entry and filled on the inside with signs pointing you to things like the Beaver Stage

If there's a particular strip club you want to visit, don't let your cabdriver talk you out of it. Clubs give cabdrivers kickbacks for delivering customers. So be leery of drivers who suggest one club over another. They may be making $20 for delivering you there. And don't accept a higher cover charge than we've listed here; the clubs are trying to get you to cover the kickback they just gave the cabbie.

and Honey Rooms. We know; we shouldn't be looking for class in a strip joint, but still. The place boasts three levels of stripper paradise, including a rooftop "oasis," multiple stages and bars, VIP booths, and a gift shop where you can pick up something special on your way home. Lap dances are $30. The Hustler Club is open daily 4pm until 9am. 6007 Dean Martin Dr. ✆ **702/795-3131.** www.hustlerclubs.com. Topless. Cover $30 (includes first lap dance).

The Palomino ★ The primary reason we are including this out-of-the-way club that is short on luxurious trappings is because it is the only one in Vegas that serves alcohol AND has totally nude dancers. Open since 1969, they are grandfathered into the laws that prevent that combo everywhere else. Beyond that, and the fact that they have male strippers too, they're essentially your basic strip club in both good and bad ways. Topless lap dances are $20; totally nude dances are $40. The Palomino is open Sunday through Thursday from 4pm to 5am and Friday and Saturday from 4pm to 7am. 1848 Las Vegas Blvd. N. ✆ **702/642-2984.** www.palominolv.com. Totally nude. Cover $30.

Sapphire Gentleman's Club ★★★ Ladies and gentlemen (particularly the latter), Las Vegas, home of the largest everything else, now brings you—drum roll—the largest strip club *in the world!* That's right, 71,000 square feet of nakedness. Expect three stages in a bridge shape (including one where gawkers who paid for the privilege can watch the action from below, thanks to a glass floor), and a fourth in a separate—and still large—room, with several poles and strippers all working it at the same time. Upstairs are incredibly posh and incredibly expensive rooms for wealthy sports and movie figures to utilize. And as if that all weren't enough, now they have a pool you can lounge by in between lap dances, which start at $20. Charlie Sheen hosted the pool's Memorial Day party. Enough said. Sapphire is open daily 24 hours. 3025 S. Industrial. ✆ **702/796-6000.** www.sapphirelasvegas.com. Topless. Cover $30 6pm–6am.

Treasures ★★★ Right now, along with Sapphire, this is our favorite of the strip clubs, for several reasons. From the outside, this looks like one of the new fancy casino-hotels (if considerably smaller), but inside it's straight out of a Victorian sporting house (that's a brothel, by the way), down to replicas of 19th-century girlie pictures on the walls. On stage, the performers actually perform; anyone who has witnessed the desultory swaying of the hips and vacant stare of a bored stripper will appreciate the bump-and-grind dance routines and special effects, from hair-blowing fans to smoke machines to a neon pole. Hungry? Forget the greasy buffets at other strip clubs, this one has its own steakhouse! Lap dances are $20 and up. Treasures is open Sunday through Thursday from 4pm to 6am and Friday and Saturday from 5pm until 9am. 2801 Westwood Dr. ✆ **702/257-3030.** www.treasureslasvegas.com. Topless. Cover $40.

DAY TRIPS FROM LAS VEGAS

T hough Vegas is designed to make you forget that there is an outside world, it might do you and your wallet some good to reacquaint yourself with the non-Vegas realm. The good news is that as the most geographically isolated major city in America, there's nothing but nature in every direction outside its neon-lit borders.

It's a startling contrast between the artificial wonders of Sin City and the natural wonders that, in some cases, lie just a few miles away. Few places are as developed and modern as Vegas; few places are as untouched as some of the canyons, desert, and mountains that surround it. The electrical and design marvel that is the Strip couldn't exist without the extraordinary structural feat that is Hoover Dam. Need some fresh air? There are plenty of opportunities for outdoor recreation, all in landscapes that are completely un-Vegas, in the best ways.

HOOVER DAM, LAKE MEAD & LAKE LAS VEGAS

30 miles SE of Las Vegas

This is one of the most popular excursions from Las Vegas, visited by upward of 7 million people annually. Why should you join them? Because Hoover Dam is an engineering and architectural marvel, and it changed the Southwest forever. Without it, you wouldn't even be going to Vegas. Kids may be bored, unless they like machinery or just plain big things, but expose them to it anyway, for their own good. Buy them ice cream and a Hoover Dam snow globe as a bribe. If you are visiting Lake Mead, it's a must.

Getting There

Drive east on Flamingo Road or Tropicana Avenue to U.S. 515 S, which automatically turns into I-93 S and takes you right to the dam. This involves a dramatic drive as you go through Boulder City and come over a rise, and Lake Mead suddenly appears spread out before you. It's a beautiful sight. After the 2010 opening of a bypass bridge (dramatic on its own for its soaring height over the canyon), vehicles no longer pass directly over the bridge to get from Nevada to Arizona, but despite hopes that the bypass would make the commute better, it hasn't helped much. On a normal day, getting to the dam will take about an hour.

Go past the turnoff to Lake Mead to Nevada State Route 172, the well-marked Hoover Dam Access Road. As you near the dam, you'll see a five-story parking structure tucked into the canyon wall on your left. Park here ($10 charge) and take the elevators or stairs to the walkway leading to the visitor center.

If you would rather go on an **organized tour,** check out **Gray Line** (www.grayline. com; ✆ **800/634-6579**), which offers a half-day tour of the dam from $47 or a day-long tour that includes a visit to the Welcome to Fabulous Las Vegas sign and a tour of the Ethel M Chocolate factory from $57.

Hoover Dam ★★★

There would be no Las Vegas as we know it without Hoover Dam. Certainly, the neon and glitz that we know and love would not exist. In fact, the growth of the entire Southwest can be tied directly to the electricity created by the dam.

Construction on the dam began in 1931. An army of more than 5,200 laborers was assembled, and work proceeded 24 hours a day. Though 96 workers were killed during construction, contrary to popular myth, none were accidentally buried as the concrete was poured (it was poured only at a level of 8 inches at a time). Look for a monument outside dedicated to the workers who were killed—"they died to make the desert bloom"—along with a tombstone for their doggy mascot who was also killed, albeit after the dam was completed. Compare their wages of 50¢ an hour to those of their Depression-era peers, who made 5¢ to 30¢.

Completed in 1936, 2 years ahead of schedule and $15 million under budget (it is, no doubt, a Wonder of the Modern Fiscal World), the dam stopped the annual floods and conserved water for irrigation, industry, and domestic uses. Equally important, it became one of the world's major electrical-generating plants, providing low-cost, pollution-free hydroelectric power to a score of surrounding communities. Hoover Dam's $165-million cost has been repaid with interest by the sale of inexpensive power to a number of California cities and the states of Arizona and Nevada. The dam is a government project that paid for itself—a feat almost as awe inspiring as its engineering.

The dam itself is a massive curved wall, 660 feet thick at the bottom, tapering to 45 feet where a road crosses it at the top. It towers 726 feet above bedrock (about the height of a 60-story skyscraper) and acts as a plug between the canyon walls to hold back up to trillions of gallons of water in Lake Mead, the reservoir created by its construction. Four concrete intake towers on the lake side drop the water down about 600 feet to drive turbines and create power, after which the water spills out into the river and continues south.

All the architecture is on a grand scale, and the design has beautiful Art Deco elements, unusual in an engineering project. Note, for instance, the monumental 30-foot bronze sculpture, *Winged Figures of the Republic,* flanking a 142-foot flagpole at the Nevada entrance. According to its creator, Oskar Hansen, the sculpture symbolizes "the immutable calm of intellectual resolution, and the enormous power of trained physical strength, equally enthroned in placid triumph of scientific achievement."

TOURING THE DAM

The **Hoover Dam Visitor Center** is a vast three-level circular concrete structure with a rooftop overlook. This facility is where you can buy tour tickets; peruse informational exhibits, photographs, and memorabilia; and view videos about the dam and its construction. The Overlook Level additionally provides an unobstructed view of Lake Mead, the dam, the power plant, the Colorado River, and Black Canyon. Have your camera ready.

Side Trips from Las Vegas

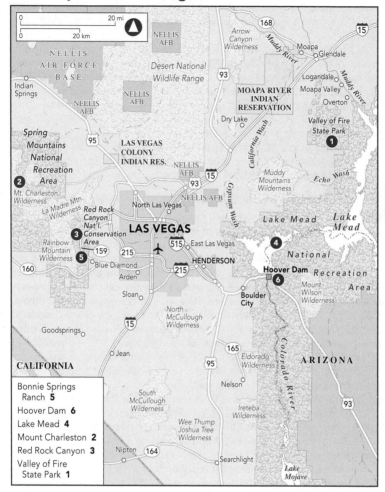

0 20 mi
0 20 km

NELLIS AFB

NELLIS AIR FORCE BASE

Indian Springs

Spring Mountains National Recreation Area

Mt. Charleston Wilderness

La Madre Mtn. Wilderness

Red Rock Canyon Nat'l. Conservation Area

Rainbow Mountain Wilderness

Blue Diamond

Arden

Sloan

Goodsprings

Jean

CALIFORNIA

Nipton

NELLIS AFB

Desert National Wildlife Range

NELLIS AFB

Dry Lake

LAS VEGAS COLONY INDIAN RES.

NELLIS AFB

North Las Vegas

LAS VEGAS

East Las Vegas

HENDERSON

North McCullough Wilderness

South McCullough Wilderness

Wee Thump Joshua Tree Wilderness

Searchlight

Arrow Canyon Wilderness

Moapa

Glendale

Logandale

MOAPA RIVER INDIAN RESERVATION

Moapa Valley

Overton

Valley of Fire State Park ❶

Muddy Mountains Wilderness

Echo Wash

Lake Mead

Lake Mead

National

Hoover Dam ❻

Mount Wilson Wilderness

Recreation Area

Boulder City

Eldorado Wilderness

Nelson

Ireteba Wilderness

Colorado River

ARIZONA

Lake Mojave

Bonnie Springs
Ranch **5**

Hoover Dam **6**

Lake Mead **4**

Mount Charleston **2**

Red Rock Canyon **3**

Valley of Fire
State Park **1**

It costs $10 to visit just this portion, but for an extra $5 you can get the Powerplant Tour as well (see below). The center closes at 6pm (5:15pm is the last admission time), though hours vary seasonally.

There are two tours available, the Powerplant Tour and the Hoover Dam Tour. The cost of the former is $15 for adults; $12 for seniors, children 4 to 16, and military personnel and their dependents; and free for children 3 and under and military in uniform. It is self-guided and takes about 2 hours if you really stop to look at and read everything (less if you're a skimmer). The more extensive Hoover Dam Tour includes the self-guided portion but adds an hour-long guided tour into the deeper recesses of the facility. It is $30 per person; no children age 7 and under are allowed. Tickets for the Hoover Dam Tour must be purchased at the Visitor Center, while admission to the Visitor Center and tickets for the Powerplant Tour are available online. Parking is $10 no matter which tour you take, and the lot takes cash only. There is no need to call ahead to reserve a place, but for more information, call © **866/730-9097** or 702/494-2517.

On the Powerplant Tour, visitors go to the center, see a movie, and walk on top of the dam. While both tours include a 530-foot descent via elevator into the dam to view the massive generators, the Powerplant Tour is a self-guided tour aided by the occasional information kiosk or guide/docent stationed at intervals along the way; the pricier Hoover Dam Tour offers the same attractions and viewing opportunities, but it is guided, lasts an hour, and is limited to 20 people. If you plan on taking that tour, be aware that it covers over a mile and a half of walking on concrete and gravel, with no handicapped access. The Hoover Dam Tour is offered every half-hour, with the last tour at 3:30pm, while the final Powerplant Tour admission is at 5:15pm.

For more information on the dam, visit www.usbr.gov/lc/hooverdam.

9 Lake Mead National Recreation Area ★★

Under the auspices of the National Park Service, 1.5-million-acre Lake Mead National Recreation Area was created in 1936 around Lake Mead (the reservoir lake that is the result of the construction of Hoover Dam) and later Lake Mohave to the south (formed by the construction of Davis Dam). Before the lakes emerged, this desert region was brutally hot, dry, and rugged—unfit for human habitation. Today, it's one of the nation's most popular playgrounds, attracting millions of visitors annually. The two lakes comprise 247 square miles. At an elevation of just over 1,000 feet, Lake Mead itself extends some 110 miles upstream toward the Grand Canyon. Its 700-mile shoreline, backed by spectacular cliff and canyon scenery, forms a perfect setting for a wide variety of watersports and desert hiking.

Having said all that, Lake Mead is in the beginning stages of a crisis so large that if unchecked, it would spell the end for Vegas entirely. The nation's largest reservoir has experienced a severe drop-off in levels since 2000, a combination of drought, global warming, and increased use. Whole portions of the lake's edges are now dry, in the process exposing the remains of some of the small towns that were flooded to build the thing in the first place. These have become tourist spots themselves. In 2010, the lake was at 39% of its capacity and hit a record low height of 1,083 feet above sea level. Things got a little better in recent years with increased water flow into the lake, but it is still a fraction of its former self and the long-term risk is still present. According to a research study published in 2008, there is a 50% chance the lake will go dry by 2021, and because it supplies water to Las Vegas (not to mention hydroelectric power), that has grave implications for that city. Let's encourage those fancy new hotels to put in drought-tolerant plants instead of more grass. And don't ask for your towels to be changed every day.

Keep in mind that if the lake water shortage continues, many of the following outdoor activities will probably be affected in one way or another, if they aren't already.

The **Lake Mead Visitor Center,** renovated and upgraded in 2013, is 4 miles northeast of Boulder City on U.S. 93, at NV 166 (© **702/293-8990**). Here, you can get information on all area activities and services, pick up trail maps and brochures, view informative films, and find out about scenic drives, accommodations, ranger-guided hikes, naturalist programs and lectures, bird-watching, canoeing, camping, lakeside

RV parks, and picnic facilities. The center has some informative exhibits about the area and is staffed by friendly folks full of local pride. It's open Wednesday through Sunday from 9:00am to 4:30pm except Thanksgiving, Christmas, and New Year's Day.

For information on camping, boat rentals, fishing, tours, and more, visit the National Parks Service website at www.nps.gov/lame.

The **entry fee** for the area is $10 per vehicle, which covers all passengers, or $5 per person if you're walking, motorcycling, or biking in. Entry fees cover 1 to 7 days and yearly passes are available for $30 per vehicle or individual.

Outdoor Activities

This is a lovely area for scenic drives amid the dramatic desert landscape. One popular route follows the Lakeshore and Northshore scenic drives along the edge of Lake Mead. From these roads, there are panoramic views of the blue lake, set against a backdrop of the browns, blacks, reds, and grays that make up the desert mountains. Northshore Scenic Drive also leads through areas of brilliant red boulders and rock formations, and you'll find a picnic area along the way.

BOATING & FISHING   The **Las Vegas Boat Harbor** (www.boatinglakemead.com; ✆ **702/293-1191**) rents powerboats, pontoon boats, personal watercraft, and watersports equipment. It also carries groceries, clothing, marine supplies, sporting goods, water-skiing gear, fishing equipment, and bait and tackle. Similar services are offered at the **Callville Bay Resort & Marina** (www.callvillebay.com; ✆ **800/255-5561** or 702/565-8958), which is usually less crowded. Nonresidents can get a fishing license here ($69 for a year or $18 for 1 day plus $7 for each additional day; discounts for children 15 and under are available; additional fees apply for special fishing classifications, including trout, which require a $10 stamp for taking or possessing that fish). Largemouth bass, striped bass, channel catfish, crappie, and bluegill are found in Lake Mead; rainbow trout, largemouth bass, and striped bass are in Lake Mohave. You can also arrange here to rent a fully equipped houseboat at **Echo Bay,** 40 miles north.

CAMPING   Lake Mead's shoreline is dotted with campsites, all of them equipped with running water, picnic tables, and grills. Available on a first-come, first-served basis, they are administered by the **National Park Service** (www.nps.gov/lame; ✆ **702/293-8990**). There's a charge of $10 per night at each campsite.

CANOEING   The **Lake Mead Visitor Center** (see above) can provide a list of outfitters that rent canoes for trips on the Colorado River. A canoeing permit ($16 per person) is required in advance and is available from livery services licensed by the Bureau of Reclamation. Questions about launch permits should be directed to Willow Beach/Black Canyon River Adventures (www. willowbeachharbor.com; ✆ **928/767-4747**). You can apply for and receive the permit on the same day that you plan to canoe.

HIKING   The best season for hiking is November through March (it's too hot the rest of the year). Three trails, ranging in length from .75 mile to 6 miles, originate at the **Lake Mead Visitor Center** (see above), which stocks detailed trail maps. The 6-mile trail goes past remains of the railroad built for the dam project. Be sure to take all necessary desert-hiking precautions. (See "Desert Hiking Advice," below.)

LAKE CRUISES   A delightful way to enjoy Lake Mead is on a cruise aboard the **Lake Mead Cruises** boat *Desert Princess* ★ (www.lakemeadcruises.com;

Hoover Dam, Lake Mead & Lake Las Vegas

DESERT hiking ADVICE

Except in summer, when temperatures can reach 120°F (49°C) in the shade, the Las Vegas area is great for hiking. The best hiking season is November through March. Great locales include the incredibly scenic Red Rock Canyon (p. 221) and Valley of Fire State Park (p. 218).

Hiking in the desert is exceptionally rewarding, but it can be dangerous. Here are some safety tips:

1. Don't hike alone.
2. Carry plenty of water and drink it often. Don't assume that spring water is safe to drink. A gallon of water per person per day is recommended for hikers.
3. Be alert for signs of heat exhaustion (headache, nausea, dizziness, fatigue, and cool, damp, pale, or red skin).
4. Gauge your fitness accurately. Desert hiking may involve rough or steep terrain. Don't take on more than you can handle.
5. Check weather forecasts before starting out. Thunderstorms can turn into raging flash floods, which are extremely hazardous to hikers.
6. Dress properly. Wear sturdy walking shoes for rock scrambling, long pants (to protect yourself from rocks and cacti), a hat, and sunglasses.
7. Wear sunscreen and carry a small first-aid kit.
8. Be careful when climbing on sandstone, which can be surprisingly soft and crumbly.
9. Don't feed or play with animals, such as the wild burros in Red Rock Canyon. (It's actually illegal to approach them.)
10. Be alert for snakes and insects. Though they're rarely encountered, you'll want to look into a crevice before putting your hand into it.
11. Visit park or other information offices before you start out and acquaint yourself with rules and regulations and any possible hazards. It's also a good idea to tell the staff where you're going, when you'll return, how many are in your party, and so on. Some park offices offer hiker-registration programs.
12. Follow the hiker's creed: Take only photographs and leave only footprints.

© **702/293-6180**), a Mississippi-style paddle-wheeler. It's a relaxing, scenic trip (enjoyed from an open promenade deck or one of two fully enclosed, climate-controlled decks) through Black Canyon and past colorful rock formations known as the Arizona Paint Pots en route to Hoover Dam, which is lit at night. Options include narrated midday cruises ($26 adults, $13 children), brunch cruises ($45 adults, $19.50 children), and dinner cruises ($61.50 adults, $25 children). Dinner is served in a pleasant, windowed, air-conditioned dining room. There's a full onboard bar. Brunch and dinner cruises run April through October, and the midday cruises run February through November. Call for departure times.

VALLEY OF FIRE STATE PARK ★★

60 miles NE of Las Vegas

The 36,000-acre Valley of Fire State Park typifies the mountainous, red Mojave Desert that surrounds Las Vegas. It derives its name from the brilliant sandstone formations that were created 150 million years ago by a great shifting of sand, and that

LEAVING (lake) LAS VEGAS

Originally created as a playground for the rich and famous (Céline Dion had a house here), Lake Las Vegas is a man-made reservoir created in a formerly dry, dusty valley about 20 miles east of the city on the way to Lake Mead. Surrounded by multi-million-dollar houses and rambling upscale condominium complexes, the bulk of the area is privately owned; but curving gracefully around the western lip of the lake is MonteLago Village, an homage to an Italian seaside community that features accommodations, dining, shopping, entertainment, and recreation options for those with a taste (and a budget) for the finer things in life.

The area was hit hard by the global economic recession, and many of the reasons to visit vanished. The fantastic Ritz-Carlton hotel, the casino, and two of the three golf courses closed. Many of the stores and restaurants went out of business, and most of the development sank into bankruptcy.

Things are improving, with the Ritz reborn as a fancy Hilton, but it's still a far cry from what its developers hoped it would be.

There are several shops and restaurants at **MonteLago Village,** Lake Las Vegas Parkway at Strada di Villagio, Henderson (www.montelagovillage.com;

© **877/997-6667**). Done as an Italianate village with cobblestone streets and candy-colored buildings, it's a nice place to stroll on spring days.

The former Ritz-Carlton is now operating as the **Hilton Lake Las Vegas Resort & Spa,** 1610 Lake Las Vegas Pkwy. (www.hilton.com; *©* **702/567-4700**). Though not much has changed in the room and amenities department, a focus on the business traveler has diminished some of the personal touches that made it special. Still the immaculate gardens are serene, the pool is a blissful retreat, and rooms are gorgeous, especially those located on the recreation of the Ponte Vecchio bridge over the lake.

On the other side of the lake, the **Westin Lake Las Vegas,** 101 MonteLago Blvd. (www.westinlakelasvegas.com; *©* **702/567-6000**), is new but in name only, having formerly been a Loews and before that a Hyatt. Not much has changed with the new ownership except the addition of their trademark "Heavenly" beds and some toning down of the Moroccan-themed decor. There are more than 500 rooms, a spa, several pools, restaurants, recreation programs, kids programs, and more, so you won't be lacking in things to do here or in ways to be pampered.

continue to be shaped by the geologic processes of wind and water erosion. These are rock formations like you'll never see anywhere else. There is nothing green, just fiery red rocks swirling unrelieved as far as the eye can see. No wonder various sci-fi movies have used this place as a stand-in for another planet—it has a most otherworldly look. The entire place is very mysterious, loaded with petroglyphs, and totally inhospitable. It's not hard to believe that for the Indians it was a sacred place, where men came as a test of their manhood. It is a natural wonder that must be seen to be appreciated.

Although it's hard to imagine in the sweltering Nevada heat, for billions of years, these rocks were under hundreds of feet of ocean. This ocean floor began to rise some 200 million years ago, and the waters became more and more shallow. Eventually, the sea made a complete retreat, leaving a muddy terrain traversed by ever-diminishing streams. A great sandy desert covered much of the southwestern part of the American continent until about 140 million years ago. Over eons, winds, massive fault action, and water erosion sculpted fantastic formations of sand and limestone. Oxidation of iron in the sands and mud—and the effect of groundwater leaching the oxidized iron—turned the rocks the many hues of red, pink, russet, lavender, and white that can be seen today. Logs of ancient forests washed down from faraway highlands and became petrified fossils, which can be seen along two interpretive trails.

Getting There

From Las Vegas, take I-15 N to exit 75 (Valley of Fire turnoff). However, the more scenic route is I-15 N to Lake Mead Boulevard east to Northshore Road (NV 167) and then proceed north to the Valley of Fire exit. The first route takes about an hour, the second, 1½ hours.

There is a $10-per-vehicle admission charge to the park ($8 for Nevada residents), regardless of how many people you cram inside.

Plan on spending a minimum of an hour in the park, though you can spend a great deal more time. It can get very hot in there (there is nothing to relieve the sun beating down on and reflecting off of all that red), and there is no water, so be certain to bring a liter, maybe two, per person in the summer. Without a guide, you must stay on paved roads, but don't worry if they end; you can always turn around and go back to the main road. You can see a great deal from the car, and there are also hiking trails.

Numerous **sightseeing tours** go to the Valley of Fire; inquire at your hotel tour desk.

What to See & Do

There are no food concessions or gas stations in the park; however, you can obtain meals or gas on NV 167 or in nearby **Overton** (15 miles northwest on NV 169).

At the southern edge of town is the **Lost City Museum ★**, 721 S. Moapa Valley Blvd. (© **702/397-2193**), a sweet little museum, very nicely done, commemorating an ancient ancestral Puebloan village that was discovered in the region in 1924. Artifacts dating back 12,000 years are on display, as are clay jars, dried corn and beans, arrowheads, seashell necklaces, and willow baskets from the ancient Pueblo culture that inhabited this region between A.D. 300 and 1150. Other exhibits document the Mormon farmers who settled the valley in the 1860s. A large collection of local rocks—petrified wood, fern fossils, iron pyrite, green copper, and red iron oxide, along with manganese blown bottles turned purple by the ultraviolet rays of the sun—are also displayed here. The museum is surrounded by reconstructed wattle-and-daub pueblos. Admission is $5 for adults, free for children 17 and under. It's open daily from 8:30am to 4:30pm, but closed Thanksgiving, December 25, and January 1.

Information headquarters for Valley of Fire is the **Visitor Center** on NV 169, 6 miles west of Northshore Road (© **702/397-2088**). It's open daily 8:30am to 4:30pm and is worth a quick stop for information and a glance at some of the informational exhibits before entering the park. Postcards, books, slides, and films are for sale here, and you can pick up hiking maps and brochures. Rangers can answer your park-related questions. For online information about the park, which is open sunrise to sunset, go to www.parks.nv.gov/vf.htm.

There are **hiking trails, shaded picnic sites,** and **two campgrounds** in the park. Most sites are equipped with tables, grills, water, and restrooms. A $20-per-vehicle, per-night camping fee is charged for use of the campground (plus $10 for utility hookups); if you're not camping, it costs $10 per vehicle to enter the park.

Some of the notable formations in the park have been named for the shapes they vaguely resemble—a duck, an elephant, seven sisters, domes, beehives, and so on. Mouse's Tank is a natural basin that collects rainwater, so named for a fugitive Paiute called Mouse, who hid there in the late 1890s. **Native American petroglyphs** etched into the rock walls and boulders—some dating from 3,000 years ago—can be observed on self-guided trails. Petroglyphs at Atlatl Rock and Petroglyph Canyon are both easily accessible. In summer, when temperatures are usually over 100°F (38°C), you may have to settle for driving through the park in an air-conditioned car.

RED ROCK CANYON ★★★

19 miles W of Las Vegas

If you need a break from the casinos of Vegas, Red Rock Canyon is balm for your overstimulated soul. Less than 20 miles away—but a world apart—this is a magnificent, unspoiled vista that should cleanse and refresh you (and if you must, a morning visit should leave you enough time for an afternoon's gambling). You can drive the panoramic 13-mile **Scenic Drive** (daily 6am–dusk, $7 per vehicle) or explore more in-depth on foot, making it perfect for athletes and armchair types alike. There are many interesting sights and trail heads along the drive itself. The **National Conservation Area** (www.nv.blm.gov/redrockcanyon) offers hiking trails and internationally acclaimed rock-climbing opportunities. Especially notable is 7,068-foot Mount Wilson, the highest sandstone peak among the bluffs; for information on climbing, contact the **Red Rock Canyon Visitor Center** at ✆ **702/515-5350.**

There are picnic areas along the drive and in nearby **Spring Mountain Ranch State Park** (✆ **702/594-7529;** www.parks.nv.gov/smr.htm), 5 miles south, which also offers plays in an outdoor theater during the summer. The entrance fee is $10 per vehicle.

Getting There

Just drive west on Charleston Boulevard, which becomes NV 159. As soon as you leave the city, the red rocks will begin to loom around you. The visitor center will be on your right.

You can also go on an **organized tour. Gray Line** (www.grayline.com; ✆ **800/634-6579**), among other companies, runs bus tours to Red Rock Canyon. Inquire at your hotel tour desk.

Finally, you can go **by bike.** Not very far out of town (at Rainbow Boulevard), Charleston Boulevard is flanked by a bike path that continues for about 11 miles to the visitor center/scenic drive. The path is hilly but not difficult, if you're in reasonable shape. However, exploring Red Rock Canyon by bike should be attempted only by exceptionally fit and experienced bikers.

Just off NV 159, you'll see the turnoff for the **Red Rock Canyon Visitor Center** (www.nv.blm.gov/redrockcanyon; ✆ **702/515-5350**), which marks the actual entrance to the park. It features outdoor exhibits on the flora and fauna found in the canyon and you can also pick up information on trails and the driving route. The center is open daily from 8am to 4:30pm.

About Red Rock Canyon

The geological history of these ancient stones goes back some 600 million years. Over eons, the forces of nature have formed Red Rock's sandstone monoliths into arches, natural bridges, and massive sculptures painted in a stunning palette of gray-white limestone and dolomite, black mineral deposits, and oxidized minerals in earth-toned sienna hues ranging from pink to crimson and burgundy. Orange and green lichens add further contrast, as do spring-fed areas of lush foliage. And formations, such as **Calico Hill,** are brilliantly white where groundwater has leached out oxidized iron. Cliffs cut by deep canyons tower 2,000 feet above the valley floor.

During most of its history, Red Rock Canyon was below a warm, shallow sea. Massive fault action and volcanic eruptions caused this seabed to begin rising some 225 million years ago. As the waters receded, sea creatures died, and the calcium in their bodies combined with sea minerals to form limestone cliffs studded with ancient fossils. Some 45 million years later, the region was buried beneath thousands of feet of windblown sand. As time progressed, iron oxide and calcium carbonate infiltrated the sand, consolidating it into cross-bedded rock.

About 100 million years ago, massive fault action began dramatically shifting the rock landscape here, forming spectacular limestone and sandstone cliffs and rugged canyons punctuated by waterfalls, shallow streams, and serene oasis pools.

Red Rock's valley is home to more than 45 species of mammals, about 100 species of birds, 30 reptiles and amphibians, and an abundance of plant life. Ascending the slopes from the valley, you'll see cactus and creosote bushes, aromatic purple sage, yellow-flowering blackbrush, yucca and Joshua trees, and, at higher elevations, clusters of forest-green pinyon, juniper, and ponderosa pines. In spring, the desert blooms with extraordinary wildflowers.

In the latter part of the 19th century, Red Rock was a mining site and later a sandstone quarry that provided materials for many buildings in Los Angeles, San Francisco, and early Las Vegas. In 1990, Red Rock Canyon became a National Conservation Area that comprises approximately 197,000 acres.

What to See & Do

Begin with a stop at the **Visitor Center;** while there is a $7-per-vehicle fee for entering the park, you also can pick up a variety of helpful literature: history, guides, hiking trail maps, and lists of local flora and fauna. You can also view exhibits that tell the history of the canyon and depict its plant and animal life, including the thousands of wild horses and burros, protected by an act of Congress since 1971. Call ahead to find out about ranger-guided tours as well as informative guided hikes offered by such groups as the Sierra Club and the Audubon Society.

The easiest thing to do is to **drive the 13-mile scenic loop ★★★** (or give it a go on your bike for a moderately difficult ride). It really is a loop, and it only goes one way, so once you start, you are committed to driving the entire thing. You can stop the car to admire a number of fabulous views and sights along the way, have a picnic, or take a walk or hike. As you drive, observe how dramatically the milky-white limestone alternates with iron-rich red rocks. Farther along, the mountains become solid limestone, with canyons running between them, which lead to an evergreen forest—a surprising sight in the desert.

If you're up to it, however, we can't stress enough that the way to really see the canyon is by **hiking.** Every trail is incredible—glance over your options and decide what you might be looking for. You can begin from the Visitor Center or drive into the loop, park your car, and start from points therein. Hiking trails range from a .7-mile-loop stroll to a waterfall (its flow varying seasonally) at Lost Creek to much longer and more strenuous treks. Actually, all the hikes involve a certain amount of effort, as you have to scramble over rocks on even the shortest hikes. Unfit or undexterous people should beware. Be sure to wear good shoes, as the rocks can be slippery. You must have a map; you won't get lost forever (there usually are other hikers around to help you out, eventually), but you can still lose your way. Once deep into the rocks, everything looks the same, even with the map, so give yourself extra time for each hike (at least an additional hour), regardless of its billed length.

A popular 2-mile round-trip hike leads to **Pine Creek Canyon** and the creekside ruins of a historic home site surrounded by ponderosa pine trees. Our hiking trail of choice is the **Calico Basin,** which is accessed along the loop. After an hour walk up the rocks (which is not that well marked), you end up at an oasis surrounded by sheer walls of limestone (which makes the oasis itself inaccessible, alas). In the summer, flowers and deciduous trees grow out of the walls.

As you hike, keep your eyes peeled for lizards, the occasional desert tortoise, herds of bighorn sheep, birds, and other critters. But the rocks themselves are the most fun, with small caves to explore and rock formations to climb on. On trails along Calico Hills and the escarpment, look for "Indian marbles," a local name for small, rounded sandstone rocks that have eroded off larger sandstone formations. Petroglyphs are also tucked away in various locales.

Biking is a tremendous way to travel the loop. There are also terrific off-road mountain-biking trails, with levels from amateur to expert.

The gleaming luxurious **Red Rock Resort** (p. 74) gives day-trippers a highly desirable refueling point on a trip to the canyon. Be sure to stop by the food court Capriotti's, the economical submarine sandwich shop. The subs are ideal for takeout for picnics in the park (buy a cheap Styrofoam ice chest at a convenience store) or for in-room dining as you rest up in your hotel post-hike.

Nearby **Bonnie Springs Ranch** (www.bonniesprings.com; ☎ **702/875-4191**) has a cute Wild West old town, horseback riding, a petting zoo, and more.

MOUNT CHARLESTON ★★

About 35 miles NW of Las Vegas

Although officially known as the Springs Mountains National Recreation Area, this region is more popularly referred to by the name of its most prominent landmark, the 11,918-foot-high Mount Charleston. Visible from Las Vegas proper, the mountain and its surrounding recreation areas have been a popular getaway for locals and vacationers alike for decades.

Comprising more than 316,000 acres of the Humboldt-Toiyabe National Forest (the largest in the lower 48), the area is practically an earth science class covering geography of such variety that it almost causes whiplash. As you start up the road toward the peak, you are surrounded by the kind of desert sage brush and Joshua trees that are most predominant at the lower levels. Suddenly the road takes a curve and a dip, and the desert gives way to a pinyon-juniper based ecosystem, full of craggy canyons and trees. Finally, you dive into the full-on forests of ponderosa and bristlecone pines, which create a lush oasis powered by more than 100 natural springs formed by water and snow runoff that soaks through the porous limestone rock and eventually bubbles to the surface.

Outdoor activities are the predominant lure and include hiking, camping, rock climbing, and, during the winter months, skiing and snowboarding.

Getting There

Head north on I-15 away from the Strip and then transition to U.S. 95 N. About 18 miles of freeway-style driving will bring you to the first of two roads up to the Mount Charleston area. Kyle Canyon Road/NV 157 will take you about 17 miles up toward the summit and is where you'll find the **Spring Mountain Visitor Center,** open 9am to 4pm daily (© **702/872-5486**), many of the campgrounds and hiking trails, the Mount Charleston Resort, and the Mount Charleston Lodge. A few miles farther is Lee Canyon Road/NV 156, which runs about 18 miles up to the Las Vegas Ski and Snowboard Resort (see "Snow Sports," below). It's only about 35 miles or so from Downtown Las Vegas, but traffic on the freeways in town is often difficult (to say the least) so plan an hour of travel time to be safe. *Note:* Chains are often required during or after snowfalls, which can be epic in the area. A December 2010 storm dumped a record 90 inches here over the course of several days.

Also note that there are no gas stations, convenience stores, or other services (and that often includes cellphone service) in the area, so be sure to fill up the tank and bring whatever supplies you may need with you.

Outdoor Activities

You might well be satisfied with a drive up to the region and, if it's wintertime, gazing at the snow from the warmth of your vehicle. We know that many of you come to Las Vegas in the winter to get away from the snow, but for those who don't get to see it very often, snow-covered peaks could very well be an entertaining sight. But if you want to actually get out of the car, there are a number of recreational activities available.

CAMPING   There are seven campgrounds in the Mount Charleston area, although only the McWilliams, Fletcher View, and Kyle Canyon sites are open year-round. Some have hookups if you are bringing your camper with you, while others are good for just tents and your sleeping bag; most have toilets, fire pits, and other outdoorsy conveniences. Fees range from around $10 to $50, depending on the number of people, type of vehicle, and facilities or hookups. A full listing of the campgrounds is available at the USDA Forest Service website at www.fs.fed.us (then search for the Spring Mountains National Recreation Area). To make reservations for any of the sites, use the National Recreation Reservation Service at © **877/444-6777** or head online to www.recreation.gov.

HIKING   Whether you are an expert hiker or a casual walker, there is probably a trail here for you—more than two dozen total. The Echo/Little Falls trail is a relatively easy mile or so through forests that lead to a small waterfall. On the other end of the scale is the South Loop, an 8-mile trek that leads you almost all the way to the summit of Mount Charleston more than 11,000 feet up. You can pick up a trail guide at the Spring Mountain Visitor Center. There is no fee to use the trails, but be sure to stick to the marked routes and follow all of the admonitions about bringing plenty of water and not drinking from the natural springs (they may contain parasites that can make you sick).

ROCK CLIMBING   There are several rock-climbing opportunities available in the Mount Charleston area, but all of them are do-it-yourself—no cushy controlled environments here. The most popular sites are the Hood along the unfortunately named

THE grand canyon

The geographically challenged among us believe that the Grand Canyon is just a hop, skip, and a jump from Las Vegas and therefore a great idea for a side trip while visiting Sin City. While this may be true from a strictly comparative basis— the canyon is closer to Vegas than it is to, say, London—it is not exactly what you might call "close." The South Rim is about 270 miles from Las Vegas via two- and four-lane highways. This equates to a solid 5-hour drive on a good day and an hour or two more than that during peak traffic times. In other words, if you want to take a quick day trip to the Grand Canyon from Las Vegas, you better accept the fact that it's going to be a very long day and you won't have much time at the park. An overnight visit or taking advantage of an air tour is probably a better bet.

But if you have the time and the energy, visiting the Grand Canyon is a breathtaking experience. There's a reason why it is considered one of

the seven natural wonders of the world.

Open year-round, the South Rim is the most popular area of the park and the one that you should visit if you have never been, as it offers the most options in terms of lodging, tours, activities, restaurants, and more. Keep in mind, however, that there are other areas of the park worth visiting. For more information on the North Rim and other Grand Canyon National Park destinations, visit www.frommers.com.

If you're taking your own car, head east on Flamingo Road or Tropicana Boulevard to I-515 S. This becomes NV 93, which crosses over Hoover Dam into Arizona and leads to I-40 at Kingman. Take the interstate east to NV 64 at Williams, Arizona, and follow the signs north. Drivers should be advised that much of the route to the Grand Canyon from Las Vegas is along narrow, twisty roads that can be a challenge and are often jammed with traffic.

Mount Charleston

Trail Canyon Trail, or Robber's Roost, accessed from the trail head along Highway 158. For more information, pick up a guide at the Spring Mountain Visitor Center.

SNOW SPORTS   The **Las Vegas Ski and Snowboard Resort,** Highway 156, Mount Charleston (www.skilasvegas.com; © **702/385-2754**), offers two chairlifts and more than a dozen trails ranging from beginner to advanced, plus terrain parks for snowboarders. Lift tickets are $40 to $60 for adults, and $30 to $45 for children 12 and under and seniors 60 and over. The facility offers a full array of equipment and clothing rentals; there's also a small snack bar and sundry shop if you forgot to bring a camera with which to record yourself in full downhill glory (or falling repeatedly, if you are like us). It is usually open late November through early April from 9am until 4pm, but that may vary based on conditions.

Where to Stay & Dine

In addition to the aforementioned snack shop at the Las Vegas Ski and Snowboard Resort, there is only one other dining option outside of the Mount Charleston Resort (see below). The **Mount Charleston Lodge,** 5375 Kyle Canyon Rd. (www.mtcharlestonlodge.com; © **702/872-5408**), has a rustic dining room with 20-foot ceilings in an A-frame, ski-lodge type building; a big bar; an open fireplace in the center of the room; and big windows and an outdoor patio from which you can enjoy the scenic views from its 7,717-foot elevation. They serve a wide range of American comfort food, from burgers to ribs, and are open for breakfast, lunch, and dinner from 8am until 8pm Sunday through Thursday and from 8am until 9pm on Friday and Saturday. The lounge is open daily until midnight.

The Resort on Mount Charleston ★   This woodsy retreat has undergone some serious improvements over the last few years that have kept the charm of the place, but modernized it and moved it upscale a notch or two. The ski-chalet style buildings (log and stone exteriors) are tucked into a canyon, providing a gorgeous backdrop for a peaceful respite. The lobby has a big fireplace perfect for warming up after a winter hike, along with a small menagerie of stuffed animals that seem *de rigueur* in a place like this.

The rooms range from standard motel size to presidential suites, all with comfortably modern furnishings, flatscreen TVs, faux fireplaces, iPod radios, DVD players, and more.

On site there is a small spa and fitness center; a full-service restaurant serving breakfast, lunch, and dinner (classic American fare); a sundry store/bistro with quick bites; and a bar and lounge complete with billiards and even a few video poker machines if you're going into gambling withdrawal.

2 Kyle Canyon Rd. ℂ **888/559-1888** or 702/872-5500. www.mtcharlestonresort.com. 61 units. $40 and up double. Resort fee $11.14 tax included. Free self-parking. Extra person $15. Children 17 and under stay free in parent's room. Pets under 25 pounds permitted, $25 per animal up to 2. **Amenities:** 2 restaurants; bar/lounge; spa; free property-wide Wi-Fi.

PLANNING YOUR TRIP TO LAS VEGAS

Whether you are visiting Las Vegas for the first time or the 50th, planning a trip here can be an overwhelming experience—as overwhelming as the city itself. With more than 150,000 hotel rooms, nearly as many slot machines, thousands of restaurants, and dozens of shows and attractions, there are seemingly endless ways to lose or waste your money. This chapter is designed to help you navigate the practical details of designing a Vegas experience that is tailored to your needs, from getting to and around the city to advice on the best times to visit and more.

Lots of people, both from the U.S. and abroad, believe that Las Vegas is the way it is portrayed in movies and television. For the most part, it isn't. Well, okay, you are more likely to run into a random showgirl or Elvis impersonator here than you are in say, Wichita, but they aren't in the background of every photo opportunity. International visitors, especially, should pay close attention to the material that follows in order to prepare for the most common nonshowgirl issues you may encounter in Las Vegas or on your way here.

GETTING THERE
By Plane

Las Vegas is served by **McCarran International Airport,** 5757 Wayne Newton Blvd. (© **702/261-5211,** TDD 702/261-3111; www.mccarran. com), just a few minutes' drive from the southern end of the Strip, where the bulk of casinos and hotels are concentrated. The airport is known by the code **LAS.**

Most major domestic and many international airlines fly into Las Vegas, and the city acts as a major routing point for low-cost Southwest Airlines.

The airport has two terminals. Terminal 1 serves mostly domestic carriers with four sets of gates. A and B gates are accessible to the main ticketing area and baggage claim by (very long) hallways, while most of the C and all of the D gates are reached by tram. The ultramodern Terminal 3 opened in 2012 and primarily services international and some domestic carriers like United with its 14 gates.

In case you're wondering what happened to Terminal 2, it closed when Terminal 3 opened. Why they didn't renumber things is a mystery.

Each terminal has its own baggage-claim facility and services such as dining, shopping, and traveler assistance, along with ground transportation areas for taxis, buses, and shuttles to the rental-car facility.

And yes, all of the terminals and baggage claims have slot machines just in case you want to lose a few bucks while you're waiting for your luggage.

By Car

The main highway connecting Las Vegas with the rest of the country is **I-15;** it links Montana, Idaho, and Utah with Southern California. The drive from Los Angeles is quite popular and can get very crowded on weekends as hopeful gamblers make their way to and from Las Vegas.

From the east, take **I-70** or **I-80** west to Kingman, Arizona, and then **U.S. 93** north to Downtown Las Vegas (Fremont St.). From the south, take **I-10** west to Phoenix, and then U.S. 93 north to Las Vegas. From San Francisco, take I-80 east to Reno, and then **U.S. 95** south to Las Vegas.

Vegas is 286 miles from Phoenix, 759 miles from Denver, 421 miles from Salt Lake City, 269 miles from Los Angeles, and 586 miles from San Francisco.

International visitors should note that insurance and taxes are almost never included in quoted rental-car rates in the U.S. Be sure to ask your rental agency about these. They can add a significant cost to your car rental.

For information on car rentals and gasoline (petrol) in Las Vegas, see "Getting Around: By Car," below.

By Bus

Bus travel is often the most economical form of public transit for short hops between U.S. cities, but it's certainly not an option for everyone. Though getting to Vegas this way is cheaper, especially if you book in advance, it's also time consuming (a 1-hr. flight from L.A. becomes a 5- to 8-hr. trek by bus) and usually not as comfortable. So you need to figure out how much time and comfort mean to you. **Greyhound** (© **800/231-2222** in the U.S.; © **001/214/849-8100** outside the U.S. without toll-free access; www.greyhound.com) is the sole nationwide bus line.

The main Greyhound terminal in Las Vegas is located Downtown next to the Plaza hotel, 200 S. Main St. (© **702/383-9792**), and is open 24 hours. Although the neighborhood around it has improved dramatically, it is still a busy bus station and so normal safety precautions should be taken in and around it.

Megabus (© **877/462-6342;** www.megabus.com) operates coaches from Los Angeles to the Regional Transportation Commission's South Strip Transfer Terminal at 6675 Gillespie St. near McCarran International Airport. From there you can easily transfer (hence the name) to many of the city's bus routes, including those that travel to the Strip (see "Getting Around: By Bus," below).

By Train

Amtrak (© **800/872-7245;** www.amtrak.com) does not currently offer direct rail service, although plans have been in the works for years to restore the rails between Los Angeles and Las Vegas. We've been hearing these reports for so long now, they just make us roll our eyes.

In the meantime, you can take the train to Los Angeles or Barstow, and Amtrak will get you to Las Vegas by bus, which takes 5 to 6 hours depending on traffic.

GETTING AROUND

It isn't too hard to navigate your way around Vegas. But do remember: Thanks to huge hotel acreage, often very slow traffic, and lots and lots of people—like you—trying to explore, getting around takes a lot longer than you might think. Heck, it can take 15 to 20 minutes to get from your room to another part of your hotel! Always allow for plenty of time to get from point A to point B.

Getting into Town from the Airport

Getting to your hotel from the airport is a cinch. You can grab one of the roughly nine gajillion cabs that are lined up waiting for you (see "By Taxi," p. 233) or you can grab a shuttle bus. **Bell Transportation** (© 800/274-7433 or 702/739-7990; www.bell-trans. com) runs 20-passenger minibuses daily (3:30am–1am) between the airport and all major Las Vegas hotels and motels. The cost is $7 per person each way to hotels on the Strip or around the Convention Center and $8.50 to Downtown and other off-Strip properties (north of Sahara Ave. and west of I-15). Several other companies run similar ventures—just look for the signs for the shuttle bus queues, located just outside of the baggage-claim area. Buses from the airport leave every few minutes. When you want to check out of your hotel and head back to the airport, call at least 2 hours in advance to be safe (though often you can just flag down one of the buses outside any major hotel).

Even less expensive are **Citizens Area Transit (CAT)** buses (© 702/228-7433; www. rtcsnv.com/transit). The no. 109 bus goes from the airport to the South Strip Transfer Terminal at Gilespie St. and Sunset Rd., where you can transfer to the Strip and Downtown Express (SDX) or Deuce line that runs along the Strip into Downtown. Alternately, the no. 108 bus departs from the airport and takes you Downtown. The fares for buses on Strip routes are $6 for adults for 2 hours or $8 for 24 hours. Other routes are $2 for a single ride. *Note:* You might have a long walk from the bus stop to the hotel entrance, even if the bus stop is right in front of your hotel. Shuttles and taxis are able to get right up to the entrance, so choose one of those if you're lugging lots of baggage.

If you have a large group with you, you might also try one of the limos that wait curbside at the airport and charge $45 to $65 for a trip to the Strip. The price may go up with additional passengers, so ask about the fee very carefully. The aforementioned Bell Transportation is one reputable company that operates limousines in addition to their fleet of shuttle buses (call in advance).

By Car

If you plan to confine yourself to one part of the Strip (or one cruise down to it) or to Downtown, your feet will suffice. Otherwise, we highly recommend that visitors rent a car. The Strip is too spread out for walking (and Las Vegas is often too hot or too cold to make strolls pleasant); Downtown is too far away for a cheap cab ride, and public transportation is often ineffective in getting you where you want to go. Plus, return visits call for exploration in more remote parts of the city, and a car brings freedom, especially if you want to do any side trips at your own pace.

You should note that places with addresses some 60 blocks east or west of the Strip are actually less than a 10-minute drive—provided there is no traffic.

Having advocated renting a car, we should warn you that traffic is pretty terrible, especially on and around the busy tourist areas. A general rule of thumb is to avoid driving on the Strip whenever you can and give yourself plenty of extra time during rush hour to get where you want to go (see p. 234 for some helpful tips on how to get around the worst of the traffic).

Parking is usually a pleasure because all casino hotels offer free valet service. That means that for a mere $2 to $5 tip, you can park right at the door, though the valet usually fills up on busy nights and is restricted at some hotels to elite players' club members. In those cases, you can use the gigantic self-parking lots (free on the Strip, nominal fees Downtown) that all hotels have.

If you're visiting from abroad and plan to rent a car in the United States, keep in mind that foreign driver's licenses are usually recognized in the U.S., but you may want to consider obtaining an international driver's license. Also, international visitors should note that insurance and taxes are almost never included in quoted rental-car rates in the U.S. Be sure to ask your rental agency about these. They can add a significant cost to your car rental.

At press time, in Nevada, the cost of gasoline (also known as gas, but never petrol) is around $3.60 per gallon and tends to vary unpredictably. Taxes are already included in the printed price. One U.S. gallon equals 3.8 liters or .85 imperial gallons. Fill-up locations are known as gas or service stations. Las Vegas prices typically fall near the nationwide average. You can also check **www.vegasgasprices.com** for recent costs.

Renting a Car

Major companies with outlets in Las Vegas include **Advantage** (© **800/777-9377**; www.advantage.com), **Alamo** (© **800/462-5266**; www.alamo.com), **Avis** (© **800/331-1212**; www.avis.com), **Budget** (© **800/922-2899**; www.budget.com), **Dollar** (© **800/800-4000**; www.dollar.com), **E-Z Rent-A-Car** (© **800/277-5171**; www.e-zrentacar.com), **Enterprise** (© **800/736-7222**; www.enterprise.com), **Hertz** (© **800/654-3131**; www.hertz.com), **National** (© **800/227-7368**; www.nationalcar.com), **Payless** (© **800/729-5377**; www.paylesscarrental.com), and **Thrifty** (© **800/367-2277**; www.thrifty.com).

Rental policies vary from company to company, but generally speaking you must be at least 25 years of age with a major credit or debit card to rent a vehicle in Las Vegas. Some companies will rent to those between 21 and 24, but will usually charge extra ($20–$30 per day) and will require proof of insurance and a major credit card; also, they may restrict the type of vehicle you are allowed to rent (forget those zippy convertibles).

All of the major car-rental companies are located at a consolidated facility at 7135 Gilespie St., just a block off Las Vegas Blvd. near Warm Springs Rd. and about 2½ miles from the airport. When you arrive, look for the signs for BUSES AND SHUT-TLES in the baggage-claim area and follow them outside, where you'll find blue-and-white buses marked MCCARRAN RENT-A-CAR CENTER. It takes about 10 minutes to make the trip, although it's worth noting that the lines for buses and at the car-rental counters can be long—budget some extra time if you have somewhere to be right after you get to town.

The rental-car facility is modern and easily navigable, and just in case you resisted while at the airport, there are slot machines next to the rental counters as well. Welcome to Vegas!

When exiting the facility, take three right turns and you are on the Strip, about 2 miles south of Mandalay Bay.

Car-rental rates vary even more than airline fares. The price you pay depends on the size of the car, where and when you pick it up and drop it off, the length of the rental period, where and how far you drive it, whether you purchase insurance, and a host of other factors. Asking a few key questions could save you hundreds of dollars:

- Are weekend rates lower than weekday rates? In Vegas this is usually true, although holiday or special events weekends can be more costly. Ask if the rate is the same for pickup Friday morning, for instance, as it is for Thursday night.

- Is a weekly rate cheaper than the daily rate? Even if you need the car for only 4 days, it may be cheaper to keep it for 5.

- Does the agency assess a drop-off charge if you don't return the car to the same location where you picked it up? Is it cheaper to pick up the car at the airport than at a Downtown location?

- Are special promotional rates available? If you see an advertised price in your local newspaper, be sure to ask for that specific rate; otherwise, you may be charged the standard cost. Terms change constantly, and reservations agents are notorious for not mentioning available discounts unless you ask.

- Are discounts available for members of AARP, AAA, frequent-flier programs, or trade unions? If you belong to any of these organizations, you may be eligible for discounts of up to 30%.

- Are there additional fees? In Las Vegas, expect to add about 35% to 40% on top of the rental fee, including a $1.60-per-day vehicle license fee, a $3.75-per-day facility fee, a 10% concession fee, and about 20% in taxes and state government surcharges. Ouch.

- What is the cost of adding an additional driver's name to the contract?

- How many free miles are included in the price? Free mileage is often negotiable, depending on the length of the rental.

Some companies offer "refueling packages," in which you pay for an entire tank of gas up front. The price is usually fairly competitive with local gas prices, but you don't get credit for any gas remaining in the tank and because it is virtually impossible to use up every last bit of fuel before you return it; you will usually wind up paying more overall than you would if you just filled it up yourself. There are several gas stations within a few blocks of the car-rental center, including three at the intersection of Las Vegas Blvd. and Warm Springs Rd. You may pay a few extra pennies at them than you would at stations elsewhere in town, but in the long run it's still a better deal.

Many available packages include airfare, accommodations, and a rental car with unlimited mileage. Compare these prices with the cost of booking airline tickets and renting a car separately to see if such offers are good deals. Internet resources can make comparison shopping easier.

Surfing for Rental Cars

For booking rental cars online, the best deals are usually found at rental-car company websites, although all the major online travel agencies also offer rental-car reservations services. **Priceline** (www.priceline.com) and **Hotwire** (www.hotwire.com) work well for rental cars; the only "mystery" is which major rental company you get, and for most travelers, the difference between Hertz, Avis, and Budget is negligible. Also check out **Breezenet.com,** which offers domestic rental-car discounts with some of the most competitive rates around.

Demystifying Rental-Car Insurance

Before you drive off in a rental car, be sure you're insured. Hasty assumptions about your personal auto insurance or a rental agency's additional coverage could end up costing you tens of thousands of dollars—even if you are involved in an accident that was clearly the fault of another driver.

DRIVE IN style

If the idea of tooling around Las Vegas in a pedestrian rent-a-box just doesn't sound appealing, you can always indulge your fantasies by going with something more exotic.

Las Vegas Exotic Car Rentals (*C* **866/871-1893** or 702/736-2592; www.vegasexoticrentals.com) has a fleet from makers such as Lamborghini, Bentley, Ferrari, and Lotus, plus a stable of classic American muscle cars like the

Chevrolet Corvette. They even feature an Aston Martin, if you want to work out your inner James Bond while buzzing between casinos. Rates start at about $300 per day and go up from there—sometimes, way up. At press time, the Lamborghini Murcielago roadster was $1,895 per day, or roughly what you'll pay for a week in a suite at a nice Vegas hotel.

If you already hold a **private auto insurance** policy in the United States, you are most likely covered for loss of or damage to a rental car, and liability in case of injury to any other party involved in an accident. Be sure to find out whether you are covered in Vegas, whether your policy extends to all persons who will be driving the rental car, how much liability is covered in case an outside party is injured in an accident, and whether the type of vehicle you are renting is included under your contract. (Rental trucks, sport utility vehicles, and luxury vehicles may not be covered.)

Most **major credit cards** provide some degree of coverage as well—provided they were used to pay for the rental. Terms vary widely, however, so be sure to call your credit card company directly before you rent. If you don't have a private auto insurance policy, the credit card you use to rent a car may provide primary coverage if you decline the rental agency's insurance. This means that the credit card company will cover damage or theft of a rental car for the full cost of the vehicle. If you do have a private auto insurance policy, your credit card may provide secondary coverage— which basically covers your deductible. *Credit cards do not cover liability* or the cost of injury to an outside party and/or damage to an outside party's vehicle. If you do not hold an insurance policy, you may want to seriously consider purchasing additional liability insurance from your rental company. Be sure to check the terms, however: Some rental agencies cover liability only if the renter is not at fault; even then, the rental company's obligation varies from state to state. Bear in mind that each credit card company has its own peculiarities; call your own credit card company for details before relying on a card for coverage. Speaking of cards, members of AAA should be sure to carry their membership ID card with them, which provides some of the benefits touted by the rental-car agencies at no additional cost.

The basic insurance coverage offered by most rental-car companies, known as the **Loss/Damage Waiver (LDW)** or **Collision Damage Waiver (CDW),** can cost $20 per day or more. The former should cover everything, including the loss of income to the rental agency, should you get in an accident (normally not covered by your own insurance policy). It usually covers the full value of the vehicle, with no deductible, if an outside party causes an accident or other damage to the rental car. You will probably be covered in case of theft as well. Liability coverage varies, but the minimum is usually at least $15,000. If you are at fault in an accident, you will be covered for the full replacement value of the car—but not for liability. In Nevada, you can buy additional liability coverage for such cases. Most rental companies require a police report in order to process any claims you file, but your private insurer will not be notified of the accident. Check your own policies and credit cards before you shell out money on this extra insurance because you may already be covered.

It's worth noting that rental-car companies seem to be pushing the extra coverage especially hard these days. Doing your research on what types of coverage you do and do not need will allow you to smile politely and decline if it is appropriate. Don't let them pressure or scare you into spending extra money for items you don't need.

By Taxi

Because cabs line up in front of all major hotels, an easy way to get around town is by taxi. Cabs charge $3.30 at the meter drop and $2.60 per mile after that, plus an additional $2.00 fee for being picked up at the airport and time-based penalties if you get stuck in traffic. A taxi from the airport to the Strip will run you $15 to $23, from the airport to Downtown $18 to $25, and between the Strip and Downtown about $12 to $18. You can often save money by sharing a cab with someone going to the same destination (up to five people can ride for the same fare).

All this implies that you have gotten a driver who is honest. Long-hauling—the practice of taking fares on a longer route to the destination to increase fares—is rampant in Las Vegas these days. A 2013 audit by the state found an estimated $15 million in overcharges and nearly 25% of all fares from the airport were charged too much.

The simplest way to avoid this is to always know where you are going and roughly how much it should cost to get there. Use the maps on your phone or online to gauge the distance and calculate the approximate fare or let a website like **taxifarefinder. com** do the math for you. When you get into the cab and state your destination, don't be afraid to add something like "that will cost about $20, right?" It puts the cabbie on notice that you are not a hapless tourist ready to be taken for a metaphorical ride.

If you suspect that you have been long-hauled, call the taxi company to complain and be sure to file a report with the Nevada Taxicab Authority at **taxi.nv.gov.**

If you just can't find a taxi to hail and want to call one, try the following companies: **Desert Cab Company** (✆ **702/386-9102**), **Whittlesea Blue Cab** (✆ **702/384-6111**), or **Yellow/Checker Cab/Star Company** (✆ **702/873-2000**).

By Monorail

The 4-mile monorail route runs from the MGM Grand, at the southern end of the Strip, to the SLS Las Vegas (formerly the Sahara), at the northern end, with stops at Paris/Bally's, the Flamingo, Harrah's, the Las Vegas Convention Center, and LVH: Las Vegas Hotel along the way. Note that some of the actual physical stops are not particularly close to their namesakes, so there can be an unexpected—and sometimes time-consuming—additional walk from the monorail stop to wherever you intended to go. Factor in this time accordingly.

These trains can accommodate more than 200 passengers (standing and sitting) and make the end-to-end run in about 15 minutes. They operate Monday from 7am until midnight, Tuesday through Thursday from 7am until 2am, and Friday through Sunday from 7am until 3am. Fares are $5 for a one-way ride (whether you ride from one end to the other or just to the next station); discounts are available for round-trips and multiride/multiday passes.

Visit the Las Vegas Monorail website at **www.lvmonorail.com** for more information.

Getting Around

TRAFFIC tips

Traffic in Las Vegas can be frustrating at times, especially near the Strip on evenings and weekends. Here are a few tips to help you get around the worst of it:

○ **Spaghetti Bowl:** The "Spaghetti Bowl" is what locals call the mess where I-15 intersects U.S. 95. Major construction in and around it is planned for 2014. Avoid it if you can.

○ **Do D.I. Direct:** Most visitors seem to get a lot of mileage out of the Strip and I-15. But if you're checking out the local scene, you can bypass both of those, using Desert Inn Road, which is now one of the longest streets running from one side of the valley to the other. Plus, the 2-mile "Superarterial" section between Valley View and Paradise zips you nonstop over the interstate and under the Strip.

○ **Grin and Bear It:** Yes, there are ways to avoid traffic jams on the Strip. But at least these traffic jams are entertaining! If you have the time and patience, go ahead and take a ride along the Strip from Mandalay Bay to the Stratosphere.

The 4-mile drive might take an hour, but while you're grinding along, you'll see a sphinx, an active volcano, a water ballet, and some uniquely Vegas architecture.

○ **Rat Pack Back Doors:** Frank Sinatra Drive is a bypass road that runs parallel to the Strip from Russell Road north to Industrial. It's a great way to avoid the traffic jams and sneak in the back of hotels such as Mandalay Bay, Luxor, and Monte Carlo. On the other side of I-15, a bunch of high-end condo developers talked the city into rechristening a big portion of Industrial Road as Dean Martin Drive. It's still called Industrial from near Downtown to Twain, and it lets you in the back entrances to Circus Circus, Treasure Island, and others. It's a terrific bypass to the Strip and I-15 congestion.

○ **Beltway Bypass:** The 53-mile 215 Beltway wraps three-quarters of the way around the valley, allowing easy access to the outskirts while bypassing the Resort Corridor.

By Bus

The Deuce and SDX (Strip to Downtown Express) buses operated by the **Regional Transportation Commission** (**RTC;** ℡ **702/228-7433;** www.rtcsnv.com/transit) are the primary public transportation on the Strip. The double-decker Deuce and double-carriage SDX run a route between the Downtown Transportation Center (at Casino Center Blvd. and Stewart Ave.) and a few miles beyond the southern end of the Strip. The fare is $6 for adults for 2 hours; an all-day pass is $8 and a 3-day pass is $20. There are no discounts for children or seniors. CAT buses run 24 hours a day and are wheelchair accessible. Exact change is required.

Although they are certainly economical transportation choices, they are not the most efficient as it relates to time or convenience. They run often but are usually very crowded and are not immune to the mind-numbing traffic that clogs the Strip at peak times. Patience is required.

There are also a number of **free transportation services,** courtesy of the casinos. A free monorail connects Mandalay Bay with Luxor and Excalibur; another connects Monte Carlo, Bellagio, and CityCenter; and a free tram shuttles between the Mirage and Treasure Island. Given how far apart even neighboring hotels can be, thanks to their size, and how they seem even farther apart on really hot (and cold and windy) days, these are blessed additions.

[FastFACTS] LAS VEGAS

Area Codes The local area codes in Las Vegas are 702 and 725. The full 10-digit phone number with area code must be dialed to complete the call.

Business Hours Casinos and most bars are open 24 hours a day; nightclubs are usually open only late at night into the early morning hours, and restaurant and attraction hours vary.

Car Rental See "Getting Around: By Car," earlier in this chapter.

Cellphones See "Mobile Phones," below.

Crime See "Safety," later in this section.

Customs Every visitor 21 years of age or older may bring in, free of duty, the following: (1) 1 liter of alcohol as a gift or for personal use; (2) 200 cigarettes, 100 cigars (but not from Cuba), or 3 pounds of smoking tobacco; and (3) $100 worth of gifts. These exemptions are offered to travelers who spend at least 72 hours in the United States and who have not claimed them within the preceding 6 months. It is forbidden to bring into the country almost any meat products (including canned, fresh, and dried-meat products such as bouillon, soup mixes, and so forth). Generally, condiments, including vinegars, oils, pickled goods, spices,

coffee, tea, and some cheeses and baked goods are permitted. Avoid rice products, as rice can often harbor insects. Bringing fruits and vegetables is prohibited since they may harbor pests or disease. International visitors may carry in or out up to $10,000 in U.S. or foreign currency with no formalities; larger sums must be declared to U.S. Customs on entering or leaving, which includes filing form CM 4790. For details regarding U.S. Customs and Border Protection, consult your nearest U.S. embassy or consulate, or **U.S. Customs** (www.cbp.gov).

For information on what you're allowed to take home, contact your home country's Customs agency.

Disabled Travelers
On the one hand, Las Vegas is fairly well equipped for travelers with disabilities, with virtually every hotel having wheelchair-accessible rooms and ramps and other requirements. On the other hand, the distance between hotels (particularly on the Strip) makes a vehicle of some sort virtually mandatory for most people with disabilities, and it may be extremely strenuous and time consuming to get from place to place (even within a single hotel, because of the crowds). Even if you don't intend to gamble, you still

may have to go through the casino, and casinos can be quite difficult to maneuver in, particularly for a guest in a wheelchair. Casinos are usually crowded, and the machines and tables are often arranged close together, with chairs, people, and such blocking easy access. You should also consider that it is often a long trek through larger hotels between the entrance and the room elevators (or, for that matter, anywhere in the hotel), and then add a crowded casino to the equation.

For more on organizations that offer resources to travelers with limited mobility, go to **www.frommers. com**.

Doctors Hotels usually have lists of doctors, should you need one, or you can use the physician referral service at **Desert Springs Hospital** (© **702/388-4888;** www.desertspringshospital. com). Hours are Monday to Friday from 8am to 8pm and Saturday from 9am to 3pm except holidays. Also see "Hospitals," below.

Drinking Laws The legal age for purchase and consumption of alcoholic beverages is 21; proof of age is required and often requested at bars, nightclubs, and restaurants, so it's always a good idea to bring ID when you go out.

10

Beer, wine, and liquor are sold in all kinds of stores pretty much around the clock in Vegas; trust us, you won't have a hard time finding a drink in this town.

Do not carry open containers of alcohol in your car or any public area that isn't zoned for alcohol consumption, which includes the Strip and the Fremont Street Experience downtown. The police can fine you on the spot. And nothing will ruin your trip faster than getting a citation for DUI (driving under the influence), so don't even think about driving while intoxicated.

Driving Rules See "Getting Around," earlier in this chapter.

Electricity Like Canada, the United States uses 110–120 volts AC (60 cycles), compared to 220–240 volts AC (50 cycles) in most of Europe, Australia, and New Zealand. Downward converters that change 220–240 volts to 110–120 volts are difficult to find in the United States, so bring one with you.

Embassies & Consulates All embassies are in the nation's capital, Washington, D.C. Some consulates are in major U.S. cities, and most nations have a mission to the United Nations in New York City. If your country isn't listed below, call for directory information in Washington, D.C. (☏ **202/555-1212**), or check **www.embassy.org/embassies.**

The embassy of **Australia** is at 1601 Massachusetts

Ave. NW, Washington, DC 20036 (☏ **202/797-3000;** www.usa.embassy.gov.au). Consulates are in New York, Honolulu, Houston, Los Angeles, and San Francisco.

The embassy of **Canada** is at 501 Pennsylvania Ave. NW, Washington, DC 20001 (☏ **202/682-1740;** www.canadianembassy.org). Other Canadian consulates are in Chicago, Detroit, Los Angeles, New York, Seattle, and many other major U.S. cities.

The embassy of **Ireland** is at 2234 Massachusetts Ave. NW, Washington, DC 20008 (☏ **202/462-3939;** www.embassyofireland.org). Irish consulates are in Boston, Chicago, New York, San Francisco, and other cities. See website for complete listing.

The embassy of **New Zealand** is at 37 Observatory Circle NW, Washington, DC 20008 (☏ **202/328-4800;** www.nzembassy.com/usa). New Zealand consulates are in Los Angeles, Salt Lake City, San Francisco, and Seattle.

The embassy of the **United Kingdom** is at 3100 Massachusetts Ave. NW, Washington, DC 20008 (☏ **202/588-6500;** ukinusa.fco.gov.uk/en). Other British consulates are in Atlanta, Boston, Chicago, Cleveland, Houston, Los Angeles, New York, San Francisco, and Seattle.

Emergencies Dial ☏ **911** to contact the police or fire department, or to call for an ambulance.

Family Travel Family travel can be immensely

rewarding, giving you new ways of seeing the world through smaller pairs of eyes. That said, Vegas is hardly an ideal place to bring the kids. For one thing, they're not allowed in casinos at all. Because most hotels are laid out so that you frequently have to walk through their casinos to get to where you are going, you can see how this becomes a headache.

Note also that the Strip is often peppered with people distributing fliers and other information about decidedly adult entertainment options in the city. Sex is everywhere. Just walking down the Strip might give your kids an eyeful of items that you might prefer they avoid. (They don't call it "Sin City" for nothing!)

On top of everything else, there is a curfew law in Vegas: Kids younger than 18 are not permitted on the Strip without a parent after 9pm on weekends and holidays. In the rest of the county, minors can't be out without parents after 10pm on school nights and midnight on the weekends.

Although still an option at most smaller chain hotels and motels, the major casino-hotels on the Strip offer no discount for children staying in your room, so you may have to pay an additional fee ($10–$40 per person per night) to have them bunk with you. You'll definitely want to book a place with a pool. Some hotels also have enormous video arcades and other diversions.

To locate accommodations, restaurants, and attractions that are particularly kid-friendly, look for the "Kids" icon throughout this guide.

Gasoline   Please see "Getting Around: By Car," earlier in this chapter.

Health   By and large, Las Vegas is like most other major American cities in that the water is relatively clean, the air is relatively clear, and illness-bearing insects and animals are rare. However, in a city with this many people coming and going from all over the world, there are a couple of specific concerns worth noting:

o **Food Poisoning** Food preparation guidelines in Las Vegas are among the strictest in the world, but when you're dealing with the sheer volume that this city is, you're bound to run into trouble every now and then. All restaurants are required by law to display a health certificate and letter grade (A, B, or C) that indicate how well they did on their last Health Department inspection. An A grade doesn't mean you won't get food poisoning, but it does mean the staff does a better-than-average job in the kitchen.

o **Norovirus** Over the past few years, there have been a few outbreaks of norovirus at Las Vegas hotels. This virus, most commonly associated with cruise ships, is rarely serious but can turn your vacation into a very unpleasant experience of intestinal illness. Because it is spread by contact, you can protect yourself by washing your hands often, especially after touching all of those slot machines.

o **Sun Exposure** In case you weren't paying attention in geography, Las Vegas is located in the middle of a desert, and so it should come as no surprise that the sun shines particularly bright here. Heat and sunstroke are dangers that all visitors should be concerned about, especially if you are considering spending any amount of time outdoors. Sunscreen (stick to a minimum SPF 30) is a must even if you are just traveling from one hotel to another, and you should always carry a bottle of water with you to stay hydrated even when temperatures are moderate. The low desert humidity means that your body has to work harder to replenish moisture, so help it along with something other than a free cocktail in the casino. The good news: Low humidity means it's hard to have a bad hair day.

Hospitals   The closest full-service hospital to the Strip is **Sunrise Hospital,** 3186 Maryland Pkwy. (🕻 **702/731-8000;** www.sunrisehospital.com), but for lesser emergencies, **Harmon Medical Urgent Care,** 150 E. Harmon (🕻 **702/796-1116;** www.harmonmedicalcenter.com), offers treatment from 8am until 5pm Monday through Friday. Additionally, most major hotels in Las Vegas can provide assistance in finding physicians and/or pharmacies that are well suited to your needs.

Insurance   Traveler's insurance is not required for visiting Las Vegas, and whether or not it's right for you depends on your circumstances. For example, most Las Vegas travel arrangements that include hotels are refundable or cancelable up to the last moment, so insurance is probably not necessary. If, however, you have prepaid a nonrefundable package, then it could be worth considering insurance.

For information on traveler's insurance, trip cancellation insurance, and medical insurance while traveling, please visit **www.frommers. com/planning.**

Internet & Wi-Fi   Most major hotels in Vegas offer wireless access as a part of their nightly resort fee, although some still require an additional fee that can run upward of $20 per day. Some hotels offer free, advertiser-supported Wi-Fi in public areas, meaning you won't have to pay to surf the Web when you're hanging out at the pool, but you'll have to put up with banner ads on your browser. In Las Vegas, you can find free Wi-Fi at most stand-alone McDonald's, Starbucks, and in the Fashion Show mall.

Most major airports have Internet kiosks that provide basic Web access for a per-minute fee that's usually higher than hotel prices. Check out copy shops, such as FedEx Office, which offer computer stations with fully loaded software (as well as Wi-Fi).

Legal Aid While driving, if you are pulled over for a minor infraction (such as speeding), never attempt to pay the fine directly to a police officer; this could be construed as attempted bribery, a much more serious crime. Pay fines by mail, or directly into the hands of the clerk of the court. If accused of a more serious offense, say and do nothing before consulting a lawyer. In the U.S., the burden is on the state to prove a person's guilt beyond a reasonable doubt, and everyone has the right to remain silent, whether he or she is suspected of a crime or actually arrested. Once arrested, a

person can make one telephone call to a party of his or her choice. The international visitor should call his or her embassy or consulate.

LGBT Travelers For such a licentious, permissive town, Las Vegas has its conservative side, and it is not the most gay-friendly city. This does not manifest itself in any signs of outrage toward open displays of gay affection, but it does mean that the local gay community is largely confined to the bar scene. See listings for gay bars in chapter 8. For gay and lesbian travel resources, visit **www.frommers.com.**

Mail At press time, domestic postage rates were 34¢ for a postcard and 49¢ for a letter. For international mail, a first-class letter of up to 1 ounce or postcard costs $1.15. For more information go to **www.usps.com.**

Always include a zip code when mailing items in the U.S. If you don't know a zip code, visit www.usps.com/zip4.

The most convenient post office to the Strip is immediately behind Circus Circus at 3100 S. Industrial Rd., between Sahara Avenue and Spring Mountain Road (✆ **800/275-8777**). It's open Monday through Friday from 8:30am to 5pm. You can also mail letters and packages at your hotel.

Medical Requirements Unless you're arriving from an area known to be suffering from an epidemic (particularly cholera or yellow fever), inoculations or vaccinations are not required for entry into the United States. Also see "Health," above.

Mobile Phones Just because your mobile phone works at home doesn't mean it'll work everywhere in the U.S. (thanks to our nation's fragmented mobile phone system). Whether or not you'll get a signal depends on your carrier and where you happen to be standing when you are trying to make a call. Hotel rooms and casinos are notoriously bad places to be if you want to chat with someone back home on your cellphone, but step outside and things usually improve dramatically. Note that if you can get a signal in a casino, don't try to use your phone while sitting at a gaming table—that's a big no-no.

Once you leave Las Vegas proper, you are in the wilds of the Nevada desert, and so unless you are near a major byway (like I-15), expect to get very few, if any, bars on your phone.

If you're not from the U.S., you'll be appalled at the poor reach of the GSM (Global System for Mobile Communications) wireless network, which is used by

THE VALUE OF THE U.S. DOLLAR VS. OTHER POPULAR CURRENCIES

US$	Aus$	Can$	Euro (€)	NZ$	UK£
1	A$1.08	C$1.10	€.73	NZ$1.16	£.60

much of the rest of the world. Your phone will probably work in Las Vegas but it probably won't once you get into more rural areas, and you may or may not be able to send SMS (text messaging) home. Check with your carrier for more information.

Money & Costs   Frommer's lists exact prices in the local currency. The currency conversions quoted above were correct at press time. However, rates fluctuate, so before departing consult a currency exchange website such as **www.xe.com** to check up-to-the-minute rates.

Because Las Vegas is a town built on the concept of separating you from your money, it should come as no surprise that gaining access to money is very easy— sometimes too easy. There are ATMs (also known as "cash machines" or "cash-points") conveniently located about every 4 feet (okay, an exaggeration, but not by a lot); and check cashing, credit card–advance systems, and traveler's check services are omnipresent. Note that using any of these to access your money will cost your money; ATMs charge upward of $6 per transaction, and that's before whatever fees your bank will add.

And while Vegas visitors used to require a great deal of change in order to play the slots and other gaming machines, few, if any, still accept coins. Gone are the once-prevalent change carts. All machines now take bills in most denominations, and

you get "change" in the form of a credit slip that appears when you cash out. You then take this slip to the nearest cashier's cage to exchange for actual money.

So getting to your money isn't a problem. Keeping it may be.

Las Vegas has grown progressively more expensive, with the concept of a cheap Sin City vacation a distant memory. The average room rate on the Strip on weekends is over $200 a night, those formerly cheap buffets have been replaced by $40-a-person lavish spreads, and top-show tickets easily surpass $100 a head. And then, of course, there are the casinos, a money-losing proposition if there ever was one.

But there are Las Vegas vacations available for just about any budget, so pay (no pun intended) close attention to chapter 4, "Where to Stay," and chapter 5, "Where to Eat," which break down your choices by cost.

Beware of hidden credit card fees while traveling. International visitors should check with their credit or debit card issuer to see what fees, if any, will be charged for transactions in the U.S.

For help with currency conversions, tip calculations, and more, download Frommer's convenient Travel Tools app for your mobile device. Go to **www.frommers.com/go/mobile** and click on the "Travel Tools" icon.

Newspapers & Magazines   The *Las Vegas Review-Journal* is the major

daily periodical in the city, which is now partnered with the *Las Vegas Sun*, its former newspaper rival. Both offer the latest news, weather, and information and can be valuable resources for coupons and up-to-the-minute show listings.

What's On Las Vegas is a local magazine listing shows, restaurants, and more, and it often features discount offers to attractions that could save you some dough.

Packing   Most Las Vegas hotel rooms are fully stocked with basics—shampoo, conditioner, hand lotion, mouthwash, and in some cases things like sewing kits and cotton swabs. If you don't have allergy or skin sensitivity issues to contend with, you may want to consider leaving those types of sundry items at home to free up some room in your suitcase. The same goes for your travel iron, as most rooms have a full-size iron and ironing board or they are available by request through housekeeping.

Comfortable walking shoes are a must for Las Vegas as you'll be doing a lot of it. Yes, your Jimmy Choo's will look fabulous for your night out at the party spots, but do you really want to navigate the crowds across a 100,000-square-foot casino in them?

Checking the weather forecast before your trip can provide you with guidance on what types of clothes to bring, but packing a light sweater or jacket even during the summer months is not a bad idea. It gets windy

What Things Cost in Las Vegas	US$
Taxi from the airport to the Strip	15.00–25.00
Taxi from the airport to Downtown Las Vegas	18.00–27.00
One-way Las Vegas monorail ticket	5.00
All-day Deuce or SDX bus pass	8.00
Standard room at Bellagio, Fri–Sat	175.00–400.00
Standard room at MGM Grand, Fri–Sat	150.00–300.00
Standard room at Bally's, Fri–Sat	100.00–200.00
Dinner for two at Picasso, prix fixe	226.00
Dinner for two at Citizens Kitchen	75.00
Wynn Las Vegas buffet, weekend champagne brunch	45.00
Main Street Station Garden Court buffet champagne brunch	12.00
Ticket to Cirque du Soleil's O	109.00–180.00
Ticket to Mac King (comedy magic show)	30.00
Domestic beer at Light	10.00
Domestic beer at the Double Down Saloon	5.00

in Las Vegas and there can be a chill in the evenings, plus many of the casinos and showrooms set the air-conditioning on "Siberia," so light layers that you can peel off when you go back outside into the heat are recommended.

If you are bringing your computer or other mobile devices, don't forget to bring your power cords, chargers, and other imperatives like an Ethernet cord. Most hotels offer Wi-Fi service, but if you can't connect and need to use their cords, you could get charged extra for it.

Lastly, consider safety when packing by tossing in a small flashlight. During an emergency, this could become invaluable in helping you navigate your way out of a 4,000-room hotel.

For more helpful information on packing for your trip, download our convenient Travel Tools app for your mobile device. Go to www.

frommers.com/go/mobile and click on the "Travel Tools" icon.

Passports Virtually every air traveler entering the U.S. is required to show a passport. All persons, including U.S. citizens, traveling by air between the United States and Canada, Mexico, Central and South America, the Caribbean, and Bermuda are required to present a valid passport. **Note:** U.S. and Canadian citizens entering the U.S. at land and sea ports of entry from within the Western Hemisphere must now also present a passport or other documents compliant with the Western Hemisphere Travel Initiative (WHTI; www. getyouhome.gov). Children 15 and under may continue entering with only a U.S. birth certificate or other proof of U.S. citizenship.

Passport Offices

o **Australia** Australian Passport Information Service

(© **131-232;** www. passports.gov.au).

o **Canada Passport Office,** Department of Foreign Affairs and International Trade, Ottawa, ON K1A 0G3 (© **800/567-6868;** www.ppt. gc.ca).

o **Ireland Passport Office,** Setanta Centre, Molesworth Street, Dublin 2 (© **01/408-2000;** www.foreignaffairs. gov.ie).

o **New Zealand Passports Office,** Department of Internal Affairs, 109 Featherstone St., Wellington, 6140 (© **0800/225-050** in New Zealand or 04/463-9360; www. passports.govt.nz).

o **United Kingdom** Visit your nearest passport office, major post office, or travel agency or contact the **Identity and Passport Service (IPS),** 2 Marsham St., London, SW1P 4DF (☏ **0300/222-0000;** www.ips.gov.uk).

o **United States** To find your regional passport office, check the U.S. State Department website (http://travel.state.gov/passport) or call the **National Passport Information Center** (☏ **877/487-2778**) for automated information.

Petrol Please see "Getting Around: By Car," earlier in this chapter.

Police For nonemergencies, call ☏ **702/795-3111.** For emergencies, call ☏ **911.**

Safety *CSI: Crime Scene Investigation,* a popular U.S. TV show, may turn up new corpses in Vegas each week, but the crime rate in real-life Vegas isn't higher than in any other major metropolis of its size.

With all that cash floating around town, pickpockets and thieves are predictably active. At gaming tables and slot machines, men should keep wallets well concealed and out of the reach of pickpockets, and women should keep handbags in plain sight (on laps). If you win a big jackpot, ask the slot attendant to cut you a check rather than give you cash—the cash may look nice, but flashing it can attract the wrong kind of attention. Outside the casinos, popular

spots for pickpockets and thieves are restaurants and outdoor shows, such as the volcano at the Mirage or the fountains at Bellagio. Stay alert. Unless your hotel room has an in-room safe, check your valuables into a safe-deposit box at the front desk.

When in your room, be sure to lock and bolt the door at all times and only open it to hotel employees that you are expecting (such as room service).

A special safety concern for women (and even men occasionally) centers on behavior at nightclubs. Do not ever accept a drink from a stranger no matter how handsome he is, and keep your cocktail in your hand at all times, even while on the dance floor. Instances of people getting something slipped into their drink are rare but they have happened—singer John Popper of the band Blues Traveler was drugged and robbed in 2014—so it's best to take precautions.

Senior Travel One of the benefits of age is that travel to most destinations often costs less—but that's rarely true in Las Vegas. Discounts at hotels, shows, restaurants, recreation, and just about anything else you want to do are rare. About the only discounts offered to seniors are at some of the local attractions, which will give a few bucks off to those over 62 or 65 (see chapter 6).

Members of **AARP,** 601 E St. NW, Washington, DC 20049 (☏ **888/687-2277;**

www.aarp.org), get discounts on hotels, airfares, and car rentals. AARP offers members a wide range of benefits, including *AARP The Magazine* and a monthly newsletter. Anyone over 50 can join.

The U.S. National Park Service (NPS) offers an **America the Beautiful—National Park and Federal Recreational Lands Pass—Senior Pass**. You'll find it useful for some of the side trips covered in chapter 9. The pass gives U.S. residents 62 years or older lifetime entrance to all properties administered by the National Park Service—national parks, monuments, historic sites, recreation areas, and national wildlife refuges—for a one-time processing fee of $10. The pass must be purchased in person at any NPS facility that charges an entrance fee. Besides free entry, the America the Beautiful Senior Pass also offers a 50% discount on some federal-use fees charged for such facilities as camping, swimming, parking, and tours. For more information, call the **United States Geological Survey (USGS),** which issues the passes, at ☏ **888/275-8747** or go to **www.nps.gov/findapark/passes.htm.**

Smoking Vegas is decidedly no longer a smoker's haven. Increasingly strict smoking laws prohibit puffing virtually everywhere indoors except in designated hotel rooms, nightclubs, bars, and on the casino floor itself. Because it's frequently hard to tell

PLANNING YOUR TRIP TO LAS VEGAS

Smoking

where a casino ends and basic public area begins, don't fret too much about stepping across some invisible line. Hotels still have dedicated floors for smokers and nonsmokers. There is a significant charge, approximately $300, for smoking anything in a nonsmoking room.

Taxes The United States has no value-added tax (VAT) or other indirect tax at the national level. Every state, county, and city may levy its own local tax on all purchases, including hotel and restaurant checks and airline tickets. These taxes will not appear on price tags.

The sales tax in Las Vegas is 8.1% and is added to food and drink bills. Hotel rooms on the Strip come with a 12% tax, while those in the Downtown area carry 13%. Taxes are also added to show tickets.

Telephones Generally, Vegas hotel surcharges on long-distance and local calls are astronomical. You are often charged even for making a toll-free or phone-card call. You're better off using your **cellphone** since pay phones are almost nonexistent these days. Some hotels are adding on an additional "resort fee" to the cost of the room, which sometimes covers local calls (as well as using the pool and other elements that ought to be givens). The fee can range from $3 to $25 per day.

Many convenience groceries and packaging services sell **prepaid calling**

cards in denominations up to $50. Many public pay phones at airports now accept American Express, MasterCard, and Visa. Most long-distance and international calls can be dialed directly from any phone. **To make calls within the United States and to Canada,** dial 1 followed by the area code and the seven-digit number. **For other international calls,** dial 011 followed by the country code, city code, and the number you are calling.

Calls to area codes **800, 888, 877, 866,** and **855** are toll-free. However, calls to area codes **700** and **900** (chat lines, bulletin boards, "dating" services, and so on) can be expensive—charges of 95¢ to $3 or more per minute. Some numbers have minimum charges that can run $15 or more.

For **reversed-charge or collect calls,** and for person-to-person calls, dial the number 0 then the area code and number; an operator will come on the line, and you should specify whether you are calling collect, person-to-person, or both. If your operator-assisted call is international, ask for the overseas operator.

For **directory assistance** ("Information"), dial 411 for local numbers and national numbers in the U.S. and Canada. For dedicated long-distance information, dial 1, then the appropriate area code plus 555-1212.

Time The continental United States is divided into **four time zones:** Eastern

Standard Time (EST), Central Standard Time (CST), Mountain Standard Time (MST), and Pacific Standard Time (PST). Alaska and Hawaii have their own zones. Las Vegas is in the Pacific Time zone, 8 hours behind Greenwich Mean Time (GMT), 3 hours behind the East Coast, and 2 behind the Midwest. For example, when it's 9am in Las Vegas (PST), it's 7am in Honolulu (Hawaii Standard Time), 10am in Denver (MST), 11am in Chicago (CST), noon in New York City (EST), 5pm in London (GMT), and 2am the next day in Sydney.

Daylight saving time (summer time) is in effect from 1am on the second Sunday in March to 1am on the first Sunday in November, except in Arizona, Hawaii, the U.S. Virgin Islands, and Puerto Rico. Daylight saving time moves the clock 1 hour ahead of standard time.

For help with time translations, and more, download our convenient Travel Tools app for your mobile device. Go to **www.frommers.com/go/mobile** and click on the "Travel Tools" icon.

Tipping Las Vegas is a hospitality-driven economy, meaning many of the people you encounter depend on tips for their livelihood. This doesn't necessarily mean you *need* to tip more than you would anywhere else, but average tips in other cities can be viewed as somewhat stingy here.

In the casinos, it's common to tip **cocktail waitresses** $1 to $2 per drink and to tip **dealers** 5% of any big wins.

In hotels, tip **bellhops** at least $1 per bag ($2–$3 if you have a lot of luggage) and tip the **chamber staff** $3 to $5 per day (more if you've left a big mess to clean up). Tip the **doorman** or **concierge** only if he or she has provided you with some specific service (for example, calling a cab for you or obtaining difficult-to-get theater tickets). Tip the **valet-parking attendant** $2 to $5 every time you get your car.

In restaurants, bars, and nightclubs, tip **service staff** and **bartenders** 15% to 20% of the check, and tip **checkroom attendants** $1 per garment.

As for other service personnel, tip **cabdrivers** 15% of the fare; tip **skycaps** at airports at least $1 per bag ($2–$3 if you have a lot of luggage); and tip **hairdressers** and **barbers** 15% to 20%.

For help with tip calculations, currency conversions, and more, download our convenient Travel Tools app for your mobile device. Go to **www.frommers.com/go/mobile** and click on the "Travel Tools" icon.

Toilets   In Las Vegas, you are almost always near a bathroom as long as you are in one of the tourist areas, with the casinos being the most obvious example. All have multiple facilities and they are usually among the cleanest you'll find in any public location. One small annoyance is that many hotel restaurants do not have their own restrooms, meaning you may need to go into the casino to find the nearest one.

Large hotels and fast-food restaurants are often the best bet for clean facilities. Restaurants and bars in resorts or heavily visited areas may reserve their restrooms for patrons.

VAT   See "Taxes," above.

Visas   The U.S. State Department has a **Visa Waiver Program (VWP)** allowing citizens of the following countries to enter the United States without a visa for stays of up to 90 days: Andorra, Australia, Austria, Belgium, Brunei, Czech Republic, Denmark, Estonia, Finland, France, Germany, Greece, Hungary, Iceland, Ireland, Italy, Japan, Latvia, Liechtenstein, Lithuania, Luxembourg, Malta, Monaco, the Netherlands, New Zealand, Norway, Portugal, San Marino, Singapore, Slovakia, Slovenia, South Korea, Spain, Sweden, Switzerland, and the United Kingdom. (**Note:** This list was accurate at press time; for the most up-to-date list of countries in the VWP, consult http://travel.state.gov/visa.) Even though a visa isn't necessary, in an effort to help U.S. officials check travelers against terror watch lists before they arrive at U.S. borders, visitors from VWP countries must register online through the Electronic System for Travel Authorization (ESTA) before boarding a plane or a boat to the U.S. Travelers must complete an electronic application providing basic personal and travel eligibility information. The Department of Homeland Security recommends filling out the form at least 3 days before traveling. Authorizations will be valid for up to 2 years or until the traveler's passport expires, whichever comes first. Currently, there is a US$14 fee for the online application. Existing ESTA registrations remain valid through their expiration dates. **Note:** Any passport issued on or after October 26, 2006, by a VWP country must be an **e-Passport** for VWP travelers to be eligible to enter the U.S. without a visa. Citizens of these nations also need to present a round-trip air or cruise ticket upon arrival. E-Passports contain computer chips capable of storing biometric information, such as the required digital photograph of the holder. If your passport doesn't have this feature, you can still travel without a visa if the valid passport was issued before October 26, 2005, and includes a machine-readable zone; or if the valid passport was issued between October 26, 2005, and October 25, 2006, and includes a digital photograph. For more information, go to **http://travel.state.gov/visa.** Canadian citizens may enter the United States without visas, but will need to show passports and proof of residence.

Citizens of all other countries must have (1) a valid passport that expires at least 6 months later than the scheduled end of their visit to the U.S.; and (2) a tourist visa.

For information about U.S. visas go to **http:// travel.state.gov** and click on "Visas." For other countries go to **www.usembassy. gov** and select your country from the list.

Visitor Information

The Las Vegas Convention and Visitors Authority (✆ **877/847-4858** or 702/892-7575; www.las vegas.com) provides information, hotel reservation assistance, show guides, convention calendars, and more.

Other popular Las Vegas travel websites include www. vegas.com, www.vegas 4visitors.com, and www. cheapovegas.com.

Many hotels have their own mobile apps that you can download for special information and offers, and you can also download the Frommer's Las Vegas app with tons of great information about the city at **www. frommers.com/go/mobile.**

Water Ongoing drought conditions mean water is a concern in terms of its long-term availability, but for now it is plentiful from faucets, drinking fountains, and endless bottles of the stuff. As in most of the United States, the drinking water is considered safe and there have been no reported instances of sickness from it. Still, bottles of water are often free in the casinos, so you might as well pick one up.

Wi-Fi See "Internet & Wi-Fi," earlier in this section.

Women Travelers

Thanks to the crowds, Las Vegas is as safe as any other big city for a woman traveling alone. A woman on her own should, of course, take the usual precautions and should be wary of hustlers and drunken businessmen. Many of the big hotels have security guards stationed at the elevators at night to prevent anyone other than guests from going up to the room floors. If you're anxious, ask a security guard to escort you to your room. *Always* double-lock your door *and* deadbolt it to prevent intruders from entering.

For general travel resources for women, go to **www.frommers.com/ planning.**

AIRLINE WEBSITES

MAJOR AIRLINES

Aeroméxico
www.aeromexico.com

Air Canada
www.aircanada.ca

Alaska Airlines / Horizon Air
www.alaskaair.com

American Airlines
www.aa.com

British Airways
www.britishairways.com

Delta Air Lines
www.delta.com

Hawaiian Airlines
www.hawaiianairlines.com

Korean Air
www.koreanair.com

United Airlines
www.united.com

US Airways
www.usairways.com

Virgin America
www.virginamerica.com

Virgin Atlantic Airways
www.virgin-atlantic.com

BUDGET AIRLINES

AirTran Airways
www.airtran.com

Allegiant
www.allegiantair.com

Frontier Airlines
www.flyfrontier.com

JetBlue Airways
www.jetblue.com

Southwest Airlines
www.southwest.com

Spirit Airlines
www.spirit.com

Volaris
www.volaris.mx

WestJet
www.westjet.com

Index

See also Accommodations and Restaurant indexes, below.

General Index

A

Absinthe, 7, 177–178
Accommodations, 36–78. *See also* Accommodations Index
  best, 4–5
  chain alternatives, 67
  under construction, 59
  Downtown, 60–64
  family-friendly, 46
  just off the Strip, 64–71
  locals', 70–71
  Mid-Strip, 47–56
  Mount Charleston, 225–226
  north and west of the Strip, 73–75
  North Strip, 57–59
  pet-friendly, 43
  pools, 53
  practical information, 75–78
  by price, 36–37
  prices, 38
  reservation services, 76–77
  resort fees, 42, 76
  south and east of the Strip, 71–73
  South Strip, 37–47
  surfing for hotels, 77
Adventuredome, 136–137
Airline websites, 244
Air tours, 14
Air travel, 227
Aliante Casino and Hotel, accommodations, 71
American Restoration, 174
Amtrak, 228
Anderson, Louie, 188
Angel, Criss, 184
Angel Park Golf Club, 163–164
Animal attractions and zoos
  Lion Habitat Ranch, 145
  Shark Reef at Mandalay Bay, 134
  Siegfried & Roy's Secret Garden & Dolphin Habitat, 136
Antiques, 6, 173
Area codes, 235
Aria Las Vegas
  accommodations, 37–38
  casino, 7, 156
  entertainment and nightlife, 184, 203, 209
  restaurants, 84, 85, 87, 95, 122, 124
Arizona Charlie's East, accommodations, 70
Arizona Paint Pots, 218
Arroyo Golf Club, 164
Artifice, 200–201

B

Baccarat, 150
Backstage Bar & Billiards, 194
Bali Hai Golf Club, 164–165
Bally's Las Vegas
  accommodations, 51–52
  Jubilee!, 187
  tennis, 163
The Bar at Times Square, 199
Bare, 208
Bars, 194–200
  hotel, 198–199
  piano, 199–200
Beacher's Madhouse, 201
Bear's Best Las Vegas, 165
Beauty Bar, 194
Bellagio, 30
  accommodations, 47–48
  bars, 199, 206
  Cirque du Soleil's *O*, 183
  restaurants, 96, 122, 125
  Spa at Bellagio, 167
  Via Bellagio, 172
  weddings, 160
Bellagio Conservatory, 5, 138
Bellagio Fountains, 138
Bellagio Gallery of Fine Art, 134–135
Bell Transportation, 229
Benny Binion's Horseshoe Club, 26
Big Apple Coaster & Arcade, 132
Big Shot, 137
Biking, 161
  Red Rock Canyon, 221, 223
Binion's, 7
Blackjack, 150–151
Blue Man Group, 178
Boating
  Lake Mead, 217
  Lake Mead National Recreation Area, 161
Bodies . . . The Exhibition, 132
Body English, 201
Bonanza Gift and Souvenir Shop, 172
Bond, 198, 210
Bonnie Springs Ranch, 223
Booking agencies, 77
Boulder Station, accommodations, 70
The Boulevard, 175
Boulevard Pool, 192
Bowling, 164–165
Brad Garrett's Comedy Club, 208
Brooklyn Bowl, 164, 192

Art museums and galleries
  The Arts Factory, 138
  Bellagio Gallery of Fine Art, 134–135
  CityCenter Fine Art Collection, 132
  Emergency Arts, 139–140
The arts, 6
The Arts Factory, 138
Atomic Liquors, 194

Buffets and brunches, 97, 124–129
Business hours, 235
Bus travel, 228, 234–235

C

Caesars Palace. *See also* The Forum Shops at Caesars Palace
  accommodations, 48–49
  casino, 6, 156
  entertainment and nightlife, 178, 180, 181, 192, 196
  food court, 104
  PetStay program, 43
  Qua Baths & Spa, 167
  restaurants, 95, 96, 99, 100, 103–105, 126
Calendar of events, 33–35
Calico Basin, 223
Calico Hill, 222
California Hotel & Casino, accommodations, 61
Callville Bay Resort & Marina, 217
Camping
  Lake Mead, 217
  Mount Charleston, 224
  Valley of Fire State Park, 220–221
Canoeing, Lake Mead, 217
Canyon Ranch SpaClub, 8
Carnaval Court, 207
Carrot Top, 188
Car travel and rentals, 228–233
  best drives, 8
  Red Rock Scenic Drive, 8, 221, 222
Casino gambling, 149–157. *See also specific casinos*
  baccarat, 150
  best, 6–7
  blackjack, 150–151
  on a budget, 6
  craps, 151
  poker, 151–153
  roulette, 153–154
  slots, 154–155
  sports books, 155–156
  video poker, 155
CAT (Citizens Area Transit) buses, 229
Cellphones, 238
The Chandelier, 199
Chapel of the Bells, 158–159
Chapel of the Flowers, 159
Chateau, 201
Cheetah's, 211
Chelsea, 192
Children, families with, 236–237
  accommodations, 46
  Discovery Children's Museum, 138–139
  entertainment and nightlife, 182
Chippendales, 183
Circus Circus Hotel & Casino
  accommodations, 46, 58–59
  restaurant, 107–108
Circus Circus Midway, 137

Restaurants